Roland Sturm | Tim Griebel | Thorsten Winkelmann (eds.)

Austerity: A Journey to an Unknown Territory

Discourses, Economics and Politics

Nomos

The Deutsche Nationalbibliothek lists this publication in the Deutsche Nationalbibliografie; detailed bibliographic data are available on the Internet at http://dnb.d-nb.de

ISBN 978-3-8487-3849-6 (Print)
978-3-8452-8172-8 (ePDF)

British Library Cataloguing-in-Publication Data
A catalogue record for this book is available from the British Library.

ISBN 978-3-8487-3849-6 (Print)
978-3-8452-8172-8 (ePDF)

Library of Congress Cataloging-in-Publication Data
Sturm, Roland / Griebel, Tim / Winkelmann, Thorsten
Austerity: A Journey to an Unknown Territory
Discourses, Economics and Politics
Roland Sturm / Tim Griebel / Thorsten Winkelmann (eds.)
306 p.

ISBN 978-3-8487-3849-6 (Print)
978-3-8452-8172-8 (ePDF)

1st Edition 2017

ZfP Zeitschrift für Politik

In Zusammenarbeit mit der Hochschule für Politik München – Bavarian School of Public Policy

Gegründet im Jahre 1907 durch Adolf Grabowsky und Richard Schmidt

Zeitschrift für Politik

Special Issue 8

Inhalt

Roland Sturm, Tim Griebel and Thorsten Winkelmann

Austerity: A Journey to an Unknown Territory

In the context of the global economic and financial crisis, banking bailouts and perceived excessive fiscal debts, many countries around the globe introduced austerity measures to rebalance their economies. But although austerity is about spending cuts and the reduction of fiscal debt, it cannot be reduced to this dimension. It has to be understood as a complex social phenomenon with consequences for many economies[1], social equality[2], politics[3] and everyday life.[4] Because of this broad range of effects of austerity, the nature of the beast is of dubious analytical status. Austerity is certainly »more than the sum of its parts«.[5]

In the context of rather unconnected disciplinary debates, austerity has been burdened with a wide range of meanings, especially when austerity is implemented. Moreover the concept is never free of political bias, negative or positive. It has been argued that we can see a »primary division in arguments« between mainstream approaches, which means »those which proceed from non-systemic accounts of the crisis to get back to ›normal‹, the ›*status quo ante*‹ or the economic situation which prevailed before the crisis«, and critical approaches, which means »those which proceed from systemic accounts of the crisis.«[6] This division of arguments between »non-systemic« and »systemic« accounts about the reasons of and remedies for the economic and financial crisis is connected with a more basic division in the social sciences between »problem-solving« approaches and »critical theory.« The former takes the current system as it is and wants to improve its functioning. Critical theory, by contrast, asks how the political, economic and discursive (sub-)systems and their specific realities came about and what power mechanisms are operating in them.[7] These general dif-

1 Alfons Weichenrieder (ed.), *Austerity and Economic Growth. Concepts for Europe*, SAFE Policy Letter Collection 1/2015; Sue Konzelmann, *The Economics of Austerity*, Centre for Business Research, University of Cambridge Working Paper No. 434 (2012); Alex Callinicos, »Contradictions of Austerity« in: *Cambridge Journal of Economics* 36, No. 1 (2012), pp. 65–77.

2 Will Atkinson / Steven Roberts / Michael Savage, *Class Inequality in Austerity Britain: Power, Difference and Suffering*, Houndmills 2012.

3 Armin Schäfer / Wolfgang Streeck (eds.), *Politics in the Age of Austerity*, Cambridge 2014.

4 Gargi Bhattacharyya, *Crisis, Austerity and Everyday Life: Living in a Time of Diminishing Expectations*, Houndmills 2015.

5 Kevin Farnsworth / Zoë Irving, »Austerity: More Than the Sum of Its Parts« in: Kevin Farnsworth / Zoë Irving (ed.), *Social Policy in Times of Austerity. Global Economic Crisis and the New Politics of Welfare*, Bristol 2015, pp. 9–41.

6 Norman Fairclough / Isabela Fairclough, *Political Discourse Analysis*, New York 2012, p. 7.

7 Robert W. Cox, »Social Forces, States and World Orders: Beyond International Relations Theory« in: *Millennium – Journal of International Studies* 10 (1981/82), pp. 126–155, pp. 128–129. Taken to the extreme, these two ideal-typical positions can lead to the »boundary of boredom« on the side of problem-solving theory or the »boundary of negativity« on the side of critical theory. Ole Wæver, »The Rise and Fall of Inter-Paradigm Debate« in: Steve Smith / Ken Booth / Marysia Zalewski (ed.), *International Theory: Positivism and Beyond*, Cambridge 1996, pp. 149–185, p. 169.

ferences of analytic expectations lead to different evaluations of austerity. Whereas non-systemic or problem-solving approaches see austerity as a rational means against temporary shortcomings of an economic system that is working in principle and against moral failings of indebted populations[8], critical or systemic theorists argue that austerity is a contradictory and »dangerous«[9] neoliberal[10] idea that »bites«[11] or even »kills.«[12]

The relationship between different disciplinary and scientific entry-points of the debate so far remained in the dark. This is disappointing because a deeper understanding of the meanings, perceptions or imaginations and realities of austerity[13] asks for an interdisciplinary approach that crosses frontiers between different landscapes of the academic debates. At the same time it has to remain sensitive to different ontological and epistemological cultures found within different intellectual »lands« of austerity. The interdisciplinary journey to the strange land of austerity this volume offers will be guided by an eclectic approach. This approach

> *»is marked by three general features. First, it is consistent with an ethos of pragmatism in seeking engagement with the world of policy and practice, downplaying unresolvable metaphysical divides and presumptions of incommensurability and encouraging a conception of inquiry marked by practical engagement, inclusive dialogue, and a spirit of fallibilism. Second, [...] eclectic inquiry takes on problems that more closely approximate the messiness and complexity of concrete dilemmas facing ›real world‹ actors. Third, in exploring these problems, eclectic approaches offer complex causal stories that extricate, translate, and selectively recombine analytic*

8 Roland Sturm, »Austeritätspolitik als gesellschaftliches Projekt« in: *Aus Politik und Zeitgeschichte* 66, No. 1–2 (2016), pp. 17–23.

9 Mark Blyth, *Austerity: The History of a Dangerous Idea*, Oxford 2013.

10 The term »neoliberalism« is as controversial as the term »austerity« itself. As a starting point we follow Harvey's definition of neoliberalism as »a theory of political economic practices that proposes that human well-being can best be advanced by liberating individual entrepreneurial freedoms and skills within an institutional framework characterized by strong private property rights, free markets, and free trade. The role of the state is to create and preserve an institutional framework appropriate to such practices.« David Harvey, *A Brief History of Neoliberalism*, Oxford, Kindle-Version, p. 2. On the language and key concepts of neoliberalism see Marnie Holborow, »Neoliberal Keywords and the Contradictions of an Ideology« in: David Block / John Gray / Marnie Holborow (ed.), *Neoliberalism and Applied Linguistics*, London/New York 2012, pp. 33–55; Matthew Eagleton-Pierce, *Neoliberalism: The Key Concepts*, London/New York 2016. Sometimes austerity is even understood *as* neoliberalism. See Heather Whiteside, »Neoliberalism as Austerity. The theory, practice, and purpose of fiscal restraint since the 1970s« in: Simon Springer / Kean Birch / Julie MacLeavy (eds.), *The Handbook of Neoliberalism*, New York 2016, pp. 50–60.

11 Mary O'Hara, *Austerity Bites: A Journey to the Sharp End of Cuts in the UK*, Bristol 2015.

12 David Stuckler / Sanjay Basu, *The Body Economic: Why Austerity Kills: Recessions, Budget Battles, and the Politics of Life and Death*, New York 2013.

13 Roland Sturm, »Heilmittel oder Spardiktat? Wahrnehmungen und Realitäten der Austeritätspolitik« in: Jürgen Rüttgers / Frank Decker (ed.), *Europas Ende, Europas Anfang. Neue Perspektiven für die Europäische Union*, Frankfurt a. M./New York 2017, pp. 213–228.

> *components – most notably, causal mechanisms – from explanatory theories, models, and narratives embedded in competing research traditions.«*[14]

Eclectic scholarship – despite its problems[15] – is the best companion for a diversified group of researchers on their way to a better understanding of economic phenomena in general[16] and of austerity in particular. Only this approach allows us both to engage in a dialogue between the three travel guides that come from different parts of the academic landscape themselves and to »come in peace« to different parts of the terrain under study and to the »cults« that are exercised there. These differences, which can be detected in every region of austerity land itself, are not just the ones between systemic and non-systemic evaluations of austerity but also the ones between different methodological approaches. Sometimes these two differences find common ground.[17]

We will begin our expedition with deliberations on the impact of austerity politics both with regard to individual states and for the European Union as a whole. The next step will be the discussion of the consequences of austerity measures for the economy. Finally, discourses and their power to shape political realities will be investigated.

1. Politics land

From the perspective of non-systemic approaches, austerity provokes the electorate to choose one of three options: acceptance (the government in office survives), opposition (a change of government) or protest (non-voting and/or strikes and forms of anomic participation[18]). Of course, these three options are not mutually exclusive. Often pres-

14 Rudra Sil / Peter J. Katzenstein, »Analytic Eclecticism in the Study of World Politics: Reconfiguring Problems and Mechanisms across Research Traditions« in: *Perspectives on Politics* 8, No. 2 (2010), pp. 411–431, p. 411.

15 The greatest problem is certainly that eclecticism runs the risk of producing an incoherent »anything-goes« mix of disparate elements. Ngai-Ling Sum / Bob Jessop, *Towards a Cultural Political Economy: Putting Culture in Its Place in Political Economy*, Cheltenham 2013, p. 482. Although this has to be accepted for a first journey to the unknown land of austerity with such a diverse and broad research group, parts of the edited volumes already go beyond eclecticism by integrating elements from different aspects of social life.

16 The analysis of austerity at the cross-roads of different disciplines is to a large extent imbedded within questions and approaches within the interdisciplinary field of International Political Economy (IPE). IPE is a field that has not only a long history of interparadigmatic arguments but also experience with eclectic approaches. See, for example, Susan Strange, »An Eclectic Approach« in: Craig Murphy / Roger Tooze (ed.), *International Political Economy*, Boulder 1991, pp. 33–50.

17 That, *by trend*, mainstream, non-systemic approaches are more sympathetic to positivist and quantitative approaches, whereas critical systemic analyses that are linked with qualitative tools had to be expected as the levels of ontology, epistemology and methodology are connected. See Nuno P. Monteiro / Keven G. Ruby, »IR and the False Promise of Philosophical Foundations« in: *International Theory* 1, No. 1 (2009), pp. 15–48, p. 33; Colin Hay, »Political Ontology« in: Robert E. Goodin (ed.), *The Oxford Handbook of Political Science*, New York 2009, pp. 460–477, p. 466. But of course, there is also room for overlap between these ideal types.

18 Marco Guigni / Maria Grasso (eds.), *Austerity and Protest. Popular Contention in Times of Economic Crisis*, London/New York 2016.

sure in form of political protest strengthens political opposition and strengthens the forces that want a change of government. It would be an exaggeration, however, to argue – as some authors have done[19] – that opposition to austerity quasi-automatically results in a party political upheaval. But even if governments stay in office, this does not exclude mass protests on the streets. It has been argued, however, that the survival of governments and especially of government coalitions after austerity policies were put in place helped to stabilize the established party system, for example in Portugal in contrast to developments in Spain.[20] Table 1 gives an overview of developments since 2008 in some of the EU countries most affected by austerity policies.

Table 1: Electoral consequences of austerity policies

Country	*Number of new governments since 2008*	*Government survival (same political family governs)*	*New governments (new political family governs)*	*Turnout (last pre-2008 election – last post-2008 election) in %*	*Anomic participation High/Low*
Estonia	5	Until 2016	Since 2016	61.9 (2007) – 64.2 (2015) = +2.3%	Low
Greece	4	Changes in government	Since 2015	74.1 (2007) – 56.6 (2015) = –17.5%	High
Ireland	1	Change in government (new Taoiseach)	Since 2011	67.0 (2007) – 61.5 (2016) = –5.5%	Low
Italy	4	No	Since 2013 (2011–2013 technocratic government)	80.5 (2008) – 75.2 (2013) = –5.3%	Low
Portugal	2	Partial comeback	2011–2015 Since 2015	64.3 (2005) – 55.8 (2015) = –8.5%	High
Spain	1	No	Since 2011	73.8 (2008) – 66.5 (2016) = –7.3%	High
UK	3	No	Since 2010 (at first coalition government)	61.2 (2005) – 66.2 (2015) = +5.0%	Low

Source: own illustration based on National Statistical Offices

19 Richard Heinisch / Bernd Schlipphak, »Wenn Europa zum Problem wird – die Effekte der Finanzkrise auf Euroskeptizismus und nationales Wahlverhalten in Mittel- und Osteuropa« in: *Zeitschrift für Vergleichende Politikwissenschaft* 8, No. 2 (2014), pp. 177–196.

20 Josif Kovras / Neophytos Loizides, »The Greek Debt Crisis and Southern Europe. Majoritarian Pitfalls?« in: *Comparative Politics* 47, No. 1 (2014), pp. 1–20.

Where evaluations of austerity were positive, as in Estonia, Ireland and, until recently, in the UK, we find a lot of electoral stability. In these countries (as for some time in Portugal[21] and even still in Spain) Conservatives successfully argued that they were the best problem solvers. In Greece (far left), Italy and Portugal (in these two cases the moderate left), parties of the left were seen as most trustworthy by the voters. On the left-right scale, electoral reactions to austerity do not produce a clear picture. A surprising result may be that mainstream centre-left parties profit much less from an anti-austerity mood than one could have expected, especially when they are not in government. Giger and Nelson have found »that religious and liberal parties systematically gained votes after they retrenched the welfare state«, whereas for all other parties they found »no significant relations between their retrenchment activities and the parties' corresponding electoral outcomes.«[22] Is the result of austerity politics »electoral confusion in Europe«, as Tony Barber wrote in the *Financial Times*[23], or do we witness more profound electoral change?

One can argue that austerity politics is not a left-right issue, because of the limited room for manoeuvre for governments, which have come under outside pressure (from the EU/the markets), and that all governments tend to give in to economic facts. Klaus Armingeon et al.[24] believe that one should even go further. Contrary to the expectation that fiscal conservatives and Conservative and Liberal parties will be the strongest advocates of expenditure cuts, they show that in periods of fiscal consolidation left-wing parties cut into expenditures more deeply than Conservative parties do, especially when the left-wing parties are part of an oversized coalition government. The authors refer to the »Nixon goes to China effect«, which means in our context that left-wing governments are not per se under suspicion that they are enemies of the welfare state. They investigated 17 OECD countries during the 1982–2009 period and found evidence for their hypothesis.

For the cases in our post 2008 sample, this may have been true for Portugal to some extent, but not for the short period (until 2010) of the Labour government of Gordon Brown in the UK.[25] To speak of more pronounced strategies of the political left to embrace austerity would be an exaggeration. Gordon Brown's government opted for the opposite, a Keynesian spending policy combined with higher taxes. It was the Conservative opposition that acted as the guardian of a balanced budget and that advocated austerity policies. Their approach firmly re-established austerity as the dominant issue

21 Catherine Moury / Adam Standring, »›Going beyond the Troika‹: Power and discourse in Portuguese austerity politics« in: *European Journal of Political Research* 56, No. 3 (2017), pp. 660–679.

22 Nathalie Giger / Moira Nelson, »The electoral consequences of welfare retrenchment: Blame avoidance or credit claiming in the era of permanent austerity?« in: *European Journal of Political Research* 50 (2010), pp. 1–23.

23 Tony Barber, »Electoral confusion in Europe is the norm after austerity fatigue« in: *Financial Times*, 1.5.2016, p. 2.

24 Klaus Armingeon / Kai Guthmann / David Weisstanner: »Choosing the path of austerity: how parties and policy coalitions influence welfare state retrenchment in periods of fiscal consolidation« in: *West European Politics* 39, No. 4 (2016), pp. 628–647.

25 See Anthony Seldon / Guy Lodge, *Brown at 10*, London 2011, pp. 193ff.

of economic discourses until David Cameron's loss of office in 2016. After the 2010 election, the coalition government of Conservatives and Liberal Democrats enjoyed a high level of support for the proposed austerity programme.[26] Over time, the conviction grew, however, that no party can manage the economy adequately. When living conditions did not improve, Labour in opposition could not profit from an anti-austerity mood, because in the minds of the voters the Labour party was still connected with the 2008 crisis.[27] Brexit and its consequences, however, opened up a new debate on a future for the »left behinds.« For electoral reasons the Conservatives tried to convince the public that they were ready to increase social expenditures for the socially disconnected strata of the British society, although for budgetary reasons austerity was not off the table.

The internal electoral consequences of austerity policies were also connected with political positions taken with regard to reform policies advocated by the EU (supported by the IMF). Austerity discourses became discourses on national sovereignty, and on Germany's sinister plans to dominate the EU. For national controversies on the acceptability and the need for austerity measures, the European dimension became crucial and shaped the electorate's perception of austerity. It turned out that the acceptability of EU austerity discourses not only depended on the strength of economic arguments but also on a national administrative dimension that reflected traditional administrative cultures. Their defence, however problematic and inefficient, was seen by the general public as a convincing stand against the foreigners' »blackmail.«[28]

Austerity policies can challenge established party systems and may even erode social cohesion. Though there may be other reasons for a lower turnout at general elections, too, Table 3 indicates that austerity policies and its consequences can have the power to delegitimize the workings of democracies. Anti-system protest has been another sign of this kind of political estrangement. An essay by a former UN diplomat, Stéphane Hessel, entitled »Indignez vous!«, became the reference point for anti-austerity protests for example in Spain, Portugal and Greece. Protests against the established parties left and right, because they were under suspicion to contribute to re-distributional policies that further disadvantage the poor, seemed to be tailor-made for new politics. But the Portuguese example shows that coalitions between the established left and anti-austerity protest (QLT-Que se Lixe a Troika) were possible, too. These coalitions gave new significance to traditional forms of protest, such as general strikes. Accornero and Ramos Pinto argue that »especially in 2012 and 2013« protest movements

26 Paul Whiteley / Harold D. Clarke / David Sanders / Marianne C. Stewart, *Affluence, Austerity and Electoral Change in Britain*, Cambridge 2013; Peter Tayor-Gooby / Gerry Stoker, »The Coalition Programme: A New Vision for Britain or Politics as Usual?« in: *The Political Quarterly* 82, No. 1 (2011), pp. 4–15.

27 Paul Whiteley / Harold D. Clarke / David Sanders / Marianne C. Stewart, »The Economic and Electoral Consequences of Austerity Policies in Britain« in: *Parliamentary Affairs* 68 (2015), pp. 4–24.

28 Kevin Featherstone, »External conditionality and the debt crisis: the ›Troika‹ and public administration reform in Greece« in: *Journal of European Public Policy* 22, No. 3 (2015), pp. 295–314, p. 313.

in Portugal »have increasingly relied on alliances with political parties and in particular trade unions for major actions, and they appear to be less likely to mobilise extensively when not backed by such established actors.«[29] One has to be cautious, however, with the assumption that there is a causal relationship between anti-austerity protest and the problems of those segments of society most affected by austerity policies. Research has shown (in this case for Spain) »that those who have suffered during the crisis are not necessarily the citizens demanding an end to austerity as it is currently practiced.«[30]

In the past, social movements often legitimized new parties and became a reservoir for their membership. Anti-austerity protests, which include political strikes, were by far most frequent in Greece. In Italy, Spain and Portugal we also find a »significant density of protests«[31] for the 2008–2013 period. What is the dimension of anomic participation? Is it high or low? Should one expect greater political unrest? Genovese et al. say yes, if a country does not have the flexibility to devalue her currency in the debt crisis. For the Eurozone, the authors try to show in their empirical research that the actions of the European Central Bank (ECB), especially the reassurance of the ECB's President Mario Draghi, were able to calm down political protest. In his statement of 2012, he had used the words to do »whatever it takes« to save the euro and had thereby taken market pressure from the EU member states in crisis. For Genovese et al. it was the policy position of the ECB that prevented large-scale public protests in the eurozone.[32]

This finding sounds too good to be true, though. But a lack of anomic participation is not the whole picture. One should not forget, however, that a significant part of anti-austerity and anti-system protest was channelled into new parties or gave existing marginal parties and protest movements a new raison d'être. Examples are Syriza in Greece, Sinn Féin in Ireland, Movimento Cinque Stelle in Italy, or Podemos in Spain. These so-called »challenger parties« feed not only on austerity but also on EU integration and immigration issues. Hobolt and Tilley neatly summarized the explanations for the success of this new type of parties, which differ, however, in some aspects not mentioned by the authors:

> *»Our argument is that defectors choose challenger parties because they offer a rejection of, and an alternative to, the mainstream response to the crisis, Whereas the mainstream left and right have converged on a policy of austerity and an adherence to the fiscal policy-making guidelines of the EU, successful challenger parties have*

29 Guya Accornero / Pedro Ramos Pinto, »›Mild Mannered?‹ Protest and Mobilisation in Portugal under Austerity, 2010–2013« in: *West European Politics* 38, No. 3 (2015), pp. 491–515, p. 508.

30 José Fernández-Albertos / Alexander Kuo, »Economic Hardship and Policy Preferences in the Eurozone Periphery: Evidence from Spain« in: *Comparative Political Studies* 49, No. 7 (2016), pp. 874–906, p. 876.

31 Federica Genovese / Gerald Schneider / Pia Wassermann, »The Eurotower Strikes Back: Adjustments, and Europe's Austerity Protests« in: *Comparative Political Studies* 49, No. 7 (2016), pp. 939–967, p. 948.

32 Genovese / Schneider / Wassermann, »The Eurotower Strikes Back «, op. cit. (note 31), p. 948.

sought to offer clear alternatives. On the left, challenger parties reject the austerity agenda and are critical of the EU's insistence on reduced government welfare spending. On the right, the focus is on the desire to reclaim national sovereignty, specifically to control immigration and repatriate powers from the EU. In both cases, challenger parties reject the ›there is no alternative‹ argument and instead claim that national governments can control their own destiny and offer distinct policies.«[33]

This anti-austerian commonality explains the 2015 coalition government in Greece of a far left party (Syriza) and a far right party (Anel), which otherwise would be difficult to understand. It is remarkable that the old hard Left did not profit much from the post 2008 »crises of capitalism.«[34] For voters the policy-oriented approach of challenger parties seems to have been more convincing than a return to »class war«. This is often overlooked if analyses clump together radical left, radical right and other non-mainstream parties.[35] Research is unanimous in that the economic crises have contributed to a long-term trend of a destabilization of European party systems, their fragmentation and the rise of the extremes.

Challenger parties had greater difficulties to succeed when the mainstream parties did no rely too much on clientelistic networks. Clientelistic networks are forms of voter mobilization based above all on implicit or explicit »treaties« with the voters. Voters believe that there is a fairly immediate trade-off between voting and social reward. In Italy and, above all, in Greece, this logic is alive, and it is respected by parties in power: Electoral success of parties is »based on building up support among discrete sections of the electorate, and consolidating it through the exercise of special privileges and access to patronage networks.«[36] Portugal is an example for the absence of clientelistic networks. In Greece, clientelism colonialized the state/public sector. Its resources became part of electoral outbidding processes.[37] Afonso et al. argue that »mass clientelism led Greek parties to systematically over-promise, and voters to over-expect, which led to brutal sanctions and anger when these promises had to be betrayed. In contrast, Portuguese parties did not promise as much, and voters did not expect much from them either.«[38] In the perspective of mass clientelism, austerity policies are a form of treason, which justifies a new orientation of the voters and their efforts to build up new net-

33 Sara B. Hobolt / James Tilley, »Fleeing the centre: the rise of challenger parties in the aftermath of the euro crisis« in: *West European Politics* 39, No. 5 (2016), pp. 971–991, p. 972.

34 Giorgos Charalambous / Iasonas Lamprianou, »Societal Responses to the Post-2008 Economic Crisis among South European and Irish Radical Left Parties: Continuity or Change and Why?« in: *Government and Opposition* 51, No. 2 (2016), pp. 261–293.

35 Enrique Hernández / Hanspeter Kriesi, »The electoral consequences of the financial and economic crisis in Europe« in: *European Journal of Political Research* 55 (2016), pp. 203–224.

36 Sebastian Dellepiane-Avellaneda / Niamh Hardiman, »Fiscal politics in time: pathways to fiscal consolidation in Ireland, Greece, Britain, and Spain, 1980–2012« in: *European Political Science Review* 7, No. 2 (2015), pp. 189–219, p. 204.

37 Josif Kovras / Neophytos Loizides, »The Greek Debt Crisis and Southern Europe. Majoritarian Pitfalls?« in: *Comparative Politics* 47, No. 1 (2014), pp. 1–20, p. 5.

38 Alexandre Afonso / Sotirios Zartaloudis / Yannis Papadopoulos, »How party linkages shape austerity politics: clientilism and fiscal adjustment in Greece and Portugal during the eurozone crisis« in: *Journal of European Public Policy* 22, No. 3 (2015), pp. 315–334, p. 329.

work structures or to strengthen alternative existing networks, in the Greek case of radical trade unions and leftist parties, for example. Austerity policies create »victims« in this context. Budgetary policies suffer from »collective action problems associated with common pool goods: everyone consumes but no one wants to pay«.[39]

Are challenger parties populist parties? This is often the case as challenger parties may use populist tactics and populist vocabulary. But populism itself is a rather vague concept and stands for a great variety of nationalist protest. The term »challenger parties« is more precise and less pejorative, and it can better be used as a category in cross-national comparisons. A causal relationship between crisis and the rise of challenger parties is, however, less than obvious.[40] There are countries in crisis that did not experience the rise of challenger parties, Portugal, for example, and less crisis-ridden countries, such as Germany or Sweden, that were confronted with new parties challenging the party political consensus.

Together with populist parties, technocratic governments are seen by parts of the literature on the quality of democracy as »the Scylla and Charybdis of democratic ideals. «[41] Since the beginning of the Euro crisis we are not only witnessing an increasing concern with challenger parties but also with technocratic governments. The installation of the latter in Italy and Greece in 2011[42] and the new technocratic rules for economic governance at the EU level have changed political life not only on the level of electoral outcomes but also on a more fundamental level. »The resulting paradox is«, as Sánchez-Cuenca argues, »that in a time of growing ›politicization‹ of European affairs, the technocratic bias of the European Union has ›depoliticized‹ economic issues.«[43] Although austerity policies are subject to national decision-making, the EU has a role as far as her instruments of economic governance are involved. All EU member states have agreed to the Maastricht criteria, which include net annual deficit limits of nation-

39 Nikolas Zahariadis, »National Fiscal Profligacy and European Institutional Adolescence: The Greek Trigger to Europe's Sovereign Debt Crisis« in: *Government and Opposition* 48, No. 1 (2013), pp. 33–54, p. 33.

40 Hanspeter Kriesi / Takin S. Pappas (eds.), *European Populism in the Shadow of the Great Recession*, Colchester 2015.

41 Giulia Pastorella, »Technocratic Governments in Europe: Getting the Critique Right« in: *Political Studies* 64, No. 4 (2016), pp. 948–965, p. 948. For a conceptional discussion of the term »technocratic governments« and empirical evidence of these in the 27 Member States of the EU between the end of the Second World War and June 2013 see Duncan McDonnell / Marco Valbruzzi, »Defining and classifying technocrat-led and technocratic governments« in: *European Journal of Political Research* 53, No. 4 (2014), pp. 654–671.

42 Pepper D. Culpepper, »The Political Economy of Unmediated Democracy: Italian Austerity under Mario Monti« in: *West European Politics* 37, No. 6 (2014), pp. 1264–1281; Susannah Verney / Anna Bosco, »Living Parallel Lives: Italy and Greece in an Age of Austerity« in: *South European Society and Politics* 18, No. 4 (2013), pp. 397–426.

43 Ignacio Sánchez-Cuenca, »From a Deficit of Democracy to a Technocratic Order: The Postcrisis Debate on Europe« in: *Annual Review of Political Science* 20, No. 1 (2017), pp. 351–369, p. 351. But the according establishment of post-politics leads to a further paradox as »the institutionalization of apolitical decision-making processes is only a detour which always leads right back into the heart of politics. There is no such thing as the politics of non-politics.«

al budgets and an overall limit of the public debt. A number of instruments were created, especially for the eurozone members, to increase the probability of compliance. Without going into detail, it can be said that the EU institutions, and above all the EU Commission, have a difficult task. There is general agreement that a common currency, the euro, should be accompanied by economic and budgetary policies that guarantee an adequate economic environment. Member states have agreed to the goal of convergence of national economies, and they expect solidarity in times of crises. It is expected that member states adjust their budgets to avoid excessive deficits when they need budgetary support by the European Stability Mechanism (ESM). The steering capacity of the EU in budgetary and economic matters is limited, however. And this is said to be true for all member states, and especially for the member states of the eurozone. The EU Commission admitted this in her 2017 paper on the future of the Economic and Monetary Union: »Member States of the euro area form a diverse group. There will never be a single approach or a ›once and for all‹ common understanding of how to advance best the EMU«. The Commission could have added that the same goes for compliance to the rules set by the EU. There are not only varieties of austerity; there are also varieties of acceptance, success and sustainability of austerity policies.

Left-wing critics interpret this context not just as one of varieties of austerity but as a systemic relationship of uneven development anchored in the structure of capitalism that shapes the European state project.[44] Following Poulantzas, this is seen as a form of »authoritarian statism«, understood as a situation in which legislatures and popular forces are blocked from effective participation in the political process: »That legitimacy embodied by parliament which had as its frame of reference a universal rationality is gradually passing over into a legitimacy characterized by the instrumental rationality of efficiency and embodied by the Executive-administration.«[45] The accompanying questions about political representation are far from being merely technical ones. According to critical and systemic approaches, the developments in the field of politics in the »age of austerity« are understood as fundamental processes that are part of a broader neoliberal transformation of social life and that have changed the quality of democracy. Colin Crouch argued already in 2004 that we are on a way to an erosion of *substantial* elements of democracy in an era that he terms »post-democracy.« But the term does not stand for an »absence of democracy or a denial of democracy; rather it describes a democracy that has become more formal than real, remains strong de jure but weakened de facto.«[46]

Ian Bruff and Lukus Oberndorfer go even further in their characterization of the essence of the current political transformation that they term »authoritarian neoliber-

44 Sune Sandbeck / Etienne Schneider, »From the Sovereign Debt Crisis to Authoritarian Statism: Contradictions of the European State Project« in: *New Political Economy* 19, No. 6 (2014), pp. 847–871; Bob Jessop, »Variegated capitalism and the political economy of austerity« in: Richard Westra / Dennis Badeen / Robert Albritton (eds.), *The Future of Capitalism after the Financial Crisis: The Varieties of Capitalism Debate in the Age of Austerity*, London/New York 2015, pp. 19–38.

45 Poulantzas, Nikos, *State, Power, Socialism*, London/New York, Kindle-Version, p. 208–209.

46 Colin Crouch, »Post-democracy and the crisis« in: *Juridikum* 1/2013, pp. 41–50, p. 41.

alism« and »authoritarian constitutionalism«, respectively. For Bruff, the authoritarian turn within the current reconfiguration of the state under the »There is no alternative« (TINA) slogan is based on

> *»(1) the more immediate appeal to material circumstances as a reason for the state being unable, despite ›the best will in the world‹ to reverse processes such as greater socioeconomic inequality and dislocation; (2) the deeper and longer term recalibration of the kinds of activity that are feasible and appropriate for nonmarket institutions to engage in, diminishing expectations in the process; and (3) the reconceptualization of the state as increasingly nondemocratic through its subordination to constitutional and legal rules that are deemed necessary for prosperity to be achieved.«*[47]

The last element of this transformation is the focus of Lukas Oberndorfer. In contrast to Crouch, he argues that not only *substantial* elements of democracy have deteriorated within the European Union after the economic and financial crisis but also even *formal* ones. We observe a process that is connected to the weakening of legislatures in favour of executive powers. With respect to austerity this process is based on four main pillars: the already mentioned ESM, the stricter rules of the Stability and Growth Pact (SGP), the Euro-Plus-Pact (EPP) and the Fiscal Compact (FC).[48] In contrast to non-systemic approaches, proponents of a critical perspective argue that instruments like the ESM do not form a safety net in the name of reciprocal European solidarity. Instead, for these critics, these mechanisms are based on a form of »competitive solidarity.«[49] The results of these developments are felt most intensively in Greece, as Gounari argues: »Under the auspices of neoliberal ideology that divests the state of any responsibility for social provisions [...] the weakened social and welfare state resorts more and more to material and symbolic violence, including increased militarization, exponential increases in the police forces and the omnipresence of police in public spaces.«[50]

2. Economics land

Austerity can be described as a budgetary policy which aims to avoid debt and to achieve a balanced budget in the mid-term. Measures grouped under the heading »aus-

47 Ian Bruff, »The Rise of Authoritarian Neoliberalism« in: *Rethinking Marxism* 26, No. 1 (2014), pp. 113–129.

48 Sandbeck / Schneider, »From the Sovereign Debt Crisis to Authoritarian Statism«, op. cit. (note 44), p. 851–854.

49 Wolfgang Streeck, »Competitive Solidarity: Rethinking the ›European Social Model‹« in: Karl Hinrichs / Herbert Kirschelt / Helmut Wiesenthal (ed.), *Kontingenz und Krise. Institutionenpolitik in kapitalistischen und postsozialistischen Gesellschaften*, Frankfurt/New York 2000, pp. 245–261.

50 Panayota Gounari, »Neoliberalism as Social Necrophilia. Erich Fromm and the Politics of Hopelessness in Greece« in: Seyed Javad Miri / Robert Lake / Tricia M. Kress (ed.), *Reclaiming the Sane Society. Essays on Erich Fromm's Thought*, Rotterdam/Boston/Taipei 2014, pp. 187–201, p. 191.

terity« can include tax increases, government expenditure cuts and structural reforms. Alternatively, austerity can be defined as a reduction in government borrowing that is associated with fiscal adjustment. Reorganization of a state budget can cause concerns that there will be cuts mainly in social welfare.[51] These cuts do not put redistribution issues on the political agenda but also lead to a polarization within society. Furthermore, cuts are made in infrastructure which normally find easier acceptance by politicians because there is no proper popular resistance.

Table 2: Austerity changes in the social and investment-related fields[52]

Country	Changes in social policies	Changes in public investment activities
Greece	---	+
Ireland	--	-
Italy	-	-
Germany	ø	+
UK	-	+
Spain	-	---
Portugal	-	--
France	++	++

Source: own illustration

The consequences of austerity policies depend on the causes of the current economic and financial crisis: Approaches that are critical of capitalism as such explain the crisis as a consequence and a strategy under a neoliberal agenda. From a Marxist perspective, the present crisis might be depicted as one in which the striving for high rates of profits in the current stage of capitalism cannot be accommodated in the »real economy. « Therefore, profits are sought in the financial sector, where immense but nevertheless fictitious rates of profit are promised. This situation leads to financial bubbles and to crises when the high levels of »fictitious capital« want to be translated into »real capital« and when the pyramid of fictitious promises breaks down, accordingly. From this perspective, austerity in the form of wage and social spending cuts is one of the mechanisms to make available funds for the cost of the massive bailouts for banks. They were necessary to liquidate the immense losses in the financial system and to keep the neoliberal system running.[53]

51 Christian Breunig / Marius R. Busemeyer, »Fiscal austerity and the trade-off between public investment and social spending« in: *Journal of European Public Policy* 19, No. 6 (2012), pp. 921–938; Arne Heise / Hanna Lierse, »The Effects of European Austerity Programmes on Social Security Systems« in: *Modern Economy* 2, No. 4 (2011), pp. 498–513.

52 Declaration: „ø" = no changes; »---« = very far savings; »++« = extensive increases.

53 See Jessop in this volume.

These critical voices argue not only that financial crises are an indicator of good capitalism gone bad[54] but that the »oscillation between bouts of austerity and laxer policies encouraging the development of asset bubbles may be built into neoliberalism as an economic policy regime.«[55] This policy is said to have significant implications, particularly on the lives of the working class: increases in prices and increased unemployment, which is connected to cuts in social welfare. It also fuels support for fascist groups and parties. These developments are also seen as a danger to the European state project as a whole, which is also threatened by the dominance of Germany in Europe.[56] For left-wing critics, Europe »is caught in an ordoliberal iron cage«[57] because of the German insistence on the acceptance of strict rules. From the perspective of critical theory, the insistence on rule following, balanced budgets and corresponding austerity measures is not just part of a legal framework that shall ensure the functioning of the European market but a power strategy. Some commentators like Paul Krugman go even so far as to argue that Berlin planned a regime change in Athens against the socialist government.[58] For critical voices, such a form of imperialism brings the current imbalances between the European core and the periphery, and the inherent contradictions of capitalism, clearly to the fore.[59] From this perspective, the only solution for the current crises can be found in the end of »neoliberalism« by means of emancipatory projects that substitute neoliberalism's keywords of competition, structural reforms (in favour of capital) and privatizations with equity, solidarity, cooperation, mutual aid and environmental sustainability.[60]

In contrast, the non-systemic approach to austerity interprets the current economic and financial turbulences either from a supply- or demand-side perspective without

54 Ian Bruff, »The rise of Authoritarian Neoliberalism« in: *Rethinking Marxism* 26, No. 1 (2014), pp. 113–129, pp. 120–125.

55 Alex Callinicos, »Contradictions of austerity« in: *Cambridge Journal of Economics* 36, No. 1 (2012), pp. 65–77, p. 65.

56 Stefan Hinsch / Wilhelm Langthaler: *Europa zerbricht am Euro. Unter deutscher Vorherrschaft in die totale Krise*, Wien 2016.

57 Magnus Ryner, »Europe's ordoliberal iron cage: critical political economy, the euro area crisis and its management« in: *Journal of European Public Policy* 22, No. 2 (2015), pp. 275–294, p. 275.

58 Paul Krugman, »The Awesome Gratuitousness of the Greek Crisis« in: *New York Times*, 29.6.2015, https://.krugman.blogs.nytimes.com/2015/06/29/the-awesome-gratuitousness-of-the-greek-crisis/ [4.7.2017].

59 Matt O'Brien, »Europe strikes back: It seems to be trying to push Greece out of the euro« in: *The Washington Post*, 25.6.2015, https://www.washingtonpost.com/news/wonk/wp/2015/06/25/europe-strikes-back-it-seems-to-be-trying-to-push-greece-out-of-the-euro/?utm_term=.a8411341da13 [4.7.2017]. For imperial austerity in Greece see Fouskas and Dimoulas in this volume.

60 Angela Wigger / Hubert Buch-Hansen, »Competition, the Global Crisis, and Alternatives to Neoliberal Capitalism: A Critical Engagement with Anarchism« in: *New Political Science* 35, No. 4 (2013), pp. 604–626; Hans-Jürgen Bieling and Ulrich Brand, »Competitiveness or Emancipation? Rethinking Regulation and (Counter-)hegemony in Times of Capitalist Crisis« in: Richard Westra / Dennis Badeen / Robert Albritton (eds.), *The Future of Capitalism after the Financial Crisis. The Varieties of Capitalism Debate in the Age of Austerity*, London/New York 2015, pp. 184–204. See also Griebel in this volume.

questioning the capitalist system. As advocates of Keynes' theory of insufficient demand[61], many economists such as Crotty[62], Pitelis and Argites[63] also believe that insufficient demand is the cause of past and present crises. Insufficient demand is said to be caused by poor macroeconomic management, restrictive monetary policy, inadequate consumption and inadequate systemic regulation. In times of crisis, monetary expansion is necessary to avoid economic stalemate and mass unemployment. The so-called »Pigou effect«, the assumption that supply creates demand, cannot be observed. Investments are not attracted and production decreases. Inflationary expectations can stimulate consumption to overcome the crisis, whereas deflationary expectations will restrict consumption due to the fact that consumers expect falling prices. If austerity is implemented at this stage of the business cycle, the capitalist economy will fall again into a deep depression with resulting mass unemployment.[64] To avoid the possibility of a great economic crash, the central banks should implement a loose monetary policy. In fiscal terms, governments should deliberately run deficits financed by borrowed money. For Keynesians, a demand-managed economic policy generates further private demand and contributes to reduced unemployment rates.

When the crisis is dealt with in a supply-side manner, deficit spending is not expected to solve the problem, as Taylor explains: »The classic explanation of financial crises, going back hundreds of years, is that they are caused by excesses – frequently monetary excesses – which lead to a boom and an inevitable bust.«[65] To put the public debt on a sustainable path and to avert a crisis, a strict monetary policy is necessary. In order to improve economic performance, deeper cuts and structural reforms are of vital importance. Carmen Reinhart and Kenneth Rogroff identify a relationship between debt and economic growth.[66] In their study they show that if public debt is more than 90% of a country's GDP, this has a detrimental impact on national economies. Alberto

61 Keynesianism is understood here as a non-systemic approach because it's proponents are – usually – not critical of the capitalist system as such. In this sense, the alternative between neoliberal austerity as a form of supply-side neoclassical economics and Keynesianism as a form of demand-side neoclassical economics is no radical alternative at all, despite public arguments to the contrary. Both approaches are connected not only theoretically but also historically as Keynesianism not only laid the ground for the rise of neoliberalism but also plays an important role within the neoliberal regime. Geoff Mann, »Keynes resurrected? Saving civilization, again and again« in: *Dialogues in Human Geography* 6, No. 2 (2016), pp. 119–134, p. 130.

62 James Crotty, *Structural Causes of the Global Financial Crisis: A Critical Assessment of the New Financial Architecture*, PERI Working Paper Series 180 (2008).

63 George Argitis / Christos Pitelis, »Global Finance and Systemic Instability« in: *Contributions to Political Economy* 27, No. 1 (2008), pp. 1–11; Robert Pollin, »Austerity is not a solution« in: *Challenge* 53, No. 6 (2010), pp. 6–36.

64 Olivier Blanchard / Daniel Leigh, *Growth Forecast Errors and Fiscal Multipliers*, IMF Working Paper WP/13/1 (2013).

65 John Taylor, *The Financial Crisis and the Policy Responses: an Empirical Analysis What Went Wrong*, NBER Working Paper 14631 (2009).

66 Carmen Reinhart / Kenneth Rogoff, »Growth in a Time of Debt« in: *American Economic Review* 100, No. 2 (2010), pp. 573–578; Carmen Reinhart / Vincent Reinhart / Kenneth Rogoff, »Public Debt Overhangs: Advanced-Economy Episodes since 1800« in: *Journal of Economic Perspectives* 26, No. 3 (2012), pp. 69–86.

Alesina and Silvia Ardagna have proven that austerity – defined here as fiscal consolidation – can encourage economic output growth, decrease inflation and strengthen a currency.[67] However, with the exception of Ireland which has successfully dealt with the crisis, this wasn't the case in Greece, Spain, Portugal and Italy, where despite austerity measures the relationship between public debt and GDP deteriorated. Therefore, according to the economists Paul Krugman, Joseph Stieglitz und Thomas Piketty, austerity has had little success.[68] Alberto Alesina and Francesco Giavazzi argue, however, that massive fiscal consolidation normally requires many years to be effective when governments propose and then implement a sequence of deficit reduction policies.[69] Austerity can reduce public debt in the long term, but in the short term it will have negative effects on GDP. As Francesco Giavazzi and Marco Pagano point out, fiscal consolidation encourages more economic growth when it involves greater spending cuts rather than more taxation.[70] Following their arguments, spending-based adjustments have proven in the past to cause mid and short-lived recessions, in many cases with no impact at all. Instead, tax-based adjustments have been followed by prolonged and deep recessions.[71] To implement such a strategy of fiscal consolidation, effective governmental structures with a functioning bureaucracy are the key.[72] These structures haven't proven to be successful in Greece and in some parts of Italy, where they have encountered many problems. In the case of Greece, many cuts were made in pensions, social welfare and salaries, and there was a massive reduction of public employment. These measures were combined with a VAT increase of 5% to 24%. However, the Greek debt ratio increased from 109% (2008) to 180% (2017). Austerity measures led

67 Alesina Alberto / Silvia Ardagna, *Large Changes in Fiscal Policy: Taxes Versus Spending*, NBER Working Paper 15438 (2009).

68 Paul Krugman, »Austerity and the Greek Depression« in: *New York Times*, 10.7.2015, https://krugman.blogs.nytimes.com/2015/07/10/austerity-and-the-greek-depression/?_r=0 [4.7.2017]; Joseph Stiglitz, »Austerity has been an utter disaster for the Eurozone« in: *The Guardian*, 1.10.2014, https://www.theguardian.com/business/2014/oct/01/austerity-eurozone-disaster-joseph-stiglitz [4.7.2017]; Thomas Piketty / Jeffrey D. Sachs / Heiner Flassbeck / Dani Rodrik / Simon Wren-Lewis, »Austerity Has Failed: An Open Letter from Thomas Piketty to Angela Merkel« in: *The Nation*, 7.7.2015, https://www.thenation.com/article/austerity-has-failed-an-open-letter-from-thomas-piketty-to-angela-merkel/ [4.7.2017].

69 Alberto Alesina / Francesco Giavazzi, »The Effects of Austerity: Recent Research« in: *NBER Reporter* 3/2015.

70 Francesco Giavazzi / Marco Pagano, »Can Severe Fiscal Contractions Be Expansionary? Tales of Two Small European Countries« in: *NBER Macroeconomics Annual* 5 (1990), pp. 75–122; Alberto Alesina / Silvia Ardagna, »Large Changes in Fiscal Policy: Taxes versus Spending« in: *Tax Policy and the Economy* 24 (2010), pp. 35–68.

71 Christina Romer / David H. Romer, »The macroeconomic effects of tax changes: Estimates based on a new measure of fiscal shocks« in: *American Economic Review* 100, No. 3 (2010), pp. 763–801.

72 Roberto Perotti, *The „Austerity Myth": Gain without pain?*, NBER Working Paper 17571 (2011); Vassilis Monastiriotis, »(When) does austerity work? On the conditional link between fiscal austerity and debt sustainability« in: *Cyprus Economic Policy Review* 8, No. 1 (2014), pp. 71–92.

to a decrease in public spending as well as a reduction in private spending. The reduction in public and private demand led to a cycle of destabilization.

Table 3: Public Debt 2008 and 2017 in relation to the GDP

Country	2008 (in %)	2017 (in %)	Changes	Deficit Peak (Year)
Greece	109	180	+71	181 (2016)
Ireland	42	75	+33	120 (2013)
Italy	102	133	+31	133 (2017)
Germany	62	68	+6	81 (2010)
UK	50	89	+39	90 (2016)
Spain	39	98	+59	100 (2014)
Portugal	72	129	+57	131 (2014)
France	68	97	+29	97 (2017)

Source: own illustration based on Statista

The macroeconomic view on austerity produces several results. Firstly, as Table 3 shows, there is no evidence of systematic austerity measures in Europe. According to the figures in this table, it is questionable whether fiscal consolidation was achieved as public debt rose so dramatically. During the recession, the slowdown in economic activity combined with increased transfer payments, financial system bailouts and fiscal stimulus programmes resulted in a great surge of public debt. This raises serious concerns about fiscal solvency, as figure 1 indicates.

Figure 1: History of 10-Year Government Bond Yields

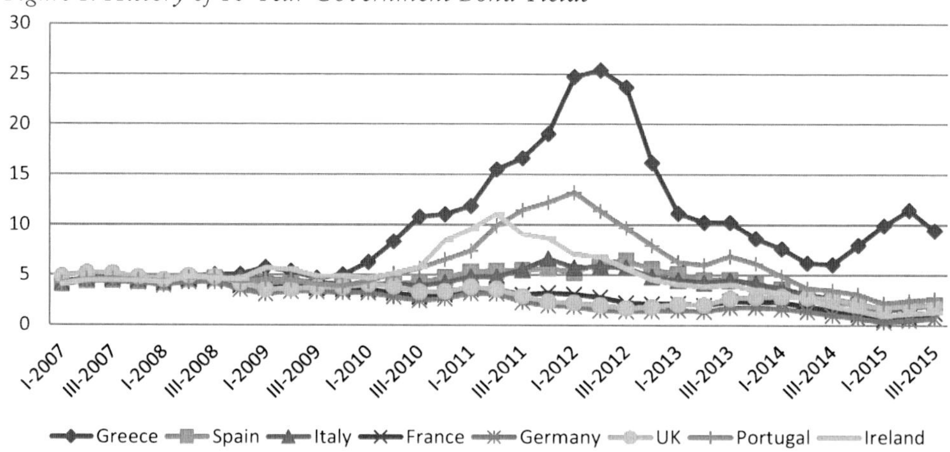

Source: own illustration based on Statista

Austerity, secondly, is implemented in countries with large and increasing levels of debt to GDP ratios. In its absence, the country would have to pay large risk premiums or even worse, be completely shut out from credit markets. An argument in support of this is that austerity creates an incentive to build a reputation of creditworthiness: By imposing unpopular austerity measures, a government indicates that it will be prepared to repay its future debt. In this perspective, austerity is part of a future-oriented policy and may help private investors to distinguish a credit-worthy government from one with a high default probability. But, as Blanchard indicates, »financial investors are schizophrenic about fiscal consolidation and growth. They react positively to news of fiscal consolidation, but then react negatively later, when consolidation leads to lower growth – which it often does.«[73] The success of austerity, therefore, depends on a number of country specific and partly unobserved factors, such as the ability to raise taxes or political stability.

Thirdly, austerity might have harsh impacts on growth, particularly during times of deep recession, when economic slack is pervasive. As a consequence, the timing of austerity is important. In economic terms, fiscal consolidation should be implemented during times of economic strength, to enhance budget surpluses and to control inflation. But no government would choose austerity measures if it was not »forced« to do so by either private (Spain) or public creditors (Greece). Based on past events, Pearlstein argues that countries like Greece, France or Italy wouldn't be willing to implement austerity measures after recovery and full employment had been achieved.[74] The reason why austerity is implemented more often in the face of high debt and sluggish growth is because of opportunism and the short-term preferences of politicians. However, the implementation of fiscal consolidation during a crisis can have dire distributional consequences. Examples of these consequences are battles over resources among various players, social unrest and riots.

3. Discourse land

The term »discourse« is at least as controversial as the term »austerity«, and in no way we intent to give final definitions of both here. We will just start with a minimal definition of discourse analysis as the study of language use or a social practice within a society.[75] However, how this social practice is understood and analysed differs significantly between different tribes in discourse land. Mainstream approaches like content analysis and critical approaches like critical discourse analysis have different ontological and epistemological standpoints regarding the nature and power of language, its

73 Blanchard, Olivier, »2011 in review: four hard truths« in: *IMFBlog*, 21.12.2011, http://blog-imfdirect.imf.org/2011/12/21/2011-in-review-four-hard-truths/ [4.7.2017].

74 Steven Pearlstein, »The case for austerity isn't dead yet« in: *The Washington Post*, 14.5.2015, http://www.washingtonpost.com/blogs/wonkblog/wp/2013/05/14/the-case-for-austerity-isnt-dead-yet/ [4.7.2017].

75 For different understandings of the term »discourse« and different ways to study discourses see Deborah Tannen / Heidi Ehernberger Hamilton / Deborah Schiffrin, *The handbook of discourse analysis*, Chichester/Malden 2015.

role in social life and the possibilities to study it.[76] Mainstream approaches, by trend, understand language as a form of variable that is *not* constitutive of social reality as a whole but is only one causal force beside many others that can be studied scientifically. These approaches are well suited to study the linguistic surface and to provide a broad overview of the discourse land of austerity. Especially researchers that use computational and quantitative tools, like cartographers, are able to provide a map of the linguistic surface and the regularities that can be found on it and will lead us to deeper levels and more substantial forms of critique of different austerity discourses later on.

In respect to parliamentary discourses, Aleksandra Maatsch, for example, has used a combination of discourse analysis and qualitative comparative analysis to find the conditions for a Keynesian or neoliberal position of a parliamentary party on anti-crisis measures in Austria, Belgium, France, Germany, Greece, Ireland, Slovenia and Spain. She detects a tendency of parliamentary parties within indebted countries »to opt for Keynesian anti-crisis measures despite their right-wing economic stance or membership in the government.«[77] A particular interesting case here is, of course, Greece, because it brings to light most clearly discursive structures that are connected with austerity policies. An investigation of the five parties in the Greek parliament, in particular during the 2009–11 period, with the help of a framing analysis of speeches delivered by the leaders of these parties, detects different forms of populism and forms of blaming for major parties and smaller parties. The argument is that

> *»blame-shifting, employed by the two major parties, is a more concentrated form of populism: blame is directed against fewer actors, concentrating upon the major contenders in the system (that is, each other as the two main parties competing for government) and external elites. [...] [B]lame-shifting, employed by the smaller parties, is a less concentrated form of populism entailing that blame is spread out, and directed against a wider range of actors including the party of government, the party of opposition, external elites, specific interest groups and the collaboration between them.«*[78]

Beside Greece, the United Kingdom is another interesting case for the study of austerity discourses.[79] Here the »age of austerity« was already welcomed by later Prime Minister, David Cameron, in 2009. Testing a large dataset of publications by think tanks between 2003 and 2013 with the help of a computer-assisted text analysis, Anstead shows that there have been three stages of the austerity discourse in Britain. Prior to

76 Cynthia Hardy / Bill Harley / Nelson Phillips, »Discourse Analysis and Content Analysis: Two Solitudes?« in: *Newsletter of the American Political Science Association Organized Section on Qualitative Methods* 2, No. 1 (2004), pp. 19–22.

77 Aleksandra Maatsch, »Are we all austerians now? An analysis of national parliamentary parties' positioning on anti-crisis measures in the eurozone« in: *Journal of European Public Policy* 21, No. 1 (2014), pp. 96–115, p. 96.

78 Sofia Vasilopoulou / Daphne Halikiopoulou / Theofanis Exadaktylos, »Greece in Crisis: Austerity, Populism and the Politics of Blame« in: *JCMS: Journal of Common Market Studies* 52, No. 2 (2014), pp. 388–402, p. 400.

79 See Grundmann / Kreischner / Scott in this volume.

2008, the term austerity was used in respect to something of the past or to something that happens in other countries. But after the financial crisis of 2007/08, right-wing think tanks used the term to attack the Labour government before left-wing political actors tried to redefine the concept once again in order to criticize the Conservative-Liberal Democrat government. Anstead also shows that right-wing articulations do »not just focus on national debt or the size of the state, but also on more long-standing ideological concerns, such as law and order, and the EU. On the left, too, divisions are evident between discussions about party and electoral politics, a more values-based approach focused on traditional concerns, and a more technocratic tendency.«[80] This study, therefore, once again points to regularities at the linguistic surface of articulations of political actors that already hint at deeper structures of political conflict although they are not addressed directly in the analysis.

But not only a look at the discursive articulations of politicians is important for an understanding of the form of austerity discourses. Because reality is always mediated, media articulations are powerful factors as well. With the help of a political claim-making analysis for traditional media texts that contain the words »crisis«, »recession« or »austerity« in nine European countries between 2008 and 2014, Sabina Monza and Eva Anduiza analysed the degree of visibility of the EU and of European actors. They found evidence for »very low levels of European visibility in the debates of the national public spheres. Overall, the results confirm the uncontested primacy of national communicative flows in every country.«[81] This analysis is another case of the detection of broader linguistic structures that hint to deeper social mechanisms at work in discourses.

Such mainstream analyses prepare the way for (more) critical approaches that leave the linguistic surface and are more directly interested in the constitutive power of discourses and their connection to ideological structures within the current economic system. Although the scope and depth of their critique differs[82], these systemic approaches are critical of the current political system, which is understood as the result of political struggles. More critical forms of discourse analysis[83] follow the signs on the linguistic surface to go deep(er) into the rabbit hole of critical theory. By doing so, quantitative tools like corpus linguistic or lexicographic methods can also be employed.[84] This path can start with the simple recognition of the ideological and corresponding emotional purposes of language use.

80 Nick Anstead, *The idea of austerity in British politics, 2003–13*, http://eprints.lse.ac.uk/72120/ [28.7.2017], p. 21.

81 Sabina Monza / Eva Anduiza, »The Visibility of the EU in the National Public Spheres in Times of Crisis and Austerity« in: *Politics & Policy* 44, No. 3 (2016), pp. 499–524, p. 518. See also Monza in this volume.

82 Andrew Sayer, »Who's Afraid of Critical Social Science?« in: *Current Sociology* 57, No. 6 (2009), pp. 767–786.

83 For an overview of different forms of Critical Discourse Analysis see Martin Reisigl, »Critical Discourse Analysis« in: Robert Bayley / Richard Cameron / Ceil Lucas (eds.), *The Oxford Handbook of Sociolinguistics*, Oxford 2013, pp. 68–90.

84 See Griebel in this volume and Paul Baker, *Using Corpora in Discourse Analysis*, London/New York 2006.

By combining corpus-based and discourse-based approaches to analyse conceptual metaphors connected to austerity, Soares da Silva et al., for example, detect differences in Portugal, Spain and Ireland: »a deep conservative morality of self-discipline and punishment, in the case of Portugal; a strong sense of outrage against austerity measures and their creditors, in Spain; and the idea that the crisis and its effects were hitting the country but not as seriously as others, in Ireland.«[85] Going down the critical route even further, Boriello has combined lexicographic methods and metaphor analysis in order to deconstruct the economic common sense and the metaphorical depiction of economics in Italy and Spain. He argues that the austerity discourse tries to construct an economic sense that is backed by the use of geological, meteorological, mechanical and clinical metaphors to describe the nature of the economy. By doing so, the political nature of economics in general and austerity in particular is hidden and a TINA world is constructed.[86]

Bickes et al. also look at metaphors. Through the lens of a critical discourse analysis they do not only find similar metaphorical structures but also offer a deeper understanding of the structure of blame in financial discourses. By looking at the metaphorical expressions in the media coverage on Greece, Spain and Italy in Germany, the United Kingdom and the United States, they show that the analysed media »avoid naming the responsible social actors, such as banks, financial markets, speculators, etc. The media construct a reality in which the European monetary union falls victim to some kind of superior power. Instead of identifiable actors, fate seems to be the guiding principle of crisis.«[87] But despite these naturalizations of the economic crisis, some populations are held more responsible than others. And for critical approaches both rhetoric strategies serve to hide the political construction of economic crises and the remedies like austerity to handle them.

In an overview of the literature about (critical) discourse analysis about financial and (anti-)austerity discourses, Kelsey et al. argue that narratives in favour of austerity are backed by a »morality tale«[88] that tells us not only that there is no alternative to spending cuts to reduce excessive and unsustainable public debt but also that the infamously called PIIGS (Portugal, Italy, Ireland, Greece and Spain) have to do their homework in order to become good pupils in the economic governance school.[89] Especially the talk

85 Augusto Soares da Silva / Maria Josep Cuenca / Manuela Romano, »The Conceptualisation of austerity in the Portuguese, Spanish and Irish Press« in: Farzad Sharifian (ed.), *Advances in Cultural Linguistics*, Singapore 2017, pp. 345–368, p. 364.

86 Arthur Borriello, »›There is no alternative‹: How Italian and Spanish leaders' discourse obscured the political nature of austerity« in: *Discourse & Society* 28, No. 3 (2017), pp. 241–261.

87 Hans Bickes / Tina Otten / Laura Chelsea Weymann, »The Financial Crisis in the German and English Press: Metaphorical Structures in the Media Coverage on Greece, Spain and Italy« in: *Discourse & Society* 25, No. 4 (2014), pp. 424–445, p. 441.

88 For an extensive discussion of the moral dimension of economics see Tomáš Sedláček, *Economics of good and evil: the quest for economic meaning from Gilgamesh to Wall Street*, New York 2011.

89 Darren Kelsey / Frank Mueller / Andrea Whittle / Majid KhosraviNik, »Financial crisis and austerity: interdisciplinary concerns in critical discourse studies« in: *Critical Discourse Studies* 13, No. 1 (2016), pp. 1–19.

of »pigs« is of interest for critical approaches as it says a lot about the ideological structures within austerity discourses. This expression hints at an even deeper understanding of blame in the austerity discourse. Like the naturalization of the causes of the crisis, this representation gives these discourses an additional anthropomorphic twist that also neglects a systemic and critical reading of austerity discourses and operates as a strategy of domination. It was argued that

> *»[w]e could, perhaps, interpret this move within the general political technology of individualising blame and guilt. If a particular country is facing difficulties this has nothing to do with systemic faults and is solely attributed to internal failings and pathologies – so the argument goes; similarly, within each country, social groups are stigmatized as irrational and immoral one after the other so that every feeling of common purpose between them is minimised and resistance to the austerity avalanche and the attacks on their rights is disarmed.«*[90]

For critical approaches these discourses are successful in minimizing resistance to austerity, because they »produce a biopolitical policing of the crisis' exceptionalized subjects (the citizens of indebted countries) and the implementation of crisis-politics by creating a public ›structure of feeling‹ related to the hegemonic crisis' rationales.«[91] The new subjectivity found and formed within austerity discourses is described by Lazzarato as the »indebted man« that is said to transform every form of subject position within the neoliberal system: consumers are transformed into »indebted consumers«, welfare beneficiaries into »indebted welfare users« and citizens into »indebted citizens.«[92] From this perspective, »[a]usterity, the demand for sacrifices, and the creation of the subjective figure of the debtor do not constitute a rough stretch as we advance toward ›growth,‹ but techniques of power whose authoritarianism, now devoid of anything ›liberal,‹ can alone guarantee the reproduction of power relations.«[93] The corresponding structure of feeling is said to be based on guilt and shame on the side of indebted citizens and anger and resentment on the side of so-called hardworking taxpayers.[94] But for critical perspectives, the notion of indebted *man* should not lead us to neglect women's special role in austerity discourses. Penny Griffin argues, for example, that austerity and its emphasis on »competitiveness« and cuts in public spending and services can be understood as part of »techniques of governance that trivialise feminist concerns while further embedding a masculinised, white and elitist

90 Yannis Stavrakakis, »Dispatches from the Greek lab: Metaphors, strategies and debt in the European crisis« in: *Psychoanalysis, Culture & Society* 18, No. 3 (2013), pp. 313–324, p. 317.

91 Yiannis Mylonas, »Austerity Discourses in ›Der Spiegel‹ Journal, 2009–2014« in: *tripleC* 13, No. 1 (2015), pp. 248–269, p. 248.

92 Maurizio Lazzarato, *The Making of the Indebted Man: An Essay on the Neoliberal Condition*, South Pasadena 2012, p. 38.

93 Lazzarato, *The Making of the Indebted Man*, op. cit. (note 92), p. 183.

94 Kirsten Forkert, »The new moralism: austerity, silencing and debt morality« in: *Soundings*, No. 56 (2014), pp. 41–53. For a more complex analysis of the emotional matrix behind austerity discourses about the »indebted citizen« they form, see Andrea Mura, »Disorienting Austerity: The Indebted Citizen as the New Soul of Europe« in: Engin Isin (ed.), *Citizenship after Orientalism: Transforming Political Theory*, London 2015, pp. 34–52.

culture of global financial privilege.«[95] In sum, these critical perspectives not only lay bare the deeper power structures that are connected with austerity discourses and thereby highlight the deeply political nature of economic phenomenon. Their paths inside the rabbit hole of critical theory also offer connections to the other lands of the territory of austerity that have been already explored above.[96]

Hopefully our challenging journey to the unknown territory of austerity, its manifold lands and research communities has provided a provisional map for our readers, which enables them to find their own way through the different regions of austerity land and to evaluate the ideas of the different tribes that can be found there.

Acknowledgments
This volume is the result of a broader research effort on austerity by the Chair of Political Science I (Professor Dr. Roland Sturm) at Friedrich-Alexander-Universität Erlangen-Nürnberg. We want to thank the *Bonner Akademie für Forschung und Lehre praktischer Politik* (BAPP) and the *Luise Prell Foundation* for supporting a conference on »Austerity and Its Social and Political Consequences« and the publication of this volume.

95 Penny Griffin, »Crisis, Austerity and Gendered Governance: A Feminist Perspective« in: *Feminist Review* 109, No. 1 (2015), pp. 49–72, p. 49.

96 The separation of discourses, economics and politics is, therefore, not sustainable for (radical) critical perspectives.

Bob Jessop

Finance-Dominated Accumulation and Enduring Austerity

This chapter applies cultural political economy to analyse crisis dynamics in selected economies in the North Atlantic region. It links this analysis to regulation- and state-theoretical arguments about kinds of austerity and their economic and political roots and repercussions. I distinguish austerity policies, the politics of austerity, and the austerity state. Each has its own conjunctural origins, dynamic, and effects in different periods, its specific implications for the relations between economics and politics, and different impacts depending on the place of the relevant economic spaces in the world market and inter-state system. After presenting some preliminary remarks on the overall approach and on the fisco-financial dimension of the modern state, I comment briefly on austerity policies in the »golden age« of Atlantic Fordism. I then discuss varieties of neoliberalism and their implications for the politics of austerity and emergence of an enduring austerity state. These ideas are explored in two kinds of post-Fordist economy, namely, neoliberal finance-dominated accumulation regimes and a eurozone economic space shaped by the overall dominance and interests of neomercantilist, profit-producing German capital.

1. Theoretical preliminaries

Cultural political economy (hereafter CPE) makes a cultural turn (understood as a concern with sense- and meaning-making as foundational to social relations) in political economy. In its analysis of political economy, it draws on the heterodox regulation school for its critique of political economy and on critical state theory and critical governance studies for its critique of politics. CPE combines an interest in the economic, political, and social imaginaries that shape capital accumulation and state projects with a critical analysis of the changing relations between the economic and political aspects of capitalist social formations. Imaginaries reflect different (and contestable) entry-points into and standpoints on a complex reality and provide the basis for societal self-descriptions and strategies for social change. One implication of this for present purposes is that austerity must be interpreted and explained in terms of prevailing economic, fisco-financial and political imaginaries, accounts of the conditions for economic and political stability and effective crisis-management when faced with instability, and views on the social repercussions of economic and political policy. However, to explain the success of some imaginaries and their overall impact, CPE also examines the structural constraints and opportunities, including specific governmental techniques and technologies that condition and mediate various agents' attempts to formulate, implement, resist, and evaluate austerity. In sum, while CPE highlights the role of imaginaries in shaping economic and political action, it insists that their impact is not explicable purely in discursive terms but needs to refer to structural, technical, and agential factors that shape their selection and retention and mediate their effects in the real economy.[1]

The regulation school seeks to explain why, despite its inherent contradictions and crisis-tendencies and its conflictual character, capital accumulation may occur relatively smoothly for long periods in specific economic and political spaces. Its answer refers in part to the discovery and eventual consolidation of institutional and spatio-temporal fixes that prioritize the handling of certain contradictions and crisis-tendencies to minimize their immediate effects and neglect, disguise, postpone or defer other sources of economic and political instability. These sources cause growing problems, limits and conflicts that eventually undermine the fixes and associated social compromises that had once seemed to many observers to secure crisis-free growth, lasting prosperity, a longed-for great moderation, and so on.[2]

The Parisian regulation school identified five key institutional (or structural) forms that characterize economic regimes: the wage relation, dominant forms of enterprise and modes of competition, the monetary and financial regime, the state form and its modes of intervention, and the place of an economic regime in the international order.[3] My analysis treats these as different sites where the inherent structural contradictions and strategic dilemmas of the capital relation are handled through specific institutional and spatio-temporal fixes. Each contradiction has two aspects, which can be linked respectively to the substantive *use-value* or monetary *exchange-value* aspects of a dualistic capitalism that involves the production, circulation, and distribution of specific goods and services within a profit-oriented, market-mediated economic regime.[4] I now present some examples, linking them loosely to the five institutional forms and, in each case, note the substantive aspect first:

- The wage is both a cost of production *and* a source of demand; similarly, wage-earners are both abstract units of labour power, substitutable by other such units (or, indeed, other factors of production), and distinct individuals with specific skills, knowledge, and creativity.
- Productive capital is a stock of time- and place-specific assets being used to produce specific goods and services for sale in expectation of profit *and* abstract value in motion (notably as realized profits available for re-investment elsewhere); like-

1 For details, Ngai-Ling Sum / Bob Jessop, *Towards a Cultural Political Economy: Putting Culture in Its Place in Political Economy*, Cheltenham/Northampton, MA 2013.

2 On the regulation approach and its different schools, see Bob Jessop / Ngai-Ling Sum, *Beyond the Regulation Approach: Putting the Economy in its Place in Political Economy*, Cheltenham/Northampton, MA 2006; Bob Jessop, »Revisiting the regulation approach: critical reflections on the contradictions, dilemmas, fixes, and crisis dynamics of growth regimes« in: *Capital & Class* 37, No. 1 (2013), pp. 5–24; on lasting prosperity, Burkart Lutz, *Der kurze Traum immerwährender Prosperität*, Frankfurt 1989; on the great moderation, Ewald Engelen / Ismail Ertürk / Julie Froud / Sukhdev Johal / Adam Leaver / Mick Morran / Adriana Nilsson / Karel Williams, *After the Great Complacence: Financial Crisis and the Politics Reform*, Oxford 2013.

3 Robert Boyer, *The Regulation School: A Critical Introduction*, New York 1990, pp. 37–42.

4 Other sites of dilemmatic contradiction are harder to align with these five forms but still affect the progress of capitalist societies. For brevity's sake, I ignore them here.

wise, knowledge circulates as part of the intellectual commons *and* can also become the object of intellectual property rights; in addition, land is a gift of nature *and* a monopolistic claim on revenues.

- Money functions both as money (medium of exchange, unit of account, store of value, etc.) *and* as capital (a hoard or credit invested for profit, interest-bearing capital, fictitious capital); in another aspect, money is a ›national‹ currency circulating within a monetary bloc that is subject to state control *and* an international money exchangeable against other monies in currency markets.
- The state is both a separate institutional apparatus that claims legitimacy on the grounds that it defends the public or general interest against particular private interests *and* a crucial support of capital accumulation thanks to its ability to deploy its own resources to secure capital accumulation, especially when this is damaged by competition and market failure; relatedly, taxation is both a source of revenue to fund the state's activities, including its self-reproduction, *and* a deduction from economic surplus generated in the private sector that would otherwise be re-invested for profit.
- International regimes are means of (peaceful) global governance *and* sites where social forces struggle over which vested interests such regimes serve.

These contradictions entail dilemmas around which of its two aspects is prioritized in efforts to secure capitalist reproduction. In each case, neoliberalism privileges its exchange-value (profitability) aspects. The politics of austerity and enduring austerity states reinforce this priority, especially regarding the wage relation (including the social wage), the monetary and fiscal regime, and taxation, often in the name of boosting economic competitiveness (see below).

Materialist state theory, critical governance studies, and research on governmentality provide analogous concepts and insights to the regulation school in the respective fields of political analysis. In their different ways, they explore what Antonio Gramsci called the state in its inclusive sense: »political society + civil society« or »hegemony protected by the armour of coercion.«[5] All three approaches focus on the modalities of political power rather than constitutional and institutional features of the state. Thus, they look beyond narrow juridico-political issues to techniques of statecraft, governance, and governmentality and to the social forces and social bases that lend provisional support to specific state projects – which typically include accumulation strategies and other economic, geo-economic, or geopolitical missions.[6]

2. *The modern tax state and fisco-financial crises*

»Public finances are one of the best starting points for an investigation of society, especially though not exclusively of its political life. [...] This is true both of the causal

5 Antonio Gramsci, *Selections from the Prison Notebooks*, London 1971, p. 263.

6 On state theory, see Bob Jessop, *The State: Past, Present, Future*, Cambridge 2015; on governance, Mark Bevir, *A Theory of Governance*, Berkeley 2013; on governmentality, Mitchell Dean, *Governmentality. Power and Rule in Modern Society*, London 1999.

significance of fiscal policy (insofar as fiscal events are an important element in the causation of all change) and of its symptomatic significance (insofar as everything that happens has its fiscal reflection).«[7]

Taxation rather than revenues from its patrimony is the lifeblood of the modern state. As a tax state, its income stems largely from its monopoly over taxation in an essentially private economic order rather than from its profitable management of public or state-controlled property.[8] Thus the modern state's performance depends on that of the market economy. A tax state can be squeezed by economic crises that weaken revenues and require more spending – thereby generating fisco-financial crises and, perhaps, legitimacy crises. This makes it vulnerable to investment strikes by industrial capital or bondholders, especially when its creditworthiness is poorly rated or otherwise distrusted. There are well-known dilemmas on how best to organize the fisco-financial regime in general and in specific regimes and distinct conjunctures. For example, whereas early debates on fiscal crisis focused on debts incurred in fighting World War One and/or resulting from the collapse of empires, later controversies addressed the Gold Standard, the Great Depression, post-war reconstruction costs, stagflation in the 1970s, Third World Debt, serious financial crises, and public debt. How fisco-financial powers come to be exercised in these critical conjunctures, including how they promote or reverse austerity policies to deal with these problems, affects the external and internal sovereignty and political legitimacy of the state.[9] Beside fisco-financial crises, the modern tax state is vulnerable to other crises. These include: challenges over the right to levy taxes (with or without representation) or crises due to tax resistance or avoidance; crises of institutional integration and coordination in the state apparatus; crises affecting the state's capacities for intervention (when, for example, this intervention weakens the tax base); legitimacy crises as the social basis mobilized behind a given tax regime fails to consolidate or breaks up; administrative demoralization or disorientation as political *esprit de corps* is weakened by a failed state project; or a hegemonic crisis over the state and its role in society.[10] This could prompt demands to redesign political representation, reform the state's internal structures and operations, alter the amount and modalities of state intervention, recompose the social bases of the state, redefine state strategies, and alter the balance between consent and coercion to address hegemonic and/or wider organic crisis.[11] Internationalization changes the relation be-

7 Joseph A. Schumpeter, »Crisis of the tax state« in: *International Economic Papers* 4 (1954), pp. 5–38. p. 7.

8 Rudolf Goldscheid, »Finanzwissenschaft und Soziologie« in: Rudolf Hickel (ed.) / Rudolf Goldscheid / Joseph Schumpeter, *Die Finanzkrise des Steuerstaates*. Frankfurt 1976, pp. 317–28; Schumpeter, »Crisis of the tax state«, op. cit. (note 7).

9 James O'Connor, *The Fiscal Crisis of the State*, New York 1973; Bruno Théret, *Régimes économiques de l'ordre politique*, Paris 1992; Wolfgang Streeck, *Buying Time: The Delayed Crisis of Democratic Capitalism*, London 2014.

10 Jürgen Habermas, *Legitimacy Crisis*, London 1975; Nicos Poulantzas, »The political crisis and the crisis of the state« in: J. W. Freiberg (ed.), *Critical Sociology*, New York 1979, pp. 373–393.

11 Gramsci, *Prison Notebooks*, op. cit. (note 5).

tween the economic and social power of money and the state's political power. The scope for capital mobility and a growing competition to attract capital undermine the effectiveness of the state's monopolies of taxation and coercion. National space is undermined as the principal site for taxation as competition intensifies to attract or retain potentially mobile capital and leads to various state-sponsored tax exemptions and exceptions and, in addition, as corporations and high net-worth households avoid or evade tax.[12] Further, state managers' fisco-financial policies must now pay more regard to international currency regimes, internationally transferable property rights, and the international political order and their impact on their ability to control national money, the domestic economy, and domestic politics. This can trigger legitimacy crises and/or create a democratic deficit as competitiveness is prioritized over other public concerns.

3. The Atlantic Fordist period

In the golden years of post-war expansion in advanced capitalist economies, the dominant accumulation regime in the interlinked economic and political space of the North Atlantic region (the USA, Canada, and Western Europe) was Atlantic Fordism. While there was specialization among these economies, growth overall rested on a virtuous circle of mass production and mass consumption. Post-war recovery and prosperity were assisted by temporary austerity measures to support reconstruction, a peacetime dividend that allowed a shift of state expenditure from warfare to welfare, a tripartite consensus behind wage-led growth, and the rising productivity of profit-producing capital thanks to Fordist economies of scale. The wage was treated mainly as a source of demand (with its cost-of-production aspect compensated by matching increases in productivity); and money was treated mainly as national money, with monetary policy supported by capital controls and guided by the commitment to promote full employment. This supported a sustainable system of wage-led growth on condition that economies were relatively closed or that, in small, open economies, supply-side measures were taken to reskill and redeploy workers and maintain competitiveness.[13] It also required cyclical austerity measures that alternated with monetary and fiscal expansion to smooth the business cycle – measures that could nonetheless prove procyclical because of bad timing and political pressures. The crisis of Atlantic Fordism emerged as continuing internationalization turned the wage (and social wage) into a cost of international production and increased competitive pressures on wages, working conditions, and welfare payments. Internationalization also undermined the conditions for Keynesian economic policies oriented to full employment in relatively closed national economies. As this virtuous Fordist growth dynamic began to reach its limits in the late 1960s and early 1970s, stagflationary tendencies triggered a fisco-financial

12 Angus Cameron, »Crisis? What crisis? Displacing the spatial imaginary of the fiscal state« in: *Geoforum* 39, No. 3 (2008), pp. 1145–1154.

13 Bob Jessop, *The Future of the Capitalist State*, Cambridge 2002.

crisis.[14] This led to a politics of austerity that was supported – reluctantly by the left, pragmatically in the centre, and enthusiastically on the right. For the last group, this became an enduring campaign. Responding to the combination of stagflation and rising peacetime debt, liberal economists and conservative politicians demanded a drastic rollback of the state to reduce inherently unproductive public sector employment[15] and/or to reverse the financial »crowding out« of private sector investment by unproductive public sector borrowing and confiscatory taxes.[16] These arguments, which are theoretically and empirically contestable[17], were used to justify monetarist shock therapy to break stagflation and weaken organized labour. Later, neoliberals proposed a politics of austerity to raise the rate and volume of profits. Relevant measures included privatization of state assets to reduce public debt, privatization of public services to lower future public spending, cuts in welfare entitlements, and attacks on public sector unions to lower wages. Paradoxically, these measures created conditions for a financial crisis due to declining growth and tax revenues and unsustainable private debt fuelled by privatized Keynesianism and financial innovation.[18]

Following the crisis of Atlantic Fordism, two new economic imaginaries became rivals for hegemony: the knowledge-based economy (KBE) and a neoliberal revival of the market economy. The former mainly reflects the interests of profit-producing capital and implicitly views the above-noted contradictions in terms of their substantive aspects. Thus, it involves a certain continuity with Atlantic Fordism but adapts its growth model to changed technological, economic, political, and social conditions. The significance of the neoliberal project lies in its consistent pursuit of the politics of austerity. It also promotes financialization and finance-dominated accumulation. This is because neoliberalism privileges the profit-oriented aspects of capital's contradictions and promotes the viewpoint of money as capital, notably interest-bearing capital. I now focus on neoliberalism and finance-dominated accumulation.[19]

4. Neoliberalism

Neoliberalism is a complex, changing, and adaptable set of projects and can be linked to quite varied political goals – illustrated by its association with Augusto Pinochet, Margaret Thatcher, Ronald Reagan, Bill Clinton, Tony Blair, Recep Tayyip Erdoğan, Binyamin Netanyahu, Lula da Silva, Wolfgang Schäuble, and Shinzō Abe. Here I dis-

14 O'Connor, *The Fiscal Crisis of the State*, op. cit. (note 9).

15 Robert Bacon / Walter Eltis, *Britain's Economic Problem: Too Few Producers*, London 1976.

16 Christopher Green, »›From tax state‹ to ›debt state‹« in: *Journal of Evolutionary Economics* 3, No. 1 (1993), pp. 23–42.

17 John D. Tomlinson, *The Politics of Decline: Understanding Post-War Britain*, London 2000.

18 Jack Rasmus, *Epic Recession: Prelude to Global Depression*, London 2010.

19 On the KBE, see Organization of Economic Cooperation and Development, *The Knowledge-Based Economy*, Paris 1996; Benoît Godin, »The knowledge-based economy: conceptual framework or buzzword?« in: *Journal of Technology Transfer* 31, No. 1 (2008), pp. 17–30; Jessop, *Future of the Capitalist State*, op. cit. (note 13).

tinguish four types, each associated with, inter alia, a different mix of austerity policies and politics.

The most radical type was the abortive attempt at *neoliberal system transformation* in post-Soviet successor states. This was based on the belief that dismantling state socialist institutions would spontaneously regenerate market forces. A second type is the *neoliberal regime shifts* that occurred in many states under centre-left or right-wing governments. Breaking with the institutionalized capital-labour compromise in postwar Atlantic Fordism, committed and newly empowered elite alliances introduced a logically coherent neoliberal policy agenda (see below). They aimed to modify the balance of forces in favour of capital and to this end promoted a vigorous neoliberal politics of austerity. The third type comprises *economic restructuring and regime shifts that were mainly imposed from outside* by transnational economic institutions and organizations backed by leading capitalist powers with support from partners among domestic political and economic elites. It adopts neoliberal policies in line with the »Washington Consensus« as a crucial precondition for financial and other aid to crisis-ridden economies in parts of Africa, Asia, Eastern and Central Europe, and Latin America. Fourth, neoliberalism can involve a more pragmatic, partial, and potentially reversible set of *neoliberal policy adjustments.* Nordic social democracies and Rhenish capitalist economies illustrate this type. In contrast to type two, only some policies from the neoliberal policy set may be pursued because this type aims at more modest and piecemeal changes to maintain existing economic and social models in the face of continuing internationalization and specific crisis-tendencies. Such adjustments can nonetheless cumulate over time and become harder to reverse.

The key planks of the neoliberal policy agenda comprise:

- Liberalization to promote free competition
- De-regulation to reduce the role of law and state in market economies
- Privatization to sell off the public sector and expand the private sector
- Market proxies in the residual public sector
- Internationalization to facilitate the inward and outward flow of money, capital, resources, goods, and services
- Lower direct taxes to boost consumer choice and shrink the state

William Black, a white-collar criminologist, adds another policy, which might be seen as part of de-regulation but is especially significant for financialization and could therefore also be counted as a seventh plank: »de-criminalization« of financial fraud.[20] Another aspect of this policy set is the loss of steering capacity, including a loss of expertise and institutional memory for handling economic crises. Paradoxically, state managers then turn to private sector financial elites to manage financial crises. The first six policies are also part of structural adjustment programmes along with an emphasis on debt repayment, which entails the pursuit of a politics of austerity.

20 William K. Black, »Posing as hyper-rationality: OMB's assault on effective regulation« in: *New Economic Perspectives*, 27.5.2014.

5. Why neoliberalism matters

To explain the renewal of neoliberalization, despite its recurrent market and policy failures, we must look beyond its intellectual appeal and domestic and international political backing. Neoliberalism has a distinct approach to capital's contradictions and dilemmas. Specifically, it privileges the exchange-value over the use-value moment of capital's dilemmatic contradictions (see above). In each case, it stresses cost reduction and cost recovery and subjects all economic activities to the treadmill pressure of matching or exceeding the prevailing world market average rate of profit. The neoliberal policy mix not only privileges capital over labour but also privileges some fractions of capital over others. For it is capital as value in motion rather than as a stock of assets that is most easily disembedded from broader socio-spatial-temporal contexts and thereby freed to »flow« relatively smoothly through space-time. In this sense, compared to the largely intermediary roles of finance in Fordist regimes or a productivist, post-Fordist KBE, neoliberalism promotes a finance-led economy with the potential to become a finance-dominated accumulation regime.

Table 1 compares priorities in the wage-led growth regime typical of Atlantic Fordism with those in the finance-led growth regime promoted under the auspices of neoliberal regimes. It is useful here to distinguish finance, finance capital, financialization, and finance-dominated accumulation. First, finance denotes money as money and money as capital (see above) and has a crucial role in the circulation and valorization of capital in all varieties and stages of capitalist development. This commonplace is often mentioned to defend the atypical dominance of finance in heavily financialized regimes by conflating the general case and a subset. Second, finance capital is a distinct fraction of capital, comprising money-dealing, bank, and interest-bearing capitals.[21] Finance capital can also assist the expansion of profit-producing capital (especially in the form of capitalist credit); and, in the form of fictitious capital (such as bonds), it joins other revenue-generating financial assets. Another aspect of finance capital is that, in certain historical or political conditions, it can become dominant and shape the entire course of capital accumulation and the wider social formation. Examples include the ways in which financialization undermined post-war growth regimes (e.g., Atlantic Fordism, East Asian exportism, Latin American import-substitution, and the KBE) and has imprinted a wide range of political, social, and economic relations (see below).[22]

21 In specific circumstances and/or theoretical contexts, finance capital can also denote a fusion of industrial and banking capital.

22 On this, see, for example, Robert Boyer, »The political in the era of globalization and finance: focus on some Régulation School research« in: *International Journal of Urban and Regional Studies* 24, No. 2 (2000), pp. 274–322.

Table 1: Wage-Led vs Finance-Dominated Growth Regimes

Wage-led growth privileges	*Finance-domination privileges*
Wage as source of demand	Wage as cost of production
Labour power as concrete skills	Labour power as abstract labour
Productive capital as stock of assets to be valorized in specific times and places	Productive capital as value in motion for profitable investment anywhere
Money as medium of exchange	Money as interest-bearing capital
Money as national (or state) money	Money as international currency

Source: own elaboration

Third, financialization involves: (1) a proliferation and expansion of financial markets; (2) new financial instruments and institutions, especially those that transform future streams of (profit, dividend, interest) income into tradable assets like stocks or bonds (securitization); (3) the dominance of finance capital over profit-producing capital, affecting investment and production, so that »profit making occurs increasingly through financial channels rather than through trade and commodity production«[23]; (4) a trend for household consumption to be sustained by extending credit, which habituates consumers to indebtedness; and (5) the colonization of economic and social reproduction by financial calculation and financial capital. As aspect two suggests, financialization generates increasingly fantastic forms of fictitious capital and, indeed, unsustainable fictitious profits.[24] The neoliberal policy set (including the de-criminalization of financial fraud) is a significant driver of financialization.

Finance-dominated accumulation occurs when the economic, political, and social power of interest-bearing capital has become hegemonic (or, at least, dominant) in the overall organization of a capitalist social formation. This is reflected, as Gerald Epstein suggests, »in the systemic power and importance of financial markets, financial motives, financial institutions, and financial elites in the operation of the economy«[25] and, one should add, its governing institutions, nationally and internationally. Finance-dominated accumulation promotes the roles of money, credit, and fictitious capital in the overall dynamic of capital accumulation and relies on deregulated financial innovation and speculation. It emerges as the circuits of interest-bearing capital as property (or fictitious capital) become increasingly autonomous from the mediating role of

23 Greta R. Krippner, »The financialization of the American economy« in: *Socio-Economic Review* 3, No. 2 (2005), pp. 173–208, p. 174.

24 Karl Marx, *Capital. Volume 1*, London 1967; Ricardo de Medeiros Carneiro / Pedro Rossi / Guilherme Santos Mello / Marcos Vinicus Chiliatto-Leite, »The fourth dimension: Derivatives and financial dominance« in: *Review of Radical Political Economics* 47, No. 4 (2015), pp. 641–662; Bob Jessop, »Credit money, fiat money and currency pyramids« in: Jocelyn Pixley / Geoffrey C. Harcourt (eds.), *Financial Crises and the Nature of Capitalist Money*, Basingstoke 2013, pp. 248–272.

25 Gerald A. Epstein, »Introduction« in: idem (ed.), *Financialization and the World Economy*, Cheltenham/Northampton, MA pp. 3–14, p. 3.

functioning finance capital in sustaining the »real economy«.[26] It also intensifies the tensions in public finance between state fiat money and private credit creation. The neoliberal form of world market integration greatly benefits interest-bearing capital (especially hypermobile financial capital) at the expense of socially and spatio-temporally embedded capitals. This is because financial capital has become the most globally integrated fraction of capital and controls the most liquid, abstract, and universal economic resource. Finance-dominated accumulation also increases inequalities of income and wealth, limiting the impact of the wage as a source of demand. This explains the emergence of financial crises that develop relatively independently, at least initially, from crisis-tendencies rooted in the dynamic of profit-producing (productive or industrial) capital.

This said, financial capital as property cannot become fully and permanently detached from the need to valorize profit-producing capital. Indeed, because continued expansion depends heavily on the pseudo-validation of highly leveraged speculative debt and unsustainable »Ponzi« debt[27], this regime has its own inherent crisis-generating mechanism. Elsner explains this as follows: financial capital in a finance-dominated regime has a target rate of return that is several times greater than the historic norm for profit-producing capital; worse still, in seeking to gain it, financial capital massively levers fictitious credit and capital. In aggregate, the eventual validation of this capital demands a total volume of surplus-value that far exceeds the productive and exploitative capacity of current profit-producing capital.[28] While finance capital remains dominant, its parasitism on the economy, the fisco-financial aspects of the state, and wider society requires austerity to continue or intensify by cutting public expenditure and privatizing infrastructure so that finance capital can continue to extract value from both private and public sectors.[29]

Such one-sided treatment or privileging can only disguise, but not suppress, the significance of the substantive or use-value aspect of these relations. Eventually the importance of these aspects to capitalist reproduction (and social life more generally) is reasserted through crises. The greater and longer the seeming independence of financial capital and the greater the resulting parasitism of finance as property, the greater and longer could the crises become. Whether and how these are then successfully resolved to rebalance the economic regime, if at all, depends on the balance of forces mobilized around rival crisis construals and crisis-management strategies and the adequacy of these strategies to the objective features of the crisis. Austerity is not an objective necessity but a political choice.

26 Ferdinando Meacci, »Fictitious capital and crises« in: Riccardo Bellofiore (ed.), *Marxian Economics: Essays on Volume III of Capital*, Vol. 1, Basingstoke 1998, pp. 189–204.

27 On Ponzi finance, where even interest payments cannot be met, see Hyman P. Minsky, *Stabilizing an Unstable Economy*, New Haven 1986.

28 Wolfram Elsner, »Financial capitalism – at odds with democracy: the trap of an ›impossible‹ profit rate« in: *Real-World Economics Review* 62 (2012), pp. 132–159.

29 Michael Hudson, *Killing the Host: How Financial Parasites and Debt Bondage Destroy the Global Economy*, Dresden 2015, pp. 59–69, 147–156, 363–398.

Attempts to overcome the contradiction identified by Elsner depend, he suggests, on three strategies that are individually and collectively unsustainable. One is to create and manage bubbles, which is the main redistribution mechanism in finance-dominated regimes, and then bail out (or get bailed out) at the right moment.[30] This requires the complicity of central banks and government in finance-dominated regimes and is generally forthcoming. Another is to invoke a system-threatening »financial emergency« that justifies austerity policies to reduce individual and social wages, impose internal devaluation and financial repression, and privatize public services and assets to pay off the public debt incurred in massive bailouts.[31] State action is crucial here, and this strategy has reinvigorated neoliberalism and supported a politics of austerity. It has a central role in the politics of austerity and the rise of the austerity state. The third approach, which partly overlaps with the second, involves state-sponsored primitive accumulation (e.g., land-grabbing, capitalizing nature and its services, and enclosing the intellectual commons). While less directly related to austerity, it plays a key role in financialization, fuelling finance-dominated predation.

6. The cultural political economy of austerity

While austerity policies differ across »varieties of capitalism« (reflecting their specific economic profiles and associated imaginaries) and different stages in business cycles and long waves, they are also shaped by interdependencies that result from interstate relations (including forms of regional and global governance and the capacity of some states to impose austerity on others, with or without help from domestic elites), foreign trade (and other features of world market integration, as reflected, say, in trade deficits, unproductive loans, or speculative inward investment), and the prevailing logic of the world market, which is currently organized in the shadow of neoliberalization even where specific economic spaces are not themselves directly based on neoliberal principles. This highlights the need to examine austerity in terms of the relations between the economic and political fields, including their basic forms and institutional architecture, and their mediation through the changing balance of forces organized behind competing economic, fisco-financial, and political imaginaries and related interests.

The policy-politics-polity triplet suggests that austerity can be studied in three ways. First, there are *conjunctural austerity policies*, which are introduced in the first instance as temporary measures in response to short-term or immediate problems. As the conjuncture becomes favourable again, these policies are suspended or reversed. Second, there is the *enduring politics of austerity* (often called »permanent austerity« in the relevant literature), which is promoted in response to a »chronic« crisis, real or manufactured, in the fisco-financial domain and/or in the economy more generally.

30 Elsner, »Financial capitalism«, op. cit. (note 28), pp. 146–147; Michael Hudson, *The Bubble and Beyond: Fictitious Capital, Debt Deflation and the Global Crisis*, Dresden 2012; Hudson, *Killing the Host*, op. cit. (note 29), pp. 285–321.

31 Philip Mirowski, *Never Let a Serious Crisis Go to Waste.* London 2013.

This enduring politics of austerity, as noted above, is intended to bring about a more lasting reorganization of the balance of forces in favour of capital rather than to make policy adjustments to safeguard existing economic and political arrangements. Third, there is the *austerity polity*. This results from a continuing fundamental institutional reorganization of the relations between the economic and political in capitalist formations. It can be a possibly unintended cumulative result of the enduring politics of austerity, especially where this aggravates the underlying causes of fisco-financial crisis. It can also result from a deliberate strategy to subordinate the polity more directly and durably to the »imperatives« of the world market as these are construed in neoliberal discourse with its one-sided emphasis on the logic of exchange-value. And, given the political, ideological, hegemonic, and organic crises that have developed in the context of the financial, economic, and fisco-financial crises, they can also be an authoritarian response to growing popular unrest (including right-wing extremism) about the technocratic and plutocratic nature of crisis responses.

Whereas conjunctural policies are associated with targeted cuts in specific areas in the pattern of neoliberal policy adjustment, neoliberal regime shifts promote an enduring politics of austerity that takes the form of general fisco-financial restraint, putting downward pressure on most areas of expenditure, especially discretionary ones.[32] This pattern can occur in normal forms of politics, in states of economic emergency or, even, in lasting states of exception. Economic emergency may be triggered by a severe crisis, a minor crisis that is deliberately exaggerated, or even one »manufactured« for political purposes. Indeed, in neoliberal regimes, whatever the state of the economy, it always seems the right time to reduce public expenditure (except for corporate welfare) through an appropriately crafted (and crafty) politics of austerity. This involves far more than quantitative cuts in spending because it is also intended to have qualitative, transformative effects. It is pursued to consolidate and extend the power of capital, especially interest-bearing capital, and to subsume ever wider areas of social life under the logic of differential accumulation. It becomes a major vector of the colonization, commodification, and, eventually, financialization of everyday life – processes subject to friction, resistance, and crisis-tendencies.

Seymour explains this well. He argues that austerity involves something much broader and more complex than spending cuts – thanks to its role in restructuring, recalibrating, and reorienting state expenditure. Indeed, for him, austerity is the dominant *political* articulation of the global economic crisis in Europe and North America. This strategy has seven aspects: (1) rebalance the economy from wage-led to finance-led growth; (2) redistribute income from wage-earners to capital; (3) promote »precarity« in all areas of life as a disciplinary mechanism and as a means to intensify the financialisation of everyday life; (4) recompose social classes, thereby reinforcing inequali-

32 Paul Pierson, »Coping with permanent austerity« in: idem (ed.), *The New Politics of the Welfare State*, Oxford 2001, pp. 410–456; Maurizio Ferrera, »The European welfare state: Golden achievements, silver prospects« in: *West European Politics* 31, No. 1–2 (2008), pp. 82–107; Richard Seymour, *Against Austerity: How We Can Fix the Crisis They Made*, London 2014.

ties in income and wealth across classes and leading to greater stratification within them; (5) facilitate the penetration of the state by business elites and the interests of corporations; (6) accelerate the turn from a Keynesian welfare state based on shared citizenship rights to a workfare regime that relies on coercion, casual sadism and, especially in the US, penality; and (7) promote the values of hierarchy and competitiveness over equality and solidarity.[33]

In many respects, these aspects were already inscribed in the politics of neoliberal regime shifts. This is reflected in stagnant real wages, cuts in welfare, increasing personal debt to invest in housing, pensions, education, and health or, indeed, maintain a previous standard of living, and growing concentration of income and assets at the top of their respective populations. However, for Seymour, they have been much reinforced following the 2007–9 financial and economic crisis. This has occurred partly because the painful measures taken to consolidate budgets in the 1990s and early 2000s were wiped out by the impact of the North Atlantic Financial Crisis (NAFC) and the eurozone crisis as governments took on more debt to bail out banks and/or engineer stimulus packages.[34]

This ramping up of the politics of austerity occurred in part because the response of financial capital to this crisis intensified the state's fisco-financial crisis. Measures were taken to rescue interest-bearing capital from the effects of its Ponzi dynamic and from the inherently unsustainable drive for financial profits.[35] This created a debt-default-deflation dynamic that has worsened public finances as well as the private sector.[36] In addition, as Seymour, among others, notes, the politics of »permanent austerity« is not just a response to economic crisis but also to political and ideological crises and, indeed, an organic crisis of the capitalist social order.[37] This is used to justify a state of economic emergency that is presented initially as a »temporary« response to immediate or chronic problems, enabling quick action because there is no time for democratic debate, but then acquires more lasting form through cumulative and mutually reinforcing institutional change, routinization of exceptional measures, and habituation – all linked to a concentration of economic policy-making powers.

The politics of austerity involves a long-term strategic offensive to reorganize the institutional matrix and balance of forces in favour of capital. It builds on the often-remarked association between the free market and the strong state. But it goes further in its efforts to rearticulate relations between (1) the social power of money as capital and of capital as property and (2) the political power of the state. Inter alia, this involves a politics aimed at *disorganizing* subaltern classes and *reorganizing* the capitalist power

33 Seymour, *Against Austerity*, op. cit. (note 32), pp. 2-4.

34 Rasmus, *Epic Recession*, op. cit. (note 18); Hudson, *The Bubble and Beyond*, op. cit. (note 30).

35 See above; and Alex Demirović / Thomas Sablowski, *The Finance-Dominated Regime of Accumulation and the Crisis in Europe*, Berlin 2013.

36 Rasmus, *Epic Recession*, op. cit. (note 18).

37 Seymour, *Against Austerity*, op. cit. (note 32), p. 4; Gramsci, *Prison Notebooks*; op. cit. (note 5); Ian Bruff, »The rise of authoritarian neoliberalism« in: *Rethinking Marxism* 26, No. 1 (2013), pp. 113–129.

bloc around interest-bearing capital (in neoliberal regimes) and export-based profit-producing capital (where neoliberal policy adjustments served to maintain a more neomercantilist accumulation strategy). In the eurozone, for example, authoritarian crisis constitutionalism seeks to deepen EU integration and govern through competitive austerity. Its aims include socializing bank losses, exploiting the sovereign debt crisis to restructure welfare states and labour markets (including further measures to weaken trade union bargaining power), and imposing shock therapy in the periphery. In both finance-dominated and export-oriented regimes, the overall approach can switch between offensive and defensive tactics (an example of the latter is the »Third Way«, with its flanking and supporting mechanisms intended to maintain the overall momentum of neoliberal transformation). The pursuit of this strategy, whose success cannot be taken for granted, leads to an *austerity state* embedded in a political system (polity) that institutionalizes a »permanent« politics of austerity.

Critics from the right and centre as well as the left have noted this trend and described it in various ways. For example, Albo and Fanelli refer to a bipartisan or pluripartisan »disciplinary democracy« as the political form of »permanent austerity«.[38] Likewise, Bruff refers to neoliberal authoritarian constitutionalism; Solty identifies an authoritarian crisis constitutionalism oriented to the economic governance of competitive austerity; and Oberndorfer describes the development of authoritarian competitive statism.[39] From a social democratic perspective, Streeck refers to a move from the welfare state to the »consolidation state«; and a (former) Fabian Socialist, Crouch, describes the transition to post-democracy.[40] On the libertarian right, there is condemnation of the strong and repressive state that emerges from allegedly unconstitutional intervention to shore up finance capital and to police dissent.[41] Most of these commentators note that the scope for material concessions to subaltern groups has shrunk and, faced with growing resentment and sometimes open resistance, capitalist states are also becoming less open and democratic, and increasingly coercive. It also creates different kinds of state and representational crisis that weaken state *power* even as its *powers* expand.[42]

38 Greg Albo / Carlo Fanelli, *Austerity against Democracy: An authoritarian phase of neoliberalism?*, Toronto 2014; Rasmus, *Epic Recession*, op. cit. (note 18); Ingo Stützle, *Austerität als politisches Projekt: Von der monetären Integration Europas zur Eurokrise*, Münster 2013.

39 Lukas Oberndorfer, »From new constitutionalism to authoritarian constitutionalism: New economic governance and the state of European democracy« in: Johannes Jäger and Elisabeth Springler (eds.), *Asymmetric Crisis in Europe and Possible Futures*, London 2015, pp. 184–205.

40 Streeck, *Buying Time*, op. cit. (note 9); Colin Crouch, *Post-Democracy*, Cambridge 2004.

41 David Stockman, *The Great Deformation: The Corruption of Capitalism in America*, New York 2013.

42 Poulantzas, »Political crisis«, op. cit. (note 10); Bruff, »Authoritarian neoliberalism«, op. cit. (note 37).

7. Debt-default-deflation dynamics in the US and UK

Neoliberal regimes in these states unwittingly created the ground for the North Atlantic Financial Crisis. Its form is typical of finance-dominated accumulation and surfaced initially in the US (thanks to the dominance of finance-dominated accumulation and financialization in that economy and its dominant global position) and then erupted for similar reasons in the UK.[43] The neoliberal regimes in both states also initiated many of the techniques of neoliberal austerity and authoritarian austerity state power that have since been refined there and elsewhere.

In the US, the crisis passed through several stages of increasing severity that would culminate in an epic recession. The response was to bailout »too big to fail« (TBTF) banks mainly as a covert strategy to recapitalize the banking system and socialize losses. This hugely increased public debt and reinforced government dependence on bondholder confidence and »Mr Market« more generally. A modest federal stimulus package to the »real economy« did not compensate for falling demand due to wage cuts plus austerity measures introduced at state and local level (where governments must balance their budgets). A scissors effect occurred as public spending and debt rose and GDP fell, so that debt grew as a proportion of GDP. Neoliberals exploited this by manufacturing a »public debt« crisis that would allegedly soon lead the federal government to fall over a »fiscal cliff«. This fuelled demands to cut the long-term costs of Medicaid, Medicare, and Social Security. Yet, of the projected 7 trillion USD deficit, some 4 trillion was due to consolidation of tax cuts introduced by the George W. Bush Administration and 1 trillion to an increased defence budget.[44] Advocates of deficit reduction never seriously examined cuts in defence spending, ending unfunded wars, halting subsidies to a broad spectrum of corporate interests (often with large reserves, often held offshore), or hiking tax rates on the rich to Reagan era levels, despite stagnant wages and increased wealth inequalities that matched those of the »roaring twenties«.[45] Indeed, despite the public theatre of the »fiscal cliff« debates, which were staged in an election period to pressure Congress to lock in bigger cuts before a potential recovery, dealing and plotting continued behind the scenes to roll out more corporate tax breaks that, if public debt was unsustainable, should have been rejected outright. Clearly, these measures reflect policy choices favoured by interest-bearing capital and transnational profit-producing capital with scant regard to policy options that might regenerate the economy, enhance competitiveness through positive measures rather than more austerity, improve conditions for the »squeezed middle«, and renew the war on poverty.

43 Rasmus, *Epic Recession*, op. cit. (note 18); Jack Rasmus, *Obama's Economic Recovery: Recovery for the Few*, London 2012; Howard Davies, *The Financial Crisis: Who is to Blame?*, Cambridge 2011; Bob Jessop, »Variegated capitalism, *Modell Deutschland*, and the eurozone crisis« in: *Journal of Contemporary European Studies* 22, No. 3 (2014), pp. 248–260.

44 Ingar Solty, »Is the global crisis ending the marriage between capitalism and liberal democracy?« in: Maximilian Lakitsch (ed.), *Political Power Reconsidered*, Berlin 2013, pp. 161–204.

45 Thomas Piketty, *Capital in the Twenty-First Century*, Cambridge, MA 2014.

Despite earlier doom-laden forecasts, the US economy is slowly recovering (although commentators doubt its robustness), and, significantly, the federal budget deficit began to fall under the second Obama Administration. Nonetheless, financialization continued as TBTF banks grew bigger and securitization reached new levels. The economic costs of this approach to crisis-management and its political blowback effects nonetheless aggravated underlying political crises and provided the seedbed for the rise of the anti-Wall Street and anti-Washington populism of Donald Trump as well as the democratic socialist campaign of Bernie Sanders and Occupy Movement. This reflects the impact of years of stagnant incomes, the fallout from the housing crisis, resentment against growing inequalities of wealth and income, and the neglect of »fly-over America«, the rustbelt, and the rural poor. After winning power through fake populism, the new Trump Administration seems determined to introduce tax cuts for corporations and the »have lots«, increase defence and infrastructure spending, unpick the already weak attempts to re-regulate finance capital, and to reduce »entitlements« even further to pay for this.

The UK also experienced a neoliberal regime shift, continued after the Thatcher years (1979–1990) under successive Conservative, New Labour, Conservative-Libdem, and Conservative regimes. The UK is even more dominated by international financial capital and more spatially polarized than the US thanks to the economic dominance of the City of London, and it also lacks the »exorbitant privilege« of having the dollar as world money and the imperial capacities to shape the global order. Other aggravating issues are the concentration of economic, political, and cultural power in London and an entrenched pattern of uneven development that favours the capital city and the rest of South Eastern England. Thus, the NAFC had a greater and more lasting impact in the UK, and this was exacerbated by the more rigid politics of austerity pursued under an austere neoliberal Chancellor (George Osborne), a Ricardian approach to workfare to reduce public spending, and preferential tax treatment of corporations and the wealthy that has led to renewed investment in profit-producing capital in the UK economy.[46] The impact of neoliberal austerity over four decades was exacerbated by Osborne's infeasible but procyclical commitment to balanced budgets. Although this commitment has been relaxed following the referendum vote in June 2017 to leave the European Union, austerity remains central to the post-referendum Conservative agenda to ensure the competitiveness of the UK economy in global markets. The weak UK recovery depends on new asset bubbles fuelled by quantitative easing and is vulnerable to secular stagnation in the eurozone and the uncertainties over British negotiations to exit the European Union.

46 Seymour, *Against Austerity*, op. cit. (note 32).

8. The eurozone crisis and the Fiscal Compact

The North Atlantic region still comprises the largest, most advanced, and most tightly integrated economic space in the global economy[47] and is powerfully shaped by the penetration of the US capital into other economies. Nonetheless European economic space is organized in the shadow of a powerful German export-led growth regime with a predisposition to pragmatic neo-mercantilism rather than principled Anglo-Saxon neoliberalism. Its entrenched export dependence has shaped the German state's post-war domestic and foreign economic policy and its general strategy for European integration for decades.[48] The prime strategic goal is to maintain Germany's export competitiveness and the regional and international stability on which its exports depend. The development of the Economic and Monetary Union (EMU) was expected to enhance the competitiveness of French and German industrial capital, especially when reinforced by direct wage restraint, a reduced social wage, and lowered domestic consumption. Reflecting German banking tenets, the EMU operated on two key principles: first, the European Central Bank (ECB) may not act as lender of last resort to insolvent banks or indebted states; and, second, sovereign debts may only be discharged by their respective member states.[49]

Before 2008, the eurozone appeared to be working smoothly thanks to global capital and trade flows and the short-term boost to growth produced by EMU, with low interest rates fuelling consumer imports and housing demand in Southern Europe. Yet structural incompatibilities and institutional design flaws were already evident before 2009, intensified in 2010–2011, and became acute in 2012. These are evident in the ensemble of incompatible growth regimes, different modes of regulation, diverging levels of competitiveness, and weak governance capacities of many eurozone member states. Other grounds for scepticism also existed. Monetary union was not accompanied by fiscal union, and no credible institutional arrangements existed to enforce long-term fiscal discipline, compensate for uneven development and economic performance, or coordinate crisis-management in a situation where conventional national crisis responses such as devaluation were ruled out. *Faute de mieux*, the enduring structural and newly intensified fisco-financial crises were managed through the imposition of neoliberal structural adjustment and austerity measures that correspond to the third type of neoliberalism identified above.

Financial and economic crises have more radical effects when there are pre-existing political crises and/or when the ways in which financial and economic crises are man-

47 Daniel S. Hamilton / Joseph P Quinlan, *The Transatlantic Economy 2013*, Brussels 2013.

48 Riccardo Bellofiore / Francesco Garibaldo / Joseph Halevi, »The Great Recession and the contradictions of European neomercantilism« in: *Socialist Register 2011*, pp. 120–146; Sergio Cesaratto / Antonella Stirati, »Germany and the European and global crises« in: *Journal of International Political Economy* 39, No. 4 (2010), pp. 56–86; Magnus Ryner, »Europe's ordoliberal iron cage: critical political economy, the euro area crisis and its management« in: *Journal of European Public Policy* 22, No. 2 (2015), pp. 275–294.

49 Yanis Varoufakis, »From contagion to incoherence: towards a model of the unfolding eurozone crisis« in: *Contributions to Political Economy* 32 (2013), pp. 51–71.

aged weaken the state, undermining its legitimacy, institutional integration, and effectiveness, and radically reduce support for all the »natural governing parties«. This is evident in the eurozone crisis, in which signs of a crisis of crisis-management are far more evident than in the USA and UK. The contagion effects of the NAFC led to the virtual insolvency of many of Europe's big banks and required urgent measures to recapitalize them and nationalize toxic assets. As in the US, this led to further concentration in banking. It also threatened a domino effect of sequential bankruptcy of vulnerable member states and their respective banking systems, starting with Greece and Eire and with the systemically important cases of Spain, Italy, and France looming on the near horizon. Without the right to exit the eurozone and regain competitiveness through devaluation (among other measures), the intensification of the eurozone crisis exposed the peripheral economies to domestic debt-default-deflation dynamics as well as to the austerity measures mistakenly adopted by other member states and European institutions in the belief that they would limit or resolve the wider crisis. Once again, crisis-management responses premised on deep cuts in spending and regressive taxation proved procyclical, triggering a mutually reinforcing downward spiral of actual or feared private and sovereign debt-default-deflation dynamics in the periphery. This has since spread to the core of the eurozone as evidenced in a triple dip recession, to which, against all the evidence, more austerity seems still to be the answer even in France, which once led the resistance to German demands for austerity.

A series of failed crisis-measures led to the Treaty on Stability, Coordination and Governance in the Economic and Monetary Union (or Fiscal Compact). If, and when, fully implemented by its signatory states, this will impose binding limits (0.5 per cent of GDP) on the structural deficits in the annual budgets of individual member-states. By extending surveillance and disciplinary neoliberalism, it constitutionalizes and entrenches the power of capital, limiting states' political autonomy, and transforms budget-making into a more technocratic process subject to legal sanctions as well as market pressures. This will block active Keynesian fiscal policy and exacerbate the underlying macroeconomic weaknesses in the eurozone. For example, to gain authority to operate as a *de facto* lender of last resort to banks, central banks, and sovereign states, the ECB had to commit to using its coercive powers in conjunction with the European Commission and the International Monetary Fund (IMF) to impose the greatest austerity upon the weakest member states.[50] To achieve the Pact's aims, however, investment must rise well above savings levels in deficit and surplus countries alike. Economic and political divisions in the eurozone make this unlikely.

9. A Greek tragedy

Greece is a small and peripheral economy with a weak and clientelist state. Although of minor economic significance in a global or European context, it has huge political significance as a laboratory for neoliberal experimentation. Thus, it is a sad example of

50 Varoufakis, »From contagion to incoherence«, op. cit. (note 49)..

the technocratic politics of austerity in southern member states, whether through EU- and ECB-inspired *coups d'état* (Greece and Italy), *de facto* or formally agreed governments of national unity (Spain, Portugal), or a coordinated war of financial manoeuvre against a radical anti-austerity regime (Syriza). The first two kinds of government are running states of economic emergency that authorize big spending cuts and neoliberal structural reforms. The failure of measures imposed on the Greek people prompted second thoughts among research staff in the IMF and the Organization of Economic Cooperation and Development (OECD) on the validity and effectiveness of austerity policies. However, despite hopes (and fears) that Greece might exit the eurozone, permanently or temporarily (to permit restructuring), the political risks and economic costs of breakup led the German government, supported by the Troika comprising the European Commission, ECB, and IMF (with US backing), to introduce exceptional measures to preserve this flawed system.[51]

Outside forces regard austerity in Greece as a price worth paying to achieve this and *encourager les autres*, especially as the excluded alternatives (Marshall-plan type capital transfers, a debt moratorium to finance contra-cyclical investment, a state role as employer of last resort, etc.) would have set bad precedents for the larger, systemically more important Spanish and Italian economies. After an initial show of resistance and a supportive referendum that backed its negotiating stance, Germany and its northern allies forced Syriza to capitulate when Greek banks were starved of liquidity. The Troika required the reversal of Syriza's reforms, dictated a legislative programme to entrench neoliberal austerity, and assumed control of Greek fisco-financial and economic policies in exchange, *possibly*, for a third bailout. The enduring paradox here is that, if Greece does not exit the eurozone, it must accept a lasting state of austerity; yet, if Grexit occurs, then a politics and policies of austerity will continue but oriented this time to creating conditions for growth rather than further shrinking the economy. This paradox is creating policy and political divisions in the Troika, with the IMF again slightly more »lenient« compared with the ECB and European Commission and their hard-line neoliberal and ordoliberal backers. Thus, in January 2017, the IMF's annual assessment of the Greek economy noted the constraints involved in resolving the crisis by continued membership of the Eurozone and added that, in these circumstances, »Greece cannot grow out of its debt problem. Greece requires substantial debt relief from its European partners to restore debt sustainability.«[52] This proposal has, unsurprisingly, been opposed by the other two Troika members.

In Greece, as elsewhere, the »There Is No Alternative« (TINA) mantra derived from the neoliberal imaginary restricts the feasible set of economic, political, and social policies unless there is countervailing pressure from other political and social forces.

51 Ryner refers to this trap as the »iron cage« of Ordoliberalism, which, paradoxically, requires neoliberal austerity to maintain the eurozone system that was designed to reproduce on a European scale the rigours of the German model; see Ryner, »Europe's ordoliberal iron cage«, op. cit. (note 48).

52 IMF, *Greece: Staff Report for the 2016 Article IV Consultation*. Washington DC, 23.1.2017, p. 1.

Growing disaffection with austerity and its social repercussions has fuelled popular unrest, including right-wing populism and xenophobia, indicating possible limits of austerity politics and policies. Past and present challenges from Syriza, *Die Linke* in Germany, and Spain's *Podemos* to the TINA cliché and ineffective austerity policies are a threat to neoliberal rule.[53] Recently, TINA has been challenged by the entry of the counter-hegemonic TATIANA (That, Astonishingly, There Is AN Alternative). This is a »blueprint for addressing the crisis through Europeanizing its four components – the crises of public debt, banks, underinvestment and the poverty explosion – while decentralizing political power through a reduction in the discretionary power exercised illicitly by the Brussels-Frankfurt-Berlin triangle.«[54] This would create a surplus recycling mechanism by adding rules that modify the operation of EU-level institutions but do not require treaty changes so that the burden of adjustment does not fall solely on deficit countries and significant power can return to national parliaments.[55] Needless to say, this proposal has fallen on deaf ears in the neoliberal centres of power, illustrating once again Deutsch's aphorism that power comprises the ability not to have to learn from one's mistakes.[56]

As in the USA and UK, right-wing populism and protectionism (such as the Front National, Five Star Movement and other parties and movements) complement the development of leftist opposition movements. The resulting threats require careful modulation of economic conditionalities to keep the electorates of »donor« states on side by avoiding what could be portrayed as handouts to feckless countries and spendthrift governments and, at the same time, to temper popular unrest that could destabilize authoritarian »regimes of economic emergency« in indebted states. The latter risk is being met, as noted above, by further steps towards authoritarian statism to limit and control popular resistance.

10. Conclusions

This chapter has analysed rapidly diverse factors relevant to describing, interpreting, and explaining the dynamics of austerity policies, politics, and polities. It has highlighted the distinctive features of neoliberal regime shifts and their role in promoting financialization and finance-dominated accumulation. It has argued that, whereas the short-lived period of apparently permanent prosperity of the Fordist period was based on the dynamic of profit-producing capital and wage-led growth, neoliberal regimes

53 Wolfgang Münchau, »Radical left is right about Europe's debt«, in: *Financial Times*, 27.11.2014.

54 Yanis Varoufakis, *And the Weak Suffer What They Must? Europe's Crisis and America's Economic Future*. New York 2016, p. 228.

55 For the details of the »modest proposal«, see Varoufakis, *And the Weak Suffer What They Must*, op. cit. (note 54), pp. 249–257.

56 Karl W. Deutsch, *The Nerves of Government*. New York 1963, p. 111.

are dominated by financial capital and involve largely debt-fuelled expansion.[57] The illusory permanent prosperity that occurred under the latter regimes (sometimes termed the Great Moderation) was actually based on unsustainable private debt facilitated by financial innovation, liberalization, deregulation and decriminalization, and the expansion of ever more fantastic forms of fictitious credit, fictitious capital, and fictitious profits. When the financial bubble burst, it wiped out any gains from the preceding period of neoliberal austerity and, thanks to the decision to bail out and recapitalize interest-bearing capital, has distorted the growth dynamic of neoliberal finance-dominated accumulation. In an ever-more integrated world economy (which has promoted calls for protectionism and isolationism), this also affects the dynamic of other varieties of capitalism because of the weight of the US and other finance-dominated regimes in the world economy and the contagion effects of their crises. This was illustrated from the eurozone crisis, which has its own dynamic but unfolds within the context of the wider North Atlantic Financial Crisis. In both cases, this is the background for the rise of the politics of austerity and the trend towards an austerity polity that represents a neoliberal variant of authoritarian statism.

The destabilizing consequences of budget-cutting in North America, Europe, and elsewhere worry even the high priests of neoliberalism in the IMF, the World Bank, the World Economic Forum, and so on. There was growing recognition in the second decade of this century about the threat to global order of extreme inequalities of wealth and income[58] as well as recognition that central bank management of the crisis has contributed massively to these inequalities whilst proving ineffective in stimulating the real economy and, indeed, even destabilizing recovery, weakening future growth prospects, and diminishing the changes for deficit and debt reduction.[59] Yet the uneven development of the world economy, the conflicting interests of different economic and political spaces in a variegated world market, and the crisis of US hegemony (compared with the Atlantic Fordist era) has blocked any serious movement by the G8, G20, or wider groupings to resolve the crisis, let alone to address the far more fundamental challenges of climate change and growing inequalities of wealth and income.

Acknowledgement
This chapter was written while I held a fellowship funded by the Economic and Social Research Council under the WISERD Civil Society programme at Cardiff University (RES-051-27-0303).

57 Jessop, *Future of the Capitalist State*, op. cit. (note 13); Engelbert Stockhammer, »Rising inequality as a cause of the present crisis« in: *Cambridge Journal of Economics* 39, No. 3 (2015), pp. 935–958.
58 World Economic Forum, *Global Risks*, Cologny/Geneva 2012, 2013, and 2014.
59 See IMF / ILO, *The challenges of growth, employment and social cohesion*, 2010, p. 10, http://www.osloconference2010.org/discussionpaper.pdf [14.6.2017].

Tim Griebel

The Cultural Political Economy of Austerity in Germany: A Corpus-Assisted Critical-Realist Discourse Analysis[1]

Economic crises, the way to understand them and the means taken to respond to them are not just naturally given or economically determined; they are always also an expression of intersubjective ideas that strive for hegemony within a discourse.[2] Austerity is, therefore, always »a site of intensive discursive struggle, through which social actors and movements seek to further specific interests and alternative visions of the future.«[3] It is not a simple rational act without alternative but »a ›morality tale‹ that exists partially detached from the pure economics – which are of course themselves open to discursive contestation.«[4] The meaning of austerity in this sense is also the expression of intersubjective meaning giving. As these meanings are never (completely) stable, it is essential not to give in to the old Greek meaning of austerity as the »dryness of tongue«[5] but to take a swig of discourse and to discover the range of possible alternative imaginaries that are articulated by nodal actors like official representatives and the press media. At the same time, it would go too far to reduce economic systems in general and austerity in particular to the level of discourse and imagination. To answer the question *why* some discourses and imaginaries are more powerful than others and why they get selected, hegemonic and institutionalized, it is necessary but not sufficient to analyse the form of meaning giving. This is even recognized by radical social constructivists like Ernesto Laclau: »[W]hat rhetoric can explain is the *form* that an overdetermining investment takes, but not the *force* that explains the investment as such and its perdurability. Here something else has to be brought into the picture.«[6] With the help of the Cultural Political Economy (CPE) approach, which is enriched by the insights of Frommian social psychology on the ground of Critical Realism, it is argued on the following pages that this ›something else‹ has to be found both in material social structures and psychological drives that are rooted in material human beings.

1 A previous version of this chapter was presented at the ECPR General Conference Prague 7–10 September 2016. I want to thank Stefan Evert, Mike Scott, Roland Sturm, Thorsten Winkelmann, Erik Vollmann, Richard Zensen, Christoph Bruckmüller, Georg Schneider and especially Kristina Chmelar for all their support. They are of course not responsible for the errors I have committed.

2 Marieke de Goede (eds.), *International Political Economy and Poststructural Politics*, Houndmills/New York 2006.

3 Rebecca Bramall, *The Cultural Politics of Austerity: Past and Present in Austere Times*, Houndmills 2013, p. 10.

4 Darren Kelsey / Frank Mueller / Andrea Whittle / Majid Khosravinik, »Financial crisis and austerity: interdisciplinary concerns in critical discourse studies« in: *Critical Discourse Studies* 13, No. 1 (2016), pp. 1–19, p. 5.

5 Florian Schui, *Austerity. The Great Failure*, New Haven 2014, p. 11.

6 Ernesto Laclau, »›Glimpsing the Future: A Reply‹« in: Simon Critchley / Oliver Marchart (eds.), *Laclau: A Critical Reader*, London 2004, pp. 279–328, p. 326, italics in original.

In the second part, the basic ideas of CPE about the interdependence of intersubjective imaginaries and material social structures will be explained first, before Erich Fromm's central ideas of different »modes of being« and the corresponding »social characters« will be used to explain why human *subjects* are not just confronted with enabling and constraining social *structures* but also »*wish* to do what they *have* to do.«[7] The following parts will discuss the corpus linguistic critical realist discourse analysis that has been used to reconstruct different economic imaginaries found within statements of the German government and texts from two newspapers. The analysis shows that the German official discourse articulates an understanding of austerity within an ordoliberal imaginary that is backed by Germany's position in the European socio-economic structure and the »having mode of existence«. In contrast to the conservative newspaper *Die Welt*, the left-wing newspaper *taz* articulates a critique of this imaginary and searches for an alternative future for Europe based on a non-competitive solidarity.

1. Cultural Political Economy – the force of social structures in meaning giving

The central idea of CPE is that the levels of semiosis, that is intersubjective meaning giving, in form of »imaginaries« and the extra-semiotic features of reality stand in a dialectic relationship. Economic imaginaries »identify, privilege and seek to stabilize some economic activities from the totality of economic relations and transform them into objects of observation, calculation and governance.«[8] Within a given society the government and the media function as »nodal actors«, who »can make a difference thanks to their different capacities to persuade, read particular conjunctures, displace opponents, and rearticulate discourses and imaginaries in timely fashion.«[9] Whereas the government is the central intermediary between domestic and international politics[10], media serve as »crisis explainer«[11] and as »crucial intermediaries in mobilizing elite and/or popular support behind competing imaginaries.«[12] But to answer the question *why* certain imaginaries – like neoliberalism – get selected and institutionalized, it is not enough to reconstruct imaginaries and discourses. The latter

7 Erich Fromm, *To Have or to Be?*, London/New York 2008, p. 109.

8 Ngai-Ling Sum / Bob Jessop, *Towards a Cultural Political Economy: Putting Culture in Its Place in Political Economy*. Cheltenham 2013, p. 166.

9 Sum / Jessop, *Towards a Cultural Political Economy*, op. cit. (note 8), p. 166.

10 International politics can be described as a »two-level language game.« See Einar Wigen, »Two-level language games: International relations as inter-lingual relations« in: *European Journal of International Relations* 21, No. 2 (2015), pp. 427–450.

11 Amelie Kutter, »A Catalytic Moment: The Greek Crisis in the German Financial Press« in: *Discourse & Society* 25, No. 4 (2014), pp. 446–466, p. 449.

12 Sum / Jessop, *Towards a Cultural Political Economy*, op. cit. (note 8), p. 167. For an analysis of the German media that is based on CPE, see Amelie Kutter / Bob Jessop, »Culture as Discursive Practice: Combining Cultural Political Economy and Discursive Political Studies in Investigations of the Financial Crisis« in: Bob Jessop / Brigitte Young / Christoph Scherrer (eds.), *Financial Cultures and Crisis Dynamics*, London 2015, pp. 64–82.

> *»must have some significant, albeit necessarily partial, correspondence to real material interdependencies in the actually existing economic and political fields and their articulation with the wider ensemble of social relations. It is the interaction between the discursive and extra-discursive that gives relatively successful economic and political imaginaries their performative, constitutive force in the material world«.*[13]

Accordingly, economic imaginaries cannot be understood by their form alone but have to be analysed as part of a »historical structure«[14], which is composed of material relations, institutions and ideas. Austerity can only be understood within a historical structure. It must, therefore,

> *»be interpreted and explained in terms of prevailing economic and fisco-financial imaginaries, accounts of the conditions for political stability and the wider social repercussions of economic and political policy. [...] But CPE also studies the structural constraints and opportunities [...] that condition and mediate agents' attempts to formulate, implement and evaluate austerity.«*[15]

The substantial arguments of CPE are based on the meta-theoretical foundation of Critical Realism. Critical Realism in general and CPE in particular make it possible to navigate between the Scylla of textualism and the Charybdis of economic determinism.[16] To be able to do so, Critical Realism distinguishes between different kinds of causal mechanisms in respect to their time-, space-, praxis- and concept-dependence,[17] which means whether they are (highly) transitive as intersubjective meaning giving or relatively intransitive, like some essential causal powers and tendencies[18] in material objects[19] *and* in material human subjects.[20] Accordingly, for Critical Realism meaning is not reducible to the level of signifier and signified but formed within a »semiotic tri-

13 Bob Jessop / Ngai-Ling Sum, »Towards a Cultural International Political Economy: Poststructuralism and the Italian School« in: Marieke de Goede (ed.), *International Political Economy and Poststructural Politics*, Houndmills/New York 2006, pp. 157–176, p. 160.

14 Robert W. Cox, »Social Forces, States and World Orders: Beyond International Relations Theory« in: *Millennium – Journal of International Studies* 10, No. 2 (1981), pp. 126–155.

15 Bob Jessop, »Neoliberalism, Finance-Dominated Accumulation and Enduring Austerity: A Cultural Political Economy Perspective« in: Kevin Farnsworth / Zoë Irving (eds.), *Social Politics in Times of Austerity. Global Economic Crisis and the New Politics of Welfare*, Bristol 2015, pp. 87–111, p. 88.

16 Sum / Jessop, *Towards a Cultural Political Economy*, op. cit. (note 8), p. 147–195.

17 Ted Benton, »Realism and Social Science. Some Comments on Roy Bhaskar's ›The Possibility of Naturalism‹« in: Margaret Archer / Roy Bhaskar / Andrew Collier / Tony Lawson / Alan Norrie (eds.), *Critical Realism. Essential Readings*, London/New York 1998, pp. 297–311.

18 The intransitive is the ontological level of referents, whereas the transitive is the epistemological level of discourse. Berth Danermark / Mats Erikström / Liselotte Jakobsen / Jan Ch. Karlsson, *Explaining Society. Critical Realism in the Social Sciences*, London/New York 2002, p. 206.

19 Clive Lawson, »An Ontology of Technology: Artefacts, Relations and Functions« in: *Techné: Research in Philosophy and Technology* 12, No. 1 (2008).

20 Kieran Durkin, *The Radical Humanism of Erich Fromm*, New York 2014, p. 152.

angle«[21] as the referents of meaning giving possess essential causal powers that are not reducible to the level of discourse. For Critical Realism non-discursive and discursive mechanisms stand in an emergent relationship; that means that »one diachronically, or perhaps synchronically, arises out of the other, but is capable of reacting back on the first and is in any event causally and taxonomically irreducible to it.«[22] Intersubjective meaning systems have to be understood on the ground of this »emergent powers materialism.«[23] Although assertions about essential causal powers and relations may just be a speculation and even wrong, Critical Realism nevertheless believes in the possibility of a rational judgment about knowledge claims and sticks to the goal of »explanatory critique for the purpose of promoting human emancipation.«[24]

2. *Enriching CPE with materialist social psychology – the force of socio-psychological structures in meaning giving*

Although the argument of emergent powers materialism holds for both social structures *and* subjects, critical realists have more often analysed the former, and the rare works on the latter have been »confined to very narrow aspects of the self, especially agency or reflexivity.«[25] Although CPE goes beyond this, by analysing the role of »technological selectivities« in order to understand subjectivations and why some individuals are »more energized affectively to maintain hegemonic modes of thinking«[26], this strand is a »relatively new feature«[27] of CPE.[28] It is, therefore, worth to further emphasize the features of human subjects, processes of subjectivities and their relation with social structures. This step will be taken with the help of the »materialist social psychology« of Erich Fromm[29], a combination of historical materialism and psychoanalysis, which will provide a more accurate view of the force behind different imaginaries.[30]

21 Roy Bhaskar, *Dialectic. The Pulse of Freedom*, London/New York 1993, p. 222–223.
22 Roy Bhaskar, *Plato Etc. The Problems of Philosophy and Their Resolution*, London/New York 1994, p. 73.
23 Roy Bhaskar, »On the Ontological Status of Ideas« in: *Journal for the Theory of Social Behaviour* 27, No. 2–3 (1997), pp. 139–147, p. 144.
24 Peter Nielsen, »Underlabouring in Empire« in: *Journal of Critical Realism* 6, No. 1 (2007), pp. 53–83, p. 55.
25 Joe O'Mahoney, »Critical Realism and the Self« in: *Journal of Critical Realism* 10 (2011), pp. 122–129, p. 123.
26 Sum / Jessop, *Towards a Cultural Political Economy*, op. cit. (note 8), p. 222.
27 Sum / Jessop, *Towards a Cultural Political Economy*, op. cit. (note 8), p. 222.
28 For an even stronger argument that CPE is »strikingly agentless« and highlights the strategic dimension in contrast to the affective dimension of subjectivity, see Krisztina Varró, »Making (more) sense of political-economic geographies of continuity and change: Dialoguing across ontological divides« in: *Progress in Human Geography* 39, No. 1 (2015), pp. 26–46.
29 Erich Fromm, »Über Methode und Aufgabe einer analytischen Sozialpsychologie: Bemerkungen über Psychoanalyse und historischen Materialismus« in: *Zeitschrift für Sozialforschung* 1 (1932), pp. 28–54.
30 Other possible routes are radical social constructivist approaches that ground their ideas about processes of subjectivation on the anti-humanist psychoanalysis of Jacque Lacan.

According to Fromm, man »is not a blank sheet of paper on which culture can write its text.« Instead, human nature can be both defined biologically and psychically[31], although social life is not determined by biology and psychology but emerges from this level of reality.[32] Man faces both *historical* contradictions, which can be solved in principle, and *existential* contradictions resulting from his self-awareness that disconnects him/her with nature. The latter lay the basis for social life:

> *»The problem of man's existence [...] is unique in the whole of nature; he has fallen out of nature, as it were, and is still in it; he is partly divine, partly animal; partly infinite, partly finite. The necessity to find ever-new solutions for the contradictions in his existence, to find ever-higher forms of unity with nature, his fellow men and himself, is the source of all psychic forces which motivate man, of all his passions, affects and anxieties.«*[33]

This situation gives rise to certain essential needs like the need for relatedness[34], which can either be stilled through man's primary potentials for reason and love or through the secondary potential for destruction.[35] These different potentialities are »formed into a set of character traits and types by social relations and social institutions«[36] and the general »mode of existence« of a society. Fromm distinguishes between two ideal types of these modes: »I refer to two fundamental modes of existence, to two different kinds of orientation toward self and the world, to two different kinds of character structure the respective predominance of which determines the totality of a person's thinking, feeling, and acting.«[37] Fromm calls these modes the *having* and the *being* mode of existence, the basic characteristics of which are summarized in table 1.

Durkin, *The Radical Humanism of Erich Fromm,* op. cit. (note 20), p. 129. But this understanding of human subjects is incompatible with Critical Realism as »realism is humanism. « Douglas V. Porpora, »Do Realists Run Regressions?« in: José López / Garry Potter (eds.), *After Postmodernism. An Introduction to Critical Realism*, London/New York 2001, pp. 260–266, p. 264. When *empirical* statements about processes of subjectivation that are grounded in a radical social constructivist ontology are used here, these statements have, therefore, to be understood as a re-articulation that fits with the ontological foundations of Critical Realism. For the idea of (re-)articulation – albeit from a radical social constructivist perspective – see Jason Glynos / David Howarth, *Logics of Critical Explanation in Social and Political Theory*, London/New York 2007, p. 181–183.

31 Fromm, *To Have or to Be?*, op. cit. (note 7), p. 11–12.

32 Durkin, *The Radical Humanism of Erich Fromm*, op. cit. (note 20), p. 152–153.

33 Erich Fromm, *The Sane Society*, London/New York 2008, p. 24, italics in original.

34 Anthony Eliot, *Psychoanalytic Theory. An Introduction*, Durham 2002, p. 48.

35 Fromm, *The Sane Society*, op. cit. (note 33), p. 36.

36 Thomas Meisenhelder, »From character to habitus in sociology« in: *The Social Science Journal* 43, No. 1 (2006), pp. 55–66, p. 58.

37 Fromm, *To Have or to Be?*, op. cit. (note 7), p. 20–21.

Table 1: Basic Elements of Different Modes of Existence

Having Mode of Existence	*Being Mode of Existence*
»In the having mode of existence my relationship to the world is one of possessing and owning, one in which I want to make everybody and everything, including myself, my property.«[38] »[T]he fundamental elements in the relation between individuals in the having mode of existence are competition, antagonism, and fear.«[39]	»[T]he being mode of existence [...] means aliveness and authentic relatedness to the world [...] and refers to the true nature, the true reality, of a person or a thing in contrast to deceptive appearances«.[40] The being mode of existence is based on the will »to share, to give, to sacrifice.«[41]»The emphasis is on a productive disposition and social relations infused with solidarity and love«[42]

Source: own illustration

Intersubjective ideas have »an emotional matrix«[43] that is rooted in the character structure, respectively the mode of existence, of a society. This is important because »individuals develop strong emotional investments in relation to economic and social structures that, in turn, support the stability of those structures.«[44] From this perspective, the social regimes and the associated ideas of neoliberalism in general[45] and austerity in particular are backed by the imagination of »an irresponsible and profligate other who stole our prosperous economy; a horrific threat of worse disaster to come if the wrong macro-economic approach is taken; but with the beatific promise of a brighter and more prosperous future waiting at the end of the path of austerity.«[46] Through this fantasy the neoliberal regime also attempts »to forge a new subject, to free the self from its old collectivist habits and to instill new habits of self-management and self-reliance, through the exercise of which the self is able to realize its economic freedom. «[47] The austerity regime specifies this general subjectivation by producing the »indebted man«[48] and the »indebted citizen« found within »a new economy of anxiety predi-

38 Fromm, *To Have or to Be?*, op. cit. (note 7), p. 20–21.

39 Fromm, *To Have or to Be?*, op. cit. (note 7), p. 20–21.

40 Fromm, *To Have or to Be?*, op. cit. (note 7), p. 20–21.

41 Fromm, *To Have or to Be?*, op. cit. (note 7), p. 86.

42 Lawrence Wilde, »A ›Radical Humanist‹ Approach to the Concept of Solidarity« in: *Political Studies* 52, No. 1 (2004), pp. 162–178, p. 171.

43 Erich Fromm, *Escape from Freedom*, New York 1941, p. 279, italics in original. As the empirical analysis of the word solidarity will show, it is therefore important to understand the mode of being or character structure behind a word. »Although the word which people of two different personality use when they speak of love, for instance, is the same, the meaning of the word is entirely different according to their character structure.« Ibid.

44 Roger Foster, »The Catastrophe of Neo-Liberalism: Finance, Emancipation and Disintegration« in: *Philosophy & Social Criticism* 43, No. 2 (2016), pp. 123–143, p. 138.

45 Jason Glynos / Robin Klimecki / Hugh Willmott, »Logics in Policy and Practice: A Critical Nodal Analysis of the UK Banking Reform Process« in: *Critical Policy Studies* 9, No. 4 (2015), pp. 393–415.

46 Crispian Fuller / Karen West, »The possibilities and limits of political contestation in times of ›urban austerity‹« in: *Urban Studies*, 2016, pp. 1–20, p. 8.

47 Foster, »The Catastrophe of Neo-Liberalism«, op. cit. (note 45), p. 125.

48 Maurizio Lazzarato, *The Making of the Indebted Man: An Essay on the Neoliberal Condition*, Soth Pasadena 2012.

cated upon the ›intensification‹ of certain affects (sacrifice, pain, restraint) and disavowal of others (indulgence, gratification, pleasure).«[49] Neoliberal and austerity regimes are, therefore, not just as stable as they are because they are backed by material power structures but also because the having mode of existence[50] and a corresponding »ascetic morality«[51] provide a kind of satisfaction for subjects within these structures: »The person with whom saving is a desire, springing from his personality, gains also a profound psychological satisfaction in being able to act accordingly; that is, he is not only benefited practically when he saves, but he also feels satisfied psychologically.«[52] The reason why this mode can become hegemonic at all is based on a paradox:

> *»[T]he frequency and intensity of the desire to share, to give, and to sacrifice are not surprising if we consider the conditions of existence of the human species. What is surprising is that this need could be so repressed as to make acts of selfishness the rule in industrial (and many other) societies and acts of solidarity the exception. But, paradoxically, this very phenomenon is caused by the need for union. A society whose principles are acquisition, profit, and property produces a social character oriented around having, and once the dominant pattern is established, nobody wants to be an outsider, or indeed an outcast; in order to avoid this risk everybody adapts to the majority, who have in common only their mutual antagonism.«*[53]

We are now in the position to translate these Frommian insights into the jargon of CPE and to connect the single elements that explain the force behind textual forms. In Fromm's terminology an economic imaginary can be understood as a »religion«, that is a *»group-shared system of thought and action that offers the individual a frame of orientation and an object of devotion.«*[54] The already discussed elements that are brought together in figure 1 are closely connected to these systems of thought: »Socioeconomic structure, character structure [*and modes of existence on a more fundamental level*, T. G.], and religious structure are inseparable from each other.«[55]

49 Andrea Mura, »Disorienting Austerity: *The Indebted Citizen as the New Soul of Europe« in: Engin Isin (ed.), Citizenship after Orientalism. Transforming Political Theory*, New York 2015, pp. 34–52, p. 34.
50 Panayota Gounari, »Neoliberalism as Social Necrophilia. Erich Fromm and the Politics of Hopelessness in Greece« in: Seyed Javad Miri / Robert Lake / Tricia M. Kress (eds.), *Reclaiming the Sane Society. Essays on Erich Fromm's Thought*, Rotterdam et al. 2014, pp. 187–201.
51 Alessandro Somma, »The biopolitics of debt-economy: market order, ascetic and hedonistic morality« in: Bertram Lomfeld / Alessandro Somma / Peer Zumbansen (eds.), *Reshaping Markets. Economic Governance, the Global Financial Crisis and Liberal Utopia*, Cambridge 2016, pp. 115–132, p. 126.
52 Fromm, *Escape from Freedom*, op. cit. (note 43), pp. 282–283.
53 Fromm, *To Have or to Be?* op. cit. (note 7), p. 87.
54 Fromm, *To Have or to Be?* op. cit. (note 7), p. 87.
55 Fromm, *To Have or to Be?* op. cit. (note 7), p. 87.

Figure 1: Building Blocks of a Textual Analysis of the Cultural Political Economy of Austerity

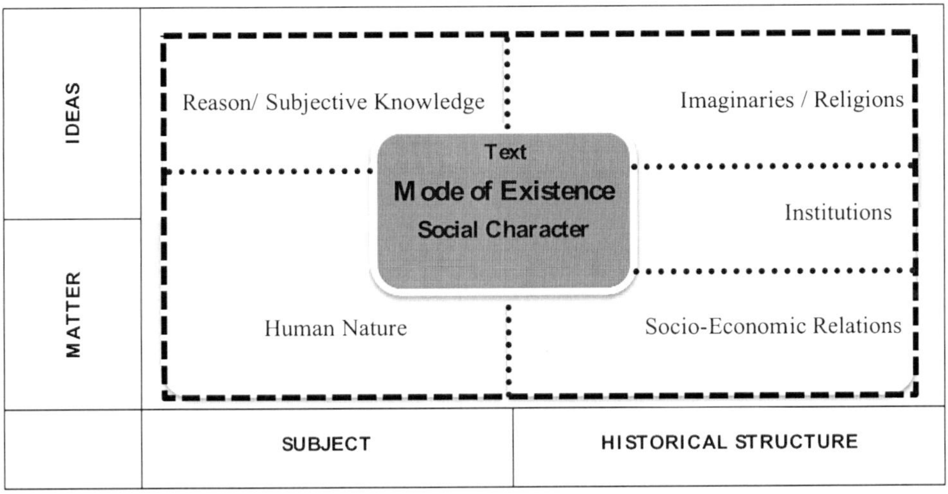

Source: own illustration[56]

In sum, austerity has, therefore, to be understood as part of the prevailing constraints and opportunities within the »asymmetrically interconnected economic space«[57] of the European socioeconomic structure as well as an expression of both the accompanying dominant having mode of existence and the economic imaginary or religious structure of neoliberalism.[58] Austerity is »a form of [un]voluntary deflation in which the economy adjusts through the reduction of wages, prices and public spending to restore competitiveness.«[59] This process is part of a broader historical structure that tries to expand the logic of the market within the realm of society and that is based on the having mode of existence. As this process also produces a certain kind of subjectivity, austerity cannot be reduced to statistical data about (un)observed cuts in state expenditure and their effect on economic growth. Such data only grasp the surface of the phenomenon within the logic of the current economic regime. But discourses are never stable and the parts of historical structures are never totalizing. There are not only va-

56 For a previous version of these thoughts in respect to questions concerning security relationships, see Tim Griebel, *Liebe und Macht in der deutsch-amerikanischen Sicherheitsbeziehung 2001–2003: Eine kritisch-realistische Diskursanalyse*, Bielefeld 2016, p. 99.

57 Bob Jessop, »Variegated Capitalism, das Modell Deutschland, and the Eurozone Crisis« in: *Journal of Contemporary European Studies* 22, No. 3 (2014), pp. 248–260, p. 249.

58 Whiteside goes so far to understand »[n]eoliberalism *as* austerity«; Heather Whiteside, »Neoliberalism as Austerity. The theory, practice, and purpose of fiscal restraint since the 1970s« in: Simon Springer / Kean Birch / Julie MacLeavy (eds.), *The Handbook of Neoliberalism*, New York 2016, pp. 50–60.

59 Mark Blyth, *Austerity: The History of a Dangerous Idea*, Oxford 2013, p. 2.

rieties of austerity *between* nation states[60] but also *within* them. It is therefore worth to examine how dominant these elements are within the cultural political economy of Germany and what kind of alternatives can be found there. Germany is a particularly important case because the political choices made in »the largest economy and creditor state in the EU«[61] have important consequences for other states as well.

3. Studying austerity – methodological considerations

To be able to uncover the spectrum of different economic imaginaries within the German cultural political economy, texts that contain *austerit**[62] and that have been published in the government bulletin[63] as well as in a conservative (*Die Welt*) and in a left-wing (*Die Tageszeitung, taz*) newspaper have been collected for the period between 1.1.2007 and 31.12.2015. The newspaper texts have been collected via *LexisNexis*.[64] The software tool *Parser*[65] has been used to extract the meta-data – like date and author – that are contained within the *LexisNexis* output.[66] The overall analysed corpus is summarized in table 2.

Table 2: Corpus

	Government	Welt	taz
Number of texts	20	243	502
Number of running words	71,378	202,265	376,702

Source: own illustration

To analyse these texts, a corpus-assisted critical (realist) discourse analysis was used that combines the strengths of quantitative corpus linguistic (CL) methods and a quali-

60 Kevin Farnsworth / Zoë Irving, »Varieties of Crisis, Varieties of Austerity: Social Policy in Challenging Times« in: *Journal of Poverty and Social Justice* 20, No. 2 (2012), pp. 133–147; Jessop, »Neoliberalism, Finance-Dominated Accumulation and Enduring Austerity«, op. cit. (note 15), p. 87.

61 Simon Bulmer, »Germany and the Eurozone Crisis: Between Hegemony and Domestic Politics« in: *West European Politics* 37, No. 6 (2014), pp. 1244–1263, p. 1245.

62 This has been done to be able to identify not only the word »Austerität« (austerity) but also its composites like »Austeritätsmaßnahmen« (austerity measures) and »Austeritätspolitik« (politics of austerity).

63 Presse- und Informationsdienst der Bundesregierung, *Bulletin 2009. Bulletin 1996–2008. CD-ROM Version*, Berlin 2010.

64 LexisNexis, »Nachrichten Datenbank«, https://www.lexisnexis.de [30.6.2016].

65 Mike Scott, *Parser*, Oxford: Lexical Analysis Software, 2016.

66 The meta-data that has not been recognized by *Parser* (for example, ›Genehmigung des taz-Verlags‹) have been deleted with the *Text Converter Tool* contained in *WordSmith*. Mike Scott, *WordSmith Tools Version 7.0*, Oxford: Lexical Analysis Software, 2016.

tative critical discourse analysis (CDA). CL methods – like a Swiss pocket knife[67] – are well suited to detect regularities at the linguistic surface that give hints to imaginaries and modes of existence[68] found within a society that might be unrecognized from a purely qualitative perspective. In contrast, CDA – like a depth driller – is able to reconstruct the social (character) structures that stand in a dialectic relation to these imaginaries while being sensitive to rare expressions of them. The two methods, therefore, stand in a »Checks and Balances«[69] relation. Of special interest on the quantitative side are keyword and collocations analyses. Keywords are understood as words that statistically occur more often in one corpus in comparison to another.[70] Like »tips of icebergs« they point to »complex lexical objects which represent the shared beliefs and values of a culture.«[71] Of special interest here is the comparison of the three different sub-corpora. A collocation is »a combination of two words that exhibit a tendency to occur near each other in natural language, i.e. to *co-occur.*«[72] Collocation analyses uncover the collocates that co-occur with a node (like »austerity«) and, as »[y]ou shall know a word by the company it keeps«[73], give, therefore, hints to the meaning of it.[74] Both kinds of analysis are conducted with the help of *WordSmith*.[75] The most interesting results of these corpus linguistic analyses from the viewpoint of the theoretical considerations described above are then – in a form of elaborated cherry-picking – interpreted qualitatively and are used to reconstruct the German cultural political economy of austerity. In order to understand and criticize the linguistic expressions of austerity, the results are connected to the social (character) structure, respectively the mode of existence, underlying them. This calls also for a qualitative interpretation of

67 Mike Scott, »Comparing Corpora and Identifying Key Words, Collocations, Frequency Distributions through the WordSmith Tools Suite of Computer Programs« in: Mohsen Ghadessy / Alex Henry / Robert L. Roseberry (eds.), *Small Corpus Studies and ELT. Theory and Practice*, Amsterdam/Philadelphia 2001, pp. 47–67, pp. 47–48.

68 Fromm himself reflected upon the changing language patterns and their connection the having and the being mode of existence. Fromm, *To Have or to Be?*, op. cit. (note 7), p. 17.

69 Gerlinde Mautner, »Checks and Balances. How Corpus Linguistics Can Contribute to CDA« in: Ruth Wodak / Michael Meyer (eds.), *Methods of Critical Discourse Analysis*, London et al. 2009, pp. 122–143.

70 Paul Baker, »Querying Keywords: Questions of Difference, Frequency, and Sense in Keywords Analysis« in: *Journal of English Linguistics* 32, No. 4 (2004), pp. 346–359.

71 Michael Stubbs, »Three Concepts of Keywords« in: Marina Bondi / Mike Scott (eds.), *Keyness in Texts*, Amsterdam/Philadelphia 2010, pp. 21–42, p. 23.

72 Stefan Evert, »Corpora and Collocations« in: Anke Lüdeling / Merja Kytö (eds.), *Corpus Linguistics. An International Handbook*, Vol. 2, Berlin/New York 2009, pp. 1212–1248, p. 1214.

73 John Rupert Firth, *Papers in Linguistics, 1934–1951*, London/New York 1957, p. 11.

74 Here only the word »Austerität« has been analysed although all the composites that begin with *austerit** and even other words that are connected to the phenomenon – like »Sparpolitik« (saving politics) and »Haushaltskonsolidierung« (budget consolidation) – will have to be examined in the future.

75 Mike Scott, *WordSmith Tools Version 7.0.0.54*, Oxford: Lexical Analysis Software, 2016. The log-likelihood (LL) measure, a threshold value of 10.83 and a minimum frequency of 3 have been used for both the keyword and the collocation analysis. For the latter, the word span has been set to five words to the left side and right side of the node.

the texts »with regard to their unconscious and unintended meaning.«[76] The overall research design is summarized in figure 2.

Figure 2: Research Design

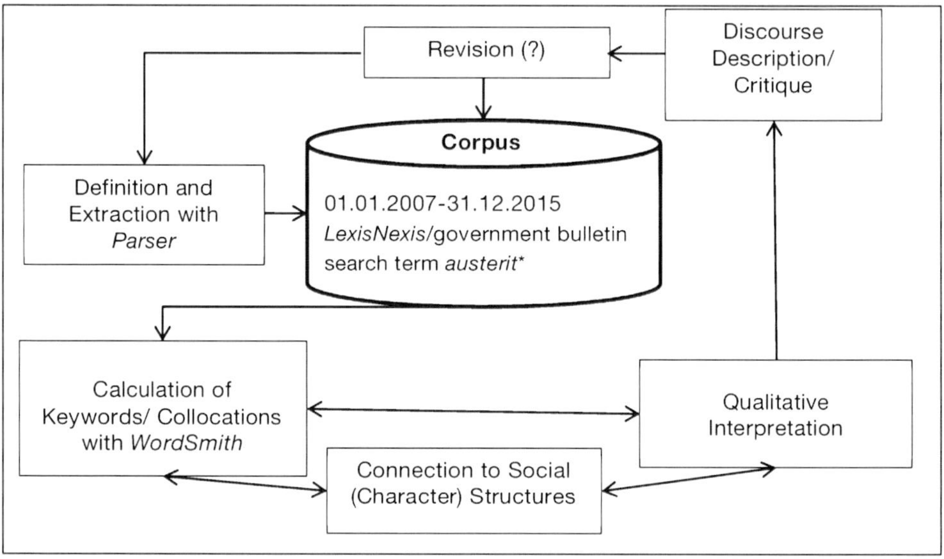

Source: own illustration

A note of caution has to be made here: Corpus linguistic tools in combination with a critical (realist) discourse analysis – like every kind of human-made text – only produce »ficts«: »A fict [...] is not a fact but rather an attempt to represent reality. Having ficts also makes it possible to observe an association of ficts without that association being an unproblematic essence.«[77] The ficts character of the results of a CL analysis is not only due to the mistakes of the researcher (for example concerning the design of the corpus[78]) and the choice of particular software settings (for example the choice of

76 Erich Fromm / Michael Maccoby, *Social Character in a Mexican Village. A Sociopsycholoanalytic Study*, kindle edition, http://www.amazon.com [29.6.2017].

77 Wendy Olsen / Jamie Morgan, »A Critical Epistemology of Analytical Statistics: Addressing the Sceptical Realist« in: *Journal for the Theory of Social Behaviour* 35, No. 3 (2005), pp. 255–284, p. 276.

78 As the root word *austerit** is quite new in German discourse and is also not directly connected to the German form of austerity conducted through *Agenda 2010*, it does not grasp the overall phenomenon of austerity in Germany. The analysis at hand will have to be expanded in the future to include other terms like »Sparpolitik« (saving politics) and »Haushaltskonsolidierung« (budget consolidation) and should, therefore, be understood as a »plausibility probe«. For the latter see John S. Odell, »Case Study Methods in International Political Economy« in: *International Studies Perspectives* 2, No. 2 (2001), pp. 161–176, p. 166.

statistical measures[79]). It is also important to keep in mind that these tools do not work like a calculation machine because the way they are programmed differs (sometimes and for some time), and »differences in the way tools are designed will have an impact on almost all corpus analyses.«[80] Although the analyses of texts and texts themselves do not contain objective facts, they are nevertheless potentially more than mere constructions: »We construct as opposed to find our data, but we make it out of something, not of nothing.«[81] The questions about the reference and adequacy of texts and scientific analyses are, therefore, crucial from a critical realist perspective: »[G]etting things right is a practical, a political, and an ethical imperative, and although achieving it may be impossible, or knowing when we have achieved it extremely difficult, we cannot give up on the aspiration.«[82]

4. The cultural political economy of austerity in Germany

Although the root word *austerit** may indeed not be totally new in the German context[83], it is in contrast to other countries nevertheless quite uncommon and only came up in the unfolding of the Euro crisis. As table 2 already showed, the root word *austerit** is not very often used. The novelty of the term is also expressed in the German official discourse, as a collocation analysis for the word »austerity« shows. The collocates BEGRIFF (term) and WORT (word) indicate the novelty of the discussion of the concept. A qualitative analysis of the collocates also shows that the term is associated with something negative. Instead of austerity, German officials prefer the more technical term HAUSHALTSKONSOLIDIERUNG (budget consolidation), highlighting that austerity is only understood as a form of fiscal austerity.

> *»It is about budget consolidation on the one hand – that is newly called austerity; that sounds even worse. I did not have fixed the word ›real economy‹ in my active language use so much before the financial crisis. And now you have the term austerity. I have never used the word in the past. It was called budget consolidation or balanced budget or sustainable financial policy. Now it is called austerity.«*[84]

79 Paul Baker, *Using Corpora in Discourse Analysis*, London/New York 2006, p. 102.

80 Laurence Anthony, »A critical look at software tools in corpus linguistics« in: *Linguistic Research* 30, No. 2 (2011), pp. 141–161, p. 151.

81 David Byrne, *Interpreting Quantitative Data*, London/Thousand Oaks, Calif. 2002, p. 15. For a critical realist analysis of media texts see Jason Toynbee, »Media Making and Social Reality« in: David Hesmondhalgh / Jason Toynbee (eds.), *The Media and Social Theory*, London/New York 2008, pp. 265–279; Eugene Flanagan, »Let's get real: a critical semiotic analysis of Irish print media discourses« in: *Social Semiotics*, 2015, pp. 1–15.

82 Colin Wight, »A Manifesto for Scientific Realism in IR: Assuming the Can-Opener Won't Work!« in: *Millenium* 35, No. 2 (2007), pp. 379–398, p. 380.

83 Boris Vormann, »Vorwort des Übersetzers. Das Spiel mit dem Feuer. Von Staaten, Märkten und dem Siegeszug der Austerität« in: Mark Blyth (ed.), *Wie Europa sich kaputtspart. Die gescheiterte Idee der Austeritätspolitik*, Bonn 2014, pp. 9–15.

84 Angela Merkel, »Rede von Bundeskanzlerin Dr. Angela Merkel beim ›Tag des deutschen Familienunternehmens‹ am 7. Juni 2013 in Berlin«, Nr. 66-3, 8.6.2013, own translation.

»This is not – I want to say that again – about the alternative: growth or austerity. – I have come to know this word only because of its retranslation from English. I have never used this word in Germany until three years ago, because you did talk of budget consolidation until then; and that has been exhausting enough. Austerity somehow sounds even more aggressive. – Such an alternative would be madness.«[85]

An analysis of the collocate WACHSTUM (growth) indicates that the German government sees no tension between austerity and economic growth and that the latter seems to be the ultimate goal. From a qualitative perspective that looks at the broader context of the discussion of austerity in the government sub-corpus, it is interesting to see what this whole discussion is »about«. It is about a neoliberal programme based on the central idea of competitiveness. In order to achieve that, austerity shall be combined with structural reforms and privatizations, two further key concepts of neoliberalism[86]:

»This is no more or no less about us following the self-given stability pact and to formulate it to be more mandatory. That is why we have introduced the Fiscal Pact in all Euro countries and furthermore in many more countries. It is also about to execute structural reforms. Because budget consolidation is a necessary but no sufficient condition to really be competitive. Efficient public structures, reasonable structural reforms in the labour market and in many other areas have to come up, too. Especially the subject of privatization plays a role in many of Europe's countries.«[87]

A collocation analysis for austerity in the *Welt*-corpus showed no statistically significant relevant results except for the collocate WACHSTUM (growth). On the surface, the *Welt* is critical of the idea that austerity can be a part of strategy to achieve growth. It cites nodal actors like Lawrence Summers (»To achieve more growth through austerity is the least plausible variant of economic policy.«[88]), the chief economist of the IWF, Olivier Blanchard[89], the Canadian Prime Minister, Justin Trudeau (»Jobs and growth of austerity and savings«[90]), and the Italian Prime Minister Matteo Renzi (» [The EU] must not only emphasize discipline and austerity but has to give greater prominence to growth«[91]) to highlight the tension between austerity and growth. At the same time, a qualitative analyse indicates that the imaginary found in the *Welt* is critical of *the critics of austerity*, as the broader context of the last two articles indicates.

85 Ibid., own translation.

86 Matthew Eagleton-Pierce, *Neoliberalism: The Key Concepts*, London/New York 2016.

87 Angela Merkel, »Rede von Bundeskanzlerin Dr. Angela Merkel beim 34. Bayerischen Wirtschaftsgespräch der Vereinigung der Bayerischen Wirtschaft am 9. Juli 2013 in München«, Nr. 81-3, 9.7.2013, own translation.

88 Anja Ettel / Holger Zschäpitz, »Top-Ökonom warnt Berlin vor Realitätsverlust« in: *Die Welt*, 30.5.2015, own translation.

89 Martina Meister, »Die Griechen sind ihr Waterloo« in: *Die Welt*, 3.7.2015, own translation.

90 Matthias Heine, »Als Kommunisten noch Sparsamkeit predigten« in: *Die Welt*, 20.10.2015, own translation.

91 Florian Eder, »Renzi: ›Europa wird Italien folgen müssen‹; Regierungschef hakt die Reformen schon ab« in: *Die Welt*, 22.1.2015, own translation.

In the text about Matteo Renzi the *Welt* discredits his talk about growth, saying that »›politics of growth‹ is a cypher to take liberties with the EU's new debt threshold. Italy has the second highest debt level in the Eurozone after Greece.«[92] In the article that cites Justin Trudeau, the reference that at least *one* communist was in favour of austerity is part of a discursive strategy to discredit the anti-austerity politics of Alexis Tsipras, the Greek Prime Minister:

> *»Thereby in 1980, the Left has been admitted to the older, more positive understanding of austerity of Stafford Cripps. A communist gushes in an edited volume of the Marxism researcher Iring Fetscher called ›Wie geht es weiter? Politische Zukunftsvorstellungen ohne Utopie‹: ›We as the Communist Party are in favour of a politics of austerity. And we need a politics of austerity for social reform.‹ Take this, Alexis Tsipras!«*[93]

Although the *Welt* discusses the term »austerity« more critically than the government, a substantive critique is only found in the *taz*. The left wing newspaper, in contrast to the government or the *Welt*, offers a narrative that highlights the fight against austerity, as can be reconstructed from the collocate KAMPF (fight) and especially the collocate GEGEN (against). The qualitative analysis shows that this struggle against austerity is described in most cases but sometimes even propagated, as is best expressed in this text:

> *»Now it looms large how thin the skin is over the combination of neoliberal recklessness and a right-wing populist, semi-fascist underground. And what miserable role Germany plays within this Europe! A left Greece government that dares to stand up against neoliberalization and austerity is stared down with truly all means, and an authoritarian and racist regime like the Hungarian one is given free reign. A chancellor that freely expresses that this is not about Europe but about the Euro.«*[94]

Similar tendencies appear by looking at some of the keywords found in the three different sub-corpora when they are compared to one another. In contrast to the *taz*, the government discourse highlights the ideas of NACHHALTIGKEIT (sustainability), HAUSHALTSKONSOLIDIERUNG (budget consolidation), WACHSTUM (growth), WETTBEWERBSFÄHIGKEIT (competitiveness) and STRUKTURREFORMEN (structural reforms). The *taz*, in contrast to the government's and the *Welt*'s discourse, highlights a critical attitude towards the NEOLIBERALE/N (neoliberal) capitalist system as such, which goes far beyond the idea of structural reforms in the government discourse. More frequently than both the government and the *Welt* it also uses words indicating that austerity is not just a rational response to the economic crisis, like PROTESTE (protests), WUT (anger), BLOCKUPY and ALTERNATIVE/N (alternative/s). Although the terms WETTBEWERBSFÄHIGKEIT (competitiveness), HAUSHALTSKONSOLIDIERUNG (budget consolidation) and WACH-

92 Eder, »Renzi: ›Europa wird Italien folgen müssen‹«, op. cit. (note 91), own translation.
93 Heine, »Als Kommunisten noch Sparsamkeit predigten«, op. cit. (note 90), own translation.
94 Georg Seeßlen, »Europa, die Killerin« in: *taz*, 9.9.2015, own translation.

STUM (growth) are also keywords for the government discourse in contrast to the *Welt*, the latter does not highlight such a system critical attitude as the *taz*, in spite of the exceptions KAPITALISMUS (capitalism)[95] and KRUGMAN. Of course, these quantitative results need further qualitative analysis to see what they mean in a particular context. How this can be done in principle can be exemplified by looking at a particularly interesting word that points to different modes of existence: the word SOLIDARITÄT (solidarity).[96] It has the potential to indicate a »special relationship«[97], which points towards an orientation to collective concerns and actions[98] and therefore a »political form or social form of love relations.«[99] In this sense, it is rooted in the will to give, to share and to sacrifice and, therefore, the being mode of existence. But the word can also point to a form of »competitive solidarity«[100], where the worth of social relations is reduced to their contribution to enhance economic competitiveness. This has also an effect on the form of solidarity that can be expressed and lived: »Competition is a pervasive force. It transforms social solidarity even where an economy successfully adjusts to intensified market pressures, and its effects extend far beyond the firms and sectors directly exposed to it.«[101] Competitive solidarity, therefore, is based on the having mode of existence. This difference can be illustrated by a comparison of the government- and the *taz*-corpus. When the *taz*-corpus is compared to the government-corpus, solidarity does *not* show up as a keyword, viz., the frequencies of the word in both corpora do not differ significantly from a quantitative perspective. But solidarity shows up as a keyword for both the government and the *taz*-corpus in comparison to the *Welt*-corpus. Yet a further analysis of the word »solidarity« shows very important differences in the meaning of the word in the government- and the *taz*-cor-

95 But capitalism is only criticized in one of these texts.

96 For an analysis of the word »solidarity« in the German political discourse that misses the important differentiation between different forms of solidarity, see Tim Griebel, »Zwischen Taschenmesser und Tiefbohrer – Eine korpuslinguistische kritisch-realistische Diskursanalyse von Solidarität in der deutsch-amerikanischen Sicherheitsbeziehung« in: *Zeitschrift für Diskursforschung*, No. 3, 2015, pp. 273–294; Griebel, *Liebe und Macht in der deutsch-amerikanischen Sicherheitsbeziehung*, op. cit. (note 56).

97 Siegfried Schieder, »Solidarität als konstitutives Element von Sonderbeziehungen: Frankreich und Schweden in den Cotonou-Verhandlungen« in: Sebastian Harnisch / Klaus Brummer / Kai Oppermann (eds.), *Sonderbeziehungen als Nexus zwischen Außenpolitik und internationalen Beziehungen*, Baden-Baden 2015, pp. 261–286, p. 263.

98 Iseult Honohan, »Metaphors of Solidarity« in: Terrell Carver / Jernej Pikalo (eds.), *Political Language and Metaphor: Interpreting and Changing the World*, New York 2008, pp. 69–82, p. 69.

99 Kathleen Lynch, »Why Love, Care and Solidarity Are Political Matters. Affective Equality and Fraser's Model of Social Justice« in: Anna G. Jóhannesdóttir / Ann Ferguson (eds.), *Love. A Question for Feminism in the Twenty-First Century*, New York/Abingdon 2014, pp. 173–189, p. 186 n. 2.

100 Wolfgang Streeck, »Competitive Solidarity: Rethinking the ›European Social Model‹« in: Karl Hinrichs / Herbert Kirschelt / Helmut Wiesenthal (eds.), *Kontingenz und Krise. Institutionenpolitik in kapitalistischen und postsozialistischen Gesellschaften*, Frankfurt/New York 2000, pp. 245–261.

101 Streeck, »Competitive Solidarity«, op. cit. (note 100).

pus. A qualitative analysis[102] of the 20 hits in the government discourse shows that there is a tendency to understand solidarity as a form of competitive solidarity. German solidarity is not so much based on the will to share, to give, to sacrifice; it is based on the ordoliberal imaginary, which demands self-responsibility, competition and rule-following. Solidarity is clearly on a form of self-responsibility. Merkel argues »that European solidarity and national self-responsibility go hand in hand. Those who undertake reform efforts are also worthy of solidarity. This is and was our maxim.«[103] But with this idea comes a certain form of hierarchy. Self-responsibility has to be understood as a form of homework[104], which is the basis for solidarity. »When homework has been done, we also show solidarity. Self-responsibility and solidarity – two sides of the same medal; solidarity to save time, to be able to fulfil one's obligations in order to have a stable currency for us all together.«[105] Self-responsible efforts serve as a means of a country to »enhance its competitiveness«.[106] German solidarity, in addition, is conditional on the adherence to rules:

> *»Solidarity is an old term used by the socialist labour movement in Europe. But it never meant chumminess. It always meant responsible behaviour towards oneself and others. [...] It is exactly here where the conflict with the actual Greece government came and comes from. It is about the adherence to this principle of solidarity. Why do we stick to these rules? Because these rules that we have in Europe and the Eurozone are just not coloured in national terms. They just do not serve the enforcement of national interests, but they shall link and ally us as Europeans.«*[107]

The government discourse also expresses a hierarchy between its different elements, as budgetary discipline through rule-following and the encouragement of competitiveness are clearly more important than solidarity, which is expressed in the order of topics and in the form of solidarity articulated here. Solidarity is discussed at the end of certain goals and only from the perspective of the market.

102 The following arguments are only based on a qualitative interpretation as a collocation analysis for the node SOLIDARITÄT (solidarity) revealed no meaningful results.

103 Angela Merkel, »Rede von Bundeskanzlerin Dr. Angela Merkel zur Verleihung der Ehrendoktorwürde der Radboud Universität zu Nimwegen am 23. Mai 2013 in Nimwegen«, Nr. 58-3, 23.5.2013, own translation.

104 For an analysis for different forms of this teacher/learner metaphor in different magazines, see Hans Bickes / Tina Otten / Laura Chelsea Weymann, »The Financial Crisis in the German and English Press: Metaphorical Structures in the Media Coverage on Greece, Spain and Italy« in: *Discourse & Society* 25, No. 4 (2014), pp. 424–445, p. 437.

105 Merkel, »Rede von Bundeskanzlerin Dr. Angela Merkel beim ›Tag des deutschen Familienunternehmens‹ am 7. Juni 2013 in Berlin«, own translation.

106 Angela Merkel, »Rede von Bundeskanzlerin Dr. Angela Merkel beim Tag der Deutschen Industrie des Bundesverbands der Deutschen Industrie e. V. am 3. November 2015 in Berlin«, Nr. 137-1, 3.11.2015, own translation.

107 Sigmar Gabriel, »Rede des Bundesministers für Wirtschaft und Energie, Sigmar Gabriel, in der vereinbarten Debatte zur Situation nach dem Auslaufen des Finanzhilfeprogramms für Griechenland vor dem Deutschen Bundestag am 1. Juli 2015 in Berlin«, Nr. 90-2, 1.7.2015, own translation.

»I believe the first question has to be: are we ready to dare more Europe? My response to that is: 2011 showed that, yes, we are ready. That's the good news. More specifically, we are ready to do so in three areas.
The first area is budgetary discipline, and not only because it concerns the budget but also because it concerns sustainability. [...]
Second, I'd like to mention the sphere of competitiveness in combination with jobs. [...]
And third, mutual solidarity, which shows that we belong together, that we want to belong together and that the outside world expects us to support each other.
If we look at what has been achieved by individual countries during the last year in respect of the first two points, budgetary discipline and competitiveness, then it's still not enough. [...]
Ladies and gentlemen, of course we are also asked: what about more commitment in Europe and more solidarity? I believe Europe has now reached a point where the boundaries between foreign policy and domestic policy are slowly blurring. We have to discuss our internal market and our common European Union.«[108]

These discursive elements are able to grip subjects not only because they correspond to the position of Germany in the European socio-economic structure and because they are therefore satisfying in an economic sense. They also provide psychological satisfaction because they are backed by the having mode of existence, which suits the needs of this structure. As competition is the principal goal, »cooperation and mutual aid – the antithesis to competition – are marginalized as organizing principles.«[109] This is amplified by the accentuation of *self*-responsibility, accompanied by a new form of subjectivity based on the having mode of existence: »The extension of market rationality into social life entails ›marketing‹ the subjective practices, that will turn subjects into entrepreneurs who rationally choose to maximize opportunity when possible and, at the same time, will agree to shoulder much of the responsibility formerly taken on by public agencies.«[110] That the government's imaginary is based on the having mode is also exemplified by the emphasis on rule-following. Rules have to be followed in order to *have* a stable currency, not in order to enhance human *being*. This does not mean that rules should be abandoned, but it is essential to reflect upon the goals behind certain rules. Fromm expresses this in his discussion of the different qualities of kinds of knowledge, which the »new man« of a new society based on the being mode should cultivate: »Knowing, also, that no growth is healthy that does not occur in a structure, *but knowing, too, the difference between structure as an attribute of life and ›order‹ as*

108 Angela Merkel, »Speech by Dr Angela Merkel, Chancellor of the Federal Republic of Germany, at the World Economic Forum Annual Meeting«, 25.1.2012.

109 Angela Wigger / Hubert Buch-Hansen, »Competition, the Global Crisis, and Alternatives to Neoliberal Capitalism: A Critical Engagement with Anarchism« in: *New Political Science* 35, No. 4 (2013), pp. 604–626, p. 608.

110 Lynne Layton, »Some psychic effects of neoliberalism: Narcissism, disavowal, perversion« in: *Psychoanalysis, Culture & Society* 19, No. 2 (2014), pp. 161–178, p. 163.

an attribute of no-life, of the dead.«[111] The *ordo*liberal insistence on rules shows signs of the latter and of a bureaucratic character: »Bureaucrats fear personal responsibility and seek refuge behind their rules; their security and pride lie in their loyalty to rules, not in their loyalty to the laws of the human heart.«[112]

The talk about self-responsibility, competitiveness and rule-following hides the fact that the European political economy in terms of its socio-economic structure is a »asymmetrically interconnected economic space«[113], where economic regimes based on an export-led growth model like Germany and such based on demand-led growth are brought together. »[T]he export-led strategies of northern Europe generated large balance of payments surpluses that the northern banks were only too happy to lend to southern firms and governments. Thus, an influx of cheap credit encouraged demand-led growth in southern Europe.«[114] A very important reason why Germany got rich is that »other countries were not doing the same at the same time.«[115] Germany's trade surplus not only depended to a very large extent on demand from the European periphery[116]; Germany's trade surplus also »meant that German investors – mainly German banks – were heavily exposed to public and private debt in the periphery nations«.[117] Not only has financial assistance to countries in trouble been given only in form of loans and guarantees. »Moreover, with this aid, much of which went to service existing debts, the countries of northern Europe were essentially bailing out their own banks, which held massive sums of southern Europeans debt«.[118]

Instead of reflecting on these conditions, the government narrative describes the structural reforms that have been introduced in Germany to enhance competitiveness under the heading of *Agenda 2010* as a role model for Europe.[119] This reform process can be understood as a basic element of Germany's »managed austerity«[120] that transformed the German welfare state in line with the idea of competitive solidarity at the

111 Fromm, *To Have or to Be?* op. cit. (note 7), p. 139, italics T. G.
112 Fromm, *To Have or to Be?* op. cit. (note 7), p. 139.
113 Jessop, »Variegated Capitalism, das Modell Deutschland, and the Eurozone Crisis«, op. cit. (note 57), p. 249.
114 Peter A. Hall, »The Economics and Politics of the Euro Crisis« in: *German Politics* 21, No. 4 (2012), pp. 355–371, p. 360.
115 Blyth, *Austerity: The History of a Dangerous Idea*, op. cit. (note 59), p. 142.
116 John Weeks, »Euro Crises and Euro Scams: Trade not Debt and Deficits Tell the Tale« in: *Review of Political Economy* 26, No. 2 (2014), pp. 171–189, pp. 174–175.
117 Richard Baldwin / Daniel Gros, »Introduction: The Euro in Crisis – What to do?« in: Richard Baldwin / Daniel Gros / Luc Laeven (eds.), *Completing the Eurozone Rescue: What More Needs to Be Done?*, London 2010, pp. 1–23, p. 12.
118 Hall, »The Economics and Politics of the Euro Crisis«, op. cit. (note 114), p. 363–364; Ian Bruff, »The Rise of Authoritarian Neoliberalism« in: *Rethinking Marxism* 26, No. 1 (2014), pp. 113–129, p. 123–124.
119 Merkel, »Speech by Dr Angela Merkel, Chancellor of the Federal Republic of Germany, at the World Economic Forum Annual Meeting«; for a critical analysis of the corresponding »Model Deutschland« see Jessop, »Variegated Capitalism, das Modell Deutschland, and the Eurozone Crisis«, op. cit. (note 57).
120 Mark I. Vail, *Recasting welfare capitalism: economic adjustment in contemporary France and Germany*, Philadelphia 2010, p. 27.

beginning of the 21st century. »[T]he main end of social policy has shifted from providing a considerable degree of equality and income security to the goal of raising the level of societal human capital and thereby increasing the international competitiveness of the German economy.[121] This transformation has been accompanied by a decline of 3.3 per cent of real wages in the period between 1994 and 2008.[122]

But although this powerful imaginary is backed by the socio-economic position of Germany in the European political economy and the according having mode of existence, it is not all encompassing in the German context. Media can enhance solidarity, but – as the discussion so far should have proven – it is important to understand what kind of solidarity is articulated.[123] The qualitative analysis shows that more than 75 per cent of the 94 hits of the keyword »solidarity« in the *taz*-corpus are directly related to the reflection of the economic situation in Europe. The kind of solidarity offered here is, in most of these topic-relevant cases, a kind of transnational European solidarity, especially with Greece, which offers an alternative to the current system. This is also indicated by a collocation analysis of the node »solidarity«. Statistical significant collocates are GERECHTIGKEIT (justice), EUROPÄISCHEN (European), GRIECHENLAND (Greece), SYRIZA, FORDERN (demand).The qualitative analysis of the word »solidarity« in the *taz*-corpus not only shows that the *taz* offers a critique of the government's narrative in terms of a critique of the overall system; it also indicates a tendency within the *taz* towards the being mode of existence. Solidarity is clearly not framed within the neoliberal rationality of the market and the idea of competitiveness, quite the contrary.

> *»The integration process follows a paradoxical course. Up to now, progress has been achieved through negative integration, in the form of market liberalization and deregulation of politics. But this is a phase-out-model, as the crisis shows. Progress is only possible in solidarity. In this case, the redistribution of income and wealth or a financial cross-subsidiary programme must not be declared a taboo. That would be a political alternative to the finance-driven, anti-political, authoritarian integration that, according to the hopes of Monetarists, would lead an economic, social and political harmonization of Europe. It would also be an actual alternative to the Fiscal Pact with its enduring saving dictate and to the enduring euro rescue mechanism ESM and to other bureaucratic monstrous products of neoliberal rationality.«*[124]

In this and other articulations the *taz* also emphasizes an imaginary that is based on the complex role that Germany's trade surpluses and the corresponding engagement of

121 Antonio Brettschneider, »On the Way to Social Investment? The Normative Recalibration of the German Welfare State« in: *German Policy Studies* 4, No. 2 (2008), pp. 1–41, p. 2.

122 Alex Demirović / Thomas Sablowski, »Finanzdominierte Akkumulation und die Krise in Europa« in: *PROKLA* 42, No. 1 (2011), pp. 77–106, p. 80.

123 Maria Kontochristou / Evi Mascha, »The Euro Crisis and the Question of Solidarity in the European Union: Disclosures and Manifestations in the European Press« in: *Review of European Studies* 6, No. 2 (2014), pp. 50–62.

124 Elmar Altvater, »Das falsche Modell. Als reine Währungsunion ohne solidarische Regulierung kann Europa nicht überleben« in: *taz*, 14.9.2012, own translation.

German banks in the periphery played within the crisis, and not on the individualistic idea of self-responsibility by particular debtor states:

> *»The enhancement of German interests since the beginning of the banking crisis in Europe is bought dearly by Mrs Merkel's government, bought more dearly than the rotten loans of the South, which have been financed through rescue packages that kept the balances of German banks clean in the end and that kept the German export industry booming. Berlin, as it operated until now, has put the EU at risk. When solidarity was called for, Germany reacted with harshness.«*[125]

In the *taz*-corpus we can also see signs of a reaction that is based on the human heart and the human condition within the crisis and not just a bureaucratic attitude:

> *»Apropos solidarity, why do so few Germans have compassion for the Greek?«*[126]
> *»In the southern countries foreign policy is more and more concerned with the question how Germany can be moved to accept concessions, that is: how it can be moved to reason in line with its own interests, European solidarity and the human race as a whole. And it is a totally open question whether and when the wounds within the emotional relationships between Germany and countries such as Italy and Greece that have been caused by the Euro can be healed.«*[127]

5. Conclusion – there is always an alternative

The analysis showed that the German official discourse articulates an understanding of austerity within an ordoliberal imaginary that is backed by Germany's position in the European socio-economic structure and the having mode of existence. But although these elements tend to reinforce each other, there is always an alternative. Discourses are never stable, historical structures are never totalizing. That is why critical voices like the left-wing newspaper *taz* still merge the articulation of critique of this imaginary and the search for an alternative future for Europe, based on a non-competitive solidarity and the being mode of existence. It is therefore essential not to give in to the old Greek meaning of austerity as the »dryness of tongue« but to take a swig of discourse and to search for alternative imaginaries. But imagination can only be a starting point in the struggle for human emancipation.

125 Miguel Szymanski, »Leitkultur der Zucht und Ordnung. Wie Deutschland Europas Wähler radikalisiert« in: *taz*, 24.11.2015, own translation.

126 Nils Reucker, »Nein zur Zwangspolitik. DISKUSSION: Blockupy möchte größere Solidarität mit den Griechen erzeugen durch Aufklärung« in: *taz*, 29.7.2015, own translation.

127 Wolfgang Streeck, »Südländer, Nordländer und der Euro« in: *taz*, 11.6.2015, own translation.

Sabina Monza

Who is in the Media? Dominant Interests in Times of Austerity

Having a voice in the national public sphere by appearing in the media is considered as a relative measure of power in a given context at a specific time. Visibility in the media gives political actors and the issues they advocate the possibility of being supported, contested, and legitimized. How do these relations develop during critical periods? The analysis of public discourse[1] during the recent economic crisis contributes to understanding the dynamics in which the austerity policies were implemented. This chapter examines the years of the financial and debt crises that led to implementing austerity policies in Europe. From 2008 to 2014, I compare across countries and over time who were the political actors and which were the subjects that dominated the national mainstream media of nine European countries. A »crisis« may be defined as a transitional period that »marks a phase of disorder in the seemingly normal development of a system«[2] and as »a moment of decisive intervention«[3] and transformation, where the narrative of the crisis searches to mobilize public perceptions crucial to influencing the trajectory of structural transformation. Crises are both real and socially constructed, i.e., events must be recognized and defined as such.[4] The subjective nature of a crisis as an interpreted threat implies a certain diagnosis/prognosis that needs to be socially shared. Conveying meaning and interpreting events in a particular way determines (and justifies) which are the procedures that might lead to overcoming it. Crises call into question the survival of a system, forcing political actors to act for their own stability while appearing effective in the eyes of public opinion. Crises are political windows of opportunity: in the first place for new actors who may advance specific interests that would otherwise remain latent or in the periphery of policy-making; yet conversely also for already powerful actors who intend to implement controversial policy changes.[5]

1 In this chapter, I use »discourse« and »discursive« or » debate« in their broader sense without distinction in order to embrace the diversity of verbal and textual interventions in the public sphere.

2 Arjen Boin / Paul 't Hart / Eric Stern / Bengt Sundelius, *The Politics of Crisis Management: Public Leadership under Pressure*, New York 2005, p. 2.

3 Colin Hay, »Crisis and the structural transformation of the state: interrogating the process of change« in: *British Journal of Politics and International Relations* 1, No. 3 (1999), pp. 317–344, p. 317; Vivien Schmidt, »Taking ideas and discourse seriously: explaining change through discursive institutionalism as the fourth ›new institutionalism‹« in: *European Political Science Review* 2, No. 1 (2010), pp. 1–25.

4 »[E]ven exogenous shocks must be endogenously interpreted.« Wesley Widmaier / Mark Blyth / Leonard Seabrooke, »Exogenous Shocks or Endogenous Constructions? The Meanings of Wars and Crises« in: *International Studies Quarterly* 51 (2007), pp. 747–759, p. 749.

5 Hanspeter Kriesi, »Political Context and Opportunity« in: David Snow / Sarah Soule / Hanspeter Kriesi (eds.), *The Blackwell Companion to Social Movements*, Oxford 2004, pp. 67–90; Sabine Saurugger, »Sociological Approaches to the European Union in Times of Turmoil« in: *Journal of Common Market Studies* 54, No. 1 (2016), pp. 70–86.

The European integration project still faces major challenges. The recent economic recession that particularly affected the Eurozone shaped exceptionally critical circumstances that jeopardized its continuity. In several countries, political crises merged with the virulence of the economic strain. Political consequences are still emerging. This turbulent period was characterized by new mechanisms of economic and political governance. It is clearly beyond the scope of this chapter to describe the policies that different European countries executed during these years. However, it is worth noticing that, in response to the recession, the EU and European governments applied highly homogeneous policies that not even partisan shifts in governments seemed to alter.[6] The initial phase (2007–2009) was characterized by expansive fiscal policies and massive bailouts of financial institutions. From 2010 onwards, fiscal consolidation became the priority. The broadened EU supranational level of political decision-making adapted and created new regulations imposed upon the national governments. Targeting deficit control, governments reduced public spending and deepened the retrenchment of the welfare system. In the most affected countries, the harshness of these policies was followed by the enforcement of unprecedented supranational political interventions. Although there is no proof of causal evidence, studies do show that loss of political support (both for national and EU institutions) has been more acute in those countries that have undergone bailouts and, in general terms, in those under critical economic conditions, namely with unprecedented high unemployment rates.[7]

This chapter provides an overview of the political information available in those years. Any kind of diagnosis/prognosis has particular implications that may affect citizens' perceptions and evaluations. If the public dominant discourses legitimize the austerity policies as a »technical« response to an economic problem framed within a particular theory, they may cancel alternative political interpretations and in-depth discussions that involve broader social statements, leaving contestation aside and limiting the

6 Jonas Pontusson / Damian Raess, »How (and Why) Is This Time Different? The Politics of Economic Crisis in Western Europe and the United States« in: *Annual Review of Political Science* 15 (2012), pp. 13–33; Klaus Armingeon / Lucio Baccaro, »Political Economy of the Sovereign Debt Crisis: The Limits of Internal Devaluation« in: *Industrial Law Journal* 41, No. 3 (2012), pp. 254–275; Christophe Degryse / Maria Jepsen / Philippe Pochet, *The Euro crisis and its impact on national and European social policies*, European Trade Union Institute, Working Paper No. 5, 2013.
From the viewpoint of how governments effectively implemented policies in each member-state under the common EU framework, the EU response to the economic crisis was differentiated and adapted to each country. These agreements and mechanisms remain beyond the scope of this chapter. See, for example, Beat Weber / Stefan Schmitz, »Varieties of helping capitalism: politicoeconomic determinants of bank rescue packages in the EU during the recent crisis« in: *Socio-Economic Review* 9 (2011), pp. 639–669; Demosthenes Ioannou / Patrick Leblond / Arne Niemann, »European integration and the crisis: practice and theory« in: *Journal of European Public Policy* 22, No. 2 (2015), pp. 155–176.

7 Klaus Armingeon T Besir Ceka, »The loss of trust in the European Union during the great recession since 2007: The role of heuristics from the national political system« in: *European Union Politics* 15, No. 1 (2014), pp. 82–107; Felix Roth / Felicitas D. Nowak-Lehmann / Thomas Otter, *Crisis and Trust in National and European Union Institutions. Panel Evidence for the EU, 1999 to 2012*, EUI Working Paper RSCAS, No. 31, 2013.

debate about social and political concerns.[8] Some recent research has investigated the effects of discourse and news in the media during the crisis, namely through content and framing analyses. In the public sphere, austerity policies were presented as an inevitable harsh stance required for overcoming the economic crisis. National stereotypes reinforced this explanation.[9] Nevertheless, as far as I know, there is not yet a systematic comparative record of which political actors addressed specific subjects in different European countries as the financial and debt crises developed and austerity policies were introduced. This chapter offers an insight, first, by evidencing the protagonists of the dominant economic discourse and, complementary, by exploring whether alternative subjects might have also gained access to the mainstream media, where and by whom. As a result, I contribute a portrayal of interests played during the most critical phase of the financial and economic crises that led the way to the implementation of austerity policies. The chapter unfolds as follows: First, I delineate a theoretical framework built upon three key elements: the public sphere as an arena for contention where social actors struggle to make visible and legitimize their own interests; the function of ideas and discourses used to validate the implementation of public policies; and availability of information as an essential constituent of opinion formation, crucial to facilitate deliberation and contestation. Second, I introduce the data and methodology. Third, I develop the analysis of claims and present the results. Last, I draw the conclusions and suggest some further research.

1. Theoretical framework

Numerous scholars have reflected upon the role of ideas and, more specifically, discourses for decision-making and political opinion formation processes. In particular, authors refer to the imperative narratives of policy-making in the context of globalization and European integration[10] and in the context of the financial and economic crises

8 From this viewpoint, the recent crisis seems a missed opportunity of enhancing the national debates about Europe and its policies, of incorporating European civil society to the discussions, and of contributing to bridge the gap between the EU and its citizens. On the contrary, the fact of embracing citizens' participation in public debates would contribute to legitimize the European integration project.

9 See, for example, Tamsin Murray-Leach (ed.), *Crisis Discourses in Europe. Media EU-phemisms and Alternative Narratives*, Background Paper, London School of Economics and Political Science, 2014, www.subterraneanpolitics.eu [12.3.2016]; Yiannis Mylonas, »Media and the Economic Crisis of the EU: The ›Culturalization‹ of a Systemic Crisis and Bild-Zeitung's Framing of Greece« in: *Triple C* 10, No. 2 (2012), pp. 646–671; Ruth Wodak / Jo Angouri, »From Grexit to Grecovery: Euro/crisis discourses« in: *Discourse & Society* 25, No. 4 (2014), pp. 417–423; Grahame Thompson »What's in the frame? How the financial crisis is being packaged for public consumption« in: *Economy and Society* 38, No. 3 (2009), pp. 520–524.

10 Vivien Schmidt / Claudio Radaelli, »Policy Change and Discourse in Europe: Conceptual and Methodological Issues« in: *West European Politics* 27, No. 2 (2004), pp.183–210; Colin Hay / Ben Rosamond, »Globalization, European integration and the discursive construction of economic imperatives« in: *Journal of European Public Policy* 9, No. 2 (2002), pp. 147–167;

that recently determined the execution of austerity policies.[11] An important argument that underlies most studies is that discourses in the public sphere are not only the expression of specific actors' interests but, furthermore, become a restrictive conception of what is possible, and what is not, in policy-making. In other words, when narratives become accepted and normalized in society, they function as a means for justifying policy-making – first and foremost among political actors themselves and likewise intended to the general public. Narratives are particularly crucial in critical periods when political decisions are expected to limit a perceived threat under conditions of uncertainty and a sense of urgency – when citizens expect political actors to act. The aim of this chapter is to contribute to the understanding of the informative contexts in which European citizens transited the financial and debt crises that justified implementing austerity policies in most European countries from 2010 onwards. I argue that the role of political actors advancing issues in the public sphere was central to underpin the crises definitions (»economic crisis«, »financial crisis«, »debt crisis«) and the consequent policy implementations.[12] But may it be that extraordinary events can alter the frequency and dominance of powerful actors and the issues they promote in the national media? In an attempt to address this question, I portray a series of pictures that illustrate the prevalence of different kinds of actors and subjects in several selected European public spheres between 2008 and 2014.

The role of the media in the process of opinion formation is well-documented. An extensive body of literature analyses the importance of public discourses and news, and it documents the mechanisms of framing, agenda-setting, and priming.[13] Unlike

Bennett W. Lance / Victor Pickard / David Iozzi / Carl Schroeder / Taso Lagos / Evans Caswell, »Managing the Public Sphere: Journalistic Construction of the Great Globalization Debate« in: *Journal of Communication* 54, No. 3 (2004), pp. 437–455.

11 Mark Blyth, *Austerity: The History of a Dangerous Idea*, New York 2013; Erik Jones, »Getting the Story Right: How You Should Choose between Different Interpretations of the European Crisis (And Why You Should Care)« in: *Journal of European Integration* 37, No. 7 (2015), pp. 817–832; Colin Hay, »Treating the Symptom Not the Condition: Crisis Definition, Deficit Reduction and the Search for a New British Growth Model« in: *British Journal of Politics and International Relations* 15, No. 1 (2013), pp. 23–37; Vivien Schmidt, »Speaking to the Markets or to the People? A Discursive Institutionalist Analysis of EU's Sovereign Debt Crisis« in: *The British Journal of Politics and International Relations* 16, No. 1 (2014), pp. 188–209; Ferdi De Ville / Jan Orbie, »The European Commission's Neoliberal Trade Discourse Since the Crisis: Legitimizing Continuity through Subtle Discursive Change« in: *The British Journal of Politics and International Relations* 16, No. 1 (2014/1), pp. 149–167; Jean-Frédéric Morin / Caterina Carta, »Overlapping and Evolving European Discourses on Market Liberalization« in: *British Journal of Politics and International Relations* 16, No. 1 (2014/1), pp. 117–132.

12 This chapter follows Widmaier et al.'s assertion that conciliates constructivist frameworks and rationalist assumptions, as explained: »To assume that agents are strategic is simply to suggest that they have consistent preferences and make choices which advance those preferences, not that they can collectively employ all available information [as in rational choice theory]«. In other words, »agents make strategic choices, given some social context.« Widmaier / Blyth / Seabrooke, »Exogenous Shocks or Endogenous Constructions? The Meanings of Wars and Crises«, op. cit. (note 4), p. 750.

13 John Zaller, *The Nature and Origins of Mass Opinion*, Cambridge 1992.

these studies, I circumscribe the media to its function of conveying visibility (required for achieving legitimacy) to the discursive activities of the dominant social actors and the subjects they put forward. To a great extent, citizens rely on the media to be informed. For ordinary people, economic subjects are usually complex. Political decisions are taken far away from their everyday lives. The EU multilevel political system adds another layer of difficulty for assessing policy-making and political responsibilities. It is through the mass media that élites, large functional interest groups, political parties, and experts strongly influence citizens' opinion formation. Similarly, in their search of public support to influence policy-making, alternative organizations, social movements, and smaller civic groups also intend to gain public visibility in the mass media. The media mediate information not only between political actors and the general public but also among political and social actors themselves.

Researchers on social movements have developed the notion of «discursive opportunity» to grasp the function of the public sphere in producing, increasing and softening events. Discursive opportunity is defined as »the aspects of the public discourse that determine a message's chances of diffusion in the public sphere.«[14] It explains the dynamics of media attention, bridging framing and political opportunity perspectives.[15] The three elements that compose discursive opportunities are visibility, resonance, and legitimacy, taking place in this order. »Visibility is a necessary condition for a message to influence the public discourse, and, other things being equal, the amount of visibility that [the media] allocate to a message increases its potential to diffuse further in the public sphere.«[16] By gaining visibility in the media, actors and subjects may either be supported or contested (resonance), opening the possibility for acquiring social legitimacy. The public sphere is as an arena for political contention that offers discursive opportunities for conflicting actors. Public discourses reflect social conflicts and symbolic struggles. Discursive opportunities are part of the political opportunity structure of a given institutional setting at a particular moment. Disruptive periods in society offer a window of opportunity for political actors (being incumbent, advocacy groups, or challengers) to advance their own interests, to redefine or prioritize subjects, and to put forward policy or organizational reforms that might otherwise be difficult to accept.[17] »Extraordinary« events provide new opportunities for new structural align-

14 Ruud Koopmand / Susan Olzak, »Discursive Opportunities and the Evolution of Right-Wing Violence in Germany« in: *American Journal of Sociology* 110, No. 1 (2004), pp. 198–230, p. 202.

15 The notion of »discursive opportunity« may answer »why certain perceptions and interpretations of political reality spread (while others do not) and why certain actors may effectively succeed in opening new windows of opportunity (when most do not). We suggest that the public sphere mediates between political opportunity structures and movement action. « Koopmand / Olzak, »Discursive Opportunities and the Evolution of Right-Wing Violence in Germany«, op. cit. (note 14), p. 201.

16 Koopmand / Olzak, »Discursive Opportunities and the Evolution of Right-Wing Violence in Germany«, op. cit. (note 14), p. 203.

17 Ruud Koopmans / Barbara Pfetsch, »Obstacles or motors of Europeanization? German media and the transnationalization of public debate« in: *Communications* 31 (2006), pp. 115–

ments and new strategic alliances. Major disruptions tend to give rise to conflicting interpretations where actors compete to impose their views.[18]

The mass media constitute a prime field where political conflict takes place. In search of public recognition, contending actors intend strategic interventions and seek media attention as a means for legitimacy. As for the media, it privileges credible and expert sources – in addition to its ideological affinity and its own interests. Not all actors make it to the news. Media news reflects which actors are successful in making public their political concerns, i.e., they reproduce the dominant positions of the most powerful actors and discourses in society. The literature indicates that governments, institutions, élites from business and elsewhere, powerful organizations, unions[19], and, in general, groups with more resources – i.e. actors at the centre of the political system and those who already have access to policy-making – are more prominent in the national media. National actors overwhelm supranational actors.[20] In contrast, weaker actors who lack not only political power but also connections and resources, among which are organizations and groups that promote public interest, social movement organizations, NGOs, group-specific organizations, and civil society as a whole – i.e. all those actors that do not usually have access to policy-making and thus try to influence the system from the periphery – rely on extraordinary events to attract media attention.[21] Could the recent crisis, then, have represented a discursive opportunity for weaker actors to become visible in the public domain? Besides the expected prevalence

138; Paul Statham / E. Gray, »The European Public Sphere and Debates about Europe in Britain: Internalized and Conflict Driven?« in: *Innovation* 18, No. 1 (2005), pp. 61–81; Hans Jörg Trenz, *In Search of the European Public Sphere. Between Normative Overstretch and Empirical Disenchantment*, Recon Online Working Paper, 2008/07; Regina Vetters / Erik Jentges / Hans Jörg Trenz, *Exploring the EU's Social Constituency: Patterns of Public Claims-Making in Constitutional Debates in France and Germany*, Working Paper, ARENA Centre for European Studies, 2006; Arjen Boin / Paul 't Hart / Allan McConnell, »Crisis exploitation: political and policy impacts of framing contests« in: *Journal of European Public Policy* 16, No. 1 (2009), pp. 81–106.

18 Boin / 't Hart / Stern / Sundelius, *The Politics of Crisis Management*, op. cit. (note 2), p. 3. Studies on media framing of crises show that financial crises are particularly susceptible to political conflict. See Eva-Karin Olsson / Lars Nord / Jesper Falkheimer, »Media Coverage Crisis Exploitation Characteristics: A Case Comparison Study« in: *Journal of Public Relations Research* 27, No. 2 (2015), pp. 158–174.

19 The declining power of labour unions through the past decades is well documented. Even so, they are still an important interest group, particularly in the European policy-making framework.

20 For a detailed description and analysis of the geopolitical scope of actors (national, EU, EU state, European, and other) and issues in the European mainstream media during 2008–2014, using the same LIVEWHAT dataset, see: Sabina Monza / Eva Anduiza, »The Visibility of the EU in the National Public Spheres in Times of Crisis and Austerity« in: *Politics & Policy* 44, No. 3 (2016), pp. 499–524.

21 A. Trevor Thrall, »The Myth of the Outside Strategy: Mass Media News Coverage of Interest Groups« in: *Political Communication* 23 (2006), pp. 407–420; Anne Binderkrantz, »Interest groups in the media: Bias and diversity over time« in: *European Journal of Political Research* 51 (2012), pp. 117–139; Anke Tresch / Manuel Fischer, »In search of political influence: Outside lobbying behaviour and media coverage of social movements, interest groups and political parties in six Western European countries« in: *International Political Science*

of economic issues in the media, did the social and political consequences of austerity become subjects of discussion as well? How did the composition of actors and subjects vary across European countries as the austerity policies were being executed? This chapter explores and maps the visibility of different types of actors, and the issues they advanced, in nine European public spheres. I trace between- and within-country differences over the period 2008–2014. All in all, I describe who »spoke« to whom over which subjects and in whose interests.

2. *Methodology and data*

This chapter follows political claims-making analysis[22], a quantitative method used to retrieve political information from news. It uses the selective function of the media to recover the information that has been made visible through the media in a given country at a particular time. Political claims-making analysis considers direct verbal or nonverbal statements (referred to as »claims«) that appear in the media with no interpretation on the part of journalists or editors.[23] In doing so, it considers that the claims that were published reveal the political power of those actors and the relevance of those issues that have succeeded in overcoming media filters. In other words, political claims analysis unveils the underlying power relationships which exist in society, thus illustrating the »political climate« of a given country at a specific time. It mirrors social cleavages and evidences the most prominent subjects and events. I use the LIVEWHAT EU-PF7 work package 3 dataset that retrieves claims published in the national media of nine European countries (France, Germany, Greece, Italy, Poland, Spain, Sweden, Switzerland, and the UK) during the recent economic crisis. These countries represent a range of political and economic contexts: EU and non-EU member states; creditors and debtors; EMU, opt-out, and non-euro countries; pro-EU and Eurosceptics; founder members and countries from subsequent accession waves; and Western and Eastern Europeans. Considering the impact of the recent economic and debt crises on the national contexts, they may be separated in three broad groups: strongly affected countries that received a bailout programme or a rescue package (Greece, Italy and Spain), intermediately affected countries (France and the UK), and countries with weak or lateral effects (Germany, Poland, Sweden and Switzerland).[24]

Review 36, No. 4 (2015), pp. 355–372; Regula Hänggli, »Key Factors in Frame Building: How Strategic Political Actors Shape News Media Coverage« in: *American Behavioral Scientist* 56, No. 3 (2012), pp. 300–317.

22 Ruud Koopmans / Paul Statham, »Political Claims Analysis: Integrating Protest Event and Political Discourse Approaches« in: *Mobilization: An International Journal* 4, No. 1 (1999), pp. 203–221; Paul Statham / Howard Tumber, »Relating news analysis and public opinion: Applying a communications method as a ›tool‹ to aid interpretation of survey results« in: *Journalism* 14, No. 6 (2013), pp. 737–753.

23 When the media is also analysed as another political actor, editorial and opinion sections might be coded too. In the LIVEWHAT dataset, claims made by the media were not coded.

24 For more details on this classification, see the contextual data collected in the work package 1 of the LIVEWHAT Project, http://www.livewhat.unige.ch [30.6.2017]; LIVEWHAT, *Codebook for Coding of Collective Responses to Crises in the Public Domain. WP3: Collec-*

The reported claims may be a political decision (e.g., law, governmental guide, implementation measure), a verbal statement (e.g., public speech, press conference, parliamentary intervention), or a protest action (demonstration, occupation, violent action). They were retrieved from any section of the main national newspapers, excluding editorials and opinions (that represent journalistic interpretations). Recovered through a keyword search, the dataset includes claims that refer explicitly to »austerity«, »crisis«, or »recession«, pertaining to the current economic crisis. They cover a variety of themes (e.g., unemployment, recession, exclusion, welfare reforms, economic stability, budget balance, and so forth). Unfortunately, with the available data it is impossible to disentangle the crisis from the recession or from austerity. I therefore explore the three concepts altogether. The unit of analysis is a political claim. A political claim is a strategic intervention, either verbal or nonverbal, in the public space made by a given actor on behalf of a group or collectivity and bearing on the interests or rights of other groups or collectivities.[25] Claims were made in one of the countries of coding.[26] They were coded by random sampling of 1,000 claims from five newspapers in each country. The LIVEWHAT dataset covers the period 2005–2014, but I discarded those claims prior to 2008 due to the scarcity of claims referring to the crisis, austerity, or recession during the initial years prior to the burst of the financial crisis. Claims were retrieved in each country from five mainstream national newspapers that cover a range of ideological preferences, selected to increase the representativeness of the sample. Despite the undeniable relevance of new media and interpersonal communications for citizens' opinion formation, mainstream newspapers are still very strong influencers of public opinion that lead news agenda-setting.[27] The newspapers selected for the LIVEWHAT dataset represent the well-established printed press of each country. I assume they reflect the views of the most powerful actors and subjects in society. Hence, it is particularly relevant to examine whether, during the crisis, challenging actors and alternative topics were able to make it through media biases in these specific newspapers. These newspapers are in France: *Le Figaro*, *La Tribune*, *Le Monde*, *Le Parisien*, *Libération*; in Germany: *Bild*, *Die Welt*, *Frankfurter Allgemeine Zeitung*, *Frankfurter Rundschau*, *Süddeutsche Zeitung*; in Greece: *Eleytherotypia*, *Kathimerini*, *Rizospastis*, *Ta Nea*, *To Vima*; in Italy: *Corriere della Sera*, *La Stampa*, *La Repubblica*, *Il Giornale*, *Il Sole 24 Ore*; in Poland: *Dziennik Gazeta Prawna*, *Super Express*, *Gazeta Polska Codziennie*,

tive Responses to Crises in the Public Domain, http://www.livewhat.unige.ch/wp-content/uploads/2014/07/Deliverable-3.1.pdf [17.3.2016].

25 See LIVEWHAT 2014, codebook, op. cit. (note 24), pp. 3.

26 Alternatively, claims were made by, or addressed to, a supranational actor of which the country of coding is a member (e.g., UN, EU, IMF), on the condition that the claim is substantively relevant for the country of coding (e.g., a decision by ECB is included if affecting one's own member state).

27 Statham / Tumber, »Relating news analysis and public opinion«, op. cit. (note 22); Rens Vliegenthart / Andreas Schuck / Hajo Boomgaarden / Claes H. De Vreese, »News Coverage and Support for European Integration, 1990–2006« in: *International Journal of Public Opinion Research* 20, No. 4 (2008), pp. 415–439; Hans Jörg Trenz, »Media Coverage on European Governance Exploring the European Public Sphere in National Quality Newspapers« in: *European Journal of Communication* 19, No. 3 (2004), 291–319.

Gazeta Wyborcza, *Rzeczpospolita*; in Spain: *ABC*, *El País*, *El Periodico de Catalunya*, *La Vanguardia*, *El Mundo*; in Sweden: *Aftonbladet*, *Dagen Nyheter*, *Göterborgs Posten*, *Norbottens Kuriren*, *Svenska Dagbladet*; in Switzerland: *Blick*, *Le Matin*, *Le Temps*, *Neue Zürcher Zeitung*, *Tages Anzeiger*; and in the United Kingdom: *Daily Mail*, *Daily Mirror*, *The Guardian*, *The Sun*, and *The Times*.

From the LIVEWHAT dataset I selected all claims published during the period 2008–14 (N = 8,707 claims). I use the following variables which respond to the questions that structure the data:

When and where was the claim made? Country of claim, date of claim;
Who made the claim? Typology of first actor;
At whom was the claim directed? Typology of addressee[28];
What was the claim about? Typology of first issue[29];
Who was affected by the claim? Typology of object.

All claims have an actor, an issue, and an object, but not all claims are explicitly directed towards an addressee; hence, the variable addressee contains many unspecified values.

3. *Typology of actors, addressees and objects*

According to the interest of this analysis, I recoded the original LIVEWHAT dataset variables that refer to types of actors, types of addressees, and types of objects. These three variables refer to political, economic, and social actors performing different roles in the flux of claims-making communications. Accordingly, »actors« refers strictly to those who begin (make) the claim, »addressees« relates to those who are targeted by the claims, and »objects« indicates those whose interests are affected by the claims. These three variables – actors, addressees, and objects – are codified in the same way. However, we must keep in mind that actors hold the most visible role as they always appear making a claim. Addressees depend on being targeted by actors, while objects are affected by the claims but not necessarily mentioned. The typology I use is adapted from previous research that analyses the relationship between interest groups and the media.[30] It is organized in three main groups: state and political actors, interest groups, and civil society. The classification criteria might result rather simplistic but illustrate well the role that different actors play in society, highlighting the relationship they hold with regard to policy-makers and the media. The first group represents the core political system and consists of state and party actors: government, parliament, courts,

28 Many claims have no specific target as actors speak in general or in an undefined way.

29 Only 10% of claims have a second actor, and slightly over 50% have no second issue. I therefore omit this information. From now onwards, in this chapter, »actor« refers to the first actor and »issue« refers to the first issue in the original LIVEWHAT dataset. See the LIVEWHAT (2014) codebook for a detailed list of all the variables in the dataset.

30 Thrall, »The Myth of the Outside Strategy«, op. cit. (note 21); Tresch / Fischer, »In search of political influence«, op. cit. (note 21); Hänggli, »Key Factors in Frame Building«, op. cit. (note 21); Koopmans / Pfetsch, »Obstacles or motors of Europeanization?«, op. cit. (note 17); see also Binderkrantz, »Interest groups in the media«, op. cit. (note 21).

other state agencies, politicians, and political parties. The second group corresponds to interest groups that have access to the policy-making process and tend to be mentioned by the media: market and economic actors, financial, business, employer's associations, labour unions, professional groups[31], think tanks, and the media. Finally, the third group includes other interest groups and civil society actors that lack access to the policy-making process and are usually excluded from the media: civil society organizations, social movement organizations, and sectional groups with limited resources. For the sake of simplicity, these three broad groups are labelled as »Core political actors«, »Interest groups« and »Civil society«. All negligible values in the LIVEWHAT dataset were incorporated into broader categories. Table 1 presents the typology used for the actors, addressees, and objects according to this classification.

Table 1: Typology of actors/addressees/objects

GROUP 1: Core political actors (at the centre of the political system)	
State actors	Executive, legislative, judiciary, economic, and others (police, military and security, welfare, and other executive)
Political parties	
GROUP 2: Interest groups (with privileged access to policy-making and the media)	
Market and finance	Market, banks, credit and rating agencies
Companies	Private companies, and employers
Labour	Unions, workers, and other work-related
Opinion leaders	Media, research institutes and think tanks, and élites
Other professionals	
GROUP 3: Civil society actors (interest groups with limited access to policy-making and the media)	
Civil society	Group-specific (women, migrants, unemployed, disabled, youth, and others), solidarity, welfare and human rights, others (anti-austerity and occupy movements, reclaim initiatives, extreme right, radical left, religious, and others), and citizens

Source: own illustration

4. Typology of issues

This recoding of the original variable of first issues reorganizes, in the first place, macroeconomic and financial categories, dissecting the nature of diverse subjects that are of special interest to this research. Two broad groups cluster the issues in order to contrast economic and financial against social and political topics. Within the second group of social subjects, I aim at distinguishing those that are more directly linked to welfare policies – housing, education, health, social policy, and labour – which were heavily hit by austerity. However, as aforementioned, the recoded categories only

31 The LIVEWHAT codebook does not indicate which professional groups are included here; nevertheless, this category is coded under the umbrella of »Professional organizations and groups« that includes all the other most powerful actors in the sample.

identify the significant data, i.e., negligible values from the original dataset were incorporated into broader groups. The low numbers of most categories do not allow distinguishing subtopics in further detail. Implications of scarce data in particular subjects will be discussed along the analysis. Table 2 presents the typology of issues.

Table 2: Typology of issues

GROUP 1: Economic and financial issues	
Macroeconomics	Inflation, prices and interest rates, unemployment rate, monetary policy, budget and debt, taxation, industrial policy, wages, and others
Banks and finance	Banking system, bank secrecy, financial markets, credit market, insurances, and bankruptcy
Business	Competition and corporate management, small business and independent workers, copyright and patents
Others	
GROUP 2: Social and political issues	
Macroeconomics	Inflation, prices and interest rates, unemployment rate, monetary policy, budget and debt, taxation, industrial policy, wages, and others
Banks and finance	Banking system, bank secrecy, financial markets, credit market, insurances, and bankruptcy
Business	Competition and corporate management, small business and independent workers, copyright and patents
Others	
Labour	
Health, education, and housing	
Social policy	
Public administration	
Others	Agriculture, environment, energy, immigration, transportation, law, civil rights, defence, science, culture, sports, foreign trade, international affairs, lands and water, urban and regional, other fields

Source: own illustration

5. Results: An overview of actors, addressees and issues, and the objects affected by the claims

When analysing this data, we should always keep in mind that all claims in the sample refer at some point either to the economic crisis, the recession, or austerity. We might therefore expect an economic bias in the subjects discussed by these actors and a strengthened role of economic (and executive) claims-makers. However, social and political issues were also extremely important amid the economic context of this period (2008–2014), presumably even more in the countries that were most critically affected by the crisis and hit by harsh austerity policies. The following exploration maps the visibility of the different kinds of players and issues, tracing opposed and complementary interests in the nine national public spheres over time. First of all, I present an overview of the sample for the whole period 2008–2014: the three main sorts of actors who made the claims (table 3) and the addressees who received them (figure 1) in each country. Then, I trace over time the issues that claims-makers proposed in each country (figure 2 and table 4), and finally I portray a general picture of whose interests were affected by these claims (table 5).

Regarding the composition of actors and addressees, in both cases, civil society organizations and groups were undoubtedly the minority type throughout the whole period, far behind core political players and interest groups. For the rest, the typology of actors and addressees evidences different patterns. Overall, actors (table 3) were quite fairly distributed between core political claims-makers (50%) and powerful interest groups (46%), while civil society was only visible in 4% of all claims. Considering the balance between the two dominant sorts of actors (core political and powerful interest groups), I identify three clusters of countries. First, there are countries where core political actors overwhelmingly dominated the media. In Germany, Greece and Spain these actors produced roughly 65% of each country's claims, whereas interest groups made around 30%. A second cluster is composed of countries that equilibrated the share of visibility among both dominant types of claims-makers. This was clearly the case of Italy (47% each type) and Switzerland (50% visible core political actors against 47% visible interest groups). Two other countries drew the transition in the limits of this middle group, not far from balancing core political and interest types of actors. On the one side, France presented 50% visible core political actors against 44% visible interest groups. On the other side, the other way round, the UK displayed 52% of its claims made by interest groups against 43% made by core political actors. The third cluster of countries, where interest groups greatly outnumbered core political actors, was composed by Poland (65% visible interest groups against 32% core political actors) and Sweden (35% against 62%). As for civil society claims-makers, despite being a very small minority in all countries, as aforementioned, they were slightly more visible in France, Italy (6% of each country's total claims), Spain and the UK (5 %). Table 3 shows how the visibility of all kinds of actors is distributed in each country during the analysed period.

Table 3: Actors 2008–2014, N = 8707

Country	Actors: Executive	Legislative	Judiciary	Economic	Other	Political parties	**State and political**	Companies	Market and finance	Labour	Opinion leaders	Other professionals	**Interest groups**	**Civil society**	**Total %**
France	26	4	1	1	3	15	**50**	11	8	14	9	2	**44**	**6**	100
Germany	33	4	1	11	2	14	**64**	10	9	4	7	2	**32**	**4**	100
Greece	30	16	1	6	4	8	**65**	5	7	10	7	4	**32**	**3**	100
Italy	28	2	1	7	2	8	**47**	20	5	15	6	1	**47**	**6**	100
Poland	14	3	-	3	4	7	**32**	26	12	5	20	2	**65**	**3**	100
Spain	34	3	-	5	4	18	**64**	9	3	6	9	4	**31**	**5**	100
Sweden	16	2	-	7	4	7	**35**	28	24	5	3	2	**62**	**3**	100
Switzerland	13	15	-	10	3	8	**50**	20	16	5	5	1	**48**	**2**	100
UK	17	2	-	8	1	16	**43**	18	12	8	9	5	**52**	**5**	100
Total %	23	6	0,5	6	3	11	**50**	16	11	8	8	3	**46**	**4**	**100**

Figures indicate percentages. Values below 1% are not displayed.

Source: own illustration

A more detailed decomposition of actors evidences that state executive actors prevailed in six out of nine countries. These actors made 23% of all claims, followed by companies (16%), then markets and financial actors, and political actors (11% each). State claims-makers were most visible in Spain (34% of the country's claims), Germany (33%), Greece (30%), Italy (28%), and France (26%). Companies, on the other hand, were the most visible actors in Sweden (where 28% of all claims in the country represented visible companies, closely followed by market and financial actors with 24% of the national share), Poland (26%), and Switzerland (20%). Markets and financial claims-makers were particularly important in Sweden (24%) where, together with companies, they represented 52% of the national visibility of actors. Other core political claims-makers were especially visible in certain countries. Hence legislative actors were most significant in Greece (16%) and Switzerland (15%), economic state agencies were distinguishable in Germany (11%) and also in Switzerland (10%), and political parties stood out in Spain (18%), the UK (16%), France (15%), and Germany (14%). In contrast, labour actors never reached this amount of visibility in any national media. Their largest numbers appeared in Italy (14%), France (14%), and Greece (10%). Finally, an interesting fact is the high visibility of opinion leaders in Poland (20%). These actors were also quite visible in France, Spain, and the UK (9% each).

The typology of addressees across countries (figure 1) exhibits certain similarities with the visibility of actors, but there are a few differences too. In the first place, civil society addressees were always the weakest sort, receiving fewer than 10% of national claims in all nine countries in the sample. The highest numbers of civil society addressees were visible in France and Greece (9% each), followed by Germany (7%) and then the rest. Second, as usual, core political addressees outstood and hence received by large the majority of claims in every country, with the exception of France. Compared to actors, the contrast between the two powerful sorts of addressees – core political and powerful interest groups – was much more exacerbated within countries, on the one hand, and much more even between countries, on the other hand. In descending order, striking within-country differences were seen in Spain (46% core political against 8% interest group addressees), the UK (31% against 7%), Greece (62% against 16%), Sweden (21% against 6%), Italy (63% against 19%), Poland (57% against 21%), Switzerland (33% against 12%), and Germany (53% against 20%). The only exception was France, where both types of addressees were almost balanced: core political addressees received 29% of all French claims against 26% that targeted interest groups. Figure 1 presents the distribution of all kinds of addressees in the sample. Countries are displayed in decreasing order according to the amount of core political addressees that were visible in each country during the whole period.

Figure 1: Addressees 2008–2014, N = 8707

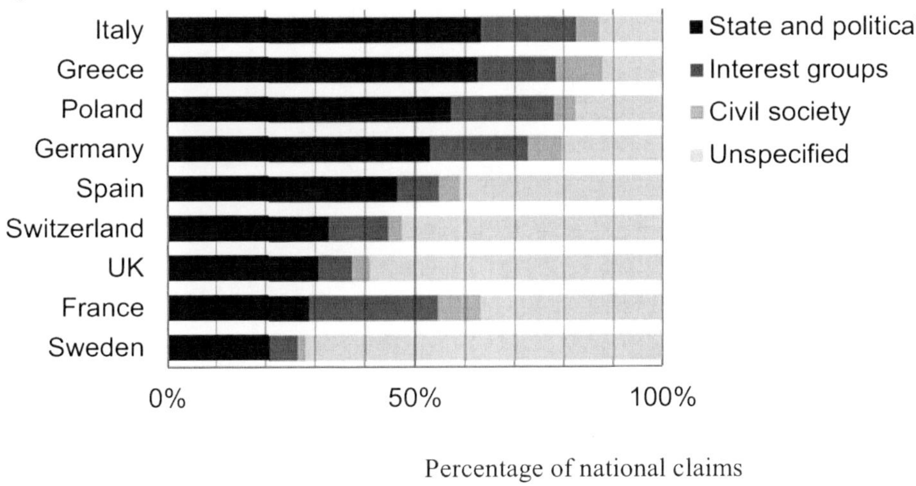

Source: own illustration

The next step of this initial overview is to compare the two broad typologies of issues – economic and financial against social and political – across countries and over time (figure 2). Economic and financial issues made up 67% of the total amount of claims during the period under review, while social and political issues represented 33% of the sample. In all nine countries, economic and financial subjects far outweighed social and political concerns. Considerable disparity appeared, in decreasing order, in the UK (81% visible economic and financial issues against 19% visible social and political subjects), Sweden (77% against 23%), Switzerland (76% against 24%), Poland (67% against 33%), Greece (62% against 38%), and France (58% against 42%). By comparison, Italy (55% against 45%) and Spain (54% against 46%) tended to balance both main types of issues through the reported period.

Figure 2: Issues 2008–2014, N = 8707

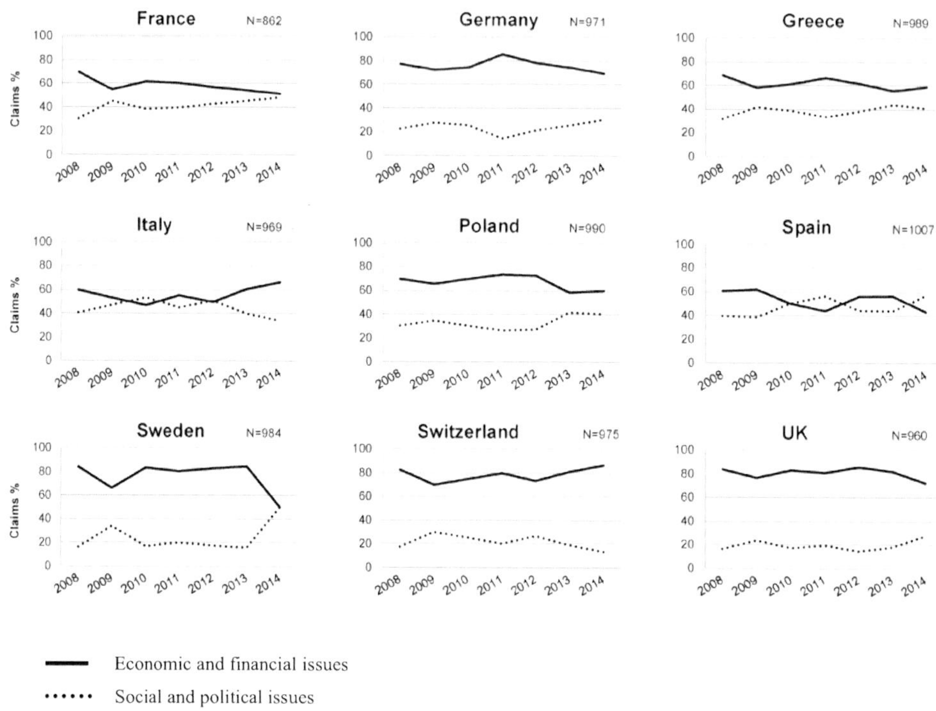

Source: own illustration

The patterns drawn by the data (figure 2) illustrate how distant these two broad groups of issues were in each country over time. During the initial years of the financial crisis (2008–2009) social and political subjects traced an upward trend in all countries except in Spain. From then onwards, only in rare occasions did social and political subjects come close to economic and financial issues. This is the case namely in Italy and Spain, and to a lesser extent in France and Greece. Exceptionally, the visibility of social and political subjects exceeded economic and financial issues in Spain in 2011 and 2014, and in Italy in 2010 (in 2012 they equalled).[32] A close-up picture of the issues (table 4) that these claims made visible reveals that macroeconomics was, by far, the undisputed subject throughout the whole period. The overall visibility was 67% for

32 I do not consider relevant the case of Sweden 2014 because, despite the convergence it shows, the amount of claims is negligible that year (under 2% of the country's sample). Switzerland presents a similar drop in the amount of claims that year, and Germany is below 4% of its sample. In contrast, France (12%) still continues active, followed by Greece (9%), Italy (8%), and the UK (7% of the country's sample).

economic and financial issues against 33% for social and political subjects. Country by country, economic and financial issues occupied 65% of all claims in the UK, 61% in Sweden, 51% in Poland, 49% in Germany, 47% in Greece, 46% in France, 44% in Switzerland, 40% in Italy, and 39% of all Spanish claims. Within this type of subjects, banks and specific financial topics stood out in Switzerland (24%), Germany (17%), the UK (14%) and Sweden (12%), while issues on businesses and other economic activities were quite relevant in Spain (11% of the country's claims). Among the social and political sort of issues, labour subjects were most visible in France and Italy (15% each), Poland (11%), and Greece (9%). Public administration topics reached considerable visibility in 16% of Spanish claims. Health, education and housing, and social policy topics were always below 7% in all countries over the whole period.

Some particularities over time may add information to the longitudinal patterns shown in figure 2. As expected, the visibility of banking and financial subjects was stronger during the first year. In 2008, these issues were particularly visible in Switzerland (37%), Italy and Germany (23% each), and Greece (27%). The peak of social and political issues displayed in France in 2009 (table 4) was due to the rise of labour topics (which represented 22% of all French claims in contrast to the previous 8% in 2008) at the expense of macroeconomic subjects (which fell to 38% in 2009 from the previous 55% in 2008). Similarly, the rise of labour subjects was mainly visible in Italy in 2012 (23% of Italian claims that year), when social and political issues (around 51%) only just surpassed economic and financial subjects (around 49%). Besides, labour topics also peaked in Greece in 2009 (visible in 14% of Greek claims that year) and 2014 (13%). In 2009, despite the sharp increase in visibility of macroeconomic subjects (up to 47% in 2009 from the previous 28% in 2008), the steep drop of topics related to banks and finance (which fell to 7% from the previous year's 27%) and businesses (which fell to 5% from the previous 13% in 2008) determined, together with the aforementioned rise of labour issues, the significant reduction of the gap between the two main types of issues in the country. In Spain, in 2010 and 2011, public administration issues increased up to 20% and 23%, respectively, while business-related and other economic activities dropped to 8% and 4%, accordingly. Also in Spain, health, education, and housing subjects steeply increased up to 20% in 2014 (from the previous 4% in 2013), while macroeconomic issues decreased from 42% in 2013 down to 34% in 2014. These facts inversed the trend, i.e., social and political subjects surpassed economic and financial issues during those years. Many more variations arise from the data, but these seem to be the most significant.

Table 4: Detail of issues by country and over time (2008–2014) N = 8707

Issues	2008	2009	2010	2011	2012	2013	2014	Total %
FRANCE								(N=862)
Macroeconomics	55	38	53	46	44	44	44	**46**
Banks and finance	14	8	3	11	6	4	3	**7**
Business and other	1	8	5	4	7	7	5	**6**
Labour	8	22	15	10	14	16	13	**15**
Health, edu, housing	5	1	3	4	8	4	8	**4**
Social policy	1	5	8	5	1	3	6	**4**
Public administration	-	1	3	1	4	5	4	**2**
Others	16	17	9	18	15	18	18	**16**
Total %	100	100	100	100	100	100	100	**100**
GERMANY								(N=971)
Macroeconomics	38	45	49	65	55	47	53	**49**
Banks and finance	23	15	18	14	18	22	14	**17**
Business and other	17	13	8	6	5	6	3	**9**
Labour	10	9	6	1	1	2	3	**6**
Health, edu, housing	2	2	2	-	-	-	6	**2**
Social policy	3	2	3	1	1	1	6	**2**
Public administration	-	2	2	4	3	7	3	**3**
Others	6	12	13	9	17	16	14	**12**
Total %	100	100	100	100	100	100	100	**100**
GREECE								(N=989)
Macroeconomics	28	47	51	58	49	48	36	**47**
Banks and finance	27	7	6	6	7	3	16	**9**
Business and other	13	5	4	3	6	5	7	**6**
Labour	4	14	9	6	8	7	13	**9**
Health, edu, housing	1	3	2	3	3	7	5	**3**
Social policy	4	3	6	2	5	5	1	**4**
Public administration	2	5	5	8	5	8	6	**6**
Others	19	16	17	15	18	18	16	**17**
Total %	100	100	100	100	100	100	100	**100**
ITALY								(N=969)
Macroeconomics	35	33	33	43	38	45	56	**40**
Banks and finance	23	14	10	7	5	6	5	**9**
Business and other	1	6	3	5	7	10	5	**6**
Labour	10	12	13	17	23	16	5	**15**
Health, edu, housing	10	13	7	2	6	8	5	**7**
Social policy	6	3	3	3	3	3	5	**3**
Public administration	3	5	9	9	6	7	6	**7**
Others	11	14	23	14	13	5	13	**13**
Total %	100	100	100	100	100	100	100	**100**
POLAND								(N=990)
Macroeconomics	51	49	62	59	55	45	42	**51**
Banks and finance	11	6	5	9	5	5	5	**7**
Business and other	8	10	3	5	12	8	13	**8**
Labour	12	9	8	9	12	15	13	**11**
Health, edu, housing	4	7	2	2	3	4	5	**5**
Social policy	1	4	10	5	1	6	7	**5**
Public administration	2	3	3	2	5	4	2	**3**
Others	10	12	8	9	5	12	13	**10**
Total %	100	100	100	100	100	100	100	**100**
SPAIN								(N=1007)
Macroeconomics	42	43	38	36	33	42	34	**39**
Banks and finance	6	7	3	4	7	3	-	**5**
Business and other	12	12	8	4	16	11	9	**11**
Labour	7	8	9	6	3	6	5	**6**
Health, edu, housing	6	3	7	5	6	4	20	**6**
Social policy	2	5	5	5	5	4	-	**4**
Public administration	12	11	20	23	15	19	20	**16**
Others	12	11	10	18	15	11	13	**13**
Total %	100	100	100	100	100	100	100	**100**
SWEDEN								(N=984)
Macroeconomics	63	52	69	62	70	69	22	**61**
Banks and finance	16	10	10	9	13	9	28	**12**
Business and other	5	4	5	9	-	7	-	**5**
Labour	5	10	4	7	5	-	6	**7**
Health, edu, housing	3	6	2	2	1	2	28	**4**
Social policy	-	2	-	2	-	2	-	**1**
Public administration	-	1	-	1	-	2	6	**1**
Others	8	15	11	7	11	10	11	**11**
Total %	100	100	100	100	100	100	100	**100**
SWITZERLAND								(N=975)
Macroeconomics	37	44	37	58	53	43	33	**44**
Banks and finance	37	18	29	15	18	27	47	**24**
Business and other	9	9	9	6	2	11	7	**8**
Labour	2	8	5	5	2	-	-	**5**
Health, edu, housing	-	2	1	2	-	-	-	**1**
Social policy	6	2	4	1	2	3	-	**3**
Public administration	4	1	3	1	-	5	-	**2**
Others	5	17	12	12	23	11	13	**13**
Total %	100	100	100	100	100	100	100	**100**
UK								(N=960)
Macroeconomics	62	61	66	69	67	74	58	**65**
Banks and finance	18	12	15	10	17	7	13	**14**
Business and other	3	3	2	1	2	1	1	**2**
Labour	1	4	6	4	2	3	3	**3**
Health, edu, housing	6	4	3	1	2	6	9	**4**
Social policy	-	-	3	1	-	1	1	**1**
Public administration	2	1	1	1	2	1	-	**1**
Others	7	13	4	12	9	6	14	**9**
Total %	100	100	100	100	100	100	100	**100**

Figures are in percentages. Values below 1% are not displayed.

Source: own illustration

The last part of this general analysis illustrates whose interests were touched by these claims. These players are the objects of the claims. As aforementioned, civil society organizations and groups gained very limited direct visibility in the national mainstream media, both as actors and addressees of the claims. Nevertheless, as table 5 evidences, 30% of all claims concerned their interests. This is a significant share that almost doubles the amount of core political actors (16%) who were affected. Yet both groups were clearly below powerful interest groups (54%), where market and financial objects received 21%, companies 16%, and labour organizations and groups 13% of claims of the whole sample. Table 5 presents the distribution of claims affecting all kinds of political, economic, and social objects during the entire period 2008–2014.

Table 5: Objects of the claims 2008–2014, N = 8707

Country	State	Political parties	**Core political actors**	Companies	Market and finance	Labour	Opinion leaders	Other professionals	**Interest groups**	**Civil society**	**Total %**
France	35	4	**39**	12	16	15	2	1	**47**	**15**	100
Germany	36	1	**37**	15	26	8	1	1	**50**	**13**	100
Greece	12	1	**12**	9	16	21	0	4	**50**	**38**	100
Italy	12	1	**13**	35	9	21	3	1	**69**	**18**	100
Poland	3	1	**4**	27	6	13	0	2	**47**	**49**	100
Spain	13	3	**16**	8	6	8	1	4	**27**	**57**	100
Sweden	6	1	**6**	23	25	11	1	0	**59**	**35**	100
Switzerland	10	2	**11**	13	42	16	4	1	**76**	**13**	100
UK	10	1	**12**	5	48	4	0	0	**57**	**31**	100
Total %	**15**	**1**	**16**	**16**	**21**	**13**	**1**	**1**	**54**	**30**	**100**

Values below 1% are not reported. Figures are in percentages

Source: own illustration

To begin with, claims affected the interests of civil society players mainly in Spain (57% of the country's claims), Poland (49%), Greece (38%), Sweden (35%), and the UK (31%). The interests of markets and financial objects were particularly affected in the UK (48% of British claims) and Switzerland (42%), followed by Germany (26%) and Sweden (25%). Labour concerns, in Greece and Italy (21% each). Last but not least, the state's interests were mostly affected by claims in Germany (36% of all German claims) and France (35%). In contrast, political parties, opinion leaders, and other professional organizations and groups that have access to policy-making were hardly affected at all.

6. Relations among actors and addressees, and actors and issues

The second part of this description takes a closer look at how these three basic components – actors, addressees, and issues – were visibly connected in the nine public spheres I explore. However, before advancing the analysis, a reminder needs to be made. A comparative analysis of nine countries over time cannot, unfortunately, develop in-depth and extensively all the richness of the data in a single contribution. Nevertheless, regardless of the limitations of scope, certain considerations that arise from the data are worth mentioning. The following description stems from the role of actors as claims-makers. Actors are the ones who begin the flux of communication; they target different kinds of addressees and promote particular issues. Consequently, I illustrate the most relevant relationships of particular kinds of actors turning to particular kinds of addressees, on the one hand, and advancing specific issues in the national public spheres, on the other hand.[33] In the first place, a more detailed analysis of the kinds of actors and addressees allows to differentiate the main competitors in the broad typology I have used so far. In the core political group I distinguish state agents from political parties; in the interest group, labour from companies and from market and finance players. In any case, first and foremost, all kinds of actors directed their claims to state actors.[34] No other type of addressee received such attention. Particularly, the state/state relationship (state actor/state addressee) was by far the most visible one in all countries – apart from a negligible difference in the UK, where state/state represented 6% of the British sample, while political parties targeted the state in 7% of British claims. In descending order, state/state claims were most visible in Greece (33% of all Greek claims), Germany (22%), Italy (20%), Switzerland (18%), Spain (16%), Poland (14%), France (10%), Sweden (7%), and the UK, as aforementioned. The state also directed its claims to civil society (6% in Greece, 5% in France). Other actors that addressed the state during the considered period were companies (14% of claims in Italy and 13% in Poland), labour actors (10% of claims in Italy, 5% in Greece), opinion leaders (10% of claims in Poland), political parties (9% of claims in Germany and Spain, 6% in Italy and Poland, and 5% in Greece and Switzerland), and market and finance (6% of claims in Poland and 5% in Sweden) claims-makers. There is hardly any other data worth stressing. However, this is neither to say that actors did not target other addressees nor that the remaining kinds of actors were not active – only that they represent either too small or negligible amounts of claims when analysed targeting particular addressees. In the second place, I highlight certain information about the actors/issues relationship. In this case, state actors advancing macroeconomic issues dominated by far the claims in all countries. In decreasing order, these represent 30% of the claims in Greece, 27% in Germany, 22% in Spain, 21% in Switzerland, 20% in

33 I do not discuss figures < 5%.

34 When the addressee is explicit in a claim. Although I maintain the representativeness of the sample including unspecified addressees in the data, I do not comment here on those claims directed to unspecified addressees, which surpass other sorts of addressees in Sweden, Switzerland, and the UK.

Sweden, 19% in the UK, 18% in France, 16% in Italy, and 15% in Poland. Other kinds of actors who also introduced macroeconomic subjects were market and finance players (15% of claims in Sweden, 8% in Poland, 7% in the UK, 6% in Switzerland, 5% in France), companies (14% of claims in Sweden, 13% in the UK, 9% in Italy, 8% in Poland and Switzerland, 5% in Germany), political parties (11% of claims in the UK, 8% in France, 6% in Germany and Spain, 5% in Poland), opinion leaders (6% of claims in the UK), and labour actors (5% of claims in the UK). For its part, state actors also proposed other kinds of issues. The most visible were banking and financial subjects (11% in Switzerland, 8% in Germany, 5% in Italy and the UK) and public administration topics in Spain (6% of all Spanish claims).

7. Conclusions

In this chapter, I presented an examination of 8,707 claims published by several European mainstream media, thus contributing to illustrate the informational contexts and the power relations developed by contending actors over the period 2008–2014 in a selected sample of nine European countries. I basically considered whether the exceptional circumstances of those years opened up the possibility for visualizing a variety of actors and issues in the national public spheres. Specifically, I explored whether social and political concerns that derived from the economic crisis coexisted with more technical economic or financial subjects. The map of successful contenders in the media mirrors power in society. The results I introduced show an overwhelming preponderance of economic matters at the expense of all other kinds of interests in all the countries of the sample.

The crisis went through different phases over the seven-year period under review. The data presents some evidence of these changing phases. Social and political concerns gained increasing visibility in the media during the initial phase of fiscal expansion (2008–2009). From then onwards, the forcefulness of the usual dominant actors and the monotony of recurrent economic subjects crystallized a uniform picture. Consequently, alternative perspectives lacked visibility. The claims published by these mainstream media provided information and aided to form the opinions of European citizens, who were directly or indirectly exposed to this particular information. The picture hence contributed to signify the complexity of extremely critical circumstances. Published issues were made visible by actors who, in turn, gained themselves visibility in the media; this way, they affected the interests of specific groups. Furthermore, the amount of visibility that state actors and macroeconomic issues enjoyed in the mainstream media increased the potential to spread their messages even further. This chapter does not analyse the resonance and legitimacy that these claims produced in the national public spheres. However, the exploration done so far reveals that state actors who advanced economic subjects largely fulfilled the first necessary condition required to influence the public sphere, i.e. visibility in the media. From this perspective, the economic crisis did neither represent a discursive opportunity for peripheral actors and challengers nor for social and political concerns.

The data shows that state actors were the most visible claim-makers in every country over the whole period, except in the UK, where they were slightly outnumbered by political parties. Quite the contrary, civil society actors were the real missing players in this story. State actors were extremely prominent in Greece and Germany, capturing over half the total amount of claims in each country, followed by Spain and Switzerland. In any case, state actors consistently proposed economic and financial issues far beyond any other subject. The dominant group that was structured around the state incorporated political parties, companies, market and financial players, and eventually opinion leaders too, with slight variations across countries. All these actors clearly advanced economic and financial issues, with two noticeable exceptions: political parties in Spain and companies in Poland – although the latter still privileged economic and financial subjects over social and political topics. On the other hand, in the case of addressees, in contrast, core political addressees (particularly the state) were always, and by far, more visible than interest groups – except in France, where both types shared similar visibility.

Undoubtedly, the state/state link (a state actor targeting a state addressee) was the most visible relationship in every country. In specific countries, other particular actors that addressed the state also had a rather significant share of visibility in the media. This was the case of business groups in Italy and Poland, labour groups in Italy, opinion leaders in Poland, and political parties in Spain and the UK. Besides, labour organizations and groups (including labour unions) gained noticeable visibility in France and, to a lesser extent, in Greece, but they remained scarcely visible in all the remaining countries. The data thus reflects the declining power of labour unions, even amidst the steep deterioration of labour conditions that followed the economic recession and the implementation of austerity policies. Namely in the countries most affected by unemployment, lowered wages, job insecurity, welfare retrenchment, and so forth, the critical social conditions of those years did not represent a discursive opportunity neither for labour groups nor for civil society organizations and groups. Labour actors, however, proposed social and political issues mostly in Italy, France, and Greece, but also economic and financial subjects. Conversely, they privileged economic and financial subjects in Sweden, Switzerland, and the UK (the amounts of visible claims are sometimes quite negligible in these cases; hence we must be cautious in drawing conclusions). The state played a double role regarding the issues it promoted. Although, as aforementioned, being the first actor and the first addressee too, it mainly advanced economic and financial subjects, and it also played an important role in posing social and political concerns. Nevertheless, these were always far below the amount of economic and financial matters it made visible in the media.

Lastly, I explored whose interests were affected by the claims in order to complement the picture of these power relationships. Overall, the interests of civil organizations and groups were affected by a third of all claims, which means a considerable share. These organizations have neither access to policy-making nor the media and were in fact unable to surmount the extremely low visibility that they enjoyed as actors and addressees. Their interests were mainly affected in Spain (where claims affecting them doubled the average in all countries), Poland, Greece, Sweden, and the UK. They were by far the most affected single type of player in the sample.[35] The second group whose interests were most affected was the one composed of market and financial players, especially in the UK and Switzerland but also in Germany and Sweden. Next there were companies, business associations, and business groups, who were particularly affected in Italy, then in Poland and Sweden. In the fourth place, the interests of the state were most affected, mainly in France and Germany. And lastly, the interests of labour organizations and groups were mostly affected in Italy and Greece, followed by Switzerland, France, Poland, and Sweden.

So far, I depicted the ability and capability of different actors in gaining visibility for themselves and their interests by being published in the national media during the recent crisis. Further research could broaden and deepen the comprehension of these strategic alignments by tracing the resonance that these claims had among economic, political, and social actors. This comprehension might lead to confirming the legitimacy of certain actors and the political concerns they succeed in making public. Similarly, timing the visibility of specific subjects in cross-national comparisons may reveal other patterns in the data. Moreover, contextual information, macroeconomic data, the identification of key political events, and, in particular, a follow-up of the implementation of austerity policies and the execution of the new European mechanisms of financial support in each country would certainly contribute to the interpretation of these claims.

35 All powerful interest groups together exceed civil society organizations.

Reiner Grundmann, Kim-Sue Kreischer and Mike Scott

The Discourse of Austerity in the British Press

As we are writing this chapter, the National Health Service in the United Kingdom is facing its worst crisis since inception. This may well be the result of several years of austerity policies, which led to underinvestment in the health sector and severe cuts to social services, exacerbating the problems faced by British hospitals. Austerity policies were introduced in the UK after the conservative liberal coalition came to power in 2010. Six years later, at the time of the Brexit referendum, major actors indicated a much longer period for fiscal consolidation, while the policy impact is still causing severe problems across the country.[1] In May 2016 an IMF paper questioned the rationale:

> *»An assessment of these specific policies (rather than the broad neoliberal agenda) reaches three disquieting conclusions:*
> *• The benefits in terms of increased growth seem fairly difficult to establish when looking at a broad group of countries.*
> *• The costs in terms of increased inequality are prominent. Such costs epitomize the trade-off between the growth and equity effects of some aspects of the neoliberal agenda.*
> *• Increased inequality in turn hurts the level and sustainability of growth. Even if growth is the sole or main purpose of the neoliberal agenda, advocates of that agenda still need to pay attention to the distributional effects.«*[2]

In this chapter we examine the discourse of austerity and its unfolding in British broadsheet papers. We present an analysis based on corpus linguistics methodology, using a full text database spanning nine years. Our approach overcomes the relatively small sample size used in previous research and the restricted time periods. In so doing, we develop an innovative method to ensure we include all relevant news items, excluding duplicates and irrelevant texts. We are interested in the semantics of austerity and in the salience of various actors visible in public discourse who are trying to influence its trajectory.

1. Our approach and previous research

Discourse analysis is a promising tool to understand the interrelation between actors, ideas, policies, and practices. In news coverage, specific actors and organizations are given prominence, either as sources, or reference points, or both. The language used by the sources, or used to describe their statements, is crucial. That is why we have under-

1 »George Osborne scraps 2020 budget surplus plan« in: *The Guardian*, 1.6.2016; »New chancellor Philip Hammond to scale back austerity« in: *Financial Times*, 14.7.2016.

2 Jonathan D. Ostry / Prakash Loungani / Davide Furceri, »Neoliberalism: Oversold?« in: *IMF Finance & Development* 53, No. 2 (2016), pp. 38–41.

taken a research project that analyses the discourse of austerity through language use by different actors in the UK. Much of our effort is focused on the construction of a robust corpus of relevant press publications and its analysis with Corpus Linguistics tools. We combine this with qualitative inspection of selected publications.

Framing analysis emphasizes the aspects of giving meaning to complex stories, defining a problem, attributing causality and blame, and identifying remedial action.[3] The importance of ideas and language in the policy process goes back to ancient times, recognized by political scientists well before the term »discourse analysis« was coined. The relation between ideas, interests, and political strategies is a well-established nexus. In political terms, the definition of options is the crucial playing field on which decisions and their consequences are played out. In 1960, E. E. Schattschneider famously wrote that »[t]he definition of the alternatives is the supreme instrument of power [...]. He who determines what politics is about runs the country, because the definition of alternatives is the choice of conflicts, and the choice of conflicts allocates power.«[4]

In combining insights from discourse analysis and political science, our analysis aims at establishing the powerful actors in the discourse and revealing how they were able to exercise this power through ideas and language. We will do this through an analysis of their visibility in the press and through their discursive performance. We realize there may be a difference between high visibility and political influence or power.

1.1 Austerity

Mark Blyth defines austerity as »the deliberate deflation of domestic wages and prices through cuts to public spending – [it] is designed to reduce a state's debts and deficits, increase its economic competitiveness, and restore what is vaguely referred to as ›business confidence‹.«[5] This means reducing state deficit through fiscal measures. The IMF has been proposing such policies, mainly for countries in the global South, for several decades.[6] The same has been suggested for developed capitalist countries after the financial crash. As has been observed, politicians have bought into these ideas:

> *»This new era of fiscal consolidation is based on two simple ideas. First, government budget deficits experienced today by many advanced countries are unsustainable. Second, fiscal consolidation measures are invariably expansionary; that is, massive cuts in government expenditures and significant tax hikes have positive effects on*

3 Robert M. Entman, »Framing: Towards Clarification of a Fractured Paradigm« in: *Journal of Communication* 43, No. 4 (1993), pp. 390–397.

4 Elmer Eric Schattschneider, *The Semisovereign People: A Realist's View of Democracy in America*, New York 1960, p. 66.

5 Mark Blyth, »The Austerity Delusion. Why a Bad Idea Won Over the West« in: *Foreign Affairs* 92, No. 3 (2013), pp. 41–56, p. 41.

6 John Clarke / Janet Newman, »The Alchemy of Austerity« in: *Critical Social Policy* 32, No. 3 (2012), pp. 299–319, p. 300.

> *output and employment. These simple ideas are wrong but very powerful. No policy-maker around the world seems immune to them.«*[7]

In the UK, austerity discourse has a historic precedent in the immediate post-war era. As Kynaston points out, »[t]he lessons of history can be overdone, but the austerity of the 1940s – a largely successfully managed operation, with society remaining broadly stable and cohesive«[8] – has four lessons to teach us: a sense of shared purpose, a perceived equity of sacrifice, an aura of hope and a degree of public confidence in the political class. Clark and Newman comment that «[t]he purpose of austerity is, at best, shared on a sort of grudging acquiescence about the condition of the global economy, the public debt and the ›necessity‹ of tough measures (producing echoes of Margaret Thatcher's claim that 'There Is No Alternative (TINA) which typically evoked grudging compliance rather than enthusiastic support).«[9]

In the early stages of UK austerity policy, the public might have been ready for this. Vis et al. report public opinion poll data from the UK showing

> *»that the UK public is willing to accept government spending cuts, but refuses to accept cuts on health care. A more recent Financial Times/Harris Poll (2010) supports this result. Only 8 per cent of Britons think that healthcare should bear the biggest part of the spending cuts burden. Interestingly, the same poll shows that a little over 50 per cent of Britons consider it acceptable that unemployment benefits get cut the most.«*[10]

This is different to other countries examined by Vis et al. They studied Denmark, Germany, the Netherlands, Sweden, the UK, and the USA, not only comparing public opinion but also austerity policies. Their verdict is, »If we examine the details of the measures taken, the UK stands out. Although the UK had the lowest score on supportive [labour market] policies of all EU 15 countries before the crisis, the government has been very reluctant to improve these policies, even temporarily.«[11]

1.2 Research on media coverage of UK austerity

Previous research on British media coverage of austerity indicates that it tends to interpret the economic crisis as a financial crisis of overspending restricted to the UK, which can, then, support the »inevitable« solutions of spending cuts and austerity mea-

7 Giuseppe Fontana / Malcolm Sawyer, »Fiscal Austerity: Lessons from Recent Events in the British Isles« in: *Challenge* 45, No. 2 (2011), pp. 42–60, pp. 57–58.

8 David Kynaston, »Austerity was a hard sell in the 40s. Today it's harder still« in: *The Guardian*, 21.6.2010.

9 Clarke / Newman, »The Alchemy of Austerity«, op. cit. (note 6), p. 307.

10 Barbara Vis / Kees van Kersbergen / Tom Hylands, »To What Extent Did the Financial Crisis Intensify the Pressure to Reform the Welfare State?« in: *Social Policy and Administration* 45, No. 4 (2011), pp. 338–353, p. 343.

11 Vis / van Kersbergen / Hylands, »To What Extent Did the Financial Crisis Intensify the Pressure to Reform the Welfare State?«, op. cit. (note 10), p. 347.

sures.[12] Fairclough[13], in developing an analytical framework for the evaluation of practical arguments in political discourse, analyses 461 press articles published in the two months following the adoption of the first austerity budget in June 2012. Her corpus is comprised of articles from newspapers with a heterogeneous political outlook: *The Guardian*, *The Daily Telegraph*, *The Daily Mail*, *The Financial Times*, and *The Sun*. Utilizing concordance lines and key words as part of her analysis, she finds that the press echoes and validates the government's framing of the crisis as one of state overspending. The arguments made in the five newspapers imbued this narrative with common sense by portraying the economy as a household that has lived outside its means and must now pay off its debt. It thus seemed natural that debt could »not be cured with more debt« but with austerity policies.[14]

Other research indicates that additional factors were the lack of alternatives and an alignment with the narrative of a fiscal crisis of the state even by British newspapers that are generally critical of Conservative policies. Pririe[15] tracks the development of how the economic crisis was presented in the British print media by comparing four 2-week sample periods from October 2008 to December 2010 for the same five newspapers as Fairclough. He claims his analysis demonstrates that it was particularly »the failure of the Labour party to offer a clear and compelling alternative«[16] that resulted in a debate in the mainstream press that was dominated by fiscal questions of public spending.

Other media outlets, such as the BBC, interpreted and presented the economic crisis in similar terms. The Frame Analysis of Kay and Salter[17] compares the framing of three online BBC news features of the government's Comprehensive Spending Review with the framing advanced by the government. They suggest that the BBC material was in line with the government and presented the economic crisis as a technical rather than a political problem and further disregarded alternatives or the moral-ethical dimension of the austerity measures.

One central concern is whether the portrayal of the economic crisis by the British press and the lack of alternatives offered both by Labour as the main parliamentary opposition and the press itself was facilitated by drawing upon specific experts, in the form of economists, business lobbies, think tanks, or scientists, who thus defined the crisis in the news. Generally those in powerful and privileged institutional positions

12 Isabella Fairclough, »Evaluating policy as argument: the public debate over the first UK austerity budget« in: *Critical Discourse Studies* 13, No. 1 (2016), pp. 57–77; Jilly Boyce Kay / Lee Salter, »Framing the cuts: An analysis of the BBC's discursive framing of the ConDem cuts agenda« in: *Journalism* 15, No. 6 (2014), pp. 754–772; Ian Pirie, »Representations of economic crisis in contemporary Britain« in: *British Politics* 7, No. 4 (2012), pp. 341–364.

13 Fairclough, »Evaluating policy as argument«, op. cit. (note 12).

14 Fairclough, »Evaluating policy as argument«, op. cit. (note 12), p. 73.

15 Pirie, »Representations of economic crisis in contemporary Britain«, op. cit. (note 12).

16 Pirie, »Representations of economic crisis in contemporary Britain«, op. cit. (note 12), p. 361.

17 Kay / Salter, »Framing the cuts«, op. cit. (note 12).

are often given preferred access to the press, which reinforces an overrepresentation of mainstream views of the elite.[18]

Pririe claims that there is a vast gulf between the dominant media and academic debates concerning the economic crisis. While a general divergence between the media and academic accounts is not exceptional, he further notes that there is »no clear relationship between the two« and that the popular media is dominated by »a narrative of crisis almost completely lacking in any form of intellectual support.«[19]

A similar picture of divergence was found by Berry[20] in his qualitative study of the deficit debate in the British Press. Berry identified peak days for each month from January to August 2009 in six national newspapers (*The Guardian*, *The Daily Telegraph*, *The Daily Mail*, *The Daily Express*, *The Sun*, and *The Mirror*) and included the coverage of the two peak days for each month, resulting in a corpus of 166 articles. He concludes in his thematic frame analysis that politicians are more often cited as experts instead of non-governmental sources, while some of the strongest advocates of neoliberalism in the press were key in defining and managing the crisis. These experts include the Bank of England, IMF, OECD, the Adam Smith Institute, and right-wing think tanks such as the Policy Exchange and the Taxpayers' Alliance. Berry[21] notes the distinctive lack of any left-wing or even Keynesian alternatives amongst the groups in his data. The representation of the crisis by drawing upon particular experts further restricts the possibility of arguing against the dominant framing of the crisis as a fiscal problem of overspending restricted to the UK.

2. Method and data collection

This section describes the construction of the corpus. We used the LexisNexis database to download news articles in the period January 1, 2007, until December 31, 2015. Our search terms were *(austerity AND chancellor) OR anti-austerity OR rating agencies*, and the sources selected in LexisNexis were UK Broadsheets:[22]

18 Mike Berry, »The UK press and the deficit debate« in: *Sociology* 50, No. 3 (2016), pp. 542–559; Stuart Hall / Chas Critcher / Tony Jefferson / John Clarke / Brian Roberts, *Policing the Crisis: Mugging the State and Law and Order*, London 2013; Hugh Heclo / Aaron Wildavsky, *The private government of public money: community and policy inside British politics*, Berkeley 1974.

19 Pririe, »Representations of economic crisis in contemporary Britain«, op. cit. (note 12), p. 343.

20 Berry, »The UK press and the deficit debate«, op. cit. (note 18).

21 Berry, »The UK press and the deficit debate«, op. cit. (note 18), p. 549.

22 For some reason these turned out to include City A. M. as well.

Table 1: UK Broadsheet articles 2007–2015 as originally downloaded

Newspapers	Number of articles
The Independent, Independent on Sunday	3,399
Daily Telegraph, Sunday Telegraph	7,765
The Guardian, The Observer	5,425
The Times, Sunday Times	6,577

Source: own

Like Dayrell[23], following Gabrielatos[24], we used a search procedure which computes the ratio between the number of texts returned by a first search within a database (on *austerity*) against the number of texts returned by the same core query set plus extra candidate terms. This gave us the additional terms *anti-austerity* and *rating agencies*. However, as will become clear below, we found that this collection of over 20,000 articles contained many where austerity was quite peripheral.

In practice, there are significant problems in managing downloads because of factors such as duplication, unevenness of formatting standards, or lack of documentation. These had caused us in previous work over the past years[25] to develop the Download Parser software.[26]

The formatting which suits one newspaper or news agency cannot be expected to correspond with that of others. Experience with LexisNexis downloads suggests that there is not much uniformity; that LexisNexis does little to unify their holdings, matching them to common standards, but instead accepts them more or less as supplied by the participating publishers. There might be little incentive for publishers to establish common standards for export of their output to LexisNexis, though mark-up standards were devised starting back in the 1960s.[27] The search options are fairly simple (Nexis shows an example with two pages outlining the various choices one may make for an advanced search), but how the search operates internally in their database is not made clear. Relevant articles appear one after the other up to the agency's limit, here 500 documents.[28]

23 Carmen Dayrell, *Working Paper #1 The Brazilian Corpus on Urban Violence*, http://cass.lancs.ac.uk/wp-content/uploads/2015/11/Working-paper-1-Corpus-Compilation.pdf [29.6.2017].

24 Costas Gabrielatos, »Selecting query terms to build a specialised corpus from a restricted-access database« in: *ICAME Journal* 31 (2007), pp. 5–44.

25 Reiner Grundmann / Mike Scott / Jin Wang, »Energy security in the news: North/South perspectives« in: *Environmental Politics* 22, No. 4 (2013), pp. 571–592; Reiner Grundmann / Mike Scott, »Disputed climate science in the media: Do countries matter?« in: *Public Understanding of Science* 23, No. 2(2014), pp. 220–235.

26 Mike Scott, *Download Parser*, Stroud 2017, http://lexically.net/DownloadParser/ [2.3.2017].

27 Charles Goldfarb, *The SGML Handbook*, Oxford 1990.

28 Nexis Advanced Search Guide, http://bisinfo.lexisnexis.co.uk/hubfs/Resources/Nexis_User_Guides_Advanced_Search_Guide.pdf [18.7.2017].

By default[29], even if a search-term occurs once only in passing, the Nexis search-engine normally includes it. For example, a *Times* article of November 10, 2015, headed »Berlusconi bounces back in rightwing pact«, was retrieved because it included a brief reference to Beppe Grillo, »a former comic whose anti-austerity Five-Star movement [...]«, although the text really concerns Berlusconi joining a coalition, hoping thereby to recover politically. The text is not about austerity, cuts, or economic problems, but about Italian politics.

A basic set of indicators can be found by searching through the text, usually indicating who wrote each article, the date, which language it was written in, or the name of the newspaper, but the number of fields used and their formats vary.

Downloads are thus a rather mixed bag of incompletely formatted data containing a lot of relevant articles with some duplication and including articles where the search-term is peripheral.

A corpus building on news resources in that way should ideally

- ensure a standard format;
- identify article features such as headlines, text boxes, sub-headings, captions of graphics, hypertext links;
- filter out duplicate articles and duplicated sections within articles;
- filter out articles where the main topic searched for is not evident;
- store individual articles so that they can be retrieved easily;
- build sub-corpora by grouping articles according to criteria such as date, publication-type, or within a set of specific publications.

In what follows we have tried to achieve these aims, addressing each of the above items in turn.

2.1 The parse process

This section describes how the downloaded plain text files are handled by the Download Parser[30], how they are cleaned up, marked-up, and sorted for corpus use. The programme operates first of all by converting all of each downloaded text to Unicode.[31] Then it goes through each download text looking for wording which marks the beginning of an article, such as »Document # of #«.[32] Once it finds where each text begins and ends, the Download Parser can keep a copy of each article and parse that copy for document fields.

In news items downloaded from Nexis, some aspects of text are typically marked up, though not always consistently. For example, a story may contain such strings as GRAPHIC, LANGUAGE, LENGTH or LOAD-DATE in capitals. But, rather surprisingly, publication names and dates are typically not marked up by such field

29 There are alternatives in a drop-down list.

30 Scott, *Download Parser*, op. cit. (note 26).

31 Unicode allows the programme to process text in most of the world's languages, because it allows a very great range of characters to be interpreted and displayed correctly.

32 Or *Dokument # von #* as the case may be.

names. Likewise, there is no explicit mark-up for the headline or any sub-headings. This is surprising because the structure of text is of professional interest to linguists, media researchers, and news publishers. For many years, the computational industry has enabled software to process text divisions, so as to query databases seeking only specific fields. Back in 1997, Peter White described the »opening nucleus« of hard news stories which typically starts articles off with what journalists call the headline and the lead (a story synthesis), after which the rest of the article goes in for what he calls »orbital textual development« where the journalist elaborates, explains cause and effect, justifies, contextualizes, and appraises.[33] The fact that there is in the 21st Century still no mark-up for the headline and the lead may be surprising in view of the potential for more effective handling of these large text resources.

After the news articles have been copied from the original download files, each article will have a set of headers gleaned from the text or any weak mark-up supplied in the download.

Figure 1: Header section in a parsed corpus file

```
00002_00002_10_05_2012___AU_02A5.TXT - Notepad
File  Edit  Format  View  Help
<HEADER>
        <Story 184 of 500 [THIS DOWNLOAD]>
        <FROM lines 29,699-29,772 of J:\austerity\download\2012\UK_Broadsheets2015-12-10_13-55.TXT>
        <SOURCE: TELEGRAPH.CO.UK>
        <DATE: MAY 10, 2012 THURSDAY 9:08 PM GMT>
        <SECTION: NEWS>
        <LENGTH: 394 words>
        <LOAD-DATE: May 11, 2012>
        <LANGUAGE: ENGLISH>
        <PUBLICATION-TYPE: Web Publication>
        <JOURNAL-CODE: WEBDTNS>
        <COPYRIGHT: Copyright 2012 Telegraph Media Group Limited>
        <COPYRIGHT: All Rights Reserved>
</HEADER>
```

Source: own illustration

Headlines (figure 2) are identified rather crudely by seeking a suitable line-break in the first complete sentence in the text.

Figure 2: Headline section in a parsed corpus file

```
<HEADLINE>
        Francois Hollande threatens to block eurozone's new financial treaty;
</HEADLINE>
```

Source: own illustration

33 Peter R. R. White, »Death, Disruption and the Moral Order: the Narrative Impulse in Mass-Media Hard News Reporting« in: Frances Christie / J. R. Martin (eds.), *Genres and Institutions: Social Processes in the Workplace and School*, London 1997, pp. 101–133.

Duplication occurs in five main ways. The same article can be retrieved in the database software if two similar search-terms are used, such as *global warming* and *climate change*. Such duplication is a simple artefact of the database search process. Other causes of duplication are where an article gets re-published at a later date either in the same paper or elsewhere, where it gets edited possibly for legal reasons, or where it is re-issued for an online edition and there are editorial reasons for altering the style, length, or accompanying images. Finally, we get unexpected duplication when a paragraph gets repeated numerous times within the same text, probably because of some programming error. A variant of the first of these happens also when two journalists are each using the same newswire source and echo wording in the newswire report. It is easy to detect duplication where the text exactly matches or where the headers plus headlines match; computers are good at such simple matching. The Parser filters out repetition within a text by simply searching for repeated stretches of 250 characters. Finding cases where there has been minor change is trickier. The Parser first compares the length of the two texts and, if the difference is slight, compares the vocabulary of the two texts taking into account each word's frequency. In practice this works reasonably well except in a growing number of cases where an online text gets added to with comments.[34]

2.2 Filtering

The filter routine, which has been developed and extended because of the perceived problem exemplified by the Berlusconi text mentioned above, attempts to determine whether any given article is really about the topic as originally specified to the online database. There are three requirements here: is the text vocabulary as expected, is it spread appropriately through the text, and is the text long enough? We decided to exclude texts of less than 400 words.

A parsing routine cannot get directly at discourse meaning. It is good at finding repeated strings of characters in text but cannot interpret meaning. A reader has the advantage of being able to read between the lines; so the challenge is to devise a parsing routine that includes articles about austerity (even if the word does not appear) and to exclude articles that are not about austerity (even if the word appears). It is not simply a question of the original search-words. A text might not contain[35] any of a given set of expected words and still be about austerity. Likewise a text might contain several words or phrases expected to typify discussion of austerity but not really be about austerity. An example from our download is a 2012 *Times* story which starts out dis-

34 However, Dayrell (personal communication) points out that, even if a text is duplicated, filtering out must be handled with caution: she argues that it is likely the different versions reached different readerships, as is evident in the difference between print and online publication.

35 In the 1980s Scott worked on *European integration*, also with news text. It was common for texts to report attitudes of *Paris*, *London*, *Bonn*, *Rome*, etc., without stating explicitly that these politicians were aiming at European integration.

cussing the European debt crisis, reporting that various Finance ministers all said their country was not in trouble[36], followed by a middle section on Eurotunnel and the New York Stock Exchange, and a final section on bargains in UK hotel chains. Another example: Peter Mandelson on the election of Jeremy Corbyn to the Labour party leadership, September 2015.[37] His 1,100 word article uses the word *austerity* twice but is not about hardship or government policies. It is regret of the choice of leader, a history of how and why he thinks that came about, and a warning for the future.

We took 100 articles at random from the output, and each read them, trying to decide whether they were really austerity articles or not. At first we had poor agreement between us: some irrelevancy was easy to agree on, but other texts were much more problematic. We had only agreed on 50 as being about austerity, and 7 as not being about austerity; for 43 others there was disagreement. Would we wish to include articles about the Eurozone's sovereign debt crisis involving terms like *Merkel*, *Tsipras* and *Greece*? What about articles where a company had made significant losses? If the company is typical of a whole sector that would have huge implications beyond its own work-force and investors, it will made sense; if not, it is merely a company profit or loss report. After much discussion and trial of various systems, we found that the austerity discourse in the downloaded stories has three components: (1) UK austerity policy; (2) market and company reports; and (3) sovereign debt crises. We agreed to attempt to eliminate (2) and (3), leaving us with UK austerity policy.

We then took a fresh set of 100 randomly selected articles from the download, trying to reach agreement between us on these three categories. With this in mind, as human readers we now reached high agreement, identifying 75 of them as fitting into three sets of texts and 25 as outsiders which did not fit any or which belonged to more than one of these categories. Our desired UK austerity texts were 21 of the 75, sovereign debt accounted for 18 and company reports for 36.

But for the Parser to do a similar identification task, homing in on UK austerity, filtering out sovereign debt, company reports, mixed-bag, and irrelevant texts would not be as straightforward. A first trial required the presence of a minimum number of required search strings, but then we hit upon a more supple strategy: giving each text a score, by counting the presence of certain search strings in it positively, and marking it down if certain other relatively undesirable strings were found. Accordingly, positive terms included *cutting spending*, *spending cuts*, *deficit reduction*, *recovery*, *The Treasury*, *Bank of England*, *The Chancellor*. Negative-scoring terms for sovereign debt included *Eurozone*, *sovereign debt crisis*, *Draghi*, *ECB*, *troika*. Negatively scoring terms for the company reports aspect of austerity included *FTSE 100*, *Standard & Poor*, *hedge fund*, *Emissions Trading System*, *Lloyd's*.

36 »›Spain is not Uganda‹ said the Spanish Prime Minister to which the Ugandan Foreign Minister said Uganda does not want to be Spain.« Martin Waller, »City Diary story« in: *The Times*, 22.6.2012.

37 Peter Mendelson, »I'm partly to blame for this mess but let's fight to win back Labour« in: *Sunday Times*, 13.9.2015.

How were these search strings arrived at? They came in two ways: firstly, identification by us as readers having read quite a number of the texts in the download. This is very intuitive selection. It is not rigorous (unless carried out by a large number of suitable informants – we were only two), but it does take advantage of human knowledge. Secondly, using WordSmith Tools, keywords were computed of the three vocabularies from the 75 texts, using the word list of the 100 texts as a reference corpus. These key words picked out terms as much more typical of each set of texts and enabled us to add less easily predictable strings to the set of search-strings, such as for company reports *VW*, *Company's*, *cent*; *bailout* for sovereign debt crisis texts; *freeze* and *families* for UK austerity.

These terms were tweaked until mechanical filtering reached reasonable agreement with our identification of the 75 texts. Sometimes a small detail makes a difference. *The Chancellor* in our texts was the UK minister for the economy, George Osborne in much of the period, while *Chancellor* alone is often Chancellor Merkel. A further detail is that the scoring mechanism added points for the spread of the desirable terms throughout the text. A total of 62 terms were used in the end.

Dayrell used a very similar clean-up and parsing process in her analysis of Urban Violence. She was downloading from a different database (Factiva) but employed very similar tactics in handling her downloads. Like ours, her filter looked for specific terms but does not seem to have used a system of scoring for filtering.

Three texts were wrongly excluded by the mechanical filter, and three texts were wrongly included (precision 18/21 = 86%, recall 21/24 = 88%). Considering that the vocabulary of all the relevant word lists overlapped considerably (all Dice[38] scores between 0.41 and 0.45 suggesting an overlap of over 40% of the vocabulary of these texts), we felt encouraged: even though nearly half the words in each type of austerity text were the same, the filter was distinguishing the UK austerity texts fairly well.[39] It reduced the original over 20,000 articles to 3,741.

38 A Dice coefficient ranges between 0 and 1. It measures the number of word types in each text and the number of words present in both texts. A score like 0.41 can be thought of like a percentage, i.e., there's about a 41% overlap between the vocabularies of the two texts being compared.

39 This not to claim perfection. For example, we still get a letters page article of December 23, 2012, in the *Sunday Times*, which contains 5 letters. The first concerns pensions and inflation, the second complains about government taxes, the third is on renewable energy, the fourth is on disputed debts, and the fifth argues for cutting spending and selling off assets. Most of them concern the UK and money issues, but only one is really about austerity.

Table 2: UK Broadsheet articles 2007–2015 after clean-up and filter

Newspapers	Number of articles
The Independent, Independent on Sunday	526
Daily Telegraph, Sunday Telegraph	1,249
The Guardian, The Observer	1,187
The Times, Sunday Times	779

Source: own

2.3 Final corpus

As shown in table 2 above, there are 3,751 individual articles[40] which can be retrieved and studied. The 3.2-million-word corpus constructed with these cleaning up and filtering operations has 35 thousand word types, with an average sentence length of 25 words. The most frequent words are grammatical; the first few lexical words are OSBORNE, TAX, SPENDING and BUDGET.

The corpus exists in two formats. Corpus Linguistics tools find it straightforward to treat one file as equal to one text when computing text statistics and the single article texts are available for those purposes. However, it may be useful to generate any number of further sub-corpora using different criteria. The procedure for constructing sub-corpora can select from a list of publications or of authors, creating a sub-corpus organized so that all the texts belonging to the same day, month, or year are grouped together in one larger text. Moreover, each text will be dated[41] so that the operating system will recognize the date appropriately.

This second format we find more useful for time-line display. It gives us a reasonable degree of delicacy[42] in research covering a decade. We have 96 monthly texts, with one file each for the 96 different months covered after filtering, with one month's file (December 2012) holding as many as 188 articles. No articles met our criteria for May to August, November and December 2007, or January, April, June, July, December 2008, or January 2009. Thereafter all months were covered up to December 2015.

A plot of hits on the term »austerity« in our corpus of UK austerity as defined above shows that the amount of wording (grey shading) grows to a peak in 2013. Likewise, the number of articles per month starts low with only one to four until April 2009 (the first visible spike in figure 3 below); thereafter it varies considerably.

40 Plus a further 53 articles from *CITY A.M.* included by mistake in the filtered corpus.

41 If covering a date from January 1, 1970. The individual texts are so dated too.

42 Term borrowed from Halliday 1961 referring to the fine detail with which one might categorize linguistic features. For Halliday, language is a cline of lexico-grammar in which lexis is the most »delicate« level. In our case we distinguished 96 different months. 9 years would be less delicate in this sense; if we distinguished individual articles, we would have greater delicacy, but it would be harder to see time-line patterning.

Figure 3: Plot of term »austerity« in the corpus

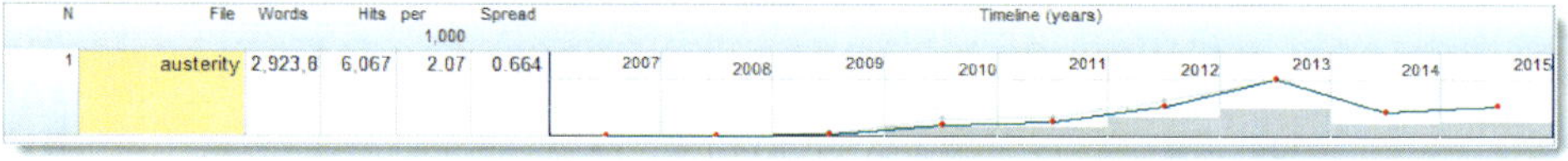

Source: own illustration

Figure 4: Number of articles per month

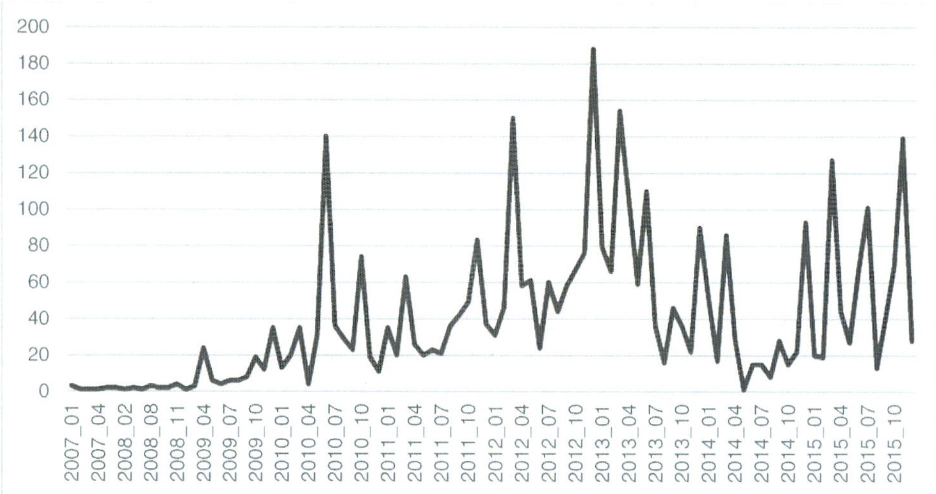

Source: own illustration

3. Results

3.1 The lexico-grammar of austerity

> *»The businesses I speak to have heard the language of austerity from ministers for three years but have not heard the language of optimism and growth nearly loud enough.« John Cridland, director-general of the CBI*[43]

The aim of this section is to discuss how austerity is discussed and presented in our corpus. In order to study it, a word list of the whole corpus was first generated; second, word-lists of each individual month.

First, the word list of the whole austerity corpus was compared with a general reference corpus (British National Corpus written text) in order to identify key words which characterize UK austerity (figure 5). These key words are mostly nouns. Some refer to chief agents who promote a policy of austerity; others refer to locations, time

43 Reported in Kathryn Cooper, »Where's the revival? Osborne ready to pass buck to Carney« in: *Sunday Times*, 17.3.2013.

periods, quantities. It is noticeable that many of these words, such as *Inflation*, *taxation*, *reduction*, *economy*, *deficit*, and *debt*, are abstractions. Austerity keeps company with processes such as increasing prices or making staff redundant, reified as abstract nouns.

Figure 5: Key words of UK austerity corpus

Source: own illustration

Figure 6: Two-word key clusters

N	Key word
1	THE CHANCELLOR
2	MR OSBORNE
3	GEORGE OSBORNE
4	THE ECONOMY
5	THE DEFICIT
6	SPENDING CUTS
7	THE TREASURY
8	THE OBR
9	THE BUDGET
10	THE COALITION
11	THE CHANCELLOR'S
12	PUBLIC FINANCES
13	THE GOVERNMENT
14	AUTUMN STATEMENT
15	DEFICIT REDUCTION

Source: own illustration

Top multi-word key clusters[44] were mostly 2 word forms starting with *the* (figure 6). But longer phraseologies, often referring to organizations, were also key: *Office for Budget Responsibility*, *The Bank of England*, *The Institute for Fiscal Studies*, *The UK economy*, *double dip recession*, etc.

What about the grammar of the word »austerity« itself? To study this, the nearly 7,000 instances of austerity were concordanced, and any collocates occurring at least 10 times were computed, as well as the statistical relation between each collocate and the term »austerity« in those instances. There are a number of statistics[45] which can be used to relate a term with its collocates. These measures use the frequency data of the term in the corpus, the frequency of the collocate in the corpus, and the number of times the term was found with the collocate within a given span (default 5 words to left and right of the search-term) and attempt to show which word-pairs are most as-

44 I.e. clusters of 2- to 5-word sequences found to occur significantly more in the austerity corpus than in the general reference corpus.

45 Dice, Mutual Information, MI3, Z scores, Log Likelihood, T scores, Log Ratio, as Scott explains.

sociated with each other based on these numbers. The words collocating with *austerity*, ordered by Z-score, can be found in table 3.

Table 3: Collocates of austerity (R1 = one word to the right of austerity, L2 = two words before austerity)

Collocate	Typical position
programme	R1
measures	R1
anti	L1
drive	R1
Government's	L1
age	L2
ease	L3
lite	R1
defeating	L1
relax	L2
years	L2
Coalition's	L1
Osborne's	L1
plans	R1

Source: own

Clearly, austerity is often followed by another noun as part of a noun phrase. The top ten R1 collocates in simple frequency order are *measures*, *programme*, *is*, *and*, *the*, *drive*, *in*, *plans*, *will*, and *to*. The open-class forms in those ten are nouns all with a similar meaning, a government policy; the others are mostly cases where austerity is a single head noun. In table 3 there is more of a mix of open-class forms, but the R1 nouns in table 3 are policy steps taken by L1 agents. We also see evidence of wider phraseology. There is pressure to *ease … austerity*:

Figure 7: Easing austerity

N	Concordance
1	we don't want the government to ease off on austerity. We want the government to
2	GEORGE OSBORNE must ease off on austerity to rescue growth and bring the
3	austerity; The Government must ease off on austerity to boost growth if the public finances
4	said as he vowed not to "ease up" on austerity. The state must be shrunk
5	has come under pressure ease back on austerity. The International Monetary Fund
6	about the need for governments to ease up on austerity, something Germany, Britain and
7	, while resisting pressure to ease his broader austerity programme.The Chancellor today
8	, while resisting pressure to ease his broader austerity programme.The Chancellor today
9	economy this year to ease the government's austerity programme.In an upbeat autumn
10	year he was urging Osborne to ease up on austerity or risk a double-dip recession.
11	that, if re-elected, Osborne will ease up on austerity. On the contrary. Chote, a journalist
12	there space for the Chancellor to ease off on austerity now? A. The short answer is no.
13	Ed Balls called on Mr Osborne to ease up on austerity measures in the hope of bolstering
14	Government has the headroom to ease up on austerity measures for the first time since
15	him to eliminate the deficit and ease up on austerity in five years' time." He added: "The
16	finance ministers. Ease off on austerity, IMF warns Chancellor George
17	moving." Britain must ease off on austerity, IMF warns; David Lipton, the
18	. George Osborne should ease off on austerity, IMF warns ABSTRACT International
19	too high for the government to ease up on austerity. He said he would support
20	, the chancellor, needed to ease up on austerity cuts in the face of a stagnant
21	into the next election vowing to ease up on austerity and take longer to wipe out the
22	woes". It wants the chancellor to ease off on austerity and focus more on jobs and spurs

Source: own illustration

Although an austerity programme can be eased transitively (lines 7–9), *austerity* mostly goes with the phrasal verb forms *ease off/up/back on*. Other verbs which belong with *austerity* are *abandon*, *defeat*, *relax*, *extend*, *protest*, *impose*, *pile on*, *fail*, *rethink*, *implement*, *urge*, *bite*, *increase*, and *preach*. *Increase*, *extend* and *implement* might be fairly unemotive, but the other verbs suggest negativity. There are no positive sounding collocates. Austerity is put forward as necessary with the phrase *stick to*, suggesting an unpleasant obligation: one sticks to piano lessons, a diet, or a course of antibiotics (figure 8).

Equally negative are most of the adjectives associated: *tough*, *harsh*, *fiscal*, *further*, *continuing*. The first two of these adjectives are explicitly negative: even its proponents do not relish austerity, of course. Some of the metaphor nouns are negative too. Someone usually specified will have to *bear the brunt* (figure 9), or they might be subjected to a kind of unpleasant medicine in the form of a *dose of austerity* (figure 10).

Figure 8: Stick to austerity

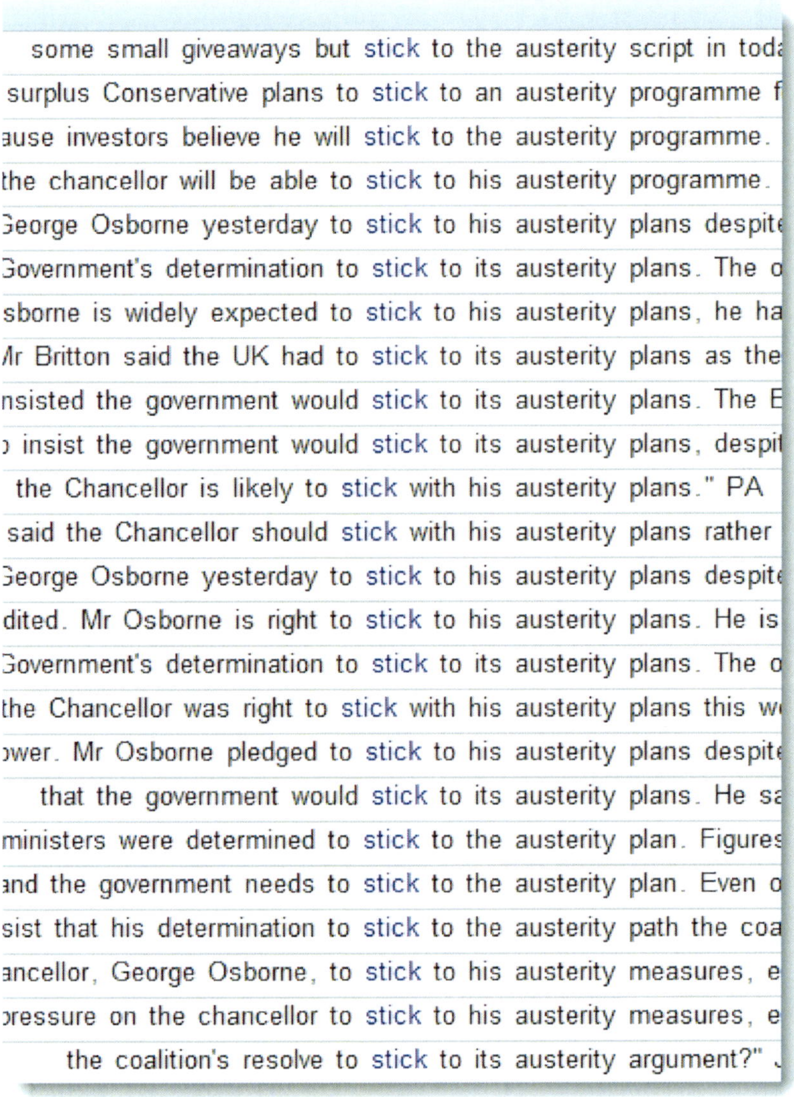

Source: own illustration

Figure 9: Bearing the brunt

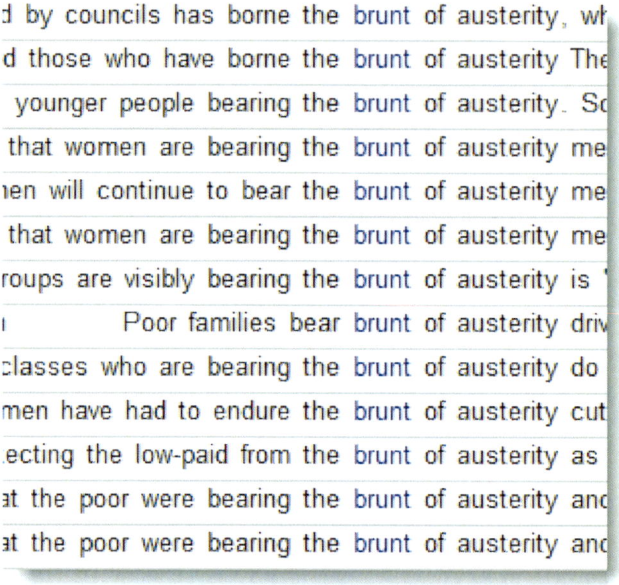
d by councils has borne the brunt of austerity, wh
d those who have borne the brunt of austerity The
younger people bearing the brunt of austerity. Sc
that women are bearing the brunt of austerity me
ıen will continue to bear the brunt of austerity me
that women are bearing the brunt of austerity me
roups are visibly bearing the brunt of austerity is
Poor families bear brunt of austerity driv
classes who are bearing the brunt of austerity do
men have had to endure the brunt of austerity cut
ecting the low-paid from the brunt of austerity as
at the poor were bearing the brunt of austerity and
at the poor were bearing the brunt of austerity and

Source: own illustration

Figure 10: Dose of austerity

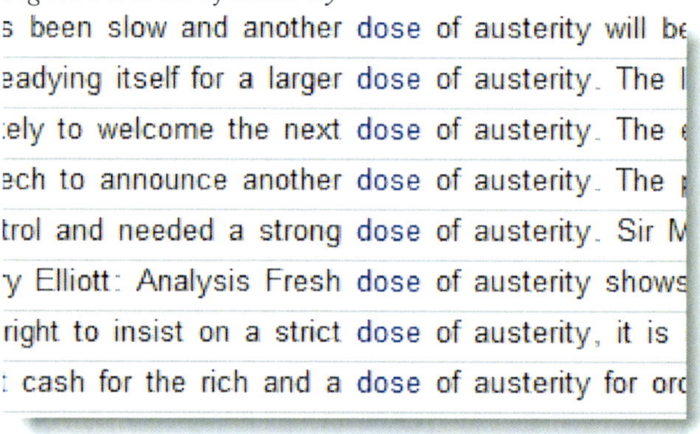
s been slow and another dose of austerity will be
eadying itself for a larger dose of austerity. The l
ely to welcome the next dose of austerity. The e
ech to announce another dose of austerity. The p
trol and needed a strong dose of austerity. Sir M
y Elliott: Analysis Fresh dose of austerity shows
right to insist on a strict dose of austerity, it is
cash for the rich and a dose of austerity for ord

Source: own illustration

To study the lexico-grammar of austerity one can also study the word clusters that it is found in. The topmost cluster was *the government's austerity*, very often part of a wider string:

Figure 11: The Government's austerity clusters

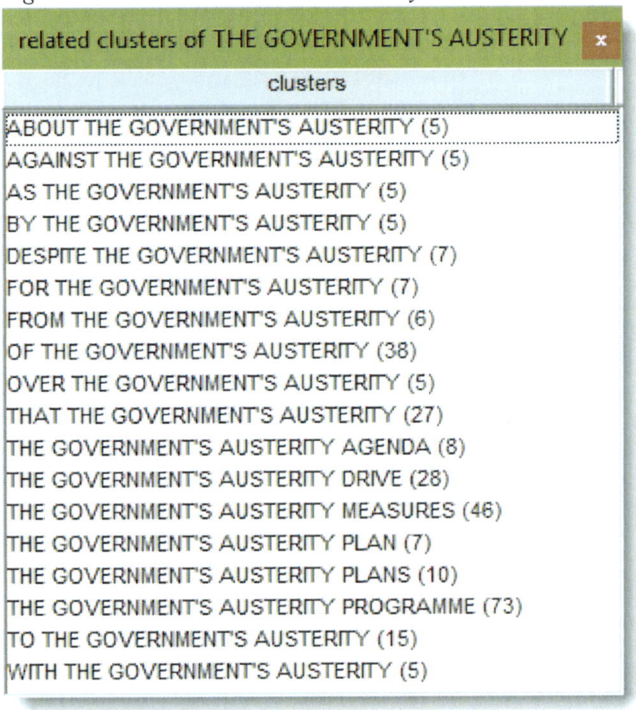

Source: own illustration

Immediately following were phrases including *years of austerity*, which cumulatively suggest an age of austerity. Austerity is thus presented as a process which goes on for a sometimes specific, but also for an extended, time period. This suggests it does not always work or at least finish on time.

Figure 12: Clusters related to years of austerity

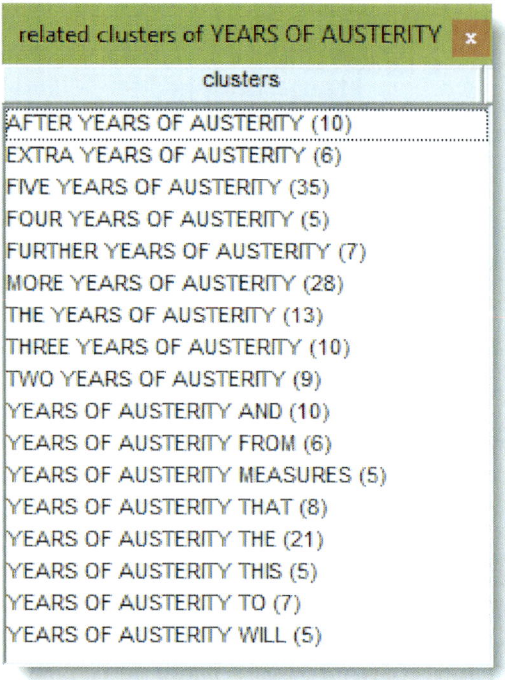

Source: own illustration

We have seen that austerity, while painted metaphorically in sombre colours and accompanied by negativity, is an abstract noun surrounded by further abstractness. One may wonder therefore: Does austerity ever get explained? To investigate this, contexts of *this austerity* were examined on the grounds that the anaphoric marker *this* plus a summary word is often used to encapsulate a previous explanation, as where an author after describing mishaps refers back to them as *the issue* or *this problem*. A *Guardian* leader article of 2010[46] provides an instance.

46 *The Guardian*, 25.8.2010; no byline.

Box 1: Austerity is cutting welfare

Now imagine your disability benefits inching up by 3% a year every year rather than 5%: within just a few years that leaves you with a big shortfall. This one fact puts in perspective the recent speculation about how Iain Duncan Smith is fighting for more generous welfare provision – a couple of billion extra does not offset the many billions being taken from society's support for the poorest. With full access to all the Treasury models, Mr Osborne will have known how much poorer he was about to make some of the most vulnerable members of society – yet he went ahead and did it anyway. *The ultimate political fact of this IFS analysis is that it deprives Mr Clegg and the Lib Dems of the fig leaf that they are the good angels in this coalition, guiding it towards progressive economic outcomes. Nor can they claim that* ***this austerity*** *is necessary. Indeed, evidence is mounting that* ***these swingeing cuts*** *leave the UK dangerously exposed to another downturn.*

Source: own illustration

Similarly a 2015 article[47] quoting a series of economists points out:

Box 2: Austerity is cutting public investment

Fiscal consolidation was introduced too early into the UK, especially in the 2010–11 and 2011–12 period. The cut of public investment by 40 per cent over this time period was the opposite of sensible macroeconomics. The OBR estimates that UK GDP was reduced by 2 per cent due to ***this austerity****.*

Source: own illustration

Finally we get a 2014 article[48] explaining austerity more jokily.

Box 3: Austerity is tightening our belts – and cutting taxes for the rich

You'll recall we have been living through a period of austerity. George Osborne has mentioned it quite a bit during his three and a half years as Chancellor: ›Hard choices‹, ›tightening our belts‹, ›all in this together‹. It's against this backdrop that the Tunics want him to show just how seriously he takes ***this austerity lark*** *by cutting taxes for rich people. Now, at this point it's important to insert a caveat. The Tunics don't say rich. They say ›people on middle incomes‹, which to them is people earning in the range 40,000 to 100,000.*

Source: own illustration

These extracts are used to remind readers that the otherwise abstract discussion often boils down to terms of effects on shortages, investments and welfare cuts.

3.2 Actors shaping the austerity discourse

We now turn to the question of who shapes the public discourse on austerity. Our aim was to identify claims makers in the news reports, either persons or organizations. We used the Stanford Named Entity Recognition (NER) software for this purpose. NER output for the monthly corpus included 425 people and 293 organizations, each mentioned at least 10 times in the set. Table 4 shows the top 40 in each category.

47 David Blanchflower in: *independent.co.uk*, 7.4.2015.
48 Dan Hodges in: *telegraph.co.uk*, 19.3.2014, pre-budget article.

*Table 4: Mentions of claims makers in the UK press: * denotes elected politician; + economic expertise, ^ independence*

Person	*Mentions*	*Organization*	*Mentions*
George Osborne*	18322	Labour Party	6165
David Cameron*	3176	Treasury	3879
Ed Miliband*	1525	Office for Budget Responsibility, OBR^	3513
Gordon Brown*	1397	Bank of England	2807
Ed Balls*	1359	International Monetary Fund, IMF	2116
Nick Clegg*	1041	Coalition	1121
Alistair Darling*	654	NHS	887
Mark Carney+	537	Office for National Statistics, ONS	777
Mervyn King+	532	Institute for Fiscal Studies, IFS^	571
Jeremy Corbyn*	440	BBC	526
Margaret Thatcher*	425	OECD	525
Paul Johnson+	437	Parliament	445
Danny Alexander*	358	CBI	391
Vince Cable*	340	SNP	376
Iain Duncan Smith*	330	MPC	329
Tony Blair*	272	The Times	214
Olivier Blanchard+	257	TUC	208
John McDonnell*	234	Cabinet	196
Christine Lagarde+	223	Capital Economics^	193
Barack Obama*	216	National Institute of Economic and Social Research, NIESR^	192
Boris Johnson*	192	AAA	183
Geoffrey Howe*	177	House of Commons	167
John Swinney*	174	Conservative Party	164
Kenneth Clarke*	165	Fitch	156
John Maynard Keynes+	165	Conservative	149
Robert Chote+	164	Moody	147
Paul Krugman+	110	RBS	113
Andrew Marr	106	National Insurance	108
Howard Archer+	105	European Union	106
Lord Lawson+	102	Resolution Foundation^	104
Chris Leslie*	101	Financial Times	102
John Cridland	101	British Chambers of Commerce	99
Theresa May*	100	HSBC	97
Angela Merkel*	94	Daily Telegraph	95
Francois Hollande*	94	BCC	93

Person	*Mentions*	*Organization*	*Mentions*
Peter Mandelson*	88	York Way	90
Michael Gove*	85	Google	90
John Major*	83	Lloyds	83
Janan Ganesh+	81	European Commission	74
Vicky Redwood+	60	House	74

Source: own

3.3 Austerity and expertise: individual actors

As our data shows, 30 out of 40 claims makers are elected politicians. George Osborne is by far the most visible claims maker on austerity in the British broadsheets. His previous roles include journalism and political speech writing, before becoming Shadow Chancellor of the Exchequer in 2005. Osborne is cited 6 times more frequently than David Cameron, the second on the list, and 10 times more frequently than Ed Miliband, Gordon Brown, Ed Balls, or Nick Clegg.

Figure 13: Most visible actors

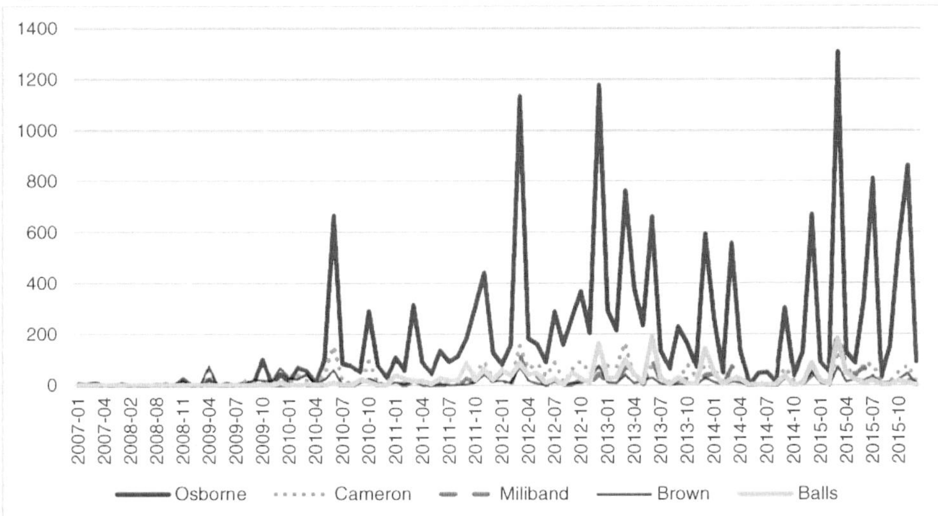

Source: own illustration

There are some highly visible persons who have expertise in the field of economics, with different roles in different organizations. The most visible is Paul Johnson, who has been Director of the IFS since 2011. He was a Member of the Economic and Social Research Council (ESRC), and Visiting Professor in the Economics department of University College London since 2013.

Olivier Blanchard was the chief economist at the International Monetary Fund, from September 1, 2008, to October 2015. He is also the Robert M. Solow Professor of Economics at MIT. Robert Chote is a British economist who started his career in journalism, then became the director of the Institute of Fiscal Studies in 2002. In October 2010, he was appointed chairman of the newly established Office for Budget Responsibility. The person with the highest reputation as economic expert is Paul Krugman, Nobel Prize winner in economics and columnist for the *New York Times*. We note that John Maynard Keynes is also on the list. The most visible non-elected politician is Christine Lagarde, who has been managing director of the IMF since July 2011, after several stints in French government (including the portfolio of Economic Affairs, Finance and Employment).

This list indicates to which extent the discourse on austerity is centred around politicians instead of economic experts. Those few that have economic expertise are also involved or have been involved with politics. Additionally, several economic experts have full-time jobs as journalists, writing for newspapers. Journalism seems to be a springboard for would-be politicians, most prominently in the case of George Osborne, who has been described as »A man with a plan.«[49]

George Osborne came to office well prepared. Before his appointment to the position as Chancellor he laid out his views on economic and financial policy in a speech in February 2010, The Mais Lecture. In it, he made a rare allusion to academic research, albeit to the later discredited work by two American economists:

> *»As Rogoff and Reinhart demonstrate convincingly, all financial crises ultimately have their origins in one thing – rapid and unsustainable increases in debt. As Ken Rogoff himself puts it, ›there's no question that the most significant vulnerability as we emerge from recession is the soaring government debt. It's very likely that will trigger the next crisis as governments have been stretched so wide.‹ The latest research suggests that once debt reaches more than about 90% of GDP the risks of a large negative impact on long term growth become highly significant.«*[50]

In this speech Osborne lays out the plan for the establishment of the OBR. He argued that »there is growing support for the concept of fiscal councils that can bring independent and forward-looking scrutiny to bear on governments... These powerful arguments, and the steady erosion of public trust in official forecasts, lie behind our proposals for an independent Office for Budget Responsibility.«

According to Osborne, the main reason for the establishment of the OBR is to restore trust through independence. One can imagine how valuable this new body would be if it was at the same time beholden to the aims and goals of the Treasury. It is inter-

49 Corpus Linguistics is a powerful tool to find language patterns in large databases of published text. It cannot tell us, however, what was going on behind the scenes. We therefore briefly look at the way Osborne was working when in office.

50 Gorge Osborne, »Speech by George Osborne on 24.2.2010«, http://conservative-speeches.sayit.mysociety.org/speech/601526 [16.7.2017]; John Cassidy, »The Reinhart and Rogoff Controversy: A Summing up« in: *New Yorker*, 26.4.2014, http://www.newyorker.com/news/john-cassidy/the-reinhart-and-rogoff-controversy-a-summing-up [16.7.2017].

esting to note that in this speech Osborne does not use the term »austerity«. The first occurrence of the term in our corpus is in January 2007 in an article about the political reactions to the IFS's Green Budget report for 2007. While journalists regularly refer to austerity to describe cuts and policies, politicians are more reluctant to use the term in their statements. Osborne did refer to an »age of austerity« for the UK in several speeches during 2009. Particularly noteworthy is a comparison of when he uses the phrase. He mentioned the »age of austerity« in a speech to the think tank Demos in August 2009, just two months before announcing wide-reaching cuts during the much publicized Tory conference in Manchester: there he refrained from using the same phrase.

Normally cabinet ministers have two special advisors, but the Treasury seems to be an exception. Gordon Brown had eleven, costing £1m (*The Telegraph*, February 21, 2007). Osborne had nine special advisors, with a preponderance of those being PR advisors.

> *»Thea Rogers, formerly Nick Robinson's producer at the BBC, who is the Chancellor's chief of staff; James Chapman, the ex-political editor of the Daily Mail, director of communications;*
> *Sue Beeby, political press officer; Simon Glasson, who handles party matters; Matt Cook, events organiser;*
> *Lisa Buckland.*
> *In addition, three special advisers are members of the Council of Economic Advisers: Richard Davies, former economics editor of The Economist, who is Mr Osborne's main economic adviser and chairs the council;*
> *Jennifer Donnellan, formerly of the Conservative Research Department;*
> *Neil O'Brien, formerly of the Policy Exchange think-tank, who is credited with the Northern Powerhouse policy.«*[51]

Richard Davies, a former economics editor at the *Economist*, seems to be the only economics expert in Osborne's team. The sheer number of PR advisors may explain his visibility in the press. It may also explain the use of pithy images and phrases with which to blame the economic situation on Labour, such as »unsustainable levels of debt« inherited from Labour; »irresponsible« or »reckless« economic behaviour; or Labour »maxing out the credit card«. The idea of a long-term economic plan (n = 101) by the Conservatives and the images of »rebalancing the economy« (n = 213) and of »fixing the roof while the sun is shining« (n = 57) seem to have particularly resonated with journalists.

51 John Rentoul, »George Osborne: Chancellor has five times the usual number of special advisers« in: *The Independent*, 31.10.2015.

3.4 Austerity and expertise: organizations

News reports not only quote persons but also organizations. The most visible organization is the Labour party, followed by the Treasury, the OBR, the Bank of England, and the IMF.

Figure 14: Most visible organizations

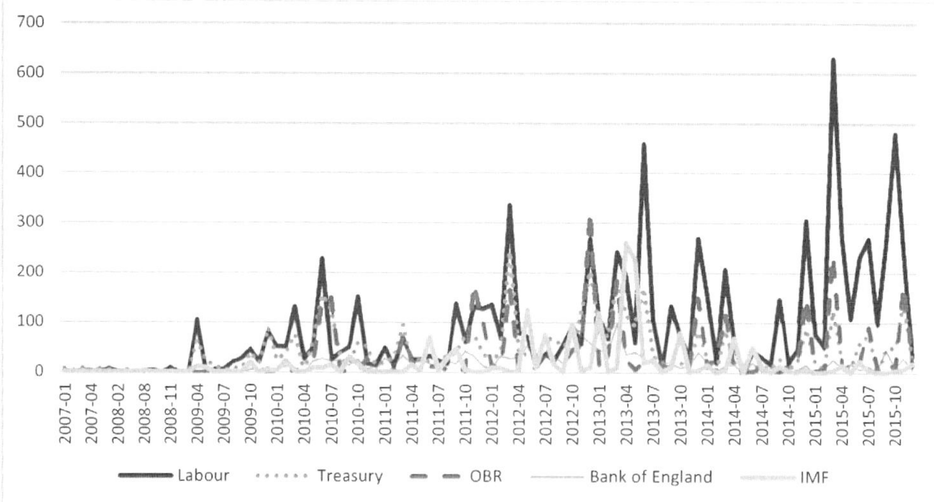

Source: own illustration

In March 2012, December 2012 and March 2015, Labour, the Treasury, and OBR show a common peak. These are the months during which also the main protagonists Osborne, Cameron, Miliband, Brown, and Balls show a peak. These are all months during which the Chancellor announced the Budget (March) or made the so-called Autumn statement (December 2012). There is a lone peak for Labour in June 2013 (*The Telegraph* has a headline on June 3, saying »Labour will work within George Osborne's spending plans, Ed Balls says«). This indicates that Labour eventually came to accept budget cuts as proposed by Osborne.

What does the press report about the Labour party? What are the topics that make it the most visible organization in our corpus? To answer these questions, we extracted the top 10 collocates of *Labour*, ordered by Z score and frequency of occurrence. As figure 15 shows, much of Labour's attention was devoted to its leadership issues.

Figure 15: Collocates of Labour

N	Word
1	LABOUR
2	LEADER
3	PARTY
4	LEADERSHIP
5	MPS
6	MP
7	SEIZED
8	CORBYN
9	UNDER
10	MILIBAND
11	ED

Source: own illustration

Figure 16: Timeline of Labour

Source: own illustration

The timeline in figure 16 shows grey blocks and a grey line for the amount of text during the period; the green line shows the amount on Labour specifically. There are some organizations that are objects of the discourse and whose fate will be affected by austerity measures, such as the NHS. The picture for the NHS is quite complex when looking at collocates and concordances. It's supposed to be protected and »ring-fenced« from spending, but those collocates only start to crop up more frequently in 2013, probably in preparation for elections.

Many other organizations, apart from government organs, may be affected by austerity but can be seen as trying to actively influence it: Parliament, CBI, SNP, MPC, *The Times*, TUC, etc. Economic expertise resides in the Treasury, but also in organizations such as OBR, Bank of England, IMF, IFS, OECD, Moody, Fitch, RBS, etc. In many cases this expertise is tied to an economic or political self-interest. The question arises which of these organizations are presented as providing impartial expertise. In table 4 we have identified five potentially relevant organizations.

First, the OBR, founded in 2010, shortly after the Conservative-Liberal Coalition came to power. It has an annual budget of about £2m. One of its tasks is to produce economic forecasts: in this process the OBR consults and agrees with three government departments, the Treasury, DWP, and HMRC, on the scope, timetable, and process for delivery of the forecast. It is supposed to be independent and transparent, but is it? Here is an assessment of its independence by Clive Cook in the *Financial Times*:

> *»The body – now established on an interim basis – is a Whitehall beast. Sir Alan Budd, OBR chief pro tem, leads a team of Treasury lifers, based in the Treasury, running Treasury models. This is all forgivable: the apparatus was set up rapidly and has yet to find its feet. It is important, however, that it does not become a permanent feature of the OBR. The most important aspect of the institution's independence is staffing. OBR staff cannot be borrowed from the chancellor, going back to the Treasury at the end of a stint at the slide-rule. Otherwise they will still be creatures of their political masters. The OBR needs its own recruitment stream.«*[52]

This was written in the early days of OBR. On February 22, 2016, *The Independent* reported on interference from the Treasury, allegedly asking for changes to aspects of language or presentation of the OBR's Economic Outlook. A parliamentary inquiry found that »officials removed key words used by the fiscal watchdog to describe spending cuts... The Treasury is allowed to fact-check OBR documents before release for ›quality assurance‹ but is not supposed to try to spin their presentation.«

The ONS does not provide economic advice, only statistical data. Nevertheless, this task has been mired in controversy and lack of credibility. In order to restore public trust in its working, former Chancellor Gordon Brown announced in 2005 that the ONS should become independent of government. However, the Statistics and Registration Service Act 2007 did not provide such independence as its status is described »to exercise its functions on behalf of the Crown.«

Second, the IFS, founded in 1969, officially politically independent. However, it has been suggested that it is politically left leaning, which prompted Osborne to establish the OBR, as a counterpart to IFS, inside government: »Fraser Nelson, the editor of the Spectator, suggests that the motivation behind Osborne's decision to create the OBR was to dent the public profile of the IFS, which many conservatives felt skewed left-

52 Chris Cook, »Is the OBR really independent« in: *Financial Times*, 20.6.2010.

wards, owing to the perceived tendency of British academic economists to favour big government and big spending.«[53]

Third, Capital Economics, a research consultancy firm. Its managing director, Roger Bootle, was an economist at the HSBC group. He has a weekly column in the *Daily Telegraph*. This indicates a political bias towards right wing and conservative policies.

Fourth, the National Institute of Economic and Social Research (NIESR), established in 1938 and claiming to be Britain's longest established independent economic research institute and think tank. It says it is »independent of all party political interests, and receives no core funding from government or other sources.« It is not affiliated to any single university, »although staff regularly undertake projects in collaboration with leading academic institutions. Funding is received through commissioned research projects from a variety of sources: government departments and agencies, the research councils, particularly the Economic and Social Research Council, the European Commission, charitable foundations, and the private sector.«[54] From the list of organizations in the business of economic expertise it would be the closest to one driven by an academically oriented research orientation.

Fifth, the Resolution Foundation, a »non-partisan and award-winning think-tank« that works to improve the living standards of those in Britain on low to middle incomes. Its executive chairman is David Willets, former minister for universities and science, 2010–2014.

Of these organizations providing economic expertise and being potentially independent (leaving aside the Bank of England), only the IFS and OBR have visible claims makers in the newspapers, Paul Johnson and Robert Chote. Osborne's decision to set up OBR as a new advisory body within government, with the aim to describe it as »independent«, has been successful. It is the most cited organization providing economic expertise and commentary. The IFS is far less visible, and NIESR pales in comparison.

Based on our corpus we tried to establish what these claims makers were saying in press publications. In order to do so, we specifically analysed collocations in which the top five claims makers (persons and organizations) appeared. We extracted the top collocations, sorted according to Z score (with a threshold above 5.0) and frequency. We distinguish between noun and verb collocates.

53 Simon Akam, »The British umpire: how the IFS became the most influential voice in the economic debate« in: *The Guardian*, 15.3.2016.

54 National Institute of Economic and Social Research, http://www.niesr.ac.uk/about-us [15.7.2017].

Table 5: Noun collocates of the five most frequently named people

Person	*Noun Collocates*
George Osborne	chancellor, david, cameron, captions, text, autumn, statement
David Cameron	george, nick, osborne, prime, clegg, quad
Ed Miliband	leader, balls, labour, joke, david, cameron
Gordon Brown	tony, blair, alistair, lawson, darling, lamont
Ed Balls	shadow, chancellor, miliband, ed, marr, labour's

Source: own

Table 6: Verb collocates of the five most frequently named people

Person	*Verb Collocates*
George Osborne	announced, unveiled & unveils, delivers, prepares, introduces, urged
David Cameron	vetoed, pledged, promised, accused, ruled, hinted
Ed Miliband	accused, attacked, tried, claims
Gordon Brown	used, introduced, was, proud, did, tried
Ed Balls	said, interviews, vindicated, described, attacked, accused

Source: own

Table 7: Noun collocates of the five most frequently named organizations

Organization	*Noun collocates*
Labour	labour, leader, party, leadership, MPs & MP, Corbyn
Treasury	treasury, spokesman, secretary, chief, committee, officials
OBR	obr, responsibility, office, forecasts & forecast, chote, budget
Bank of England	governor, king, mervyn, policymaker, carney, setter
IMF	christine, lagarde, olivier, fund, report, washington

Source: own

Table 8: Verb collocates of the five most frequently named organizations

Organization	Verb collocates
Labour	seized, inherited, accused & accusing, trusted, demoralised, claims
Treasury	select, said, transferred, estimates, insisted, entering
OBR	revise, predicted, according, said, downgraded, expected
Bank of England	incoming, restart, easing, pump, rates, printing
IMF	managing, said, urged, arrives, warns, tells

Source: own

The results indicate an interesting contrast between Gordon Brown, the Chancellor in the period 2007–2010, and his successor George Osborne. While Brown's collocations point to other Labour politicians, Osborne's indicate initiative, partly associated with the preparation of the autumn/March statements. Ed Balls and Ed Miliband *accused* and *attacked* the government, whereas Cameron *vetoed*, *pledged* and *promised*. He also *accused* the opposition. Compared to the other politicians, Osborne seems to be above the fray.

The most frequent collocates for the Treasury are linked to Danny Alexander who was its chief secretary. The OBR's *forecasts* show up as expected, and Mr *Chote*, but also its *responsibility* is a topic. The Bank of England is associated with its *governors*, and the IMF with its *managing director Lagarde* and chief economist *Blanchard*.

The Labour Party seems to be inward looking and occupied with its leadership crisis. It is represented in the press as part of the cause of the fiscal crisis: the Conservative government has *inherited* the debts and deficits from Labour. Most of the actions in the form of verbs collocating with Labour are relatively spread out over the corpus data and are not concentrated during a particular time period. The image of Labour *accusing* the government, being the actual progenitors of the debt crisis, and that they »cannot be trusted on the economy« is ever present. Labour is characterized in 2011 and 2015 as a *demoralized* party that could »scarcely oppose« the Conservatives. An interesting case is the collocate *claims*, which expressly posits Labour as a claims maker and which can function as both a noun and a verb. It is typically used in our data as a verb, with Labour making claims in reference to the plans and actions of the Tory government, most frequently during 2015. Labour is here reacting instead of providing alternatives. Their role as the opposition is limited to straightforward opposing and accusing. Furthermore, phrases such as »undermining claims by Labour« or »despite claims by Labour« indicate that their claims are rebutted or not taken seriously.

Because of the close link between knowledge and self-interest, much expertise runs the danger of being dismissed as mere »lobbying«. It is an essential trait of credible expertise to be able to claim independence, and to be seen, by relevant stakeholders in public discourse, as independent. As the history of ONS, IFS, and OBR indicates, this is contested. The OBR is an especially interesting case as it was established by George Osborne, with the official aim to provide »independent advice«. However, as a parliamentary hearing has established, the Treasury violated its independence on at least one occasion.

To sum up this section, one could conclude that the visibility and status of key actors indicates their influence in policy making. However, there is a paradox: George Osborne is the most frequently mentioned actor in the press and Labour the most frequently mentioned organization. Labour, as opposition party, did not have the power to introduce new policies. It could have made proposals that put government under pressure, presenting reports and alternatives, something that did not happen. So it saw its role to attack and accuse the government and to find a new leader.

4. Discussion

The austerity discourse in Britain is closely linked to the role of George Osborne and the Labour party. The Chancellor of the Exchequer has a powerful role in government, and the annual confirmation of his budget establishes the operating licence for government. But the office alone does not lead to high visibility in the press. Osborne got much higher press attention than his predecessor. The Labour party as main opposition party in Westminster tried to challenge his policy but failed. Most of the press attention to Labour was about its alleged responsibility for causing the budget deficit and about its own leadership problems.

In their classical study on the discourse on nuclear power, Gamson and Modigliani had this to say about the relation between discourse and policy making:

> *»Public discourse is carried on in many different forums. Rather than a single public discourse, it is more useful to think of a set of discourses that interact in complex ways [...] there is the specialist's discourse using journals and other print media aimed at those whose professional lives involve them in the issue. There is the largely oral discourse used by officials who are directly involved in decision-making roles on the issue and by those who attempt to influence them. There is the challenger discourse, providing packages that are intended to mobilize their audiences for some form of collective action. General audience media, then, are only some of the forums for public discourse on an issue. If one is interested in predicting policy outcomes, they are not necessarily the most important forums. But if one is interested in public opinion, then media discourse dominates the larger issue culture, both reflecting it and contributing to its creation. Journalists may draw their ideas and language from [...] other forums, frequently paraphrasing or quoting their sources. At the same time, they contribute their own frames and invent their own clever catchphrases, drawing on a popular culture that they share with their audience.«*[55]

This highlights an interesting lesson for our combined framework of discourse analysis and political science approaches. Journalists seem to have taken up Osborne's »clever catchphrases« without developing many of their own. The framing of an issue matters; it was Osborne and his team who came up with diagnoses of the problem, the attribution of causes and blame, and the development of policy alternatives. The institutional resources available to him and the use of political rhetoric were decisive. These resources were the establishment of an advisory team with ample experience in the media landscape of Britain; the setting up of the OBR as an ostensibly independent body, supporting his policies; the majority in parliament as part of the liberal conservative coalition (and latterly with a much reduced majority as part of a conservative government); and the deployment of austerity policy as a necessary measure, a bitter medicine, to restore trust of financial markets and business enterprises. In addition, he

55 William A. Gamson / André Modigliani, »Media Discourse and Public Opinion on Nuclear Power: A Constructionist Approach« in: *American Journal of Sociology* 95, No. 1 (1989), pp. 1–37, pp. 2–3.

was able to tap into a public mood which had previous experience with unpleasant austerity measures after WWII that were seen as necessary. This post-war experience may have left a lasting impression on the national psyche.

The challenger discourse mentioned by Gamson and Modigliani did not show prominently in our data. There was no highly visible anti-austerity movement, and Labour restricted itself to challenging Osborne and the government through normal political forums. Rallies and marches have been used by politicians in the past as means of political participation apart from normal political forums, but also as a tool to increase support amongst the electorate. Concordances of the words *rally* and *demonstration* show limited to no involvement of Labour politicians in the anti-austerity marches in March 2011, October 2012, and March 2013. An exception is the rally organized by the People's Assembly Against Austerity in June 2015. Jeremy Corbyn, among few other Labour politicians, attended the rally, gave a speech, and was consequently supported by the People's Assembly in his bid for the Labour leadership. This public stance and form of challenger discourse against austerity may in part have helped Corbyn to become elected as the Labour leader.

Our analysis partly confirms previous findings in the literature. Fairclough's finding that the press »validates the government's framing of the crisis as one of state overspending« seems to be borne out by our data. We also confirm Pririe's suggestions about »the failure of the Labour party to offer a clear and compelling alternative« and his claim that there is a vast gulf between the dominant media and academic debates concerning the economic crisis, and that the popular media is dominated by »a narrative of crisis almost completely lacking in any form of intellectual support«.

However, we provide a more nuanced analysis of the coverage of austerity which provides metaphors linked to medicine and disciplinary measures. It also reveals the structure of the discourse in terms of visible actors, both on the level of individuals and organizations. We concur with Berry that politicians are more often cited as experts and that »some of the strongest advocates of neoliberalism in the press were key in defining and managing the crisis.« But we only partly agree with his finding that these experts include the Bank of England, IMF, OECD, the Adam Smith Institute, and right-wing think tanks such as the Policy Exchange and the Taxpayers Alliance. As our analysis shows, the main organizations shaping the discourse were the OBR, the Bank of England, the IMF, and the IFS. The absence of the Adam Smith Institute and other right-wing think tanks could be due to the different sample, as Berry analysed four tabloids but only two broadsheets. Perhaps most importantly, our analysis shows what importance one central actor had in this discourse.

The absence of a counter-frame and the absence or low visibility of credible voices, including independent research outfits, may have contributed to Osborne's dominance. He came to power with a clear plan of how to persuade the British press, and the British public, of his austerity policy. The defeated Labour party did not rise to the task, and there was no alternative discourse emerging in the left leaning press.

There is a prevalence of political voices in the discourse we analysed, and a relatively low visibility of independent expertise and of the political left. The Labour Party is the most frequently mentioned organization because of its leadership crisis, not because of its proposals regarding austerity. Expertise based on academic research is virtually absent. Perhaps this is due to a mixture between low levels of advocacy of economists and other social scientists, combined with a media bias of the British press to give prominence to non-academic sources, following a tradition of anti-intellectualism. And it may be due to Labour's defeat in the general election of 2010, from which it did not recover. Labour certainly failed to develop a counter narrative that opposed Osborne's message about the need to swallow bitter medicine. Be that as it may, Osborne and Treasury PR spin doctors have developed a narrative which defined the policy alternatives. An important role was played by the newly established OBR with its alleged independence. This was Osborne's brainchild, and, together with his team of experienced spin doctors, he was an expert in using its reports to legitimize his policy proposals.

5. *Limitations*

Our aim was to build a corpus that is a true reflection of the available data from a news archive. By this we mean that we wanted to include *all* stories that deal with austerity in the UK, and *only* stories that deal with austerity in the UK. The challenge was to develop a filtering routine that does the job. We think we have made an important innovation in this regard. Nevertheless, there are limitations which still need to be addressed. The Parser programme has grown over the past five years or so; it will continue to develop as necessary. Most of the objectives set out in the Method and Data section where it was presented have been met, but there are still improvements to be made.

The filter for duplicate articles (objective 3) needs to be improved as and when better means of getting at discourse meaning become available; moreover, the issue of comments needs to be addressed because of the growing amount of online publication with comments included in the database output. These are the new voices, not the established journalist, sub-editors, and editors, but voices who are not on the payroll and for which the publication is only partly responsible. They are also clearly variable in quality, language, and tone. This is not to reject a corpus which contains them, but ideally such sections should be identified and marked up explicitly.

Another limitation is our focus on selected UK broadsheets. Our results do not allow us to generalize to other newspapers, or to other forms of media. However, given the towering visibility of some actors, it would be highly unlikely for this result to be invalidated by a different sample. We do not know what language patterns other media outlets would have shown. We would speculate that less quality media would have even less input from journalists and would repeat prefabricated statements. This is a task for further research.

Filtering out texts which make merely partial or peripheral mention of austerity can be argued to risk downplaying some of the language of austerity which comes from peripheral mentions. Costas Gabrielatos (personal communication) argues that these mentions »reveal a) acceptance of the term's prosodies/discourses (even outside the particular topic) and/or b) the extent to which such uses/prosodies/discourses have become conventionalized and entrenched in a wide variety of topics/discourses.« Thus he points out that the Mandelson article links »far-left activists with their latter-day equivalents in the anti-austerity and other activist movements« and young activists today, while saying that »confronting inequalities and extreme austerity with an equally potent response seems not only right but also contemporary«, thus twice relating austerity to extremism as well as inequality, confrontation, and youth.

In terms of Corpus Linguistics, our corpus with less than 4,000 articles and 3.2 million words is quite small. In comparison with other work not relying on corpus methods, it is a huge corpus, too big to read and digest fully. Our aim was to get into the text trying to winkle out patternings of discourse and meaning, identifying chief players and how they get represented in UK broadsheet press. As we have shown above, there is a fundamental difficulty in getting at meaning by simply observing words in text without taking into account the wider context, reading and interpreting relevant sources. To get an even better grasp on the issue, one would need to develop a case study methodology, including not only news archives but interviews with relevant voices in British society.

6. Conclusion

Despite these limitations we want to highlight three points: First, we have made a serious attempt to construct a valid corpus on the discourse of austerity in the UK broadsheets, as available in the LexisNexis database. To do that required a mix of corpus analysis and manual inspection in an iterative process of refinement. As a result, we can offer a new method of potential interest to the numerous researchers who carry out meaning-oriented investigations using databases such as LexisNexis.

Second, in terms of determining the actors shaping the discourse on austerity, we have demonstrated how corpus analysis can identify relevant actors and their narratives. This goes beyond existing scholarship on the austerity discourse in Britain. Based on our methodology, we offer a way of getting beyond the linguistic patternings of grammar and phraseology. These illustrate a phenomenon which has causes and agents who can be tracked.

Third, we need to emphasize that salience in the news discourse does not necessarily translate into political influence, as we have seen clearly with the Labour party. The power relations between government and opposition are a major structural determinant. But these relations need not be stable over time. In parliamentary democracies, power needs to affirm itself through the definitions of alternatives. These definitions are embedded in narratives that are intended to appeal to the public. In turn, the detail of causes of austerity, of agents implementing austerity, and of citizens experiencing it, but also how they operate and react at different moments over recent years can be shown by these linguistic patternings and fitted into a wider political narrative.[56]

56 We are grateful to Costas Gabrielatos and Carmen Dayrell for their comments on a draft of this text.

Klaus Gretschmann

The Austerity-Prosperity Controversy: Cutbacks Between Necessities and Fallacies

1. Austerity: old debate and new dispute

The »ideological« discussion about the right size of the government sector as compared to the private market economy as well as about the sustainability of taxation and public debt goes back a long time in the history of economic thought.[1] Even though subject of a long and persistent debate among scholars of public finance and macroeconomics, it was the international economic and financial crisis of 2007/2008 and the following years that has brought the politics of fiscal management, retrenchment and austerity to the forefront of a harsh economic and political debate.

Looking further back in history, ideas and theories about the economics of austerity as well as concerns about overly high levels of government activity and debt produced in the 1920s the so-called »Treasury view«, viz. that government deficits are economically damaging and austerity is required to control and constrain them. During the 1930s' Great Depression, this view was challenged by the »Keynesian approach«, namely that government deficit spending could be economically necessary during a slump, as the private sector could not activate sufficient effective demand to keep the economy going. Another swing of the pendulum of arguments occurred during the »stagflation« crises of the 1970s, when government stimulus proved ineffective with regard to growth and at the same time produced unintended inflationary side-effects. Eventually, the politics of fiscal consolidation was salient yet again during the 1980s and 1990s, notably when countries in Europe were eager and striving for eligibility for membership of the Economic and Monetary Union, involving the euro, by means of fulfilling the well-known convergence criteria.[2]

However, the debate about fiscal consolidation in the wake of the economic crisis that began in 2008 is an entirely different story both in quality and significance.[3] The choice between fiscal stimulus and fiscal consolidation was considered a trade-off. Whilst fiscal retrenchment was the tall order of the day for some economists and politicians, for others it was the very source of serious trouble and a self-defeating strategy. Economists such as Eichengreen, O'Rourke and others maintained that a much larger

1 Alain Parguez, »The Fundamental and Eternal Conflict: Hayek and Keynes on Austerity« in: *International Journal of Political Economy* 41, No. 4 (2013), pp. 54–68.

2 Klaus Gretschmann, *Economic and Monetary Union: Implications for National Policy Makers*, Dordrecht 1993.

3 Sebastian Dellepiane / Niamh Hardiman, *The New Politics of Austerity: Fiscal Responses to the Economic Crisis in Ireland and Spain*, UCD Geary Institute Discussion Paper Series No. 7, 2012.

fiscal stimulus would have been required to cope with the crisis, notably in Europe, whereas economists such as Barro argued for the contrary.[4]

As the sovereign debt crisis results from crises in banking, currency, balance of payments, and economic trust and confidence and led to a crisis of financial capitalism. In this situation, the unprecedented and paramount, even perhaps sky-rocketing, importance of alternative concepts of economic policy-making such as austerity are by no means a surprise. No wonder that austerity moved from an instrument in the toolkit of economic policy makers to the very objective itself – demanded by actors in the international financial markets as evidence that governments are serious about managing their deficits and paying back their debts, thereby protecting the financial interests of investors in sovereign debt. The catalyst for austerity was the Greek sovereign debt crisis. Fears of a possible Greek default raised concerns about the ability of other weak Eurozone countries to manage their deficits. However, critics often used morality rather than economic arguments and attributed the crisis primarily to a lack of fiscal discipline in the profligate southern states.

As a matter of fact, public debt was to a large extent a result of financial disruption and of the rescue operations of governments *vis à vis* their banking and financial institutions. Consequently, both in theoretical economics and in practical policy-making there was a sharp U-turn as calls for fiscal austerity clearly replaced stimulus as the one and only recipe. Notably the morality camp was inclined to see austerity measures and stricter fiscal discipline as the solution.

As Konzelmann so distinctly put it: »Thus, what had begun as a private debt crisis morphed into a European sovereign debt crisis; and in an effort to calm the bond markets [...]. This effectively shifted the burden of the crisis from the private (financial) sector to the state.«[5] This further contributed to a deepening of the crisis, because we know from several studies that fiscal stabilization is more problematic where there is also a problem of financial sector indebtedness.[6]

2. *What about austerity: curtailing the public sector or just coping with debt?*

Austerity is a concept that has proved difficult to either define formally or to measure properly. Typically, it refers to a substantial fiscal adjustment measured against any government performance indicator.

Austerity has been defined in a broader version as follows: »Austerity measures refer to official actions taken by the government, during a period of adverse economic

4 Barry Eichengreen / Kevin O'Rourke, »A Tale of Two Depressions« in: *VOX. CEPR's Policy Portal*, 8.3.2010, http://www.voxeu.org/index.php?q=node/3421 [12.6.2016]; Robert J. Barro, »Rare Disasters, Asset Prices, and Welfare Costs« in: *American Economic Review* 99, No. 1 (2009), pp. 243–264.

5 Suzanne Konzelmann, *The Economics of Austerity*, 1.6.2012, https://ssrn.com/abstract=2127567 [16.6.2017].

6 Olivier Blanchard / Carlo Cotarelli, »Ten Commandments for Fiscal Adjustment in Advanced Economies« in: *IMF Blog*, 24.6.2010, https://blog-imfdirect.imf.org/2010/06/24/ten-commandments-for-fiscal-adjustment-in-advanced-economies/ [3.7.2017].

conditions, to reduce its budget deficit using a combination of spending cuts or tax rises.«[7] While definitions vary slightly, there are some common elements: Austerity describes decisions made by the government with the aim of reducing the amount of government borrowing, or cutting the size of the fiscal deficit, over a given time period adjusting for effects of the economic cycle. Austerity is implemented by cuts in government spending such as welfare caps, wage moderation, defence expenditure and an increase in taxes. All of these often come under the heading of »sound public finance«. A narrower version is focused on debt and deficits exclusively (see section 2.1 below).

However, the very notion of austerity is murky and multi-dimensional to say the least. One could even talk about multiple austerities: Savings policy, budget consolidation, deflationary policy, restrictive incomes and labour market policy are often used as synonyms meant to define and delineate the overall context of the debate. In political terms, the notion of austerity has become a political weapon on the discursive battlefield of legitimizing economic policy concepts, such as de-leveraging on the one hand and compensatory finance on the other hand.

Fiscal conservatives argue that a deficit reduction and balancing of budgets through a fiscal austerity programme will help maintain a country's international credit rating as well as improving confidence among domestic and foreign investors, thus encouraging an inflow of capital which could result in an increase in aggregate demand and aggregate supply (economic growth). The maintenance of a good credit rating should lower interest rates on bonds.

If a nation faces ever-mounting debt, this development could make investors nervous and prevent them from buying the country's currency. So, as a nation can help push interest rates lower by getting its fiscal house in order, it alleviates concerns that it might default on its debt.

If nations can't get their budget deficits under control, their amount of debt increases and servicing debt[8], i.e. paying interest and redemption, will require a steadily increasing budget expenditure. In addition, rising government debt can place upward pressure on the yields of government bonds. The higher these yields go, the more a country will need to pay every time it wants to borrow money. In addition, rising yields could hinder private investment (crowding-out).

2.1. The debt and deficit problem

A more focused variant of austerity policy deals with the particular significance of public debt and deficit financing. The traditional approach in economics holds that balanced budgets require »consolidated« public revenues, i.e. raised through taxation to cover all public expenditures. This approach would imply a public net debt position

7 »Definition of austerity measure« in: *Financial Times*, http://lexicon.ft.com/Overview [12.4.2017].

8 James A. Gwartney et. al., Economics – Private and Public Choice, Stanford 2015, pp. 645

of zero. However, experts in public finance usually accept two basic exceptions to the rule:

1. The »pay as you use« principle saying that the future users of public goods and infrastructure should contribute to the costs of providing such goods and not leave the funding entirely to those who are presently taxed. Already in 1871, Lorenz von Stein stated, ›A state without national debt either is doing too little [in terms of investments, K. G.] for the future or is extracting too much [in terms of taxes, K. G.] from the presence.»
2. There is also consensus that anti-cyclical deficit spending may be necessary for reasons of stabilizing the economy in times of depression: If the state would cut expenditure (in the wake of receding tax revenues) or increase the tax load in order to compensate for a loss of tax revenues in a slump, both would unduly restrict and hamper domestic demand in times when a fiscal impulse is badly needed.

Public debt is created through government borrowing from economic agents such as individuals, corporations, institutions or foreign governments. The lenders transfer funds to the borrowing government; in return, the government offers a liability item representing a claim on future government (tax) revenues.

The basic rationale for public borrowing is in classical economics the possibility of payment delay in time, meaning a shifting forward of the tax burden intertemporally. Expenditures to be debt-financed are restricted to those that are extraordinary or temporary, are productive over time and could not be financed through tax revenues without putting an excess burden on taxpayers and economic agents. Moreover, a scheme for reliable debt repayment must be in place to ensure lenders that governments could service their debts as promised.

The idea of pump priming an economy in depression or in a slump was to be developed only with the advent of Keynesian economics. Whereas classical principles of public debt limited debt financing to non-recurrent, extraordinary or temporary demands, Keynesian macroeconomics viewed budget deficits as the only means of financing demand-increasing expenditures during depressions. According to a simple Keynesian model, higher aggregate demand leads to higher levels of employment and income and triggers the workings of the so-called multiplier, i.e. that the outcome may be amplified as compared to the initial effect.

It was Abba P. Lerner (1943), the founder of the school of »functional finance«, who ascribed the theoretical underpinnings of his theory to Keynes himself.[9] Although the Keynesian revolution is indeed the starting point of any deficit financing or deficit spending in practice, it may be interesting to note that Keynes himself – as argued by Jan Krekel – never explicitly recommended government deficits as a means of stabilization policy.[10]

9 Abba P. Lerner, »Functional Finance and the Federal Debt« in: *Social Research*, 10, No. 1 (1943), pp. 38–52.

10 Jan Krekel, »Budget Deficits, stabilization policy and liquidity preference: Keynes postwar proposals« in: Fausto Vicarelli (ed.), *Keynes relevance today*, London 1985, pp. 28–50.

Government budget deficits directly and indirectly affect a whole series of economic variables, notably the level of aggregate demand and its composition, by influencing national savings and investment, and also the growth rate of national income. Borrowing can influence the division of today's production between consumption and investment. If public consumption crowds out private investments, which is primarily the case when there is full employment, this diminishes later generation's potential output and – *ceteris paribus* – reduces their consumption opportunities.

However, the precondition of a balanced Keynesian policy set, viz. deficits in depression and surpluses in boom, proved to be unworkable in democratic systems. Permanent debt financing was on the cards including the financing of public consumption outlays and social transfer payments. However, such an approach was not sustainable as default on government debt became more and more tempting for politicians confronted with ever higher interest charges and increasing amounts of debt resulting from efforts to debt-finance former debt. Attempts to restore balanced budgets and to reduce deficit spending over time started to encounter massive political opposition. Tax increases and spending cuts were difficult to realize; therefore politicians often resorted to inflation as a means to devalue the repayment burden. In as much as additional debt leads to an increase in inflation, this is at the expense of the recipients of nominally fixed incomes.

The development of many industrial countries over the last few decades was associated with relatively high public deficits, causing further rises in public debt and, therefore, a deterioration of the countries' fiscal positions.

Figure 1: Debt as a share of GDP in EU MS Q3/2016

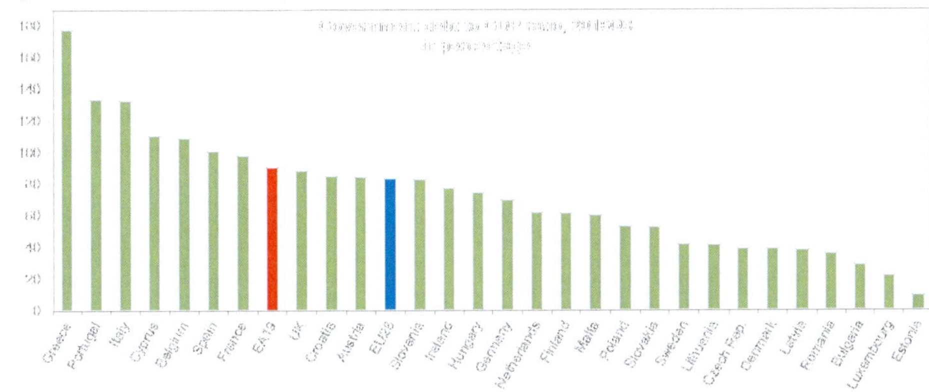

Source: Eurostat

According to Tanzi and Schuknecht, these former debt build-ups were generally accompanied by an expansion of general government expenditures.[11] In addition, in re-

11 Vito Tanzi / Ludger Schuhknecht, »Reconsidering the Fiscal Role of Government: The International Perspective« in: *American Economic Review* 87, No. 2 (1997), pp. 164–168.

sponse to the financial crisis, governments have employed fiscal measures to revive aggregate demand by recapitalizing banks and adopting sizeable fiscal stimulus packages mostly based on higher government expenditures. This has created serious concerns about fiscal sustainability, which has an adverse impact on the financial markets and causes distortions in economic plans of individuals and firms. Yet, there may be more: As pointed out by Holtfreirich et al., debt financing holds both possible intergenerational and interpersonal, i.e. intra-generational, burden shifting.[12]

Burden shifting involves intergenerational distribution problems. The reduction of the tax burden today benefits those who due to their age will not contribute to repayments, especially if maturities are long. At the same time, the unborn are burdened. Effects from public borrowing can also be found regarding interpersonal income distribution. Borrowing tends to lead to a redistribution in favour of capital owners, at least when the factors of production are being used to capacity. As capital ownership is positively correlated with high income, it can be assumed that income distribution becomes more unequal with additional borrowing. This also largely depends, though, on how interest payments are funded: through (progressive) income tax or, for instance, a (regressive) value added tax.

In recent years, the dominance and attractiveness of functional finance and deficit spending has declined, and its theoretical foundations have come under attack, notably from Barro and the Rational Expectations School, who argued that deficit finance is equivalent to taxation, as the issue of bonds creates expectations on the part of economic agents that in order to service future debt, i.e. repayments plus interest, tax liabilities will arise. All economic agents, notably also lenders, know that they themselves or their descendants will later have to pay higher taxes to cover for today's tax breaks (rational expectations). They will therefore make provisions for this in the form of savings. Additional private sector savings today will be effected in order to cover the future tax load from present deficit spending. Through public borrowing the distribution within later generations is skewed toward bondholders and at the expense of taxpayers. In such models, it is essential whether deficit financing leads to a deceleration of overall growth either through crowding-out of private economic activity or through doubts and uncertainty about the long-term sustainability of debt with strong effects on financial markets.

Against the above backdrop, the call for a »deficit- and debt-reduction-based austerity« policy rests upon the following points:

- a lack of debt sustainability in the short, mid and long term;
- concerns that a financial breakdown could be imminent – as in the financial crisis of 2008;

12 Carl Ludwig Hotfreirich / Lars P. Feld / Werner Heun / Gerhard Illing / Gebhard Kirchgässner / Jürgen Kocka / Moritz Schularick / Wolfang Streeck / Uwe Wegschal / Stefanie Walter / Carl Christian von Weizäcker, *Government debt: Causes, effects and limits*, German National Academy of Science Leopoldina, 2016, https://www.leopoldina.org/uploads/tx_leopublication/3Akad_Bericht_Staatsschulden2015_EN.pdf [2.7.2017].

- worries that in a Monetary Union weaker Member States could go for a »free-ride«, i.e. over-indebting themselves while counting on others to bail them out;
- fears that profligate countries might choose an overly lax expenditure policy accompanied by fiscal irresponsibility.

2.2 Retrenchment of the public sector – the unlimited austerity?

A decisive element in the discussion about austerity policy is the issue of whether and, if so, to what extent public spending and financing may impact upon economic growth.

In the second half of the 20th century there has been a general growth in the size and aims of government, due to the institution of modern welfare state systems and to the intervention of the public economy in the economic process. The rate of economic growth in the EU countries has undergone a systematic reduction through time. Several factors, including the aging of the population, the preference for leisure and low risk, the excesses of regulations in the real economy together with a lack of regulation in the monetary and financial sector may have been among the causes of falling growth rates. However, there are reasons to believe that an excessive increase in the ratio of public expenditure to GDP reduces the growth rate, because the costs for the market economy of financing public spending may exceed its marginal productivity. Moreover, the productivity of private firms exposed to competitive pressure, tends to grow more than that of the public sector, which is not exposed to these pressures.

Growth theory is an important yet long neglected part of modern macroeconomics. The neoclassical analysis of growth has long been based on the Solow approach, according to which growth occurs as a result of exogenous technological change.[13] Since, in the Solow world, determinants of growth are exogenous, government policy cannot affect growth rates, except temporarily. This has changed drastically with the works of Romer, Lucas, Barro and Rebelo[14], by which a new, endogenous growth theory emerged, accompanied by a changing view on the role of government in growth processes: In all endogenous growth models, government can influence growth, either directly or indirectly, with – as Dar and Amir Khalkhali convincingly argued – major implications for government policy on a country's long-term growth.[15]

13 Robert M. Solow, »A Contribution to the Theory of Economic Growth«, in: *Quarterly Journal of Economics* 70, No. 1 (1956), pp. 65–94.

14 Paul M. Romer, »Increasing Returns and Long-Run Growth« in: *Journal of Political Economy* 94, No. 5 (1986), pp. 1002–1037; Robert E. Lucas, »On the mechanics of economic development« in: *Journal of Monetary Economics* 22, No. 1 (1988), pp. 3–42; Robert J. Barro, *A Cross-Country Study of Growth, Saving and Government*, NBER Working Paper, 2855 (1989), mimeo; Sergio Rebelo, »Long-Run Policy Analysis and Long-Run Growth« in: *The Journal of Political Economy* 99, No. 3 (1991), pp. 500–521.

15 Martijn Brons / Henri L. F. M. de Groot / Peter Nijkamp, *Growth Effects of Fiscal Policies: A Comparative Analysis in a Multi-Country Context*, Tinbergen Institute Discussion Papers, 42 (1999/3); Atul A. Dar / Amir Khalkali, »Government size, factor accumulation, and eco-

Three main fiscal instruments – taxation, expenditure and the aggregate budgetary balance, i.e. debt – affect long-term growth and determine the optimal size of government.[16] The notion of optimal size of government has been subject to a long debate in economics and public finance. Authors such as Armey and Rahn argue that the hypothetical absence of government as an ordering force would imply a state of anarchy and consequently low levels of economic output and societal welfare, because, without the state as enforcer of the rule of law, property rights could not be safeguarded and consequently transaction costs in the private economy would be soaring. In such circumstances, there is no incentive to save and invest, because the threat of expropriation exists.[17] This argument had been put forward by the New Institutional Economics: Already in the 80s, scholars such as Oliver E. Williamson, Douglas North and others had sharpened our focus on the social and legal norms and rules (which are institutions) that underlie economic activity. Alternative institutional designs – i.e. state and market – and their interplay determine conflicts, externalities and efficiencies.

Just like in the case of no government where output per capita is low, the reverse holds true as well: In a situation where all input and output decisions are made by government, economic growth and welfare efficiency are also low. Accordingly, expansions in governmental size should be associated with expansions in output and increase in efficiency. However, at some point growth-enhancing elements of government should diminish and further expansion of government should no longer lead to output expansion. As spending rises, additional government spending becomes increasingly less productive, and the taxes and borrowing levied to finance government impose increasing burdens. At some point, the marginal benefits from increased government spending become zero (point 1 in figure 2).

The Rahn curve indicates that there is a level of government expenditure that maximizes economic growth and welfare. This approach is often used to argue for a decrease in overall government spending and taxation. The inverted U-shaped curve sug-

nomic growth: evidence from OECD countries« in: *Journal of Policy Modeling* 24, No. 7–8 (2002), pp. 679–692.

16 Literature abounds: Phillip J. Grossman, »The Optimal Size of Government« in: *Public Choice* 56, No. 2 (1987), pp. 193–200; Bernhard Heitger, *The Scope of Government and Its Impact on Economic Growth in OECD Countries*, Kiel Institute of World Economics; Kiel Working Paper No. 1034, 2001; Dimitar Chobanov / Adriana Mladenova, *What Is the Optimum Size of Government*, Institute for Market Economics, 2009; Vito Tanzi / Ludger Schuhknecht, »Reconsidering the Fiscal Role of Government: The International Perspective« in: *American Economic Review* 87, No. 2 (1997), pp. 164–168; George Tridimas / Stanley L. Winer, »The Political Economy of Government Size« in: *European Journal of Political Economy* 21, No. 3 (2004), pp. 643–666; Richard K. Vedder / Lowell E. Gallaway, *Government Size and Economic Growth*, https://www.jec.senate.gov/public/_cache/files/da82f715-a9d3-4625-8cf2-264b11153962/government-size-and-economic-growth.pdf [13.6.2017].

17 Dick Armey, *The Freedom Revolution: The New Republican House Majority Leader Tells Why Big Government Failed, Why Freedom Works, and How We Will Rebuild America*, Washington 1995; Richard W. Rahn / H. Fox, *What Is the Optimal Size of Government*, www.ime.bg/uploads/335309_OptimalSizeOfGovernment.pdf [17.6.2017].

gests that the optimal level of government spending is 20–25% of GDP.[18] The notion is that when government is very small, its expansion makes a positive contribution to the economy. The rationale behind this is that when government protects life, liberty and property – and provides infrastructure – it builds a safe framework for the productive private sector to operate. At a certain point the positive influence of government fades away, and it becomes – through the imposition of taxes necessary to finance government activities – a burden on the economy.

Larson has used an extended Rahn curve to demonstrate the effects of austerity policies. Based on his line of argumentation, I have modified the analysis as follows:

Figure 2: The Extended Rahn Curve

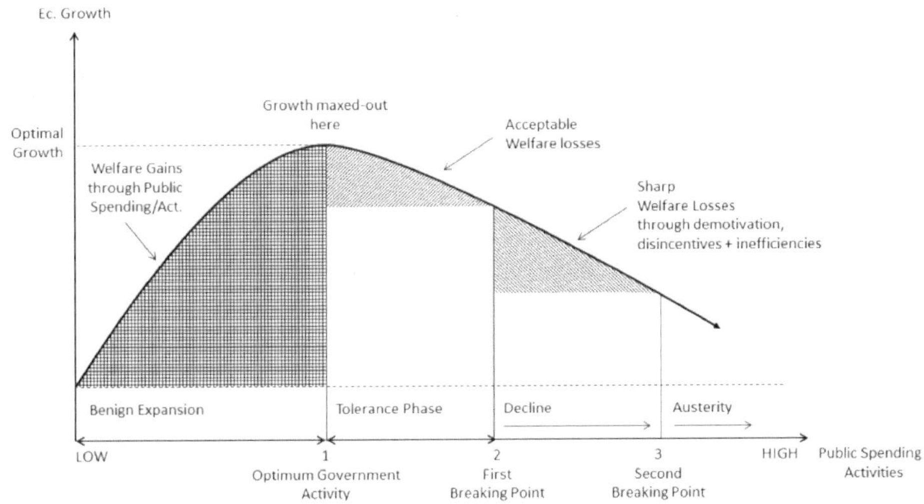

Source: own illustration

Basically, the curve differentiates between four different phases. The »Benign Expansion Phase« is located between zero public activities (point 0) and point 1, the latter representing the optimal amount of government spending/activities. Increases in government activities trigger overproportionate increases in economic growth and societal welfare. In the »Tolerance Phase« between points 1 and 2, further government expansion impacts negatively on growth and welfare. However, this is the phase of government growth where the productive sector of the economy is resilient enough to adjust to the burden of government without any major toll on its productivity. This is followed by the »Decline Phase« between points 2 and 3: Government continues to expand. As the decline phase accelerates (steep negative slope of the curve), it becomes

18 Gerald W. Scully, »The Size of the State, Economic Growth and the Efficient Utilization of National Resources« in: *Public Choice* 63, No. 2 (1989), pp. 149–164.

increasingly difficult to safeguard both economic growth and tolerance for losses. Economic actors are demotivated by high tax burdens to finance additional public spending. Consequently, disincentives to work and invest are triggered, confidence of economic agents in public activities is undermined and politicians used to resort to policy measures aimed to preserve the welfare state at the costs of sacrificing infrastructure, defence and other expenditure.

The most difficult is the »Austerity Phase«: When an economy passes point 3, GDP strongly shrinks, and so do tax revenues. Consequently, efforts to balance the budget will take precedence, and the bigger the deficit, the more panic-oriented the attempts at closing the gap become. In practice this means that legislators will desperately resort to the kind of spending cuts we classified as harmful above. Its cuts drain the private sector of resources, thus causing a net reduction of economic activity. Consequently, government spending increases again, though at a much lower level of economic activity and growth. This implies that the composition of government spending is changed, moving away from hard infrastructure or public goods and towards entitlement programmes in order to evade social unrest.

According to Chao and Grubel, economics suggests, first, that government policies leave their long-term impact primarily on the level of economic activity, not the growth rate; and, second, that the sources of this impact are multi-dimensional and not necessarily well measured by conventional measures of »size«, such as the share of government spending in GDP.[19]

Using time-series and panel data methodologies, Forte and Magazzino have analysed the existence and shape of a »BARS curve«[20], an extension of the original Armey and Rahn approach for EU countries in the period 1970–2009, connecting the size of government (measured by the share of public expenditure on GDP) to the rate of economic growth. The results show that the shares of actual public expenditures generally exceed substantially those related to the maximization of GDP growth. Results highlight that European countries are very heterogeneous in terms of the peak of the curve. The authors found that the latter ranges from 35.39 for Belgium and 35.52 for the Netherlands to 43.50 for UK and 44.47 for Ireland.

Pevcin – also using an Armey-Rahn-Curve approach – investigates the relationship between government spending and economic growth, using data for 12 European countries (Austria, Belgium, Denmark, Finland, France, Germany, Ireland, Italy, the

19 Jonny C. P. Chao / Herbert Grubel, »Optimal Levels of Spending and Taxation in Canada«, in: Herbert Grubel (ed.), *How to Use the Fiscal Surplus: What is the Optimal Size of Government?*, Vancouver 1998.

20 Francesco Forte / Cosimo Magazzino, »Optimal Size Government and Economic Growth in EU Countries« in: *Economica Politica* XXVIII, No. 3 (2011), pp. 295–321. The BARS curve relates to the interdependence between public expenditure and global output. Robert J. Barro, »Government spending in a simple model of endogenous growth« in: *Journal of Political Economy* 98, No. 5 (1990), pp. 103–125; Armey, *The Freedom Revolution*, op. cit. (note 17); Rahn and Fox, »What Is the Optimal Size of Government«, op. cit. (note 17); Scully, »The Size of the State, Economic Growth and the Efficient Utilization of National Resources«, op. cit. (note 18).

Netherlands, Norway, Sweden and the United Kingdom) from 1951 to 1995, based on an ARIMA (Autoregressive Integrated Moving Average) regression model.[21] The results suggest that the curve peaks where the government spending equals around 40 per cent of GDP. If these results are correct, the size of government in the countries analysed has been too large from the standpoint of growth or output optimization, since their government contributed to, on average, 52.02 per cent of GDP in 1996. Therefore, potential scope for reduction of government spending is estimated from approximately 19 per cent up to approximately 30 per cent. The author insists that huge scope exists for spending reduction and austerity measures; approximately 19 per cent on average.

This evidence of widely varying national peaks leads to an interesting question, i.e., whether the fiscal adjustment through austerity should be the same for all the states or whether it should depend on the weight of the public sector on GDP in each country.[22]

3. Austerity between purgatory, ineffectiveness, self-defeat or stairway to heaven?

3.1 The dubious case of »Expansionary Austerity«

Let us backtrack for a second: We discussed above that public debt might, under specific circumstances, stifle economic growth for reasons being that either large deficits and debt may raise interest rates and crowd out private investment, or that high debt and high interest payments may require large distortionary taxes eventually leading to a fiscal crisis (debt service being unsustainable), which in turn may trigger a financial crisis and require painful adjustments. Albeit these »mechanisms« have been criticized in a multitude of studies both on theoretical and on empirical grounds[23], the debt-growth relationship has been at the starting point for what is called »expansionary fiscal consolidation« or »expansionary austerity«.

The expansionary austerity hypothesis holds that a reduction in government spending changes expectations of rational economic actors about future taxes and public spending cuts and may thus expand private consumption and overall economic activity by raising expected private income and by increasing investor's confidence.[24] By raising the expected income of the private sector in the future and by increasing investors'

21 Primož Pevcin, *Does optimal size of government spending exist?*, University of Ljubljana, 2015, pp. 1–12.

22 Brons / de Groot / Nijkamp, *Growth Effects of Fiscal Policies*, op. cit. (note 15); Dar / Khalkali, »Government size, factor accumulation, and economic growth«, op. cit. (note 15); Romer, »Increasing Returns and Long-Run Growth«, op. cit. (note 14).

23 See Thomas Herdon / Michael Ash / Robert Pollin, »Does high public debt consistently stifle economic growth? A critique of Reinhart and Rogoff« in: *Cambridge Journal of Economics* 38, No. 2 (2014), pp. 257–279.

24 The expansionary austerity hypothesis is derived from the Ricardian equivalence proposition, involving a generalization of the intertemporal theory of choice, which is substantially undermined by factors such as uncertainty or liquidity constraints.

confidence, fiscal consolidation will clearly stimulate private consumption and growth. Thus, the short term effects of fiscal consolidation are expansionary. Contractionary effects may be reversed either by a sharp decline in interest rates or by moving to a positive trade balance.[25] The proponents of »expansionary fiscal contractions« argue that even the supposedly short-run damage of fiscal austerity according to the Keynesian model would be limited or wouldn't arise at all; instead, recovery should follow very soon if consolidations are credible, decisive and of the right kind.

But how could fiscal contractions be expansionary? This seems to be a contradiction in terms. Three arguments hold sway: (1) Severe budget problems could be damaging to confidence; getting deficit under control improves confidence. (2) Budgetary problems lead to raising interest rates and hurt the financial system. Fiscal retrenchment would lower rates and allow firms and consumers to borrow at reasonable conditions. (3) Budget problems often are a symptom of dysfunctional government. Fiscal consolidation is a sign that the government is functioning, and so it may be correlated with other measures that are good for growth.

Expansionary austerity forms the main dogma of the European economic policy today. The main theoretical imperative is to avoid any damage to »credibility«, notably on financial markets. It is indispensable to inspire the »confidence« of bond investors to offset any contractionary impact of public expenditure cuts or increased taxes. The key link here is between debt costs and bond market confidence.[26] In the most favourable case of austerity-based fiscal consolidation, non-Keynesian effects (from greater credibility and investor confidence) exceed contractionary Keynesian effects of reduced public spending, thus resulting in higher growth.

By taking tough and often unpopular austerity decisions, a government also signals it will be prepared to honour its future debt obligations. Thereby, a government's decision to go for austerity measures can help creditors to screen governments seeking fresh funds. This is particularly relevant for high debt countries in a fiscal squeeze which badly need to tap financial markets. As regards the empirical evidence of the economic effects of budget cuts, it is mixed, with some studies observing an expansionary effect and others a contractionary one.

Studies about the empirical effects from austerity policies are copious. However, there is no robust empirical evidence that supports the expansionary austerity hypothesis. Giavazzi and Pagano show that fiscal consolidations are sometimes correlated with an expansion of private consumption within one year. Alesina and Perotti find that reducing public expenditures is superior to raising taxes in any fiscal consolidation strategy meant to trigger rapid growth. Finally, Alesina insists that many sharp reductions of budget deficits have been accompanied by »sustained growth rather than recession even in the short-run«. Reinhart and Rogoff maintain that in only very rare

25 For a critical review see George D. Demopoulos / Nicholas A. Yannacopoulos, *The myth of expansionary austerity*, Athens University Department of Economics Working Paper Series No. 9, 2012, http://www.econ.aueb.gr/uploadfiles/AllRP092012.pdf [4.7.2017].

26 It thus differs from the neo-Ricardian equivalence idea or hopes for positive »supply-side effects« from shrinking public spending.

cases countries may be able to resuscitate their economy by deficit spending; usually they can't escape the debt trap.[27]

The results outlined above are differentiated in the IMF's World Economic Outlook, which emphasizes that austerity programmes walk a fine line because they are contractionary in the short run, though they may be expansionary in the long run. Similar results have been put forward by Guajardo, Leigh and Pescatori, who found that fiscal consolidations are contractionary even in economies with high perceived sovereign default risk.[28]

Fazzari et al. find that tax cuts and spending increases have similarly greatly stimulating effects in periods of excessive slack but are much less effective when the economy is close to or above potential. In terms of austerity measures designed to reduce the debt-to-GDP ratio, tax increases and spending cuts are most contractionary and largely self-defeating in periods of excessive slack, while only spending cuts lead to any significant reduction in the debt-to-GDP ratio when the economy is close to or above potential.[29]

One thing can be deduced from the various studies: There is *no clear cut and one-dimensional link of the kind »cuts lead to growth«*. Therefore, austerity may not be regarded as a hazard-free and non-dangerous strategy; some even call it a *»poisoned medicine«*.[30]

3.2 Fallacies and the pros and cons of austerity policy

The analyses outlined above cast doubt on at least some versions of the »expansionary fiscal consolidations« hypothesis, notably on its applicability to many countries in present circumstances. Austerity arguments are compelling only in extreme circumstances and under fragile assumptions.[31] As explained in Botta, path-dependency and cumulativeness make the short-run impulse effects of fiscal consolidation of

27 Francesco Giavazzi / Marco Pagano, »Can severe fiscal contractions be expansionary? Tales of two small European countries« in: *NBER Macroeconomics Annual* 5 (1990); Alberto Alesina / Roberto Perotti, »Fiscal Adjustments in OECD Countries: Composition and Macroeconomic Effects« in: *NBER Working Papers* 44, No. 2 (1997), pp. 210–248; Alberto Alesina, *Fiscal adjustments: lessons from recent history*, Cambridge 2010, http://scholar.harvard.edu/files/alesina/files/fiscaladjustments_lessons-1.pdf [5.6.2017]; Carmen M. Reinhart / Kenneth S. Rogoff, »Growth in a time of debt« in: *The American Economic Review* 100, No. 2 (2010), pp. 537–578.

28 Jaime Guajardo / Daniel Leigh / Andrea Pescatori, *Expansionary Austerity: New International Evidence*, IMF Working Paper, WP/11/158, 2011, pp. 1–40.

29 Steven M Fazzari / James Morley / Irina B. Panovska, »When Do Discretionary Changes in Government Spending or Taxes Have Larger Effects?, UNSW Business School Research Paper, No. 4, 2017, http://dx.doi.org/10.2139/ssrn.2921667 [5.3.2017].

30 »Do budget cuts lead to growth?« 18.4.2012, https://www.youtube.com/watch?v=mJhDMBjekUc [27.6.2017]; Mark Blyth, *Austerity: The History of a Dangerous Idea*, Oxford 2013; Mark Thornton, »Real Austerity: Procesos de Mercado« in: *Revista Europea de Economia Politica* 10, No. 1 (2013), pp. 269–173, p. 269.

31 Roberto Perotti, *The ›Austerity Myth‹: Gain Without Pain?*, BIS Working Paper No. 362, 2011, pp. 1–60.

paramount importance in obtaining any appreciable medium-to-long-run benefit. Moreover, beyond pure economic reasoning, other problematic effects play a crucial role.[32] Against this background, Boyer has pointed out four major fallacies of austerity policies:

(1) The first fallacy derives from false diagnosis that the present crisis is the outcome of lax public spending policy, whereas in many cases it is actually the outcome of a private credit-led speculative boom.

(2) The second fallacy assumes universal validity of the so-called »expansionary fiscal contractions«: this neglects the short-term negative effects on domestic demand and overestimates the generality of Ricardian equivalence.

(3) Also the third fallacy, namely that »one size fits all«, is problematic since, for example, countries such as Greece or Portugal cannot simply replicate a German-like model of austerity success. Their productive, institutional and political configurations differ drastically; thus they require different policies.

(4) The fourth fallacy states that inefficient and politically risky »beggar my neighbour« may result from one-sided application of austerity.[33]

Chowdhury and Islam have added another weak link, i.e. the highly contentious and shaky relationship between debt and growth.[34] Beyond pure economic reasoning, other crucial effects come into play. Ponticelli and Voth ask whether budget cuts may cause social unrest, thereby imposing both economic and political instability costs on a society.[35] As various examples from Argentina in 2001 to Greece in 2010–11 show, austerity measures have often created waves of protest and civil unrest. Economic conditions often deteriorate further and faster if political and social chaos follows attempts to influence spending in order to reduce debt and deficits. Therefore, in political practice there is a tendency to refrain from austerity measures as far as possible. Fiscal consolidation is often delayed or only implemented half-heartedly. Woo has found that financial depth, income inequality, political assassinations, cabinet size and centralization of authority in budgetary decisions are significant and robust determinants of public deficits. He also demonstrated conclusively that countries with higher levels of unrest usually resort to more deficit-spending and are also more indebted.[36]

In a similar vein, Vivian Schmidt argues that despite lip service and legislative action to the contrary, real world politics largely refrains from implementing hard austerity measures and rather shows quite some degree of resilience with respect to the theoreti-

32 Alberto Botta, *The Short- and Long-run Inconsistency of the Expansionary Austerity Theory: A Post-Keynesian/Evolutionist Critique*, Levy Economic Institute, Working Paper No. 878, 2016, pp. 1–33.

33 Robert Boyer, »The four fallacies of contemporary austerity policies: the lost Keynesian legacy« in: *Cambridge Journal of Economics* 36, No. 1 (2012), pp. 283–312.

34 Anis Chowdhury / Iyanatul Islam, »The fallacy of austerity-based fiscal consolidation« in: *VOX. CEPR's Policy Portal*, 2010, http://voxeu.org/debates/commentaries/fallacy-austerity-based-fiscal-consolidation [18.7.2017].

35 Jacopo Ponticelli / Hans-Joachim Voth, *Austerity and Anarchy: Budget Cuts and Social Unrest in Europe, 1919–2008*, CEPR Discussion Paper No. 8513, 2011, pp. 1–28.

36 Jaejoon Woo, »Economic, political, and institutional determinants of public deficits« in: *Journal of Public Economics* 87, No. 3–4 (2003), pp. 387–426.

cally underlying (neoliberal) ideas. The latter are first oriented towards strict austerity and then shifted to a discourse of growth and then to flexible application. Decision makers try to reinterpret the rules »by stealth«, that is, by not admitting to their constituencies that their ideas about austerity weren't working in practice and that the rules therefore needed to change.[37]

In summing up, we can enumerate a number of arguments in favour, i.e. pro, austerity policies and an equally weighty number of arguments against, i.e. contra, austerity as follows:

Arguments for austerity

- Budget deficits are too high and need to be reduced.
- If budget deficits are not cut, it will lead to higher bond yields. Higher bond yields increase cost of financing the deficit. (Future generations will be paying interest on current levels of debt.) Higher bond yields and interest rates on other bonds can crowd-out private investment.
- Cutting budget deficits will give investors greater confidence about the long-term performance of the economy. Lower debt levels will encourage the private sector to invest.
- Government spending as a percentage of GDP has grown too high, crowding out the more efficient private sector. Many claim that governments with lower shares of GDP tend to be more successful, though evidence is very mixed.

Arguments against austerity

- In a recession there is a rise in private sector savings and therefore a strong demand for government bonds.
- In a recession you have the private sector paying off debt (leading to lower private sector consumption and investment). This leads to a fall in aggregate demand. If the government also cuts spending, there will be an even bigger fall in demand.
- Austerity measures lead to higher bond yields. This is because markets see that austerity has caused lower growth and lower tax revenues; therefore, with a shrinking economy, markets can't see how governments can repay debts.
- Austerity is self-defeating. In a recession, governments who cut spending dramatically have seen a large fall in nominal GDP. In other words, austerity has reduced economic growth so much that the budget deficit has failed to improve.
- Recession is not the time for austerity. Austerity should be pursued when there is strong economic growth.
- There is no compelling empirical evidence that cutting spending creates increased confidence.

In the policy debate there are two camps.[38] The pro-austerity camp claims – as discussed above – that the main function of austerity is to help establish and signal a gov-

37 Vivian Schmidt, *The Resilience of ›Bad Ideas‹ in Eurozone Crisis Discourse, Even as Rival Ideas Inform Changing Practices*, TLI Think Paper No. 52, 2017.

38 Harris Dellas / Dirk Niepelt, »Austerity« in: Alfons Weichenrieder (ed.), *Austerity and Economic Growth: Concepts for Europe*, Frankfurt 2015, pp. 12–19, p. 12.

ernment's level of creditworthiness and, thus, suppress sovereign debt default *premia* and increase the flow of fresh funds. Consequently, such confidence-inspiring policies increase investment and thus foster rather than hamper economic performance even in the short run.[39] They have an even stronger positive effect on medium-long term growth. The opponents of austerity, on the other hand, while recognizing its direct contribution to credibility, argue that this effect may be overwhelmed by negative macroeconomic implications. Austerity is thought to depress economic activity through standard spending (Keynesian) multiplier effects and thus to lower a country's debt repayment ability. Consequently, in their view, severe austerity could actually reduce the flow of fresh funds by making default more, rather than less, likely.

The ultimate promise an austerity approach holds is indeed that cut-backs and debt reductions instill confidence into investors and convey the message of a revival of a flourishing economy. Uhlig argued that, the higher probability the markets ascribe to the default risk for government bonds, the more urgent fiscal consolidation may become.[40] On the other hand, austerity not only holds promises but also risks, notably the risk of self-defeat: A reduction of public expenditure will negatively affect the overall effective demand and have ample contractive effects (reinforced by a negative multiplier[41]) on economic activity. Böttger et al. substantiated the argument that even in a long-term depression or stagnation characterized by investment reluctance and a savings glut, idle capital might be flooding the markets, capital which the government can and should tap, activate and allocate to productive use without countervailing and negative effects such as crowding out.[42]

39 The empirical literature has been primarily pre-occupied with short term effects, while the policy debates have involved both short and particularly long term effects. According to the IMF study mentioned above (2010), a fiscal consolidation equivalent to 1% of GDP leads on average to a 0.5% decline in GDP after two years and to an increase of 0.3 percentage points in the unemployment rate.

40 Harald Uhlig, »Default risk and banks in a monetary union« in: *German Economic Review* 15, No. 1 (2014), pp. 23–41.

41 Paul Krugman, »Airbrushing Austerity« in: *New York Times*, 22.4.2015, krugman.blogs.nytimes.com/2015/04/22/airbrushing-austerity [2.7.2017]; Christina Romer / Jared Bernstein, »The Job Impact of the American Recovery and Reinvestment Plan« in: *Council of Economic Advisers*, 2009, have estimated that one additional euro of deficit spending could trigger a multiplier of 1.5, i.e. increase income to 1.5 euros; more sceptical economists argue the factor would be only 0.6.

42 »Crowding out occurs when expansionary fiscal policy reduces investment spending by the private sector. The Government is ›crowding out‹ investment because it is demanding more Loanable Funds and it is increasing interest rates from the borrowing. Much of the debate in the 1970s was based on the assumption of a fixed supply of savings within a single country, but with the global capital markets of the 21st century international capital mobility completely undermines a simple model of crowding out«. Oliver J. Blachard, »Crowding-Out« in: Steven N. Durlauf / Lawrence E. Blume (eds.), *The New Palgrave Dictionary of Economics*, Houndmills/New York 2008, pp. 728–730; Jim Tomlinson, »Crowding-Out« in: *History & Policy*, 5.12.2010, http://www.historyandpolicy.org/opinion-articles/articles/crowding-out [2.7.2017]; Wolfgang Stützel, »Zum Einfluss der öffentlichen Verschuldung auf den Kapitalmarktzins« in: Diethard B. Simmert / Kurt-Dieter Wagner (eds.), *Staatsverschuldung kontrovers*, Köln 1981; Francis Coppola, »The ECB and the Eurozone Credit

Almost all proponents and opponents of austerity policy agree on one thing: The right management and control of public debt and deficit is essential, but it can work both ways: toward more or less deficit-spending. The intellectual controversy is basically about the speed, the when and the extent of it. »The austerity debate is about different timings and extents of budget cuts or increase.«[43] Stringent criteria to apply in order to make the right decisions include the following:

- What kind of expenditure are we talking about: productive or consumptive ones?
- Is the level of national public indebtedness still within reasonable limits?
- Will there be debt repayment when tax revenues rise beyond expectations in a boom?
- What is the political situation like in individual countries?
- Can monetary policy support fiscal policy and vice versa?
- Can we control and adequately guide financial markets?
- What is the sign (positive/negative) and what the size of the multiplier effect?
- Is the weak national demand just temporary of persistent?
- Are markets – labour markets, commodity markets and financial markets – overregulated and distorted?
- Is the tax system fair and tolerable?

4. Rhetoric or reality – is the end of austerity near?

As pointed out above, the very notion of austerity policy is actually a *political battle cry* in the discursive fight between activist economists and fiscal abstainers! The debate itself is not new in substance. What is new is the intellectual doggedness and fierceness of the discussion. This appears not only in the academic discussions about the best economic strategies but also in the media coverage: On the one hand, a »neutral« and »impartial« coverage and comments elaborating the pros and cons of austerity are missing. Rather, according to the political colour and position and the economic understanding of both individual journalists and the press, austerity is being lauded or condemned. On the other hand, many of the very complicated and highly differentiated arguments, which in their majority require quite a lot of knowledge, explanation and qualification, are dispensed with because the media think the normal proverbial (wo)man in the streets will not (wish to) understand them.

This creates a most complexly intricate situation and a *maelstrom* of conflicting interests. In view of the hefty debate about austerity versus stimulus in the Eurozone crisis, there is a lot of pressure in the pot of international cross-border policy making: In

Crunch« in: *Credit Writedowns*, 6.3.2014, https://www.creditwritedowns.com/2014/03/the-ecb-and-the-eurozone-credit-crunch.html [25.6.2016]; Geert Böttger / Klaus Gretschmann / Paul Helmut Hupperzt, »Finanzierungspotentiale kompensatorischer Staatsbudgets« in: *Konjunkturpolitik* 27 (1981), pp. 207–226.

43 See »Austerity a double edged sword?« in: *BBC*, 17.10.2010, http://www.bbc.com/news/business-11555481 [4.7.2017].

the Anglo-American world pressure is mounting on Europeans and others to recant austerity measures. As a former secretary of the treasury has put it loud and clear:

> »*We continue to believe that more countries have room to enact pro-growth policies. We also see the choice of using fiscal or structural tools as a false choice. [...] But it is clear that macroeconomic support is essential [...] to boost an economy during an adjustment period when necessary structural changes can lead to a short term decline in economic activity, such as when excess industrial capacity is retired.*«[44]

There seems to be a high probability that, in applied policy-making in several countries, expansive and activist fiscal policy may play a much bigger role in future. This can be derived from several observations: The new US President, Trump, plans to lower tax rates across the board to increase infrastructure spending massively, while at the same time increasing the defence budget drastically. But also in other countries the mantra of spending and deficit reductions and the reduction philosophy has lost quite some support and appeal and has come under severe political attack.

In the UK and in the wake of Brexit, Prime Minister May has announced a »fiscal reply« to the implicit pre-negotiation threats by the EU to restrict the access of UK enterprises to the single European Market. May has been playing with the idea of replacing the trade-related export effects which may cease to exist in a post-Brexit world by deficit-financed stimulus programmes. At the same time, a broad strategy of tax relief for business and consumers is supposed to lure enterprises from within the EU to the UK by means of tax competition and lower corporate and income tax rates. As the treasury secretary Hammond put it so nicely: »We are ready to ›reset‹ Britain's fiscal policy if needed to respond to turbulence caused by the decision to vote to leave the European Union.«[45]

Similar voices and noises are heard from southern Member States of the EU: Former Italian Prime Minister Renzi, Greek Prime Minister Tsipras or various leading French politicians argue with extraordinary abrasiveness in favour of a more flexible interpretation of the deficit spending limits of the Stability and Growth Pact and in favour of a more activist fiscal policy in order to resuscitate their economies. Also, the President of the EU Commission Juncker put it quite bluntly: »It should no longer be said that this Commission continues the austerity measures applied in the past.«[46]

In other words, many signposts point in the direction of a trend reversal. And even if Schopenhauer is right that no signpost walks the way it guides, there is a certain probability that a turning of the tide is on the cards – away from recipes such as auster-

44 Jakon J. Lew, *Remarks at the Brookings Institution: From Pittsburgh to Hangzhou: The Past, Present, and Future of the G-20*, Washington, U.S. Department of the Treasury, 31.8.2016, https://www.treasury.gov/press-center/press-releases/Pages/jl0544.aspx [3.5.2017].

45 Joe Mayes, »U.K. Chancellor Ready to ›Reset‹ Fiscal Policy on Brexit« in: *Bloomberg*, 22.6.2016, https://www.bloomberg.com/news/articles/2016-07-22/u-k-chancellor-ready-to-reset-fiscal-policy-after-brexit-vote [18.7.2016].

46 Francesco Guarascio, »Stop attacking EU Commission on fiscal policy, Juncker tells Renzi« in: *Reuters Business News*, 7.11.2016, http://www.reuters.com/article/us-eurozone-italy-budget-idUSKBN13228R [18.7.2017].

ity, fiscal abstinence and a comprehensive retrenchment of government and towards fiscal expansion, stimulus setting and much more activist governments.[47]

47 Klaus Gretschmann, »The European Union in Stormy Seas« in: Bruno Dallago / Gert Guri / John McGowen (eds.), *A Global Perspective on the European Economic Crisis*, New York 2016, pp. 33–47.

Erik Vollmann and Wolfram Ridder[1]

Neither the Devil, nor a Saint – Macroeconomic, Social, and Political Implications of Fiscal Austerity in Europe between 2001 and 2015

Over the recent years, various contributions in the fields of, among others, political science, economics, and sociology have argued or highlighted the fact that Western societies have entered a so-called Age of Austerity.[2] While therefore much has been said about the causes, political aims, and likely or actual implications of a policy of fiscal austerity[3], there still is no epistemic consensus regarding the relationship of fiscal austerity measures and various parts of society. Furthermore, it is likely to happen that two people, speaking about austerity, will end up talking about entirely different topics, due to the various conceptions and »images« of austerity that are out in the debate.[4] Not only has the scientific community led controversial debates about the »true nature« of austerity. An even fiercer discussion has enflamed political elites and media in the course of the financial and fiscal crisis. While proponents of fiscal austerity measures in Europe have proposed the concept as the one and only possibility to master the critical situation and save the common currency[5], opponents predicted devastating consequences of austerity, with some (quite renowned) commentators describing austerity measures harshly as »delusion«[6], »madness«[7] or the economic equivalent to the Versailles treaties[8]. A calmed consideration on the implications of fiscal austerity in its various alleged areas of consequence seems necessary. Therefore, departing from the

1 The authors would like to express their gratitude to Sarah Kolling for her assistance with the preparation of this contribution.

2 Marcos Ancelovici / Pascale Dufour / Heloise Nez, *Protest and Social Movements: Street Politics in the Age of Austerity: From the Indignados to Occupy*, Amsterdam 2016; Richard Westra (ed.), *The Future of Capitalism after the Financial Crisis: The Varieties of Capitalism Debate in the Age of Austerity*, London 2015; Thomas Byrne Edsall, *The Age of Austerity: How Scarcity Will Remake American Politics*, New York 2012.

3 In addition to the contributions indicated in note 2, see, for instance, the more focused studies by Kevin Featherstone, »The Greek Sovereign Debt Crisis and EMU. A Failing State in a Skewed Regime« in: *Journal of Common Market Studies* 49, No. 2 (2011), pp. 193–217; Howard Karger, »The bitter pill. Austerity, debt and the attack on Europe's welfare states« in: *Journal of Sociology & Social Welfare* 41, No. 2 (2014), pp. 33–53.

4 For a discussion on four different possible conceptualizations of the term austerity, see Roland Sturm, »Austeritätspolitik als gesellschaftliches Projekt« in: *Aus Politik und Zeitgeschichte* 66, No. 1–2 (2016), pp. 17–23.

5 For an overview see Sturm, »Austeritätspolitik als gesellschaftliches Projekt«, op. cit. (note 4).

6 Paul Krugman, »The austerity delusion« in: *The Guardian*, 29.4.2015, https://www.theguardian.com/business/ng-interactive/2015/apr/29/the-austerity-delusion [15.10.2016].

7 Paul Krugman, »Europe's Austerity Madness« in: *New York Times*, 27.9.2012, http://www.nytimes.com/2012/09/28/opinion/krugman-europes-austerity-madness.html [15.10.2016].

8 Paul Krugman, »Weimar and Greece, Continued« in: *New York Times*, 15.2.2015, http://krugman.blogs.nytimes.com/2015/02/15/weimar-and-greece-continued/ [17.2.2016].

assessment that austerity has profound consequences on people's lives and at the same time neither has an unambiguous meaning been found nor is there a common understanding of the political, economic, and societal consequences of this term, we undertake the attempt of bringing more clarity into the question of the implications of adopting a policy of fiscal austerity.

In doing so, we first develop hypotheses regarding the relationship between austerity and three »sub-sectors« of Western societies, namely macroeconomics, the social and welfare sector, and general politics. Second, we lay out how to measure the relationship between austerity and the variables contained in our hypotheses. Afterwards, we introduce the reader to our results and interpret them. Then, we will discuss the actual meaning of our findings and will conclude this contribution with a short summary and some final remarks.

1. Formation of hypotheses

In order to analyse the relationship between fiscal austerity and the wider public, we have subdivided the receiving end of austerity measures into three parts and have built hypotheses for each of these:

First, we hypothesize that austerity measures will overall be beneficially correlated with the sector of macroeconomics, by analysing the relationship of the adoption of austerity with economic growth in countries having introduced such programmes, with sovereign debt levels, with sovereign interest rates, and also with unemployment rates. Second, we hypothesize that fiscal austerity measures will overall be negatively correlated with social and welfare policy. Here, we again subdivide this general interaction by forming sub-hypotheses regarding the relationships of the adoption of fiscal austerity measures with, first, governmental spending levels on welfare and social policies, and, second, with income distribution. Third, we hypothesize that austerity will overall be negatively correlated with variables representing its political implications. Specifically, we ask for the connection between such a policy on the one hand and voter turnout and the share in parliamentary seats gained by so-called »challenger parties« on the other. Additionally, we assume that fiscal austerity measures will be in some way related to the satisfaction with democracy in affected countries and finally also with an increase in Euro-scepticism.

How do we arrive at these hypotheses and what specific interactions do we assume? The assumption that fiscal austerity measures will be positively correlated with macroeconomic indicators is at the core of the scientific debate of economists and has been fervently supported as well as denied by different authors – while at times drawing different conclusions from the usage of the very same data and principal approach. The latter is true of an IMF-inspired debate starting with the controversial work of Alesina and Ardagna in their 2009 study.[9] They have suggested economically positive

9 Alberto Alesina / Silvia Ardagna, »Large Changes in Fiscal Policy. Taxes versus Spending« in: *Tax Policy and the Economy* 24 (2010), pp. 35–68.

effects of fiscal austerity (preferring spending cuts over tax increases), specifically arguing that »spending cuts adopted to reduce deficits have been associated with economic expansions rather than recessions.«[10] In response, Guajardo et al.[11] came to the conclusion of negative implications of fiscal austerity in the same data set – only narrowing the definition of fiscal austerity shocks by including explicit intention. While Alesina and Ardagna's approach might tend, as Guajardo et al. have suggested, to overestimate the positivity of austerity's impact on macroeconomics, the more narrow approach of their critics might very well underestimate it.[12] Another argument for macroeconomic benefits through induction of austerity measures has been made by Reinhart and Rogoff in their studies from the years 2012 and (obnoxiously famous) 2010.[13] They argue that indebting a country beyond a certain threshold, indicated as 90% of GDP, will have some serious adverse implications for economic growth for market economies. Those assumptions have had a broad audience not only in scientific debate but also to policy makers and austerity proponents. While both these studies have, unfortunately, been linked to serious methodological issues, the principal direction of their conclusions has been upheld by critics.[14] The fluent state of the debate asks for new evidence using alternative measures. The well-being of the macroeconomy does undoubtedly lie

10 Alesina / Ardagna, »Large Changes in Fiscal Policy«, op. cit. (note 9), p. 37.

11 Jaime Guajardo / Daniel Leigh / Andrea Pescatori. »Expansionary Austerity? International Evidence« in: *Journal of the European Economic Association* 12, No. 4 (2014), pp. 949–968.

12 See also the replication of Guajardo et al. by Òscar Jordà / Alan M. Taylor, »The Time for Austerity: Estimating the Average Treatment Effect of Fiscal Policy« in: *The Economic Journal* 126, No. 590 (2016), pp. 219–255. They also report negative effects of fiscal austerity during times of economic recession as well as booms.

13 Carmen Reinhart / Kenneth Rogoff, »Growth in a Time of Debt« in: *American Economic Review* 100, No. 2 (2010), pp. 573-578; Carmen Reinhart / Vincent Reinhart / Kenneth Rogoff, »Public Debt Overhangs: Advanced-Economy Episodes since 1800« in: *Journal of Economic Perspectives* 26, No. 3 (2012), pp. 69–86. For an overview over the arguments proposed by Reinhart and Rogoff, see also Karger, »The bitter pill«, op. cit. (note 3), p. 34–35.

14 Thomas Herndon / Michael Ash / Robert Pollin, »Does high public debt consistently stifle economic growth? A critique of Reinhart and Rogoff« in: *Cambridge Journal of Economics* 38, No. 2 (2014), pp. 257–279; Paul Krugman, »The Excel Depression« in: *New York Times*, 18.4.2013; Robert Pollin / Michael Ash, »Austerity after Reinhart and Rogoff« in: *Financial Times*, 17.4.2013. Herndon et al. also find an – although less dramatic and more differentiated as well as nuanced – relation between high public debt and reduced growth levels. There are suggestions that this »more temperated« relation in the long run did not uphold in the financial and public debt crises hitting Europe after 2007. Erik Vollmann, »Wirtschaftliche und soziale Implikationen fiskalischer Austerität in Europa«, in: Roland Sturm / Tim Griebel / Thorsten Winkelmann (eds.), *Austerität als gesellschaftliches Projekt*, Wiesbaden 2017, pp. 103–128, p. 113. Furthermore, Pescatori, Sandri and Simon not only argue that there is no »magic threshold« at all for the relationship between sovereign debt and economic growth, but they also argue that debt trajectories can be as important as debt levels themselves. Andrea Pescatori / Damiano Sandri / John Simon, *Debt and Growth. Is There a Magic Threshold?*, IMF Working Paper Series No. 34, 2014. For a discussion of the more general relationship between fiscal policy and public debt, see Alan Sutherland, »Fiscal crises and aggregate demand. Can high public debt reverse the effects of fiscal policy?« in: *Journal of Public Economics* 65, No. 1 (1997), pp. 147–162.

at the heart of the debate for and against the implementation of fiscal austerity measures. Consequentially, we formulate Hypothesis H1.1 as follows:

H1.1: Fiscal austerity measures will be positively correlated with economic growth, measured by an increase in GDP.

One could even argue that public debt is the »root« of austerity in current EU-politics. Fiscal austerity has been proposed as a means (or »the« means) to reduce sovereign debt levels that have been perceived as excessive. Besides this mostly political discourse, the argument is substantiated scientifically: Philip R. Lane[15], as well as others, argues that fiscal austerity measures might be accompanied by a reduction in sovereign debt. There certainly is no deterministic relationship between these two variables, especially because even if fiscal austerity measures are in the short term successful in affecting debt-GDP ratios, as it is proposed, among others, by Roberto Perotti[16], there then still »remains the post-crisis adjustment challenge of gradually reducing government debt to safer levels«. Since this is mainly the case due to the political elite's aim of improving the governmental position vis-à-vis rating agencies, the bond market, and capital suppliers[17], there is some good reason to hypothesize that fiscal austerity measures will be correlated with a decrease in the sovereign debt/GPD ratio. Therefore, hypothesis H1.2 will be formulated as follows:

H1.2: Fiscal austerity measures will be negatively correlated with the sovereign debt/GDP ratio.

Positive correlation between fiscal austerity and lowered interest rates, that has been implied in the section above, is also indicated by Alesina and Ardagna[18], who argue that such an introduction of spending cuts will, in a very similar way to the remarks made for the relationship between fiscal austerity measures and sovereign debt levels, serve primarily to placate bond markets, which in turn will additionally be followed by an improvement of the ratings and assessments offered by rating agencies and an overall increase in loan offerings made available by private investors. We therefore additionally theorize as hypothesis H1.3:

H1.3: Fiscal austerity measures will be negatively correlated with interest rates.

Our fourth and last hypothesis concerning the relationship between fiscal austerity measures and macroeconomics pertains to changes in unemployment rates in countries

15 Philip R. Lane, »The European Sovereign Debt Crisis« in: *The Journal of Economic Perspectives*, 26 (2012/3), pp. 49-67.

16 Roberto Perotti, »The Austerity Myth. Gain without Pain« in: Alberto Alesina / Francesco Giavazzi (eds.), *Fiscal Policy after the Financial Crisis*, Chicago 2013, pp. 307–354, p. 307.

17 Alesina / Ardagna, »Large Changes in Fiscal Policy«, op. cit. (note 9). See also Peter Coy, »Keynes vs. Alesina. Alesina Who? Economist Alberto Alesina argues that austerity triggers growth« in: *Bloomberg Business Week*. https://www.bloomberg.com/news/articles/2010-06-29/keynes-vs-dot-alesina-dot-alesina-who [17.1.2017].

18 Alesina / Ardagna, »Large Changes in Fiscal Policy«, op. cit. (note 9).

adopting such reforms.[19] Especially because the introduction of fiscal austerity measures is expected by proponents of austerity to significantly encourage investments by the private sector in the economy[20], we assume that the adoption of such programmes will positively correlate with a decline in unemployment rates. However, one has also to take into account that there are contributions casting doubt on this unilinear relationship between fiscal austerity measures and the unemployment, particularly indicating that at least in some cases there can also be quite weak effects of fiscal austerity measures on the share of unemployed people, or even none at all.[21] Still, our fourth and final sub-hypothesis in the area of macroeconomics can be formulated in the following way:

> *H1.4: Fiscal austerity measures will be positively correlated with a decline in unemployment rates.*

With regards to the implications of fiscal austerity measures for social and welfare policies, we first assume that the introduction of such measures will negatively correlate with overall governmental spending in these policy fields, implying that fiscal austerity measures can also be interpreted as structural adjustments and efforts to increase the competitiveness of one country's economy.[22] An austerity-critical approach would expect negative consequences of its implementation. In that regard, austerity has been characterized as a neoliberal project to redistribute wealth from the »poor« to the »rich«.[23] It is furthermore logical to assume that reductions in government deficit will negatively affect social expenditure as one of its large factors. We therefore suppose that the relationship between the adoption of fiscal austerity measures and social spending by governments can be conceived of as follows:

19 While unemployment is a macroeconomic variable, it could also have been used to measure social implications of fiscal austerity because of its severe interconnectedness with humans' ability to participate in the social (and even political) life of their society. Ann-Helén Bay / Morten Blekesaune, »Youth, Unemployment and Political Marginalisation« in: *International Journal of Social Welfare* 11, No. 2 (2002), pp. 132–139; Berthold Vogel, »Wege an den Rand der Arbeitsgesellschaft – Der Verlust der Erwerbsarbeit und die Gefahr sozialer Ausgrenzung« in: Eva Barlösius / Wolfgang Ludwig-Mayerhofer (eds.), *Die Armut der Gesellschaft*, Wiesbaden 2001, pp. 151–168.

20 Alesina / Ardagna, »Large Changes in Fiscal Policy«, op. cit. (note 9).

21 Reinhard Neck / Dmitri Blueschke / Klaus Weyerstrass, »Trade-offs of Fiscal Austerity in the European Debt Crisis. The Case of Slovenia« in: *International Advances in Economic Research* 19, No. 4 (2013), pp. 367–380.

22 Michael Dauderstädt / Ernst Hillerbrand, »Vorwort: Jenseits der Austeritätspolitik« in: Michael Dauderstädt / Ernst Hillerbrand (eds.), *Alternativen zur Austerität. Progressive Wachstumsstrategien für Europa*, FES survey, 2013, pp. 2–6, http://library.fes.de/pdf-files/id/ipa/10409.pdf [12.3.2014]; Annina Kaltenbrunner, »Strukturelle Ungleichgewichte und Austerität. Gibt es eine Zukunft für periphere Länder in der Eurozone?« in: *Kurswechsel. Zeitschrift für gesellschafts-, wirtschafts- und umweltpolitische Alternativen* 1 (2012), pp. 114–121; Kevin Farnsworth / Zoë Irving, »Varieties of Crisis, Varieties of Austerity. Social Policy in Challenging Times« in: *Journal of Poverty and Social Justice* 20, No. 2 (2012), pp. 133–147.

23 For an overview see Sturm, »Austeritätspolitik als gesellschaftliches Projekt«, op. cit. (note 4).

H2.1: Fiscal austerity measures will negatively correlate with governmental spending in the areas of social and welfare policies.

One very powerful argument about the implications of fiscal austerity which can be identified in the literature concerns the effects of such measures on income distribution. Amongst others, Klatzer and Schlager[24] argue that the adoption of fiscal austerity is in the end nothing more than a euphemism for an enrichment of the wealthier to the detriment of the poorer strata of society. In order to control for this, we develop our second sub-hypothesis for the relationship between fiscal austerity and social policies, namely:

H2.2: Fiscal austerity will be positively correlated with an increase in income inequality.

The third and final area in which we expect distinct effects of fiscal austerity measures is politics itself. The most evident consequences of implemented austerity measures in Europe have been widespread protests against those politics, especially in southern Europe.[25] There have also been government changes or the rise of new protest parties that have often been associated with anti-austerity (or anti-EU) protests, thus suggesting consequences of austerity measures on voter behaviour and electoral outcome.[26] Some authors even state negative effects on people's support for their respective democracy.[27] Therefore, we first assume:

H3.1: The adoption of fiscal austerity measures will be negatively correlated with voter turnout, both on the national level and in elections to the European Parliament.

24 Elisabeth Klatzer / Christa Schlager, »Fiskalpakt – immerwährende Austerität, Demontage von Wohlfahrtsstaat und sozialen Rechten« in: *Die Zukunft. Die Diskussionszeitschrift für Politik, Gesellschaft und Kultur* 4 (2012), pp. 16–23, p. 16.

25 Guya Accornero / Pedro Ramos Pinto, »›Mild Mannered‹? Protest and Mobilisation in Portugal under Austerity, 2010–2013« in: *West European Politics* 38, No. 3 (2015), pp. 491–515; Neil Hughes, »›Young People Took to the Streets and All of a Sudden All of the Political Parties Got Old‹: The 15m Movement in Spain« in: *Social Movement Studies* 10, No. 4 (2011), pp. 407–13.

26 Paul Whiteley / Harold D. Clarke / David Sanders / Marianne C. Stewart, »The Economic and Electoral Consequences of Austerity Policies in Britain« in: *Parliamentary Affairs* 68, No. 1 (2015), pp. 4–24; Enrique Hernández / Hanspeter Kriesi, »The Electoral Consequences of the Financial and Economic Crisis in Europe« in: *European Journal of Political Research* 55, No. 2 (2016), pp. 203–224; Anna Bosco / Susannah Verney, »Electoral Epidemic: The Political Cost of Economic Crisis in Southern Europe, 2010–11« in: *South European Society and Politics* 17, No. 2 (2012), pp. 129–154; Georgios Karyotis / Wolfgang Rüdig, »Blame and Punishment? The Electoral Politics of Extreme Austerity in Greece« in: *Political Studies* 63, No. 1 (2015), pp. 2–24.

27 Klaus Armingeonn / Kai Guthmann, »Democracy in Crisis? The Declining Support for National Democracy in European Countries, 2007–2011« in: *European Journal of Political Research* 53, No. 3 (2014), pp. 423–442; Thomas Biebricher / Frieder Vogelmann, »Die Zukunft Europas zwischen Demokratie und Kapitalismus« in: *Politische Vierteljahresschrift* 55, No. 1 (2014), pp. 1–17; Wolfgang Streeck »The Crisis of Democratic Capitalism« in: *New Left Review* 71 (2011), pp. 5–29.

This hypothesis is based upon, amongst others, the remarks by Verney and Bosco[28] and, with a special emphasis on highly educated citizens, Silja Häusermann, Bruno Wueest, and Thomas Kurer[29], who generally assume that a reduction in governmental activity in certain fields and similar content of austerity policies will result in frustration by citizens with the record of political elites, which in turn will lead to a widespread trend by the people to stay at home on election day.

However, the adoption of fiscal austerity measures might also, at least to some degree, correlate with an increase in voter turnout, then coinciding with more or less frequent decisions by voters to deprive »established« parties of their vote and instead cast their vote for so-called »challenger parties.«[30] With this term, scholarship refers to a newly emerging party or an already well-established party which is fundamentally opposed to the fiscal austerity measures, adopted and implemented by the government, as well as being EU-sceptic. In order to control for differences between the national and the EU level, we include both elections to the national parliament and to the European Parliament during the time period in question. Therefore, assuming that both former non-participants in elections and frustrated traditional voters of established parties might be tempted to cast their vote for a party which questions either the necessity or inescapability of the introduction of fiscal austerity measures, we theorize as our preliminary hypothesis H3.2:

H3.2: The adoption of fiscal austerity measures will correlate with an increase in the parliamentary seats gained by »challenger parties« in national and EU elections.

In order to account for possible differences between the national and the EU level with regards to the voters casting their vote for challenger parties, we further subdivide this hypothesis into two sub-hypotheses:

H3.2.1 The adoption of fiscal austerity measures will correlate with an increase in the parliamentary seats gained by »challenger parties« in national elections.
H3.2.2 The adoption of fiscal austerity measures will correlate with an increase in the parliamentary seats gained by »challenger parties« in EP elections.

In some way, our sub-hypothesis H3.2 is interrelated with our sub-hypothesis H3.3. Here, we suppose that the introduction of fiscal austerity measures will negatively affect trust in democracy. The close connection between the adoption of fiscal austerity measures and trust in democratic institutions is put forward by both Bieling, Haas and

28 Susannah Verney / Anna Bosco, »Living Parallel Lives: Italy and Greece in an Age of Austerity« in: *South European Society and Politics* 18, No. 4 (2013), pp. 397–426.

29 Silja Häusermann / Bruno Wueest / Thomas Kurer, *The hidden side of turnout. How constrained government depresses participation among highly educated citizens*, Paper submitted for presentation at the 2013 EUDO Dissemination Conference Elections in Europe in Times of Crisis at the European University Institute in Florence on 28–29.11.2013.

30 Sarah B. Hobolt / James Tilly, »Fleeing the Centre. The Rise of Challenger Parties in the Aftermath of the Euro Crisis« in: *Journal of European Public Policy* 39, No. 5 (2016), pp. 971–991.

Lux[31], and Genovese, Schneider and Wassmann.[32] And still more: There is even some indication that already the announcement of spending cuts in, e.g., the areas of social and welfare policies might negatively affect trust in democratic institutions.[33] Consequently, our sub-hypothesis is phrased as follows:

H3.3: The adoption of fiscal austerity measures is negatively correlated with trust in national democracy.

Our final sub-hypothesis, H3.4, is again somewhat interrelated with the previous two. Here, however, we do not any longer assume that the adoption of fiscal austerity measures will be to the detriment of trust in democratic institutions or negatively affect the decisions by voters, but we hypothesize that the citizenry will react to the introduction of such measures with a general increase in Euro-scepticism. This possible tendency of blaming the European Union for spending cuts in the area of social and welfare policies might both be caused by voters' impression that fiscal austerity is a direct consequence of specific integration steps on the European level, resulting in Euro-sceptical positions by the citizenry,[34] or by the widespread impression of citizens in austerity-affected countries that these measures are in the end nothing more than fiscal constraints imposed from abroad or above, to the detriment of their own country.[35] In order to control for whether or not the adoption of fiscal austerity measures is related to an increase in Euro-scepticism, we therefore phrase our fourth and final sub-hypothesis, H3.4, as follows:

H3.4: Fiscal austerity will be negatively correlated with the image of the European Union.

As additional explorative approach, we look into (in-)consistent effects of the two component strategies of fiscal austerity as put forward by, among others, Thomas I. Palley or Kevin Featherstone[36] – decreasing public expenditure (»spending austerity«)

31 Hans-Jürgen Bieling / Tobias Haas / Julia Lux, »Die Krise als Auslöser eines neuen europäischen Konfliktzyklus?« in: *Zeitschrift für Außen- und Sicherheitspolitik* 6, No. 1 (2013), pp. 231–249.

32 Federica Genovese / Gerald Schneider / Pia Wassmann, »The Eurotower Strikes Back. Crises, Adjustments, and Europe's Austerity Protests« in: *Comparative Political Studies* 49, No. 7 (2016), pp. 939–967.

33 Thorsten Winkelmann / Wolfram Ridder, »Die makroökonomischen und politischen Konsequenzen von Austerität«, in: Sturm / Griebel / Winkelmann (eds.), *Austerität als gesellschaftliches Projekt*, op. cit. (note 14), pp. 69–101, p. 85.

34 Matthias Ruffert, »The European Debt Crisis and European Union Law«, in: *Journal of Common Market Studies* 48, No. 6 (2011), pp. 1777–1806, p. 1777.

35 Beyza Ç. Tekin, »Rethinking the Post-National EU in Times of Austerity and Crisis«, in: *Mediterranean Politics* 19, No. 1 (2014), pp. 21–39.

36 Thomas I. Palley, *The Simple Macroeconomics of Fiscal Austerity, Public Sector Debt and Deflation*, IMK Working Paper 8/2010, p. 8–9; Featherstone, »The Greek Sovereign Debt Crisis and EMU«, op. cit. (note 3), p. 195–200.

and increasing government revenues (»tax austerity«) – for the hypothesis above.[37] This allows us to contribute further evidence to the suggestions that tax increases (as opposed to expenditure cuts) have less desirable covariations with growth[38] – and possibly with more aspects of our research scope.

2. *Method*

This study tries to settle some of the aforementioned scientific discussions and even conflicts on the »good« or the »bad« empirical relationship of fiscal austerity and the three sectors most significant to political science. Thus it contributes to the existing but very fuzzy findings on the empirical relationship between implementation of fiscal austerity and (macro-)economic development, the mainly negative consequences attributed to austerity measures, and the people's protest resulting in negative consequences for the relative reputation of democracy, European Union, elections, and mainstream parties.

We choose a correlative approach using individual country-years in a time sample consisting of the period 2001 to 2015 and choosing a country sample including Greece, Spain, Germany, the UK, France, Ireland, Portugal, and Italy, thus integrating all Eurozone members that have been denominated as »crisis states« for having (temporarily at least) been subject to the crisis programmes and mechanisms of the Union or Eurozone[39] as well as the three largest economies in the EU. The latter also include both the two main proponents of austerity in the EU (UK and Germany) and the two principal agents for deepened European Integration in the recent past (France and Germany).[40] While this approach does not allow for prescription or prognosis, as do the main-event-centred regression designs of contributions like Alesina and Ardagna[41] or Guajardo et al.[42], we argue that our continuous correlations are better suited to retrace the continuing implementation of fiscal austerity measures in the (post-)crises era in Europe. The following section will specify the measurements we employed to cover the *explanans* and our three dimensions of *explanandum* that has been aggregated into figure 1.

37 For a quite similar distinction within the realm of (near) sovereign defaults, one of the certainly most important reason for the initial adoption of fiscal austerity measures by governments, namely fiscal defaults and aggregate defaults, see Cristina Arellano / Yan Bai, *Fiscal Austerity during Debt Crises*, Minneapolis Fed Research Staff Report No. 525, 2016.

38 Alesina / Ardagna, »Large Changes in Fiscal Policy«, op. cit. (note 9); William Easterly / Klaus Schmidt-Hebbel, »Fiscal Adjustment and Macroeconomic Performance: A Synthesis« in: William Easterly / Carlos Alfredo Rodríguez / Klaus Schmidt-Hebbel (eds.), *Public Sector Deficits and Macroeconomic Performance*, Oxford 1994, pp. 15–78, p. 24.

39 Cyprus has been excluded due to its minor size.

40 Douglas Webber, »Introduction« in: Douglas Webber (ed.), *The Franco-German Relationship in the European Union*, London 1999, pp. 1–20, pp. 3–5.

41 Alesina / Ardagna, »Large Changes in Fiscal Policy«, op. cit. (note 9).

42 Guajardo / Leigh / Pescatori, »Expansionary Austerity?«, op. cit. (note 11).

Figure 1: Assumptions about the relationship between austerity and three core dimensions of societal live, variables and indicators

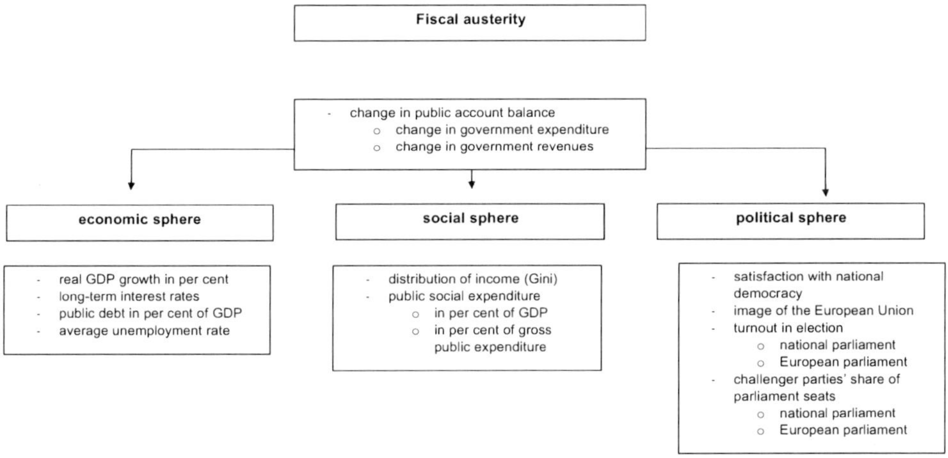

Source: own illustration

Explanatory variables

Measuring fiscal austerity. The measurement of fiscal austerity is non-trivial. We consider fiscal austerity as a process of inducing measures to either reduce public expenditure or increase its revenues. Naturally both aspects can occur in a parallel manner.

Fiscal austerity therefore is measured by using yearly changes in the government account balance. This is consistent with early findings.[43] Moreover, this is in principle in line with the current IMF-internal debate on measuring austerity except for the selection of choosing country-years.[44] While those articles use distinctive episodes of high fiscal shocks induced by austerity packages to project austerity's impact on growth over time, we have chosen a more continuous understanding of austerity. As our units are consecutive country-years in the period 2001 to 2015, we cannot focus on long-term effects of austerity. This is nonetheless necessary to account for the more continuous implementation of fiscal austerity in the crisis-driven recent history of Europe: The measures to manage the crises are overlapping. Therefore, considering the medium- to long-term effects of one year's fiscal austerity would rather muddy the water than reveal clear insights.

Changes in public account balance do cover the *general level* of the fiscal austerity process. As there are rather well elaborated arguments for a distinction to be made between both components of austerity, i.e. *increasing revenues* opposed to *decreasing ex-*

43 Easterly / Schmidt-Hebbel, »Fiscal Adjustment and Macroeconomic Performance «, op. cit. (note 38).

44 Alesina / Ardagna, »Large Changes in Fiscal Policy« op. cit. (note 9); Guajardo / Leigh / Pescatori, »Expansionary Austerity?«, op. cit. (note 11).

penditure, those changes have also been implemented into our approach. This allows us to test our hypotheses not only in respect to fiscal austerity in general but also to the two principal strategies of that phenomenon. Note that *negative* changes in expenditure indicate austerity, while *positive* changes in revenues indicate the same.

Dependent variables

Measuring macroeconomic performance. After defining the indicators used to measure our explanatory variables, our first set of dependent variables has to be operationalized. The most common indicator used to get insights on the general state of one country's economy is real growth of this country's GDP. As the discourse on threats from the financial and euro-currency crises have revolved about, first, countries' debt levels and, second, exploding interest rates as the markets' response to tumbling nations as well as unemployment, those two elements have also been taken into account: Our empirical analysis focuses on (1) yearly real GDP growth, (2) average long-term interest rates for ten-year government bonds for each country-year, (3) the yearly public debt to GDP ratio, and (4) the yearly average of unemployment rates.

Measuring changes in social state activity. The second domain that is in want of operationalization is concerning the social sphere. To test the widespread – and logically coherent – assumption of austerity being connected to or even having caused negative effects on social protection and equality, we use (1) the individual state's overall social expenditure in each year. Here we measure both public social expenditure's ratio to GDP and its ratio to overall public expenditure to check for the relative impact of fiscal austerity in comparison to other policy fields. Furthermore, we draw (2) on changes in distribution of income (Gini coefficient) to also account for austerity's connection to social (in-)equality.[45] Of course these indicators cannot account for all social hardships experienced by people in the crises or under austerity. Since the correlative approach of this contribution is designed to analyse direct and measurable changes in state activity, it is partially blind to its indirect effects diminishing social wellbeing, e.g. downfalls of public services' quality or reaction time after the reduction of public service staff or wages (further see discussion).

Measuring political protest and approval. Our third set of indicators tries to capture two crossing dimensions of possible empirical connections of fiscal austerity and political participation: First, there is a difference between attitude, or expressed opinion (more passive), and actual behaviour (more active). Second, we need to separate the national level from the EU-level. We have therefore selected indicators for each category of the combined dimensions: We (1) measure the attitudes concerning the national level by the satisfaction with national democracy as surveyed by the Eurobarometer. For each country-year, the average of both survey rounds' share of satisfied and very satis-

45 This indicator is used despite some minor issues with coverage of the country-years in focus. We believe that deeper insights could have been derived from also correlating to changes in distribution of *savings*, not only *income*. Unfortunately, data coverage does not allow for the use of that additional indicator.

fied responses has been used. For (2) the public opinion on the European Union, we also draw on Eurobarometer data on the perceived image of the EU, averaging the share of both yearly survey rounds' share of a positive and very positive image of the EU. As to the dimension of actual behaviour, we focus on voter turnout in (3) national and (4) European elections as well as on the seats share of challenger parties, as defined by Hobolt and Tilly[46], after elections to (5) the national parliament and (6) the Parliament of the European Union (EP). These parties reject what the authors describe as a »mainstream consensus«[47] of austerity and European Integration. Drawing upon actual voting behaviour greatly reduces our number of cases in the respective correlations. An alternative measurement to circumvent this could have drawn on opinion polls only. But since, *first*, polls often deviate from actual voting behaviour and, *second*, only the latter – channelled through the respective voting systems that have to be strategically considered by the electorate – is transferred into *real* political influence, i.e. mandates, polls cannot be considered as a fully adequate substitute.[48] This strict distinction between attitude or opinion and behaviour further complicates our correlative design: Since elections do not follow the continuous country-year logic of the other indicators deployed, we only correlated them with the austerity indicators in the year of the election. This derives from the assumption that the most recent austerity measures, i.e. the balance changes adopted in the year before and executed in the year of election, should have the major influence on behaviour.[49]

3. Results

The empirical results (see table 1) of our correlative design are quite diverse and far from unanimously backing either the radical proponents of austerity or its fundamental antagonists. The empirical relationship between fiscal austerity and economic, social, and political changes in our European sample is not an easy one: It's complicated.[50]

46 Hobolt / Tilley, »Fleeing the Centre« op. cit. (note 30).

47 Hobolt / Tilley, »Fleeing the Centre« op. cit. (note 30), p. 3.

48 It needs to be mentioned that even the definition of challenger parties in the applicated form is not without problems: One could argue that parties that have repeatedly held governmental responsibilities, e.g. the Greek *Syriza*, are not so much challenging the European Integration (or even efficaciously rejecting austerity) as becoming part of the establishment.

49 All indicator data have been derived from the World Bank, Eurostat, and OECD Stat Datasets apart from the opinion data (national democracy satisfaction, negative image of the EU) that originate from the Eurobarometer survey and data on national and European elections (turnout and seat shares) that draw on data from the »Parties and Elections in Europe« Dataset.

50 But at least it is fairly consistent. A reduction of the sample to a period after 2007 reveals the same tendencies in correlations of austerity indicators with macroeconomic indicators, with social indicators, and with both democracy satisfaction and Euro-scepticism. The same would be true for the election-related indicators. Due to differentiation of actual voting behaviour and mere opinion, the sample sizes are already stretched thin and results have to be taken with caution. A further reduction of cases would be meaningless.

Austerity and macroeconomic performance. The process of austere politics in general is positively correlated with real GDP growth on a weak but significant level. This is somewhat backing our first assumption (pro H1.1). While there are no significant effects concerning either long-term interest rates or unemployment (contra H1.2 and H1.4), changes in the public balance are positively and significantly correlated with the debt-to-GDP ratio. Even though the correlation is only weak, it contradicts our hypotheses H1.3, for greater austerity is associated with rising debt ratios and not, as predicted, with decreasing ones (all n = 120).

Differentiating between the components of austerity yields further insights: Whereas the only correlation getting significant with expenditure cuts is GDP growth, all chosen macroeconomic indicators show significant correlations with revenue changes. The correlation of expenditure-related austerity with GDP growth is highly significant and negative on a weak to medium level. Due to coding this means that growing public expenditure is associated with sinking GDP growth and *vice versa*. Contrary to this result, increasing public revenues are empirically associated with sinking GDP growth on a weak level. Also, there is a positive and most highly significant correlation with interest rates that is medium in strength, i.e., increased public revenues are related to rising interest rates on long-term government bonds. The correlation of public revenue changes with public debt ratios is also statistically significant and positive with a weak to medium strength. This implies that rising public revenues are empirically connected to increased public debt burdens. Also, we report a marginal significant and weakly positive correlation of the revenue indicator with average unemployment, meaning that increasing public revenues is connected to rising unemployment. This indicates that, while expenditure cuts seem to have positively related on macroeconomic performance (or GDP growth at least), tax increases are (consistently) associated with negative economic developments (all n = 120).

Austerity and social state. The second set of indicators yields a modest harvest regarding the hypotheses of austerity as neoliberal bottom-up redistribution of wealth: Neither fiscal austerity in general nor the component indicators are significantly correlated to the Gini coefficient (n = 102 due to coverage issues mentioned above). Therefore, hypothesis H2.1 has to be rejected for our sample. There is also no significant correlation of any austerity indicator used in this study with the social expenditure in relation to the GDP. With Social expenditure's share of all public expenditure there is a significant (respectively highly significant) weak to medium positive (respectively negative) correlation with public balance changes (respectively public expenditure changes, all n = 112 due to social expenditure data having only been available until 2014). In this sense, fiscal austerity measures in general as well as expenditure-related austerity as negative public expenditure changes are statistically associated with a – counterintuitive – rise of the social expenditure in relation to the whole public expenditure (contra H2.2). This can be interpreted as a pattern of »social-friendly austerity« in which social government is relatively (if not absolutely) protected in comparison to other branches of public spending.

Austerity and political change. Considering the most native domain of the political scientist, there is no correlation whatsoever with fiscal austerity indicators and voter turnout on either national or European level (contra H3.1, all n_{nat} = 34; n_{EP} = 24). Alas, we report a small positive correlation of general fiscal austerity with a more negative EU-image, indicating evidence for H3.4, but none with democracy satisfaction (contra H3.3, *n* = 120). Moreover, we report no significant correlation of fiscal austerity with challenger parties' seat shares in national parliaments (contra H3.2.1) but a highly positive (and highly significant) correlation with challenger seat shares of the EP-contingent of our country-sample (pro H3.2., n_{EP} = 22).

Taking into consideration the two components of fiscal austerity, we only report a most significant and very strong negative correlation between expenditure changes and challenger parties in the EP, implying that expenditure-based austerity is related to high increases of challenger parties' seat shares on that level. Whereas the correlation of revenue changes and the challenger parties' seat share in the EP is not significant, we find a highly significant and weak to medium negative correlation with democracy satisfaction, a highly significant and weak to medium positive correlation with Euroscepticism (both *n* = 120), and a significant and medium positive correlation with the challenger parties' seat share on the national level. Whilst there is a consistency of the general austerities' as well as the possible pathways' association with »negative« political outcome, tax increases are associated with the most.

Table 1: Correlations of fiscal austerity and its components with macroeconomic, social, and political indicators

	Fiscal austerity indicator		
	Public balance changes	Public expenditure changes	Public revenues changes
	Macroeconomic indicators		
GDP growth	**.191***	**–.273****	**–.221***
Interest rates	.085	.018	**.320*****
Debt ratio	**.199***	–.133	**.227***
Unemployment	.116	–.064	**.171+**
	Social indicators		
Gini coefficient	.012	.022	.108
Social expenditure per GDP	.029	.009	.120
Social expenditure by public expenditure	**.238***	**–.243****	.023
	Political indicators		
Turnout, national	–.031	–.027	–.196
Turnout, EP	.242	–.199	.163
Satisfaction with national democracy	–.096	.018	**–.259****
Negative image of EU	**.191***	–.105	**.284****
Challenger seat share, national	–.079	.186	**.344***
Challenger seat share, EP	**.629****	**–.727*****	–.274

Notes: Expenditure-based austerity is reversely coded in relation to the other explanatory variables, i.e., while *positive* values of public balance and revenue changes indicate austerity, the same is true for *negative* values of public expenditure changes.

*** $p < 0.001$; ** $p < 0,01$; * $p < 0.05$; + $p < 0.1$ (two-tailed tests).

Source: own illustration

4. Discussion

The macroeconomic indications of our findings are quite diverse. While there is a small positive effect for the relation of austerity and growth, the other hypothesis towards the macroeconomic dimension cannot be upheld. For debt ratio, there is even a negative relation. Considering expenditure cuts, the résumé is only slightly better because its association with rising debt ratios is not significant – though it has the same direction. Looking at tax increases, the picture is even more sombre, since there are negative implications for all our performance indicators, though most are weak. This implicates that the overall fiscal austerity is not a miraculous healing of all things suffering in the realm of economy – there might even be some side-effects. This might be true for the state's influence as a principle. There are some positive (and negative, depending on the means) implications of fiscal austerity. Alas, there is much variance left to be explained.

The same seems to be valid for the social dimension. We found no evidence for a rise in income inequality under austerity. There is, however, an interesting phenomenon concerning social expenditure: Our assumption of decreasing social expenditure's share of GDP has not been confirmed, and there even is a positive correlation of fiscal austerity and the social expenditure's percentage of gross public expenditure. As has been stressed before, the correlative design employed in this contribution is necessarily simplistic and cannot account for indirect effects of fiscal austerity, such as shrinking quality of public services due to staff reductions. Neither we have taken the discursive aspects of austerity into consideration[51], nor does social expenditure cover all social protection of the state. Our conclusion must therefore necessarily be fragmentary. Our empirical findings furthermore do *not* implicate an *absolute* preservation of social state activity rather than a protection *relative* to other domains. That seemingly illogical finding of a »social state-friendly« austerity might be hinting to a strategic implementation of austerity rather than the dealing of sweeping blows. As the social sector is a sensitive issue for the electorate, politicians might pursue vote and office seeking motives rather than implementing pure austerity doctrine.[52] Spending cuts might prioritize other policy fields less on display.[53] Despite other framings, political decisions are therefore not dead in the Age of Austerity.[54]

Variance continues when one moves on to taking a look at the implications of fiscal austerity for the political sector. While much has been published on fiscal austerity measures precipitating public discontent, violence, and infuriation[55], our findings indicate the need of being careful with overemphasizing the consequences of fiscal austerity for the political realm. While, for instance, we identify no drop in turnout both with regards to the national and the EU level, we still do identify an interesting difference between the two levels: namely, the obviously much higher tendency or inclination of

51 Confer the relevant contributions in this volume.

52 For first findings in respect to strategic timing of consolidating austerity measures by governments, see D. Pascal König / Georg Wenzelburger, »Honeymoon in the Crisis: A Comparative Analysis of the Strategic Timing of Austerity Policies and Their Effect on Government Popularity in Three Countries« in: *Comparative European Politics* 15, No. 6 (2017), pp. 991–1015.

53 Such as gross capital formation and investments into transport infrastructure, for instance. See the contribution by Thorsten Winkelmann in this volume for an extensive discussion.

54 For an overview over history and varieties over the assumption of austerity being an end of political decisions or without alternatives, see Mark Blyth, *Austerity: The History of a Dangerous Idea*, Oxford 2013; Roland Sturm, »Die Entdeckung einer Politik des Unpolitischen. Zur Institutionalisierung der List der Vernunft in der Fiskalpolitik« in: *Politische Vierteljahresschrift* 54 (2013), pp. 403–414; Roland Sturm, »Doch nicht alternativlos? Die EU-Krisenpolitik im Parteienwettbewerb« in: Eckhard Jesse / Roland Sturm (eds.), *Bilanz der Bundestagswahl 2013. Voraussetzungen, Ergebnisse, Folgen*, Baden-Baden 2014, pp. 511–530.

55 Dimitrios Theodossopoulos, »Infuriated with the Infuriated? Blaming Tactics and Discontent about the Greek Financial Crisis« in: *Current Anthropology* 54, No. 2 (2013), pp. 200–221; Japhy Wilson / Erik Swyngedouw (eds.), *The post-political and its discontents: spaces of depoliticisation, spectres of radical politics*, Edinburgh 2014.

voters to cast their vote for a so-called »challenger party« when participating in EU elections. This finding, which first can also be highlighted by the highly significant and very strong negative correlation between austerity conceived of as changes in public expenditure and an increase in challenger parties' seat share in the EP, and second also indicates that EU institutions are generally on the receiving end of the blame game around fiscal austerity, can very well be harmonized with the overall finding that public satisfaction with European integration suffers in times of austerity, while on the other side there is no general negative impact of fiscal austerity on trust in democracy. Implications of fiscal austerity measures on the national level, however, become more visible when one focuses on austerity as changes in public revenues. Here, voters no longer resort to »punishing« the EU by casting their vote for a challenger party but still clearly become more sceptical vis-à-vis the EU in general. In addition to this, now voters also become far more sceptical with national politics in general and also far more often arrive at the decision to vote for a national challenger party. In general, therefore, with regards to the political sphere and its relationship to fiscal austerity, we arrive at a result being in need of explanation: The EU heavily suffers when people are confronted with the public expenditure-paradigm of austerity, as they vote for an anti-establishment party in EP elections, while at the same time we do not identify a significant drop in the overall image of the EU. As soon as we flip things around and look at the public-revenues paradigm of austerity, things change remarkably. There is no longer any significant effect on EP elections, but now we suddenly identify negative implications for the EU image. Quite in contrast to this, we cannot identify any significant importance of distinguishing between the expenditure-paradigm and the revenue-paradigm of austerity for turnout, both on the national and the EU level.

Additionally, we have to acknowledge the fact that our possible insights are restricted due to methodological issues. This is, for instance, the case with an analysis of turnout in EP elections when conceiving of fiscal austerity both according to the public expenditure-paradigm and the public revenue-paradigm. Here, insights into the implications of fiscal austerity could be strengthened by broadening the number of cases included in our sample.

5. Conclusion

Our study of macroeconomic, social, and political implications of fiscal austerity urges to a cautious and differentiated observation of fiscal austerity. Though it has been implemented as *ultima ratio* in the Eurozone and has launched impressive de jure and de facto institutional alterations on the national and European level, our findings suggest that its scope is finite. There have been heated political, medial, and scientific discussions on austerity. It has been super-elevated and demonized alike. Our purpose was not to choose sides – as it is often done in more normatively biased contributions to this topic[56] – but to test a set of common assumptions on possible implications of austerity under a common correlative framework. We found evidence for empirical associations of austerity both to positive and negative issues. This cautious assessment can be highlighted for our macroeconomic indicators by pointing out that there is no significant relationship between spending cuts and the debt ratio or that revenue increases also turn out to be anything but a panacea, but also for the social dimension by our necessarily fragmentary conclusions due to the inability to take into account indirect effects of fiscal austerity measures. And while we do see some interesting results with regards to the political dimension, in especially when comparing »tax austerity« and »spending austerity«, we are still far away from satisfyingly understanding the relationship between political indicators and fiscal austerity measures.

Furthermore, we would argue that the power of the state (or its fiscal austerity) is not infinite and has limited scope. As so often, therefore, we need to conclude our remarks by arguing that there is no easy and clear answer to our research question. However, in any case, we have identified additional puzzles in need of an explanation, which in turn both can significantly enrich our understanding of the precise effects and implications the age of austerity is likely to have on and for Western societies and enable us to better comprehend the importance of the two paradigms located within austerity, namely the public-expenditure paradigm and the public-revenue paradigm.

56 Karger, »The bitter pill«, op. cit. (note 3); Blyth, *Austerity: The History of a Dangerous Idea*, op. cit. (note 54); or Klatzer / Schlager, »Fiskalpakt – immerwährende Austerität, Demontage von Wohlfahrtsstaat und sozialen Rechten«, op. cit. (note 24).

Thorsten Winkelmann

Lost highway: Implications of Austerity in Infrastructure Policies

1. Austerity in the infrastructure sector

Public infrastructure – defined as those institutions whose services are used by almost all sectors of the economy and which therefore constitute a central prerequisite for the economic activity of a country – can be understood as a necessary remit of the state. High-quality and well-developed infrastructure is one, if not the essential, condition for the performance and competitiveness of an industrial site, and it is the foundation for prosperity and social harmony. The requisite institutions are, despite material-technical and organizational-institutional differences, characterized by certain common features: they cannot arise from the private sector, as this would result in societally undesirable infrastructural facilities with regard to allocation, distribution, or stability.[1] The public sector therefore usually assumes responsibility for the provision of such institutions and their funding.[2] These expenditures are under increased pressure as a consequence of the economic and financial crisis. Austerity – defined here as government budget policies that have to make do without generating new debt and in the middle-term aspire to a balanced budget – can, in the area of transportation infrastructure, in the first instance affect either the entirety of the available resources for new construction or the available resources for infrastructure maintenance. The resulting relative and absolute changes can be estimated over time, based upon official investment rates. The use of additional official investment means to overcome the current weak growth in the European region could trigger multipliers or (regional) spill-over effects, which in turn, in neo-Keynesian fashion, contribute to stimulation of aggregate demand.[3] Such effects are, among other reasons, attributable to the fact that, during construction, jobs are created or retained, while transport costs sink in the middle and long term, which not only improves the competitiveness of a national economy but also the entire

1 Robert Musgrave / Peggy Musgrave / Lore Kullmer, *Die öffentlichen Finanzen in Theorie und Praxis*, Tübingen 1990.

2 Thorsten Winkelmann, *Public-Private Partnership. Auf der Suche nach Substanz*, Baden-Baden 2012.

3 David Aschauer, »Does Public Capital Crowd out Private Capital?« in: *Journal of Monetary Economics* 24, No. 2 (1989), pp. 171–188; James Heintz / Robert Pollin / Heidi Garrett-Peltier, *How infrastructure investments support the US economy: employment, productivity and growth*, Washington, D.C. 2009; Ionna Glykou / Christos Pitelis, »On the political economy of the state, the public-private nexus and industrial policy« in: *Policy Studies* 32, No. 4 (2011), pp. 461–478; Joseph Francois / Miriam Manchin, *Institutions, Infrastructure and Trade*, World Bank Policy Research Working Paper No. 4152, 2007; Christos Pitelis, »European industrial and competition policy: perspectives, trends and a new approach« in: *Policy Studies* 28, No. 4 (2007), pp. 365–381; Valeria Ramey, »Can Government Purchases Stimulate the Economy? « in: *Journal of Economic Literature* 49, No. 3 (2011), pp. 673–685.

internal market, for example with regard to trans-European networks.[4] In addition to the economies of scale thus realized, a number of indirect effects arise for the labour market and productivity, but also for private investment activity, which, especially in times of economic stagnation, can contribute to overcoming a crisis.[5] As Andy Walker puts it, »[i]nfrastructure investment is the best way to avoid austerity.«[6] Such a proactive long-term growth strategy, which would have to take the existing inefficiencies in the provision of public infrastructure and of value-adding investments into account, would (still) require farther reaching cuts in other areas, as otherwise the solidity of the public budget would suffer. It is, therefore, also conceivable that austerity can be accompanied by sinking public investment costs, without triggering any appreciable societal resistance. While cuts in social services are equated with impoverishment of entire social strata[7], the public is seldom exercised by cuts in infrastructure investments.[8] Moreover, according to the Ricardian equivalence theorem, public investments result in crowding out, so that the growth effects associated with infrastructure expenditure can in this way be guaranteed. Flyvbjerg raises the question of which infrastructure investments in developed economies yield any growth effects at all, because in saturated markets projects are sometimes undertaken without any attention to need.[9] »Ghost infrastructures« proof that infrastructure investments do not always serve the intended purpose, particularly as these often exceed initial timetables and budgets.[10] In sum, *Austerity has an impact on capital expenditures, wherein both cuts and excessive expenditure are conceivable.*

4 See for example Glykou / Pitelis, »On the political economy of the state, the public-private nexus and industrial policy«, op. cit. (note 3); Francois / Manchin, »Institutions, Infrastructure and Trade«, op. cit. (note 3); Debra Johnson / Colin Turner, *Strategy and Policy for trans-European Networks*, Basingstoke 2007.

5 TUC, *The price of austerity. How spending cuts damaged the economy, and how they could do so again*, 2015, https://www.tuc.org.uk/sites/default/files/ThePriceofAusterity.pdf [1.1.2017].

6 Andy Walker, » Infrastructure investment is best way to avoid austerity says World Bank« in: *Infrastructure Intelligence*, 2016, http://www.infrastructure-intelligence.com/article/jun-2016/infrastructure-investment-best-way-avoid-austerity-says-world-bank [1.1.2017].

7 See Mark Blyth, *Austerity: The History of a Dangerous Idea*, Oxford 2013; Hans-Jürgen Bieling / Tobias Haas / Julia Lux, »Is the Crisis Triggering a New European Cycle of Conflict?« in: *Zeitschrift für Außen- und Sicherheitspolitik* 6, No. 1 (2013), pp. 231–249; Paul Krugman, »Austerity's Grim Legacy« in: *New York Times*, 6.11.2015, http://www.nytimes.com/2015/11/06/opinion/austeritys-grim-legacy.html [1.1.2017]; Owen Jones, »We must stop Angela Merkel's bullying – or let the forces of austerity win« in: *The Guardian*, 28.1.2015.

8 Roland Sturm / Thorsten Winkelmann, »Contested Infrastructures – Citizen Protest and the Response of Political Parties« in: Hanns Seidel Foundation (ed.), *Political Parties and Citizen Movements in Asia and Europe*, Stockholm 2014, pp. 23–37, pp. 23–25; Thorsten Winkelmann, »Zwischen Kostenexplosion und bürgerlichem Protest: die Erstellung öffentlicher Infrastrukturen« in: GWP 62, No. 4 (2013), pp. 493–502, pp. 493–495.

9 Bent Flyvbjerg, »Policy and planning for large-infrastructure projects: problems, causes, cures« in: *Environment and Planning B: Planning and Design* 34, No. 4 (2007), pp. 578–597.

10 Thorsten Winkelmann, *Defizite bei der Erstellung öffentlicher Infrastrukturen*, Aachen 2014.

In addition to these supply-side changes, strategies to attract additional private resources can be implemented. These can encompass both the financing of the requisite institutions through private investors and the change of use to an increased user-financing.[11] If, for example, toll-model based user-financing is not accounted for, individualized cost allocations, at the end of which a self-financing infrastructure could be based[12], enable the substitution of public capital by private. Here, partial and full privatization, fund solutions, or different cooperation models with the private sector are all conceivable options. Public-private partnerships, so-called long-term infrastructure contracts (LTICs), based on contractually agreed exchange relationships between public contractors and private implementers, can be inter-organizationally reconstructed as Principal-Agent relationships.[13] In these, the public principal assigns a compilation of required services (Design-Build-Finance-Operate DBFO) to an external private agent to implement.[14] The private agent plans, builds, finances, and operates a public institution over a contractual period of twenty to thirty years. At the same time the private agent assumes certain risks for which s/he receives regular compensation. Such partnerships are attractive to public actors not least because in individual cases they are associated with provable/proven economic advantages (value for money).[15] The use of commercial operational rationales is, therefore, primarily oriented towards accepted cost-cutting potential in public expenditure. Grimshaw et al. posit that the increasing expansion of PPPs is evidence of »a growing belief that national economies increasingly face an inbuilt incapacity to finance the provision of public services.«[16] It can be inferred that privatization and PPP models will increasingly be used as a consequence of

11 The Economist, *Future-Proofing Infrastructure Assests. Building capital-efficient infrastructure in the age of austerity*, 2014, https://www.eiuperspectives.economist.com/sites/default/files/FUTURE-PROOFING%20INFRASTRUCTURE%20ASSETS%20-%20Building%20capital-efficient%20infrastructure%20in%20the%20age%20of%20austerity.pdf [1.1.2017].

12 Justin Yifu Lin / Doerte Doemeland, *Beyond Keynesianism. Global Infrastructure Investments in Times of Crisis*, The World Bank Policy Research Working Paper No. 5940, 2012, p. 2. There they argue that »under current economic circumstances, however, investing in bottleneck-releasing infrastructure projects that are self-financing may be the best option. « For a similar argumentation see Thorsten Winkelmann, »Auf dem Weg zu einer modernen Infrastrukturpolitik? Die PKW-Maut für Ausländer« in: GWP 63, No. 2 (2014), pp. 253–261.

13 Thorsten Winkelmann, »Neue Wege der Haushaltspolitik im Föderalismus: alternative Beschaffungsformen in Nordrhein-Westfalen« in: EZFF (ed.), *Jahrbuch für Föderalismus*, Baden-Baden 2013, pp. 286–300.

14 Edward Yescombe, *Principles of project finance*, Amsterdam 2008; Thorsten Winkelmann, *Public-Private Partnership*, op. cit. (note 2); Thorsten Winkelmann / Birgit Pickenäcker / Rainer Korte, *PPP – Vergleichsring Evaluierungsprogramm PPP Schulstudie*, Köln 2012.

15 David Osborne / Ted Gaebler, *Reinventing Government – How the Entrepreneurial Spirit Is Transforming the Public Sector*, New York 1993; Nicholas Deakin, »Public-Private Partnerships: a UK case study« in: *Public Management Review* 4, No. 2 (2002), pp. 133–147, p. 135; Thorsten Winkelmann, »Erfolgsfaktoren von vertraglichen PPP-Projekten auf kommunaler Ebene« in: *Moderner Staat* 6, No. 2 (2013), pp. 1–42.

16 Damian Grimshaw / Steve Vincent T Hugh Willmott, »Going privately: partnership and outsourcing in UK public services« in: *Public Administration* 80, No. 3 (2002), pp. 475–502.

austerity, because these approaches allow public indebtedness to remain unchanged, and as such they do not impact upon the statutory and in some cases legally anchored upper-limits for credit. Because of this, according to Dexter Whitfield, austerity also leads to an increased integration of private actors into public service provision, as these services afford new opportunities for accumulation of capital.[17] Put it in other words: PPP as an alternative to immediate full public financing might be particularly attractive to governments with high deficits because the necessary credits for a project are made from private sector and are not fully included in the public accounts at the beginning of a project. It can be hypothesized that governments with high annual deficits have bigger incentives to avoid fiscal stress and therefore make greater use of PPP. Raising additional private investment is another argument in support of PPP.[18] Nevertheless, counter-effects are conceivable, as the economic and financial crisis has exposed political risks (to the states). These uncertainties are to a degree so significant because, for private investors, investments in infrastructure only amortize over the long term.[19] Such »long-term assets« are consequently linked to such considerable risks that austerity politics do not necessarily lead to increased participation of private actors as operators and/or funders of public institutions. A working hypothesis is therefore: *Austerity can both promote and hinder the integration of private economic actors in public infrastructure.*

2 Infrastructure politics in the European perspective: comparisons between Greece, Spain, France, Portugal, Italy, Germany and the United Kingdom

2.1 Capital expenditure in the Age of Austerity

Investment rates allow first impressions whether austerity was implemented within a given period or not. The following indicators give insight: if expenditures for consumption purposes are subtracted from total public expenditure, the result is the – inflation-adjusted – capital expenditure (including investment expenditures) of all public authorities. They cover all those expenditures accrued currently – that is at the point of their incurrence – but primarily intended for later tangible benefits for the economy or later fiscal years by stimulating aggregate demand. Capital expenditures are primarily invested in fixed assets. Investments in fixed assets are concretized by the relative, and

17 Dexter Whitfield, *In Place of Austerity. Reconstructing the economy, state and public services*, Nottingham 2012, p. 1.

18 Furthermore PPP has also been discussed in the context of the New Public Management reforms in the 1990s. This reform debate creates an atmosphere which transferred managerial ideas and practices from the private sector to the public sector bureaucracy. NPM and PPP seemed to be promising answers to the most urgent problems of public sector bureaucracy: exploding costs and inefficiency.

19 Nicolas J. Firzli / Vincent Bazi, »Infrastructure Investments in an Age of Austerity: The Pension and Sovereign Funds Perspective« in: *Turkish Weekly*, 30.6.2011, http://www.turkishweekly.net/2011/07/30/op-ed/infrastructure-investments-in-an-age-of-austerity-the-pension-and-sovereign-funds-perspective/ [1.1.2017].

absolute, public gross investments, which are defined as the totality of all annual investments – that is gross investments – made by public authorities.

Changes in stock include acquisitions less disposals of valuables.[20] Gross capital investments also correspond to the difference between acquisitions and the disposal of fixed assets.[21] However, only a fraction of public gross investments flows into transport infrastructure. This includes all public expenditure for rail-, traffic – and waterways.

Figure 1: Gross public investment as a % of GDP

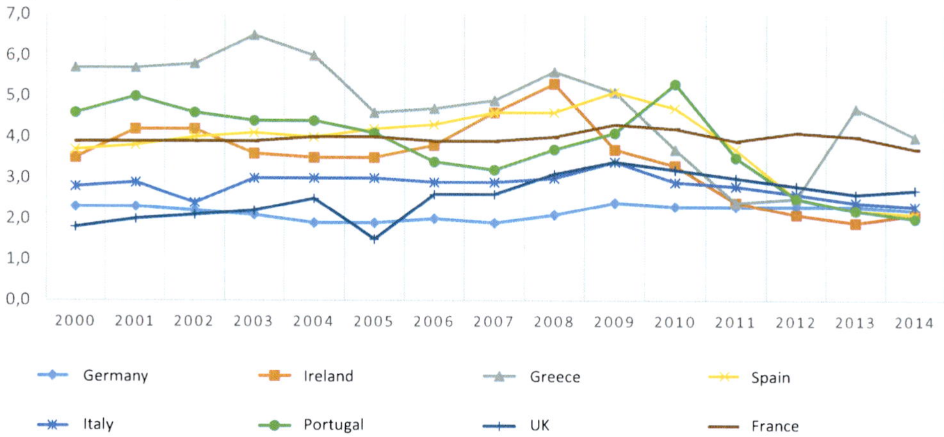

Source: own illustration based on OECD-Stat

20 Karel Havik / Kieran Mc Morrow / Fabrice Orlandi / Christophe Planas / Rafal Raciborski / Werner Röger, *The Production Function Methodology for Calculating Potential Growth Rates & Output Gaps*, European Commission Economic Papers No. 535, 2014).

21 OECD, *Investitionsquoten – Die OECD in Zahlen und Fakten 2010: Wirtschaft, Umwelt, Gesellschaft*, 2010, http://dx.doi.org/10.1787/9789264087552-15-de [29.6.2017].

Figure 2: Gross investment per GDP (before/after 2010)

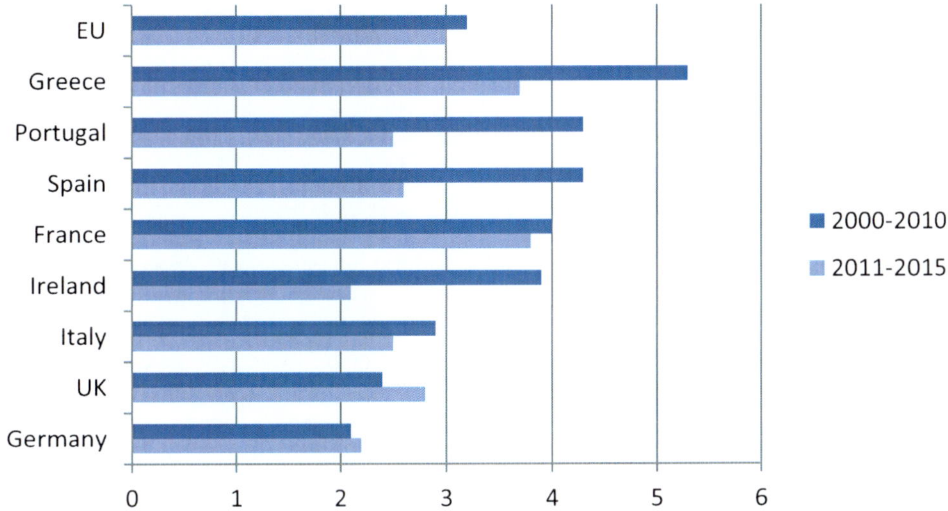

Source: own illustration based on OECD-Stat

Figure 1 illustrates the percentage change in public gross investments in relation to GDP, while figure 2 illustrates this relationship before and during the crisis. There were significant differences in levels in the countries included in the study, which, quite apart from austerity, reflect, in the first instance, the different levels of development of the various economies. The expenditure corresponds to the area, population, and level of development of a given economy. National differences can also be attributed to the specific initial conditions, political cultures, balance of power, and constellation of actors; in short, the respective roles and significance of the public sector are reflected here to a certain degree.[22] Highly developed economies, like the UK or Germany, invest a much lower percentage, because in these economies tendencies to saturation and sinking economies of scale exist, which means that, with a few exceptions, capital-intensive new infrastructure construction is no longer necessary; instead, restoration, maintenance, and modernization are more important.[23] The comparatively low German and, to a lesser degree, British investment rates can be traced back to the observed

22 Helmut Cox, *Daseinsvorsorge und öffentliche Dienstleistungen in der Europäischen Union*, Baden-Baden 2000; Florian Mayer, *Vom Niedergang des unternehmerisch tätigen Staates: Privatisierungspolitik in Deutschland, Frankreich, Italien und Deutschland*, Wiesbaden 2006.

23 DIW Berlin / Handelsblatt Research Institute (HRI), *Private Investitionen in Deutschland, Studie im Auftrag des Gemeinschaftsausschusses der Deutschen Gewerblichen Wirtschaft*, Düsseldorf 2014; Martin Gornig / Alexander Schiersch, »Investitionsschwäche in der EU: ein branchenübergreifendes und langfristiges Phänomen« in: *DIW Wochenbericht*, No. 27, 2014, pp. 653–660; Guido Baldi / Ferdinand Fichtner / Claus Michelsen / Malte Rieth, »Schwache Investitionen dämpfen Wachstum in Europa« in: *DIW Wochenbericht*, No. 81, 2014, pp. 637–651.

capital exports that resulted from the introduction of the Euro, which profited the southern periphery. In the past, the corruption-prone »building« frenzy resulted in comparatively higher investment rates for the public sector.[24] These refinanced investments, primarily financed by government borrowing, resulted in higher gross fixed capital investments in other European countries than in Germany.

A temporary adjustment resulted from the advent of the economic and financial crises and the steps taken to overcome them: here in Germany as in the UK, Portugal, and Ireland this can be traced back to the increase in investment rates in the stimulus packages concluded nationally between 2008 and 2010 (figure 1). In the context of these »neo-Keynesian« crash programmes, considerable resources were made available in the short term for infrastructure development to use public resources to stimulate the crisis of private demand, with which the expectation of positive employment and growth effects were associated. A detectable Europe-wide correction in public sector involvement in building activity set in when these time- bound stimuli expired, which by percentage was highest in Portugal, Spain, Ireland, and Greece. As a result, most countries are far removed from their own pre-crisis levels, because, as previously, total economic uncertainty and worsened financial conditions still exist, now accompanied by significant restrictions in capital expenditures: In Greece, Italy, Spain, and Portugal, these approach minus 30%, whereas France has attained the pre-crisis levels, and Germany and the UK have slightly exceeded these levels.[25]

While gross fixed asset investments include all expenditures of tangible and intangible fixed assets, so, for example, such categories of goods as software or military equipment and buildings that can be used for civilian purposes, infrastructure investments are specifically those expended for the renovation, construction, and modernization of roads, bridges, rails, civil engineering works, etc. Cuts in these areas are typical in especially Spain and Portugal, while in Greece such savings were made *before* the onset of the crisis (see figure 3). Whereas in 2003 Greece invested 1.9% of her GDP in infrastructure, by 2005 this had fallen to only 0.8%. In Germany, by contrast, investments remained persistently low, which does nothing to close the widely acknowledged investment gap.[26] Whereas in 2011 only 0.45% of GDP was invested here at home in the

24 »Gefährliche Bauwut – Spaniens Schienennetz viel zu schnell gebaut?« in: *Focus-Online*, 26.7.2013, http://www.focus.de/panorama/welt/gefaehrliche-bauwut-spaniens-schienennetz-viel-zu-schnell-gebaut_id_3020562.html [1.1.2017].

25 IMF, »Private Investment: What's the holdup?« in: IMF (ed.), *World Economic Outlook*, April 2015, Washington, D.C. 2015, pp. 111–143; Ryan Niladri Banerjee / Jonathan Kearns / Marco Jacopo Lombardi, »(Why) Is investment weak?« in: *BIS Quarterly Review*, March 2015, pp. 67–82; Narcissa Balta, »Investment dynamics in the euro area since the crisis« in: *European Commission Quarterly Report on the Euro Area* 14, No. 1 (2015), pp. 35–42; Bergljot Barkbu / Pelin Berkmen / Pavel Lukyantsau / Sergejs Saksonovs / Hanni Schoelermann, *Investment in the Euro Area: Why Has It Been Weak?*, IMF Working Paper WP/15/32, 2015).

26 Pällmann-Kommission, *Schlussbericht*, 2000, http://www.binnenhaefen.de/fileadmin/user_upload/download_alteSeite/all/paellmann_kommission_abschlussbericht.pdf [1.1.2017]; Bodewig-Kommission, *Konzeptdokument »Nachhaltige Verkehrsinfrastrukturfi-*

road network, Spain (0.56%), and France (0.59%) invested significantly more, while the UK and Ireland (both 0.29%) invested significantly less.

Figure 3: Investments in transport infrastructure as a percentage of GDP

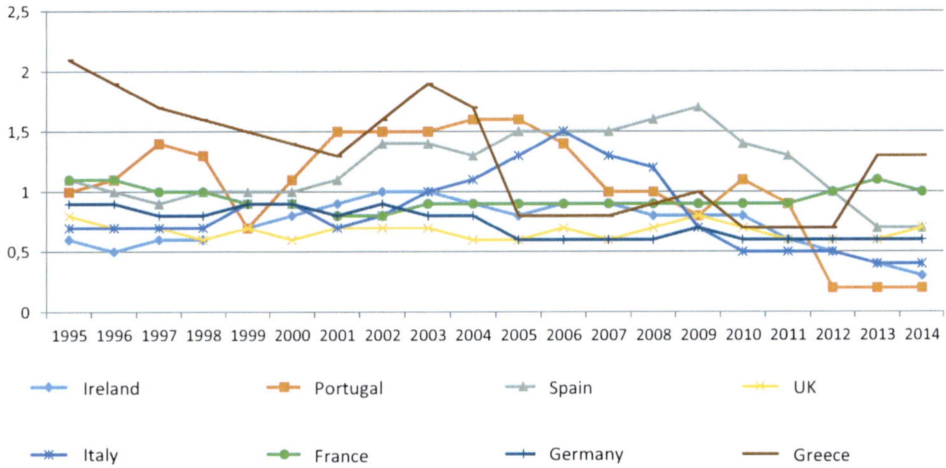

Source: own illustration based on International Transport Forum

Taken together, this confirms the thesis that, in the area of transport infrastructure, austerity already affects the level of funds made available. The changes are however by no means uniform: if the especially in 2009 effective temporarily additional expenditure, implemented in the wake of the stimulus packages, is discounted, the financial resources for Germany and the UK remain broadly constant. That means that austerity measures, in as much as they followed in these countries, do not affect the investment sector but exclusively the social and consumption sectors. So although the rate of investment in both countries develops independent of the crisis, and therefore the empirical evidence of a systematic savings or austerity policy is lacking, the public perception is of dilapidated bridges, roads filled with potholes, construction sites, traffic congestion, and a general state of disrepair.

In France and, to a degree, in Greece, investments have been increased since 2013, either to generate economic momentum or to drive strategic plans. Several consequences have resulted: France has invested in her infrastructure and has, for that rea-

nanzierung«, 2013, http://www.vifg.de/_downloads/service/Bericht_Bode-wig-Kommission_13-10-02.pdf [1.1.2017]; Daehre-Kommission, *Bericht der Kommission »Zukunft der Verkehrsinfrastrukturfinanzierung«*, 2012, http://www.bundesrat.de/VMK/DE/termine/sitzungen/12-12-19-abschlussbericht-komm-zukunft-vif.html [1.1.2017]; Uwe Kunert / Heike Link, »Verkehrsinfrastruktur: Substanzerhaltung erfordert deutlich höhere Investitionen« in: *DIW Wochenbericht*, No. 26, 2013; Institut der deutschen Wirtschaft (IW), *Infrastruktur zwischen Standortvorteil und Investitionsbedarf*, Cologne 2014; DIW (Deutsches Institut für Wirtschaftsforschung), »Investitionen für mehr Wachstum – Eine Zukunftsagenda für Deutschland« in: *DIW Wochenbericht* 80, No. 26 (2013).

son, had to be prepared to assume additional debt. France has sought to overcome the crisis through expansive budgetary measures, that is, through the opposite of austerity.[27] This »deficit spending« has, however, not contributed to a significant improvement in GDP by comparison within Europe but has certainly increased the French debt ratio.[28] A significant decline in capital expenditure in Greece is noticeable, but this had already occurred *before* the onset of the economic- and financial crisis. Only public gross investment (see figure 1) declined as a consequence of the crisis and has promptly recovered, although without attaining pre-crisis levels. From mid-2012, expenditure for transport infrastructure increases, from which two conclusions can be drawn: First, isolated observation of consumption and capital public expenditure, austerity, and saving measures must almost exclusively be implemented in the social sector. Second, savings and investment are not mutually exclusive. Rather, national spending cuts are accompanied by European investment measures. In this fashion, on average 25% of all investments in Greek transport infrastructure between 2007 and 2013 were earmarked/made available from the Cohesion Fund.[29]

The third sample includes countries like Spain, Portugal, Ireland, and Italy, in which comprehensive cuts were made for budget consolidation. With these actions, each government tries to generate long-term growth.[30] There is reason to believe that the concurrent decline in both public and private building activity in Spain has aggravated the crisis, deepened the economic downturn, and increased unemployment. As documented in the capital expenditure, in no other country such cuts have occurred. This allows the conclusion that in Spain austerity has particularly affected public capital expenditure and undermined the fundament of pre-crisis success. To put it in numbers: The Spanish economic boom was based, in the first instance, upon the hypertrophied building sector, which has since 2004 contributed more than 10% to gross value added and, at its peak, employed more than 2.7 million people. With the onset of the crisis, the PP government, in place since Christmas 2011, under Prime Minister Mariano Rajoy has instituted wide-ranging austerity measures, especially in the area of infrastructure investments. The *Ministerio de Fomento* has had to reduce its expenditure by 35% in comparison with the previous year (2011), which amounts to cuts of about €33 bil-

27 Dorothée Allain-Dupré / Claudia Hulbert / Camila Vammalle, *Public Investment at Central and Sub-national Levels: An Adjustment Variable for OECD Countries in the Present Context of Austerity?*, 2012, https://www.oecd.org/gov/regional-policy/Effective-Public-Investment-Overview-Paper.pdf [1.1.2017].

28 Esther Pérez Ruiz, *The Drivers of Business Investment in France: Reasons for Recent Weakness, France Selected Issues*, Country Report No. 14/183, Washington, D.C. 2014.

29 John Finnegan / Richard Redfern / Jacopo Signorile, *Transport. Final Report – Ex post evaluation of Cohesion Policy programmes 2007–2013, focusing on the European Regional Development Fund (ERDF) and the Cohesion Fund (CF)*, 2015, http://ec.europa.eu/regional_policy/sources/docgener/evaluation/pdf/expost2013/wp5_final_report_en.pdf [1.1.2017], p. 28; Christophe Kamps / Nadine Leiner-Killinger / Reiner Martin, »The cyclical impact of EU cohesion policy in fast growing EU countries« in: *Intereconomics* 44, No. 1 (2009), pp. 23–29, pp. 23–25.

30 Deutsche Bundesbank, »Zur Investitionstätigkeit im Euro-Raum« in: Deutsche Bundesbank (ed.), *Monatsbericht Januar (33)*, Frankfurt/Main 2016, pp. 33–52.

lion within two years.[31] This has resulted in a decline in investment rates of about 10% in comparison to the pre-crisis levels, putting it just under the eurozone average. Similar developments can be seen in Ireland. In Portugal, the government also curtailed the volume of investment in public roadwork and, at the same time, increased tolls.[32] However, through the use of the EU Structural Funds it was able to compensate for additional declines. Greece also decreased capital goods investments but invested much more than the EU-average.[33]

2.2 Integration of private actors in the Age of Austerity

Politically instituted austerity programmes must find a balance between increased expectations of public services and the capacity to finance them. Against this background, alternative procurement models, which are not only based on financing of public institutions but also on partnerships in operation of institutions and services, become more significant. Political decision makers want to cover the growing need for extension, replacement, and modernization of infrastructure through PPP approaches.[34] In as much as these procurement approaches could, as a result of austerity, increase in importance, investments can apparently be achieved without the incurrence of new debt.

31 Lothar Witte, *Austeritätspolitik in Europa: Spanien. FES International Policy Analysis*, Berlin 2012, http://library.fes.de/pdf-files/id-moe/09290.pdf [9.1.2017], p. 3; Allain-Dupré / Hulbert / Vammalle, *Public Investment at Central and Sub-national Levels*, op. cit. (note 27), p. 13.

32 José Castro Caldas, *The Consequences of Austerity Policies in Portugal. FES International Policy Analysis*, Berlin 2012, http://library.fes.de/pdf-files/id-moe/09311.pdf [10.01. 2017], p. 2.

33 Barkbu et al., *Investment in the Euro Area: Why Has It Been Weak?*, op. cit. (note 25).

34 Darrin Grimsey / Mervyn Lewis, *Public Private Partnership: the worldwide revolution in infrastructure provision and project finance*, Cheltenham 2004, p. 105.

Figure 4: The PPP market in Europe[35]

Source: own illustration based on European Investment Bank

As figure 4 illustrates, this assumption is not reflected on the European level. Since the onset of the economic and financial crisis in 2007/2008, fewer and fewer public construction projects have been organized as PPPs. The European Investment Bank has calculated that the PPP market has collapsed by 50% since 2008.[36]

35 When performing empirical social research on PPP, data problems do often arise. In some countries, PPP units such as Partnership UK, the MAPPP in France, ÖPPP Deutschland AG in Germany, and the construction industry's SEOPAN in Spain provide useful quantitative and qualitative project information.

36 Andreas Kappeler / Mathieu Nemoz, *Public-private partnerships in Europe – before and during the recent financial crisis*, EIB Working Papers, No. 4, 2010, p. 9.

Figure 5: Scale and Number of PPP projects implemented (2015)

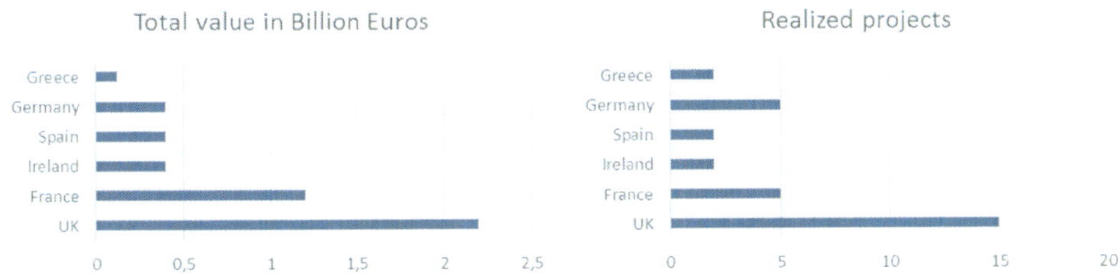

Source: own illustration based on European Investment Bank

Of the countries studied, the UK has topped the ranks of the number of such projects instituted. In no other country so many projects have been implemented. As the National Audit Office (NAO) found in its report »The choice of finance for capital investment«, PFI (Private Finance Initiative) investments with a volume of over €78 billion have been achieved since their introduction 25 years ago. The result is that one-tenth of all public infrastructure investments are organized as PFIs. Significant changes have become evident as a result of the economic- and financial-crisis-related austerity policy.

Figure 6: Number of PFI Projects implemented

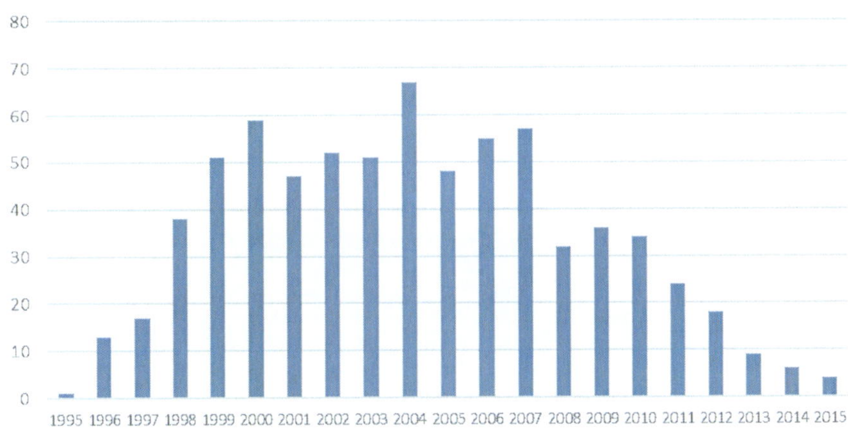

Source: own illustration based on Partnership UK

In the last five years, the average annual volume of capital acquired through PFI has sunk from nearly €6 billion to €2.98 billion in 2015. These changes can be traced back to the six to seven per cent increases in the cost of refinancing means/capital.[37] Through these expenses, PFI procurement has lost its greater efficiency in comparison with conventional credit-financed solutions. But because the British government still wants private participation in public infrastructure and wants to increase this, comprehensive measures have been adopted to increase the integration of private capital and know-how. In the context of these strategies, characterized by Hellowell (2010) as a neoliberal Agenda[38], a new authority, the »Infrastructure and Projects Authority« (IPA), has been established under the direct remit of the Finance Ministry, with the goal of spurring private participation in large infrastructure projects in particular. For projects at the communal level, the relevant authority is the »Local Partnerships« authority, also under the remit of HM Treasury, whose mandate it is to support the implementation of PFI projects across the board. In order to enable this, the British government has reformed the PPP/PFI concept. A range of structural reforms have been consolidated under the description »PF2 Finance«, which, among other things, streamlines the tendering process and simplifies procedures for the allocation of risk.[39] The »National Infrastructure Plan«, on the other hand, outlines the long-term strategic goals of the government until 2021. Private and public infrastructure expenditures of £483 billion are envisioned in the sectors »Transport«, »Energy«, »Communications«, »Flood Defence«, »Water«, »Waste«, und »Science«.[40] The goal is that ca. 50% of all projects are privately financed and operated. The Cameron government of the time accompanied this ambitious goal with a fund-based investment offensive, the so-called »Infrastructure and Capital Investment Framework«, in the amount of €17 billion. These resources come from a range of sources: the National Pensions Reserve Fund, the European Investment Bank/Council of Europe Bank, domestic banks, and foreign investors.[41] In sum, the British government sees both the application of PFI and the private financing of public infrastructure as a part of its austerity policy.[42] This policy follows a more pragmatic than dogmatic strategic direction and does not exclude the nationalization of PPP projects, as can be seen in the example of the London

37 National Audit Office, *Financing PFI projects in the credit crisis and the Treasury's response*, London 2010; Rien Wagenvoort / Carlo De Nicola / Andreas Kappeler, *Infrastructure Finance in Europe: Composition, Evolution and Crisis Impact*, EIB Papers, No. 1, 2010.

38 Mark Hellowell, »The UK's Private Finance Initiative: history, evaluation, prospects« in: Graeme A. Hodge / Carsten Greve / Anthony E. Boardman (eds.), *International Handbook on Public-Private Partnerships*, Cheltenham 2010, pp. 307–332, p. 307.

39 HM Treasury, *Reform of the Private Finance Initiative*, London 2011; HM Treasury, *Private Finance 2 (PF2)*, 2013, http://www.hmtreasury.gov.uk/infrastructure_pfireform.htm [12.1.2017].

40 Infrastructure and Projects Authority, *National Infrastructure Delivery Plan 2016–2021*, 2016, https://www.gov.uk/government/uploads/system/uploads/attachment_data/file/510525/2904569_NIDP_2016-2021_updated.pdf [12.1.2017], p. 9.

41 Matthias Beck / Gail Sheppard, *A Public Private Partnership Revival?*, 2015, http://qpol.qub.ac.uk/a-public-private-partnership-revival/ [13.1.2017].

42 For a critical view on this, see UNISON Scotland, *COMBATING AUSTERITY. Signposting the ways Scotland could limit some of the damage*, 2015, http://www.unison-scotland.org.uk/publicworks/CombatingAusterity_Sep2015.pdf [13.1.2017], pp. 9–11.

Tube, which after significant budgetary overspend and poor quality will be administered by the state in the future.[43]

The extent of PPP projects implemented has also declined in the other countries in the study. Although the Irish government expended a total of €1.183 billion in PPP projects in the school sector between 2010 and 2016[44], it did not realize either the »Dart Underground« (€2 billion project volume) or the »Metro North« (€3 billion) through PPPs; neither project will be advanced further, even using conventional means.[45] Private investments in infrastructure also declined as a result of considerable risk of default and additional uncertainties, especially those particularly prevalent in the period between 2010 and 2014. The National Roads Authority (NRA) had to make compensation payments as private toll incomes of both Highway M3 (Dublin-Cavan) and the Limerick Tunnel were 20% lower than contractually agreed. In addition, financing problems delayed public tendering for PPP projects (e.g., Gort to Tuam highway), while other projects are now publicly organized (e.g., the Thoronton Hall prison). To further stimulate investment in infrastructure, the Irish government plans, in collaboration with the European Investment Bank, to establish her own infrastructure fund, in which private actors can participate – so far with moderate success. Public institutions are to be sold as part of the austerity policy negotiated with the Troika. The intention is to achieve privatization revenues of about €3 billion, of which so far only €1 billion have actually been raised.[46]

Although France has a long statist tradition, it has implemented a, by comparison, large number of PPP projects in roadwork as well as in energy and water provision, predominantly on a concessional basis. France has a fund in the amount of €8 billion, managed by the public bank *Caisse des Dépôts et Consignants*, to guarantee the tendering process and the financing of PPP projects, from which the numerous concessional roadwork projects particularly profit.[47] These public guarantees, which are also employed in other countries, are intended to establish confidence in PPP approaches and are used primarily for large volume projects like the Tours–Bordeaux high-speed railway (€5.4 billion) or the Bretagne–Pays de la Loire high-speed railway (€1.2 billion). In order to enable investment in infrastructure and in particular highways and high-speed rail networks, President Hollande has recommended increasing the participation of private actors in public concerns, because without PPPs numerous projects could

43 House of Commons, *London Underground PPP: background*, 2012, http://researchbriefings.files.parliament.uk/documents/SN01307/SN01307.pdf [14.1.2017].

44 http://ppp.gov.ie/ppp-projects/.

45 PPP Bulletin, »A PIIGS ear« in: *Partnerships Bulletin*, 1.2.2013, http://www.partnerships-bulletin.com/features/view/1057 [14.1.2017].

46 Julien Mercille / Enda Murphy, *Deepening Neoliberalism, Austerity, and Crisis: Europe's Treasure Ireland*, Basingstoke 2015, p. 101.

47 CMS, *PPP in Europe*, 2010, https://cms.law/en/content/download/81910/3036167/version/2/file/NEU%202012%20PPP_in_Europe_Guide_v-1.pdf [14.1.2017], p. 52; Sophie Pignon-Xardel / Stéphane Manoukian / Laurent Vitse, *Le financement des partenariats public-privé*, La Croix de Berny 2010, p. 52.

not be realized by conventional means.[48] This has caused a fundamental shift in the political discourse: discussions about the integration of private actors have always been less about privatization than about the »financialization of public procurement.« Government austerity measures have now caused a shift in the discussion from institutional arrangements, which are now hardly ever discussed, to the consideration of the desired benefits (»value for money«).[49]

The implementation of PPP projects in Greece was already compromised by considerable problems even before the onset of the economic and financial crisis, in particular in connection with the lack of standardization of such procurement models and the protracted approval process.[50] Although numerous projects, like the »Athens International Airport«, the »Athens Ring Road«, the »Rio-Antirio Bridge«, the »Maliakos-Kleidi Motorway«, the »Moreas Motorway«, the »Central Greece Motorway (E65 motorway)«, or the »Port of Piraeus Transhipment Terminal«, had been successfully realized in the past, and although PPPs seemed to have been seen as a practicable option for infrastructure development, such projects as the »Thessaloniki Metro«, the »Container Terminal of Port of Thessaloniki«, and the submerged »Tunnel of Maliakos« have failed, largely as a result of political-administrative incompetence. The political risks have only increased since then. Government instability, mass protests, postponed elections, and the current discussion about the possibility of exit from the Euro have contributed, as much as the erratic politics – from the perspective of investors – of the Leftist Syriza-government of Alexis Tsipras and Yanis Varoufakis, to a hardly quantifiable uncertainty which presents a disadvantage for long-term private infrastructure investments. The privatization agreed with the international donor community also remains sluggish. The initial target of €50 billion from privatization revenues has been decreased to €15 billion, and even this seems ambitions, given that so far only €2.5 billion have been taken in.[51] As a result of austerity, payments to private enterprises that have engaged in PPs have been problematized.[52] »Non-payment-of-toll« movements against fee-charging infrastructures have developed into mass phe-

48 Géraldine Bonnet / Gilles Chomat, »France« in: Koen Verhoest / Nunzia Carbonara / Veiko Lember / Ole Helby Petersen / Walter Scherrer / Martijn van den Hurk (eds.), *Public Private Partnerships in Transport: Trends & Theory*, 2013 Discussion Papers Part I Country Profiles, Bari 2013, pp. 42–54, p. 47.

49 Elisabeth Campagnac, »The challenges of implementing new forms of PPP in France« in: M. Winch Graham / Masamitsu Onishi / Sandra Schmidt (eds.), Taking Stock of PPP and PFI around the World, London 2012, pp. 27–43.

50 Athena Roumboutsos, »Greece« in: Verhoest et al. (eds.), *Public Private Partnerships in Transport*, op. cit. (note 48), pp. 107–125.

51 Werner Mussler / Philipp Plickert, »Griechenland sperrt sich gegen Privatisierung« in: *Frankfurter Allgemeine Zeitung*, 5.4.2016, http://www.faz.net/aktuell/wirtschaft/eurokrise/griechenland/in-der-krise-weicht-griechenland-von-privatisierungsziel-ab-14162026.html [14.1.2017].

52 Roumboutsos, »Greece«, op. cit. (note 50), p. 112.

nomena in Greece.[53] Such acts of civil disobedience limit the attractiveness of private investment in public infrastructure.

In Spain and Portugal, the austerity measures were applied especially to capital means, with the result that very few tenders were issued for PPP projects. The considerable surcharges of private capital investors in their longstanding engagements in both countries are an additional hindrance.[54] Before the onset of the crisis and the measures taken to overcome it, Portugal had used PPP approaches particularly as a result of the positive experience in the timely establishment of badly needed infrastructure. Within a very short time, private actors had invested €30 billion in the country, and projections of future investment were estimated at approximately 1% of GDP.[55] Sarmento and Reis were of the view that »considering the high values of public payments regarding the assets and the services, governments in Portugal were more concerned about public deficits than with value for money.«[56] A further motive may have been that payments to private actors – apparently – did not touch the national debt and so made additional capital expenditure in infrastructure possible. As a share of GDP, no country chose to use PPP models for the establishment of public infrastructure more than Portugal. The austerity measures had different consequences: on the one hand, PPP projects could not be followed-up (e.g., high-speed rail link between Lisbon and Porto or the new Lisbon Airport); on the other hand, the problem meant that in the Portuguese banking and finance sector the European Investment Bank assumed the role of primary lender in those PPP projects that were already in advanced stages of delivery of tender.[57] The government had, as part of its austerity policy, increased the number of toll networks and turned to user-financing in certain sections of »shadow tolls.«[58] This caused the previously cross-party support for PPP use to falter. In the Memorandum of Understanding (MoU), Portugal had signed in April 2011 as part of the stability-and-growth pact. The Troika had recommended that Portugal issue no new PPP contracts until a requisite »legal and institutional framework« was in place, in order to have a more solid footing for economic feasibility studies of the various procurement

53 CWI, *Mass road toll non-payment campaign*, 2011, http://www.socialistworld.net/doc/4828 [15.1.2017].

54 Directorate General of Treasury and Finance, *PPP: Parcerias Público-Privadas, Relatório 2011*, Lisbon 2012, http://www.peprobe.com/wp-content/uploads/2014/04/2012-10-23_Relatorio_Anual_PPP_2012.pdf [21.1.2017].

55 EPEC, *European PPP Report 2009*, London 2009, p. 83.

56 Joaquim Miranda Sarmento / Ricardo Ferreira Reis, »Buy back PPPs. An arbitrage opportunity« in: *OECD Journal on Budgeting* 12, No. 3 (2013), pp. 1–14.

57 Rosário Macário / Rui Couchinho / Joana Ribeiro, »Portugal« in: Verhoest et al. (eds.), *Public Private Partnerships in Transport*, op. cit. (note 48), pp. 142–162, p. 160. They have listed some further problems. Among others, risk sharing between public and private partners has been characterized as inappropriate. Policy makers were often biased towards new projects instead of optimizing old ones. Regulation was regarded as weak and lacking pressure for performance, thus leading to non-efficient delivery and delays.

58 Joana Costa / Rui Couchinho / Joana Ribeiro / Rosário Macário, »A22 – Algarve Portugal« in: Athena Roumboutsos / Sheila Farrell / Champika Lasanthi Liyanage / Rosário Macário (eds.), *COST Action TU1001. Public Private Partnerships in Transport: Trends & Theory. P3T3*, Brussels 2014, pp. 159–169, p. 165.

models. It was in addition recommended that existing contracts be renegotiated in order to reduce excessive public payments.[59] Renegotiation led in the case of the »Pinhal Interior highway« to a reduction of payments of €500 million.[60] Through the use of arbitrage, the liquidity problems of the private sector, together with the contemporary relatively favourable public refinancing conditions, open up furthermore the possibility of repurchase of PPP contractual objects. Thus arise two advantages: liquidity flows into the economy and the financial cycle, while future public expenditure is reduced.[61] The bailout programme prompts the government, with regard to booking, to treat PPP-generated expenditures as »on-balance-sheet« in order to guarantee completeness and transparency of budgetary principles.[62] Despite this critical orientation against PPPs, the MoU admonished Portugal to privatize, among other sectors, the energy, water, and transport sectors. Chinese, Angolan, and Brazilian capital invested in the privatization advanced by the socialist government.[63]

In the area of toll roads and bridges, Spain also has long experience in integrating private actors into the planning, financing, and subsequent operation of such institutions. Across all parties, the use of PPPs is seen as a means to overcome existing infrastructure gaps and to support the (domestic) construction industry. Sanz Menéndez sees the rapid spread of PPP in Spain in the context of path dependency, »but also in functional terms due to the ›benefits and gains‹ that they bring to innovation policies. [...] PPP results from a more politically-oriented process, with the initiative being taken either by government or from below, and aim at consensus and compromise.«[64] The austerity policy of the Spanish government included cuts in capital expenditure, which also limited the scope of implemented PPP projects.[65] At its peak, this increased private refinancing costs by up to 40%. As such, it became hardly possible to undertake new projects. The transfer of utilization risks to private concession holders resulted, in light of the economic-crisis-related downturn in traffic, in PPP projects being thrown out of kilter. Subsequently, the Spanish government – for example in the context of the General State Budget Act of 2010 – has secured these with guarantees or, where the liquidity risks threaten the existence of private actors, has sought to wind up contracts. A further option has been to extend the life of contracts in order to compensate for the

59 Ricardo Ferreira Reis, *The impact of PPPs contracting on Portugal's fiscal position. Presentation at the 4th Annual OECD Symposium on PPP Working Party of Senior Budget Officials (SBO)*, 2011, http://www.oecd.org/gov/budgeting/49945426.pdf [15.1.2017].

60 PPP Bulletin, *Portugal begins PPP overhaul*, 2012, http://www.partnershipsbulletin.com/news/view/24221 [15.1.2017].

61 Sarmento / Reis, »Buy back PPPs. An arbitrage opportunity«, op. cit. (note 56).

62 EPEC, *New Eurostat rules on contracts that fund the major part of availability payments using tolls collected by or on behalf of the government. The case of the SCUT motorway contracts in Portugal*, London 2011.

63 Caldas, *The Consequences of Austerity Policies in Portugal*, op. cit. (note 32), p. 3.

64 Luis Sanz Menéndez, Public/Private partnerships and innovation policy: The Spanish experience, Unidad de Políticas Comparadas Working Paper No. 03-01, 2003, p. 10.

65 Felix J. Villalba-Romero, »Spain« in: Roumboutsos et al. (eds.), *COST Action TU1001. Public Private Partnerships in Transport*, op. cit. (note 58), pp. 55–81; EPEC, *Market Update. Review of the European PPP Market First half of 2013*, London 2013.

loss of income of private partners. The *Plan de Infraestructuras, Transporte y Vivienda* (PITVI), concluded in 2012 and running until 2024, has formulated strategic goals, in parallel with a broad liberalization of the transport sector and, in particular, the increased integration of private actors in infrastructure.[66] PPP models have been developed to reduce the public debt, which, on the one hand, can integrate means from both the structural and cohesion funds and the EIB – an area in which Spain had previously already very successfully competed for. On the other hand, in accordance with the European stability-and-growth pact, refinancing is increasingly passed on to the user.

Italy counts as something of a special case, because here the use of PPP models afforded only moderate economic advantages, by comparison with the other countries, and this even before the onset of the crisis. Iossa and Russo attribute this to the complexity of administrative procedures, financing problems, and political interventions during the tendering process.[67] According to Rossi and Civitillo, PPP projects in Italy are seldom financed via the capital market but instead through the issuance of bonds and loans, thus resulting in higher refinancing costs; therefore such projects are accompanied by fewer PPP-inherent economic advantages.[68] The austerity measures of the Italian government covered various aspects (Resolution No. 32009 of March 6, 2009): the establishment of an infrastructure fund, alternative financing options in the form of project bonds, support measures through public banks.[69] As Carbonara showed with the example of the »Bre.Be.Mi« toll-road project, a ca. €2.2 billion large project to build 100 km of highways between Milan, Bergamo and Brescia, even existing projects were subject to considerable uncertainties associated with the Italian banking and finance sector.[70]

In contrast, the additional costs caused by political uncertainty play only a minor role in Germany. Nevertheless, as illustrated in figure 7, fewer and fewer public projects are organized as PPPs. This was initially due to the means from the »Second Stimulus Package« (*Konjunkturpaket II*), for it had to be allocated rapidly, for which the complex partnership contracts were unsuited. In addition, the debt ceiling made unclear which projects the public sector could afford. The current interest levels make the financing of traditional procurement processes at favourable rates unrivalled, which to a degree costs the PPP model its particular economic advantage[71] In the middle term, a significant increase in the PPP market is foreseen, because on the one hand

66 Ministerio de Fomento, *Sociedad Estatal de Infraestructuras del Transporte Terrestre. Plan de Infraestructutras Transporte y Vivienda 2012–2024 (PITVI)*, Madrid 2012.

67 Elisabetta Iossa / Federico Antellini Russo, »Potenzialità e criticità del Partenariato Pubblico Privato in Italia« in: *Rivista di Politica Economica*, Maggio–Giugno 2008, pp. 125–158.

68 Matteo Rossi / Renato Civitillo, »Public Private Partnerships: a general overview in Italy« in: *Procedia – Social and Behavioral Sciences* 109 (2014), pp. 140–149.

69 Nunzia Carbonara / Roberta Pellegrino, »Italy« in: Verhoest et al. (eds.), *Public Private Partnerships in Transport*, op. cit. (note 48), pp. 126–141, p. 134.

70 Nunzia Carbonara, »Bre.Be.Mi Toll road Italy« in: Roumboutsos et al. (eds.), *COST Action TU1001. Public Private Partnerships in Transport*, op. cit. (note 58), pp. 125-132.

71 Fabina Möpert / Peter Witz, »Federal Republic of Germany« in: Roumboutsos et al. (eds.), *COST Action TU1001. Public Private Partnerships in Transport*, op. cit. (note 58), pp. 10–25.

the federal government and the states aspire towards standardization of procurement processes[72]; on the other hand, the Parliament concludes a comprehensive promotion law, which expressly serves to allow the pre-financing of PPP projects.

Figure 7: PPPs in Germany

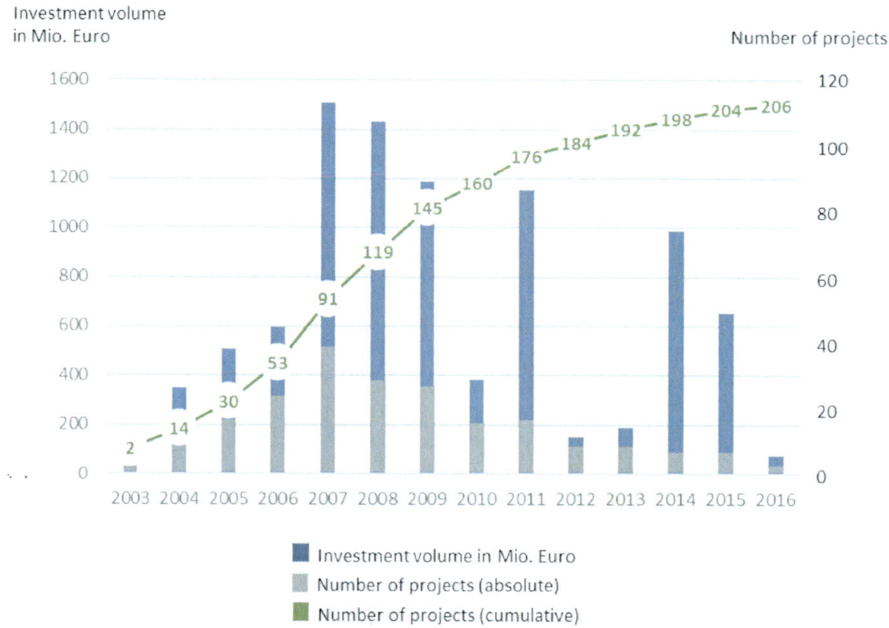

Source: own illustration based on Partnerschaften Deutschland

As Turner shows, private financing and participation in public infrastructures almost entirely succumbed to the combination of austerity measures and risk reassessment of credit-issuing banks, especially between 2010 and 2012.[73] Wagenvoort et al. estimated the collapse at between 15 and 20%, and a recovery of the market is expected in 2017 at the earliest.[74]

72 Roland Sturm / Thorsten Winkelmann, »Deep Federalism bei PPP-Programmen. Vorgaben des Bundes und der Länder und die Handlungsspielräume der Kommunen« in: Elisabeth Alber / Caroline Zwilling (eds.), *Gemeinden im Europäischen Mehrebenensystem: Herausforderungen im 21. Jahrhundert*, Baden-Baden 2014, pp. 249–269, pp. 249–251.

73 Colin Turner, *The European Infrastructure (EIS) and the Challenges of the Austerity Consensus*, 2013, http://speri.dept.shef.ac.uk/wp-content/uploads/2013/06/Turner-C-The-European-Infrastructure.pdf [15.1.2017].

74 Wagenvoort / De Nicola / Kappeler, *Infrastructure Finance in Europe*, op. cit. (note 37).

3. Discussion

If here the question of which infrastructure investments create growth impulses at all is left aside, then infrastructure influences the amount and the scope of means for capital expenditure. Supply-side changes are captured by means of public capital expenditure, gross investments, and expenditure for transport infrastructure. At the time, the governments of the countries in the study tried first, through demand-oriented politics, to master the coming crisis. Significant means for infrastructure development were made promptly available in the hope to (over-)compensate the decline in private demand. The current crisis is linked to structural causes rather than to a private consumption crisis in the Schumpeterian sense or to a capitalism-immanent accumulation crisis in the neo-Marxist reading of events. A lack of competitiveness, construction mistakes in the common currency, and budget deficits have limited the capacity of the state to act. Instead of growth effects, higher indebtedness took root in public budgets. Countries like Spain, Portugal, Italy, and Ireland reduced their capital expenditure budgets as a strategy to take account of existing debts and of future income expectations. In absolute terms, Spain and Italy in particular cut their gross investments. In both countries austerity was primarily anchored in the capital expenditure sector. This could be due to a number of factors: before the onset of the crisis, Spain and Ireland (with exceptions Italy and Portugal as well) experienced a credit-finance real-estate boom, which was reinforced by public investment.[75] The resulting austerity measures correct earlier exaggerations and lead to a »natural« market consolidation. If this argument is accepted, then austerity can be seen as a virtue of »good« governance, even if the Aristotelian virtue doctrine cautions against the dangers of self-indulgence. With this in mind, restraint remains far removed from the ideal of debt-financed excesses in real estate and infrastructure. Restraint means in this context not inner-worldly asceticism but rather discipline and self-control in public infrastructure construction. Furthermore, both the pressure to reduce debt by restricting access to financing means and political uncertainty as a result of economic policy played a role in the reduced public capital expenditures[76], which, as Barkbu et al. established empirically, were particularly evident in Spain, Italy, Greece, and Ireland.[77]Austerity measures have contributed to a correction in the real-estate- and infrastructure-dominated model of growth in a number of Euro member states, without, however, any demonstrable evidence of more sustainable

75 Alvaro Pina / Ildeberta Abreu, Portugal: *Rebalancing the Economy and Returning to Growth Through Job Creation and Better Capital Allocation*, OECD Working Paper No. 994, 2012.

76 Christopher Baum / Mustafa Caglayan / Oleksandr Talavera, »On the investment sensitivity of debt under uncertainty« in: *Economics Letters* 106, No. 1 (2010), pp. 25–27; European Investment Bank, *Investment and Investment Finance in Europe*, FSC Paper 11, 2013, http://www.eib.org/attachments/efs/investment_and_investment_finance_in_europe_en.pdf [15.1.2017].

77 Barkbu et al., *Investment in the Euro Area: Why Has It Been Weak?*, op. cit. (note 25).

growth paths.[78] Fiscal consolidation measures led directly to a new recession and to adjustment costs in the form of unemployment and wage loss.[79] There are political, social, and economic risks associated with this, thus destabilizing long-term investments in infrastructure.

Figure 8: Relation between state gross capital formation and next year's change in GDP growth

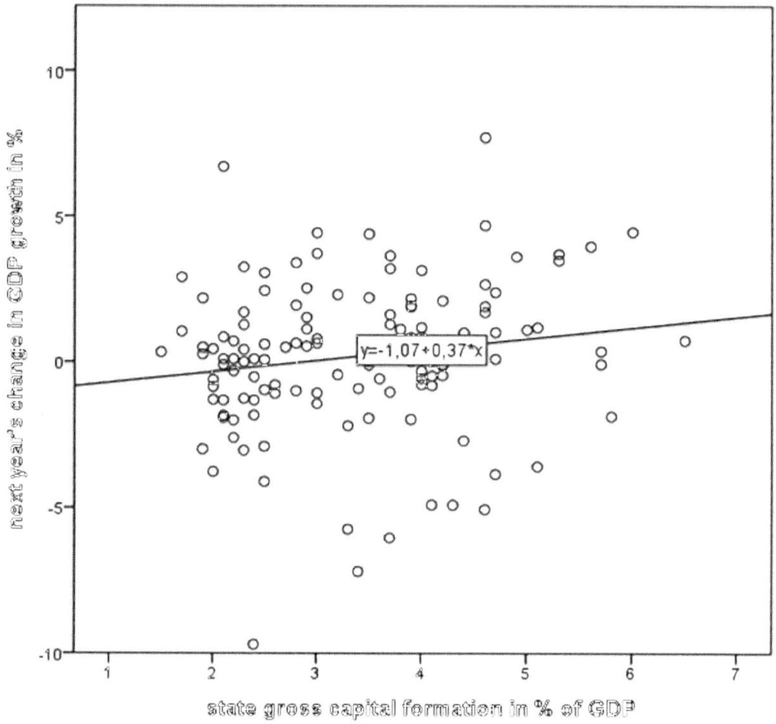

Source: own illustration based on OECD-Stat

Such austerity policy reduced public demand and, as figure 8 illustrates, influenced economic growth negatively. Thereafter, cuts in the capital expenditure sector led to low GDP growth in the following year. Corresponding cuts can also be interpreted in the light of societal resistance, because, in contrast to the social sector, the negative consequences here have less impact on individuals. Politicians cut capital expenditures because the adverse consequences are only evident in the long term, if at all. Such

78 For a divergent opinion see Deutsche Bundesbank, »Zur Investitionstätigkeit im Euro-Raum«, op. cit. (note 30), p. 39.

79 Deutsche Bundesbank, »Anpassungsprozesse in den Ländern der Wirtschafts- und Währungsunion« in: Deutsche Bundesbank (ed.), *Monatsbericht Januar (66)*, Frankfurt/Main 2015, pp. 13–83.

short-term opportunistic savings-logic-bound policies contradict growth paths and gamble away Europe's future, especially when depreciation (wear and tear) is greater than the investments made and, as a result, capital stock sinks.[80] As increasing gross investment- and transport-infrastructure expenditures show, France has chosen a structural policy of expansive budgetary measures without having realized the desired growth effects to date. Greece can be seen as something of an exception among the countries in the study: public gross expenditures sank even before the crisis both in relative and absolute terms, only for these to rise again during the crisis. The conclusion can be drawn that the capital made available by international donors (the Troika) was at least partially reinvested and that austerity in the context of a dichotomous juxtaposition of capital expenditure and consumption spending cuts almost exclusively occurred in the consumption and social sectors, respectively. But in comparison to pre-crisis levels, the European economies invested on average 15% less in their infrastructures. The sinking capital expenditure budgets raise the question of whether, in future, Europe will be understood as a (transport-)political project. At the same time a turnaround is on the horizon: the OECD, IMF, and European Commission are unanimous that the historically low interest levels should be used to increase public infrastructure investments and to end austerity at least in this sector.[81] The Investment Plan of the European Commission (the so-called »Juncker-Plan«) will make €315 Billion available in the coming three years in order to overcome the existing sluggish growth in the Euro region. It is unclear, however, which concrete investments could have growth-stimulating effects, because without course correction of structural policies these measures reveal themselves to be short-term Keynesian flashes-in-the-pan. In other words: neither anticyclical factors to stimulate the overall economic demand nor the impact of accommodating monetary policy will sustainably improve the investment.[82] Turner points out that austerity measures in the capital expenditure sector must therefore take middle- to long-term effects on growth. If that is done, in addition to the costs incurred, the planned usage comes to the fore.[83] He argued, »in reflection, the focus on infrastructure within the current austerity debate reflects more of an attempt to offer a supply side remedy when fiscal discretion is limited. The theme is that to counter the pro-cyclical effects of austerity, states will have to be more efficient in their activities and use that as a basis of growth.« Moreover, the growth effects vary according to the level of development of an economy, so that the countries of the southern and eastern peripheries of Europe should be considered for the relevant in-

80 Anthony Deutsch, »Austerity threatens EU's competitive edge in infrastructure«, in: *Reuters*, 28.3.2013, http://www.reuters.com/article/us-europe-infrastructure-slowdown-idUSBRE92R04H20130328 [15.1.2017].

81 For a critical voice see Daniel Gros, *Investment as the key to recovery in the euro area?*, CEPS Policy Brief, No. 326, 18.11.2014.

82 OECD, *Economic Policy Reforms 2015: Going for Growth*, 2015, http://dx.doi.org/10.1787/growth-2015-en [15.1.2017]; IMF, *Euro Area Policies: 2014 Article IV Consultation-Staff Report*, IMF Country Report No. 14/198, Washington, D.C. 2014.

83 Turner, »The European Infrastructure (EIS) and the Challenges of the Austerity Consensus«, op. cit. (note 73).

vestments, because the West European countries are, by comparison, at the international forefront when it comes to the quality of public infrastructure.

In addition to the supply-side changes outlined above, strategies for the mobilization and integration of private actors in infrastructure are conceivable. Austerity thus covers partial and complete privatization, fund solutions, and a range of cooperation models with the private sector. Two contrasting effects associated with austerity are conceivable. If, first, the arguments of the critics of austerity are followed, such a policy would lead to increased privatization of public services, because the dominant neoliberal paradigm would amount to the economization of the public sphere and the organization of society according to market criteria.[84] Formulated positively: »selling the idea of productivity improvement is easier in hard times than in good [times].«[85] In view of the state of affairs in national debt and the attempts to reduce this, private capital could ideally be used to drive growth. The IMF also considers the PPP approach an anticyclical instrument »that can be used to support private sector recovery and generate employment.«[86]

Nonetheless, – and, second – contrary effects are conceivable if the economic and financial crisis has indeed led to a new assessment of risks and improved public refinancing models in at least some EU countries. Even higher demands on capital resources and revised sovereign risks make such »long term assets less attractive«. In view of erratic market fluctuations, the typical infrastructure investment periods of several years or even several decades are associated with significant risks for private investors. Uncertainty in relation to political stability in general, and about the future orientation of public infrastructure policy in particular, could also contribute to a wait-and-see approach of potential investors, so that austerity policy would not necessarily lead to stronger participation of private actors as operators and/or funders of public institutions.[87] As proven by the number and scope of PPP projects implemented in Europe before and during the crisis, private participation in public infrastructure has fallen since 2008. This trend is evident in all the countries in the study, even if, »in political economy terms, it is clear that PPPs have been attractive for governments trying to make their accounts look good, thereby (ab)using public accounting rules that do not correctly capture government assets and liabilities.«[88] In other words: even though PPP projects make »off-the-balance-sheet« strategies possible, these procurement models are used less and less frequently during the debt crisis! The reasons for this are,

84 Colin Crouch, *The Strange Non-Death of Neoliberalism*, Cambridge 2011; Joseph Vogel, *Der Souveränitätseffekt*, Zürich 2015.

85 Georg Kuper, »Productivity. A national concern« in: Joan Wolfe / John Heaphy (eds.), *Readings on Productivity in Policing*, Lexington 1975, pp. 1–10, p. 5.

86 Philippe Burger / Justin Tyson / Izabela Karpowicz / Maria Delgado Coelho, *The Effects of the Financial Crisis on Public-Private Partnerships*, IMF Working Paper No. 144, 2009, p. 3.

87 Wagenvoort / De Nicola / Kappeler, *Infrastructure Finance in Europe*, op. cit. (note 37).

88 Mathias Dewatripont / Patrick Legros, »Public-private-Partnerships: contract design and risk transfer« in: *EIB Papers* 10, No. 1 (2005), pp. 120–145, pp. 132–133.

on the one hand, political risks which have a deterrent effect on private capital[89], which affected especially Greece, but also Italy and Spain.[90] Such uncertainties are multidimensional: government instability, the rise of populist forces, or a lack of clarity about the future orientation of infrastructure policy impede long-term investments from private investors. Closely connected to this is, on the other hand, the significant increase in refinancing costs elsewhere, which has caused the PPP procurement model, through the increased expenditures, to lose its demonstrably higher efficiency in comparison to conventional credit-financed processes. The austerity measures taken in the wake of the economic crisis also had a negative impact on the volume of traffic, as a result of which PPP projects, which had transferred utilization risks to private actors, for example in toll models, fell out of kilter. Such problems were evident in Spain, Portugal, and Greece, without the problems having affected public supply.[91] Rather, each government took different steps in the short term to provide support measures, ranging from providing guarantees through contract extensions to toll increases. Nevertheless, private partners were less willing to assume certain risks, so that planned projects had to make do with lower risk transfer. Such market conditions as the slowdown of real GDP growth, sinking rates of utilization, or increased refinancing costs have not yet responded to legislative interventions like the UK »Infrastructure and Projects Authorities« or the »Local Partnerships« Authority, even when, as illustrated by the »Nabarro Infrastructure Index«[92], these would in the long-term increase the attractiveness of private infrastructure investments. Since 2007, the biennially compiled index has determined the attractiveness of private infrastructure investments through an indicator-based model. While such countries as Greece, Ireland, and Portugal are not included, the United Kingdom has taken first place, whereas France, owing to a lack of

89 Deutsche Bundesbank, »Zur jüngeren Entwicklung der Buchkredite an nichtfinanzielle Unternehmen im Euro-Raum« in: Deutsche Bundesbank (ed.), *Monatsbericht September* (15), Frankfurt/Main 2015, pp. 15–42; Sarah Holton / Martina Lawless / Fergal McCann, »SME financing conditions in Europe: credit crunch or fundamentals?« in: *National Institute Economic Review* 225 (2013); European Investment Bank, *Investment and Investment Finance in Europe*, op. cit. (note 76); Ritva Reinikka / Jakob Svensson, *How Inadequate Provision of Public Infrastructure and Services Affects Private Investment*, World Bank Policy Research Working Paper No. 2262, 1999.

90 Deutsche Bundesbank, »Zur Investitionstätigkeit im Euro-Raum«, op. cit. (note 30), pp. 49–50.

91 Turner, »The European Infrastructure (EIS) and the Challenges of the Austerity Consensus«, op. cit. (note 73).

92 In the Global Investment Index investment conditions in infrastructure are also analysed. In 2016, the following ranking was made: UK (9th place), Germany (13th); France(19th), Spain (24th), Portugal (31st), Italy (34th?) Greece (39th). For this see Arcadis, *Third Global Infrastructure Investment Index 2016*, 2016, https://www.arcadis.com/media/3/7/E/%7B37E96D-F6-82D5-45A6-87D8-5427637E736D%7DAG1015_GIII%202016_ONLINE%20FINAL_SINGLE%20PAGES.pdf [15.1.2017], p. 7. An alternative ranking can be found in Klaus Schwab, *The Global Competitiveness Report 2012–2013 Insight Report. World Economic Forum*, 2012, www3.weforum.org/docs/WEF_GlobalCompetitivenessReport_2012-13.pdf [1.1.2017].

reform, and Spain, owing to political uncertainty about the future direction of infrastructure policy, continue to slip down in the rankings.

Table 1: Nabarro Infrastructure Index

Rank	*Country*	*Index Score*
1	UK	174
6	Germany	128
8	France	109
14	Italy	94
18	Spain	84

Source: own illustration

In summary, the hypotheses of, for example, Roentgen that »the fewer financial resources the state has to fulfil tasks, the more likely she is to rely on the PPP-procurement approach«[93] do not hold.[94] On the contrary: the upheaval caused by the economic and financial crisis appears to have resulted in a contribution of a renaissance of in-house production by the State. The current crisis and the reactions to it therefore return the State to its role as an actor in the financing of infrastructure! Considerations of how to finance new infrastructure without incurring additional debt have in general (still) failed to prevail. What is more: traditional procurement models have recently increased in importance, not least because the use of PPPs as anticyclical stimuli is wholly inappropriate.[95]

93 Frederik Roentgen, *PPP – Eine effizienzorientierte Analyse kommunaler Aufgabenerfüllung unter Einbeziehung erwerbswirtschaftlicher Unternehmungen*, Aachen 2001, p. 136.

94 Similiarily argues Achim Albrecht, »Rechtliche Problemstellungen bei Public Private Partnership Projekten« in: *Neue Wirtschafts-Briefe* (NWB) 48, No. 29 (2004), pp. 1637–1648, p. 1637.

95 Thomas Krumm, *The Politics of Public-Private Partnerships in Western Europe. Comparative Perspectives*, Cheltenham 2016.

Vassilis K. Fouskas and Constantine Dimoulas

Imperial Bondage: Austerity in Greece, 2008–2018

Austerity is a dependent variable of supply-side economics. It is a form of deflation in which the economy attempts to adjust through policies and legislation that reduce wages and welfare spending while increasing taxation, the rate of unemployment and precarious employment. The aim, presumably, is to restore competitiveness via »structural adjustment«, that is, reducing a state's deficits and debts by way of privatizations and liberalization of markets.[1]

Since the 1980s, austerity has become the dominant form of socio-economic policy in the West.[2] At the European level, one can find it enshrined in the Maastricht Treaty (1992) and the »Stability and Growth Pact« (SGP, 1998), both of which aimed, among others, at streamlining the budgetary process of the member states in order to optimize monetary integration by avoiding currency crises and minimizing risk (the euro was introduced in 1999 in eleven European countries and in 2001 in Greece). Exchange rate stabilization was paramount. Austerity was thus institutionalized in the EU policy regimes well before the onset of the global financial crisis and the eurozone crisis in 2008–09. What happened after that, especially in the beleaguered periphery of the EU, was the severe intensification of austerity. This was to be expected because the ruling financial and political elites of the West, contrary to the way their predecessors reacted in the aftermath of the global financial crisis in 1929, took the strategic decision not to alter the principle upon which globalization and European integration has been developing since the 1980s, namely, that of continuous support for the supply-side of the social economy and the embedded regime of austerity in it. In the wake of the eurozone crisis, new, stricter versions of austerity policies came into force in the form of »European Semester« and »Fiscal Compact« programmes.

Austerity takes different forms and intensity levels in different countries. This is because capitalism, as a (global) social system, is developing in an uneven way. It is very important to recognize this, because it challenges head-on neoliberal policy. This approach brushes aside uneven development and core-periphery dynamics, in which public and private agencies of the core extract rents and profits from peripheral countries via value transfer mechanisms. Imperialism comes via a variety of means and methods. In the context of the EU/eurozone, this can take the form of recycling of the surpluses of the core and the financialization of various commercial transactions (e.g., purchasing of T-bills of peripheral states enabling those states to import and consume

1 Mark Blyth, *Austerity. The History of a Dangerous Idea*, Oxford 2013, pp. 1–21, pp. 51–95; Wolfgang Streeck, *How will Capitalism End?*, London 2016, pp. 73–164.

2 There are exceptions, such as the Scandinavian countries. But Greece, too, had not been served by austerity cabinets in the 1980s and early 1990s, although there were strong factions within the ruling parties of PASOK (left-wing) and New Democracy (right-wing), representing specific business groups calling for supply-side policy. For a full exposition, see Vassilis K. Fouskas / Constantine Dimoulas, *Greece, Financialization and the EU. The Political Economy of Debt and Destruction*, Basingstoke 2013, pp. 109–133.

industrial and financial products of the core). For neoliberals, imbalances and asymmetries are seen at the state level alone and should be rectified at that level, because state profligacy is the culprit. External disequilibria, such as current account deficits reflecting developmental cleavages, are disregarded. In short, in order to use the nation-state executive as an instrument of austerity *par excellence*, core states offload the debt resulting from structural asymmetries and monetary and trade interactions onto the peripheral states. Whereas for heterodox economists austerity became synonymous with the era of neoliberal globalization and the deeply uneven developmental processes it generated between core and periphery, whether globally or within the eurozone, neoclassical approaches that dominate the views of the ECB, the EU and the IMF see austerity as the necessary policy tool to fight state profligacy, recklessness, tax evasion, high wages and inflation in view of improving competitiveness and growth rates. As the German Minister of Finance, Wolfgang Schäuble, put it: »It is an undisputable fact that excessive state spending has led to unsustainable levels of debt and deficits [...]. Governments in and beyond the Euro-zone need not just to commit to fiscal consolidation and improved competitiveness – they need to start delivering now.« Schäuble argued that this is the only way to achieve sustainable development, thus taking a clear position against a fiscal union at the European level because, as he wrote, it would make the crisis worse by »removing a key incentive for the weaker members to forge ahead with much-needed reforms«. After all, he continued, the fiscal union is »against the very nature of European integration.«[3]

Austerity in Greece took an unprecedented form. This is because Greece was the worst of all peripheral countries in terms of both internal (budget deficit) and external liabilities (current account deficit). As a result, the crisis took a very acute form. Under the treble discipline of the IMF, the ECB and the EU, Greek cabinets have since 2010 pursued a most peculiar and acute form of bondage, that of *internal devaluation*, and by way of accepting a direct *colonial* regime within Greece proper. True, *all* eurozone members are, as per Treaty, in one way or another, subject to controls and budgetary discipline by EU authorities. But the crisis in Greece revealed that even specific departments and branches of the Greek state are controlled *directly* by the creditors, or the »Troika« (ECB, IMF EU). For example, when Yanis Varoufakis tried to test his »Plan B« when he was Minister in January–July 2015, he found out that even the General Secretariat for the Public Revenue based in his Ministry of Finance was controlled by the creditors, who refused to provide him with the tax codes he wanted in case Greece's negotiations with the Troika failed.[4] Thus, austerity in Greece can only be analysed as *imperial* austerity, which is the worst form of externally imposed deflationary bondage in a political democracy.

3 Wolfgang Schäuble, »Why austerity is only cure for the Euro-zone« in: *Financial Times*, 5.9.2011.

4 Yanis Varoufakis, ›Conversation with Lamond and Mars‹ (in Greek), in: *Dromos tis Aristeras*, 17.7.2015. Varoufakis has repeatedly made this claim and none has disputed or denied it to date.

This chapter aims at exploring the social and economic consequences of this type of austerity in Greece (we have dealt with the political transformations caused by the crisis in other venues).[5] We will become aware that imperial austerity is being applied to Greek society via institutionalized forms of governance *merging* the »national« (the Greek government), the »European« (the EU and the ECB) and the »global« (IMF) into a single executive committee of policy imposition, regardless of liberal-democratic processes.[6] The forms of governance we are referring to are the so-called »bailout agreements« with the creditors, which we will examine briefly in the first part of our contribution. We will then move on to look at key macro-economic features and economic trends in order to decipher and expose the impact of those austerity arrangements between successive Greek governments and the creditors. The argument advanced is that imperial austerity is the worst form of bondage, failing to improve competitiveness and sustainable development as argued by neoliberals. In addition, it creates material conditions for unpleasant political turns resembling, *mutatis mutandis,* the failure of the Gold Standard in the inter-war period and the rise of new authoritarianism in Europe and beyond.[7]

5 See, for instance, Fouskas / Dimoulas, *Greece, Financialization and the EU*, op. cit. (note 2), passim.

6 »Dependency« may no longer be an adequate term to describe Greece's position in the international system. During the Cold War, core-periphery theories of international relations and political economy used the term to describe the political and economic control of the periphery by core imperial powers, chiefly the USA. The collapse of the Soviet bloc, the process of European integration and the relative decline of the USA have led to the advancement of new forms of governance and rule of the periphery by the core, effectively reducing even the minimal relative autonomy they used to enjoy during the Cold War to zero. Apart from the forms of political dependency that are clear and need no further explanation, one should consider the total loss of monetary sovereignty of all countries that are either members of the eurozone or have their currencies pegged to the euro. Thus, in periods of crisis in which the sharp terrain of structural contradictions dissipate any liberal ideological pretext of »equality« and »solidarity« and makes all actors appear in clearly defined *class* terms and roles, one distinguishes clearly the imperial from the subaltern. In this class equation, imperial forces forge a *subordinate merging* of the executive of the subaltern state with the *imperial-dictating* posture of the dominant state, creating a unique form of governance that some scholars defined as »new Constitutionalism«; see, for example, Stephen Gill / A. Claire Cutler (eds.), *New Constitutionalism and World Order*, Cambridge 2014, pp. 29–76, 126–142.

7 Arguably, the eurozone is a form of Gold Standard in which external devaluation is disallowed in case issues related to democracy (e.g., pursuing inflationary/high wage policy in order to address the demand problem in the economy) that need to be addressed head-on. Given the lack of fiscal and/or banking union, the EU is a collection of states operating as an intergovernmental organization and not as a federal state. Whereas the Gold Standard regime before the First World War was somewhat successful due to low wages, high exploitation and the limited participation of the people in national politics, the Gold Standard of the inter-war period collapsed because it could not address the issue of democracy and mass politics at the level of nation-state. That is how fascism and Nazism triumphed; see, Mark Blyth, *Austerity*, op. cit. (note 1), pp. 180–206.

1. The three bailouts, 2010–2015

From May 2010 to August 2015, Greece had signed up to receive three bailout funds from its creditors corresponding to three »economic adjustment« (read: bondage and imperial austerity) programmes. However, whereas the programmes were and are being implemented without any major deviation, almost none of the funds disbursed trickled down to the real economic sector or contributed to any decrease of the public debt. Just a year before the first bailout, the debt/GDP ratio was at 126.7%. After six years of harsh austerity, it soared up to 177.4% in 2015. GDP growth was also negative (table 1). But let us see briefly where the funds came from and where they went covering the years 2010–2010.[8]

The first programme started in May 2010 but ended prematurely in March 2012, followed by the second adjustment programme, which was planned to end in December 2014. However, it was extended until June 2015 after a second bailout agreement in March 2012, which involved debt restructuring and the involvement of the private sector, the so-called PSI. These discontinuities were due to political conditions in Greece. Political instability and social unrest obstructed the review process by the creditors, and funds stopped being disbursed. The Greek government of Syriza (Coalition of the Radical Left), succumbing to the creditors, requested a new programme in July 2015, which is scheduled to run until May 2018.

The funds for the first programme derived from the EU (80 billion euros) and the IMF (30 billion euros). However, Slovakia, Portugal and Ireland did not participate, thus the amount lowered to 107.3 billion euros. The disbursed volume was 73 billion euros, leaving 34.3 billion undisbursed. The funds of the second programme totalled 172.6 billion euros, which included the undisbursed funds from the first programme, 130.1 billion euros of new funds and an additional IMF loan of 8.2 billion euros. Overall, the first and the second programmes amounted to 226.8 billion euros in disbursed funds, the IMF's contribution being 32 billion euros. The amount agreed to be loaned with the third programme is 86 billion euros and, as with the first and the second ones, it will be distributed in tranches and on the proviso that the Greek government pursues concrete austerity measures and structural reforms, meeting specific targets. Greek government policy will be periodically reviewed by the creditors before release of next tranche. Clearly, the creditors hold Greece hostage to their policy according to the strict monetarist/deflationist rules of the eurozone and the new agreements signed, especially since liquidity can be provided only by the ECB. But what is even more intriguing is *where* the bailout funds went to.

8 We are drawing here mainly from European Commission, Directorate-General for Economic and Financial Affairs, for the years 2011–2015, as well as from various statements made by the so-called »Eurogroup«, an informal institution which played a major role in negotiating with Greece in 2015; the IMF Country Reports on Greece, especially reports 13/241 and 14/151, covering the years 2010–2010; very helpful also the paper by Jeromin Zettelmeyer / Christoph Trebesch / Mitu Gulati, *The Greek debt restructuring – an autopsy*, Peterson Institute for International Economics, Working Paper No. 13-8, 2013; also, Jörg Rocholl / Axel Stahmer, *Where did the Greek Bailout Money Go?*, ESMT White Paper No. 16-02, 2016.

Table 1: Evolution of key macroeconomic indicators before and after the crisis in Greece

Year	GDP (current prices in million euro)	GDP in market prices per capita	Real GDP growth (%)	Debt as % of GDP	Deficit as % of GDP
2004	193,715.00	17,700	5.1	102.9	–8.8
2005	199,242.30	18,100	0.6	107.4	–6.2
2006	217,861.60	19,800	5.7	103.1	–5.9
2007	232,694.60	21,100	3.3	103.1	–6.7
2008	244,990.40	21,800	–0.3	109.4	–10.2
2009	237,534.20	21,400	–4.3	126.7	–15.1
2010	226,031.40	20,300	–5.5	146.2	–11.2
2011	207,028.90	18,600	–9.1	172.1	–10.3
2012	191,203.90	17,300	–7.3	159.6	–8.8
2013	180,654.30	16,500	–3.3	177.4	–13.2
2014	177,940.60	16,300	–0.4	179.7	–3.6
2015	175,697.40	16,200	–0.2	177.4	–7.5

Source: own illustration based on Eurostat

Estimates made by the Commission, the IMF and other sources rather favourable to the creditors suggest that of the 215.9 billion euros of the first and second bailouts, some 86.9 billion euros were used to repay maturing government debt; 52.3 billion euros were paid for interest on existing government debt; 37.3 billion euros were paid for the recapitalization of the Greek banks and 29.7 billion euros were paid for the involvement of the private sector, the so-called PSI. Yanis Varoufakis, Greece's former Finance Minister, also tells us that the money from the first bailout helped mainly the recapitalization of French and German banks, whereas those of the second bailout went mainly to the assistance of Greek banks.[9] Thus, almost none of the funds trickled down to the real economy or contributed to lowering the country's debt. Further, one of the most interesting aspects of the Greek case was that, »before the debt restructuring [of March 2012], the Greek government had 205.6 billion euros in outstanding government bonds owed to private investors.«[10] Thus, effectively, the second bailout programme transferred the debt from the private sector to public agencies forcing the taxpayer, especially the Greek one, to pay for it.

The third bailout programme is signed by the leftist government of Syriza, a party of 4% in 2009 that grew out of the opposition to the two bailout agreements and the harsh austerity conditions attached to them. After catapulting the Greek party system by reaching 36% of the vote in the election of January 2015 on a moderate Keynesian agenda, it capitulated to the creditors after seven months of relentless bargaining and a

9 Yanis Varoufakis, *Adults in the Room. My Battle with Europe's Deep Establishment*, London 2017, pp. 23–25. His claim has not been contested.

10 Rocholl / Stahmer, »Where did the Greek Bailout Money Go?«, op. cit. (note 8), p. 13.

referendum. The referendum, held on July 5, 2015, asked the Greek people whether a third bailout programme with the same harsh austerity conditions attached to it should be accepted. But whereas the Greeks voted overwhelmingly against austerity, thus refusing a third programme, the Syriza ruling group, having previously sidelined its chief negotiator and Finance Minister, Yanis Varoufakis, a pro-Keynesian economist, accepted an equally harsh programme. Of the 86 billion euros agreed between Syriza and the creditors in July–August 2015, 35.9 billion euros is planned to go to debt amortization; 17.8 billion euros will go to interest payment; 7 billion euros to clearing arrears, and 25 billion euros is planned for a new recapitalization of the banks.

2. Boom to bust, 1995–2009

As we have shown elsewhere, Greece entered the constellation of neoliberal globalization in earnest only after the second half of the 1990s, when veteran socialist leader and Prime Minister, Andreas G. Papandreou, passed away.[11] Greece, having essentially pursued an inflationist, pro-Keynesian policy from 1974 to the mid-1990s, was under enormous pressure by the EU to open up its market to the deflationary policy of low wages and welfare cuts. The artificial boost to the economy came under the two consecutive cabinets of Costas Simitis (1996–2004), who succeeded Papandreou, followed by the right-wing cabinet of Costas Karamanlis (2004–2009). The economy was liberalized further, and public assets floated on Athens's Stock Exchange (ASE), which saw its share price index peak in September 1999 with 6335 points, before it crashed down to1748.4 in 2001, never to recover at the 1999 level again. Taking advantage of low interest rates, both the private and the public sectors began borrowing heavily to finance consumer demand, government requirements and major infrastructural works, such as the Athens Olympics projects of 2003–04. Throughout the 1980s and beyond, Greece financed its welfare state via external and internal borrowing, not taxation. The privatization of financial markets opened up new opportunities to European banking capital, which could now use Greek banks to penetrate Balkan and Near Eastern markets. With globalization and European »integration« at their apex, Greece's GDP and gross capital formation witnessed a remarkable increase from the mid-1990s to the onset of the crisis in 2008 (tables 1 and 2 and figure 4). However, as elsewhere in the

11 Vassilis K. Fouskas / Constantine Dimoulas, »The Greek workshop of debt and the failure of the European project« in: *Journal of Balkan and Near Eastern Studies* 14, No. 1 (2012), pp. 1–31; Fouskas / Dimoulas, *Greece, Financialization and the EU*, op. cit. (note 2), pp. 134–185. Most scholars agree that Greece entered the cycle of neoliberal financialization/ globalization in the mid-1990s. The disagreements concern the »nature« of the crisis, for example, whether the crisis is primarily fiscal or a balance-of-payments crisis; and the actual *source* of the crisis, for example, whether the crisis emanated from the financial sector or from the accumulation process per se, in which case it concerns fall in profitability; for a thorough Marxian discussion of the crisis as a profitability issue, see the interesting contributions in Turan Subasat (ed.), *The Great Financial Meltdown. Systemic, Conjunctural or Policy Created?*, Northampton, M.A. 2016; for Keynesian approaches to the crisis as a financialization issue, see Martin H. Wolfson / Gerald A. Epstein (eds.), *The Political Economy of Financial Crises*, Oxford 2013.

West, this growth was driven by debt and consumption, especially since Greece's neoliberal reforms, unlike Germany's and other core countries, were not accompanied by wage stagnation or significant cuts in public and welfare spending.[12] The official average unemployment rate in the eurozone between 2002 and 2006 stood at 8.8%, whereas in Greece it was a bit higher at 9.9%. Net profits, especially in financial services, grew, FDI inflows increased and a limited number of companies began dominating the market by creating conglomerates in banking services, construction, media and tourism. A handful of those multi-sectional enterprises networked with state authorities and foreign investors, displacing traditional small-to-medium size domestic firms, themselves contributing very little to state finance as their brands were registered offshore. Given the lack of a robust industrial and manufacturing sector, a comprador element has historically dominated Greece's economy.[13] Embracing the era of globalization, this element shifted its profiteering activities into trading of financial commodities, now acting as a mediating agent not just between material commodities but mainly fictitious ones (e.g., insurance, equity, bonds, derivatives, special vehicles, etc.).

The global financial crisis was transplanted into the eurozone via the banking sector. German banks, in particular, were the first to fail as they had been exposed to US financial products, especially CDOs (Collateralised Debt Obligations).[14] The strain across the banking-financial sector of the eurozone reverberated immediately to the weak links of the financialized periphery, with Greek government bonds coming under extreme pressure.[15] By February–March 2010, the spread between the yields on 10-

12 Martin Wolf, *The Shifts and the Shocks: What We've Learned – and Have still to Learn – from the Financial Crisis*, London 2014, pp. 45–88; Robert Brenner, *The Economics of Global Turbulence*, London 2016, pp. 22–24, passim. Despite the fact that they belong to different traditions – Wolf is a liberal-Keynesian and Brenner a Marxist economic historian – both accept the artificial over-pricing of assets in the era of globalization/financialization, something which Brenner, rather misleadingly, calls »asset-price Keynesianism«.

13 For a definition of »comprador bourgeoisie« see Nicos Poulantzas, *Classes in Contemporary Capitalism*, London 1975, p. 71. Poulantzas, who borrowed the term from Andre Gunter Frank, argues that this »go-between« character of the comprador, which represents agents situated within a peripheral national formation that imports goods and technology from the core, makes the periphery completely *dependent* on the core in three ways: ideological, political and economic. For further discussion on this and the transformation the Greek comprador element underwent in the era of neoliberal financialization ushered in after the mid-1990s, see Fouskas / Dimoulas, *Greece, Financialization and the EU*, op. cit. (note 2), pp. 156–159.

14 William K. Tabb, »The international spread of financialization«, in: Wolfson / Epstein (eds.), *The Political Economy of Financial Crises*, op. cit. (note 11), pp. 528–540.

15 As Lapavitsas et al. note, financialization has developed in both core and peripheral countries of the eurozone. This can be seen from the rising volume of financial assets relative to GDP. By 2008, Germany, Holland, Austria and Ireland were the most financialized countries with a ratio of 316%, 376%, 379% and 760%, respectively. No accident that the crisis in Ireland hit severely the banking sector. In fact, by the same year, Greece, Portugal, Italy and Spain enjoyed far lower levels of financialization at 190%, 290%, 231% and 309%, respectively. As we can see, Greece had had the lowest level of financialization. See, Costas Lapavitsas / Annina Kaltenbrunner / Duncan Lindo / J. Michell / Juan Pablo Painceira / Eugenia Pires / Jeff Powell / Alexis Stenfors / Nuno Teles, »Euro-zone crisis: beggar thyself and thy neighbour« in: *Journal of Balkan and Near Eastern Studies* 12, No. 4 (2010), pp. 351–352.

year Greek bonds and German bunds became untenable. In this context, the claims of the financial sector of the core on Greece's financial sector intensified. Increased demand for liquidity by Greece's banking sector was temporarily provided by the Greek state, contributing to the worsening of the public debt. Effectively, the virtuous cycle of borrow-to-consume boom came to a halt, and the debt-cum-consumption-driven GDP collapsed overnight. The virtuous cycle became a vicious one: As expenditure rose to rescue the banks, sovereign debt rose at a time when claims on Greece's T-bills and CDS intensified. At that point in time (February–March 2010), Greece had two complementary choices that could alternate as bargaining chips in the negotiations: either push for a reasonable bailout agreement demanding at the same time a generous write-off of its debt so that she could hope to absorb the effects of the ensuing austerity; or threaten, meaningfully and in an organized manner, for a debtor-led default and exit from the eurozone having previously established a new set of international alliances within and outside the EU. It did none of this. Following the complete failure of the then Greek PM, George A. Papandreou, to stick to his word and call a referendum on the issue, Greece's ruling elites of PASOK and New Democracy just accepted what the creditors offered. In July 2015, Syriza, too, capitulated to the EU, the ECB and the IMF and against a referendum result which Syriza itself called and which overwhelmingly refused a third bailout programme. The Syriza government is now inserted in the imperial coalition for the implementation of »structural adjustment programmes« dominated by the chief creditor power, Germany. We can now move on to examine the social and economic consequences of imperial austerity in Greece.

3. Imperial austerity and its consequences

As we argued above, monetarist deflation was inserted in the institutional framework of the European project from the early 1990s, *pari pasu* with the collapse of the Soviet bloc and the »shock therapy« programme there pursued under the guidance of Jeffrey Sachs.[16] The Maastricht Treaty foresaw a path in which the euro was to compete with the dollar in global currency markets, trade, denomination of assets and international transactions. As such, there was no room for any putative inflationary policy of high wages and fiscal expansion whether at the European or nation-state level. Beyond the fact that such a policy would have undermined the aspiring international role of the euro, there was no mechanism invented at the European level to impose such form of intervention in the management of aggregate demand, and the European budget was and remains very small.[17] In addition, it would have been against the very structural

16 The best critique on the neoliberal »shock therapy« platform for Eastern Europe put forth by Jeffrey Sachs remains that by Peter Gowan, »Neo-liberal theory and practice for Eastern Europe«, in: *New Left Review*, No. 213, 1995, pp. 3–60.

17 In 2009 it was just 1% of the aggregate GDP of all EU states, which was a small fraction of the German budget.

logic of the capitalist enterprise, which is the increase in the rate of profit via a reduction of wages accompanied by an increase in the rate of exploitation.[18]

Periphery countries with high inflation and generous spending, such as Greece, entered the eurozone at high exchange rates in order precisely to curb the anomaly of inflation and reverse public expansion. The monetarist benchmarks limiting fiscal deficit to 3% and the public debt to 60% of GDP provided the weak economies of the periphery with a straightjacket impossible to cope. For Greece and other countries that had faced competitive pressures from Germany forcing them to devalue their currencies to improve competitiveness, the eurozone created an unbearable situation essentially because the option of (external) devaluation became unavailable. Soon after the introduction of the euro, Germany, whose two-thirds of trade was with eurozone countries, began registering massive surpluses. Periphery countries, on the contrary, multiplied their current account deficits as their competitive position worsened sharply. In this context, Germany, together with the IMF and the ECB, found itself leading a coalition of deflation dictating to the periphery the only programme she could see – as Schäuble put it – bringing about »sustainable development«: that of *internal* devaluation. Typically, all three bailouts prescribed *fiscal consolidation* amounting to cuts in public spending, reduction in public sector employment and severe welfare retrenchment; *labour market and social security reform*, such as increasing labour flexibility and precarious employment, lowering wages and the minimum wage; and deepening of *structural reforms*, such as privatization of public assets and infrastructure (e.g., airports, Greece's national electricity grid) in order to service debt payments. Legal and pension systems would also have to be reformed. How did the programmes work in practice?

4. *Fiscal consolidation*

The first »adjustment programme« of 2010 pushed the ratio of debt to GDP even higher at 172.1% in 2011, whereas by 2013, that is after the second »adjustment programme«, it went further up to 177.4%. From 2009 to 2015 the country lost 26% of its GDP, effectively losing in less than six years all what it gained in the previous twelve. Despite the fact that public expenditure was reduced up to almost 16% of GDP during 2008–2013[19], the fiscal deficit remained well above the benchmarks set at the Maastricht and SGP Treaties (table 1). Typically, the general government expenditure, as

18 If possible, capital wants to have zero production costs and zero risk. As Marx put it: »[This] zero cost for labour is therefore a limit in a mathematical sense, always beyond reach, although we can always approximate more and more nearly to it. The constant tendency of capital is to force the cost of labour back towards this absolute zero.« Karl Marx, *Capital*, v. 1, London 1867/1976, p. 748.

19 These are the highest cuts among the countries pursuing structural adjustment during that period, such as Ireland (11,3% cuts), Spain (5,9% cuts) and Portugal (2,7% cuts). See, Yiannis Tolios, *The Transition to the ›National Currency‹* (in Greek), Athens 2016, p. 14.

percentage of GDP, year after year increased due to the sharp drop in real and nominal GDP, from 244.9 billion euros in 2008 to 175.7 billion in 2015 (table 2).

Table 2: Evolution of government spending and income in Greece before and after the crisis

Year	General Government Expenditure as % of GDP	General Government Expenditure on Social Security Funds as %of GDP	Gross Minimum Wage in euro	Real Adjusted Disposable Income of household per capita in PPS	GDP per capita in PPS (EU28 = 100)
2004	47.6	14.3	630.77	16,629	96
2005	45.6	15.2	709.71	16,591	91
2006	45.1	15.6	730.3	17,801	94
2007	47.1	16.1	794.02	18,685	92
2008	50.8	17.4	817.83	19,519	94
2009	54.1	18.5	862.82	19,304	94
2010	52.5	19.0	862.82	17,966	87
2011	54.4	20.7	876.62	16,437	77
2012	55.4	20.0	683.76	15,709	74
2013	62.3	18.1	683.76	15,196	74
2014	50.6	17.8	683.76	15,064	73
2015	55.4	18.4	683.76	n.a.	71

Source: own illustration based on Eurostat

To the extent that tax collection did not relate to GDP or contribute substantially to state expenditure but relate instead to debt servicing according to the bailout programmes, tax on income, wealth, property, housing and VAT increased significantly. These increases did not sap tax evasion. Quite the opposite: they encouraged it (figure 1).

Figure 1: Evolution of taxes and GDP growth in Greece

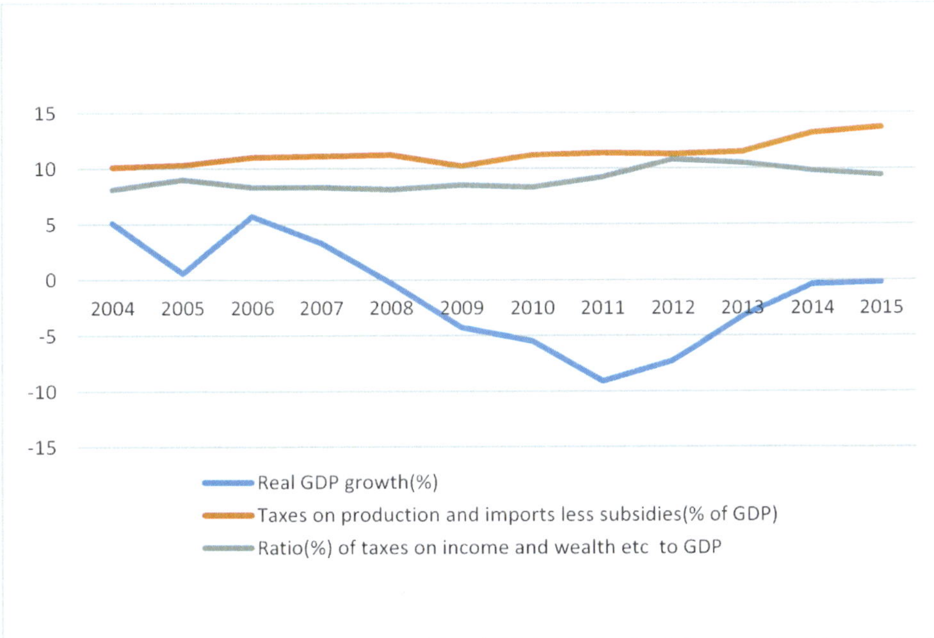

Source: own illustration based on Eurostat

Further, according to the dailies *To Vima* and *Kathimerini*, the underground economy increased from 27% to 37% with some 6,000 firms owing to the Greek state more than 30 billion euros.[20] Overdue debts of private firms and households are nearly 150 billion euros in 2016, of which 60 billion are non-performing loans, 58.5 billion overdue taxes, 27.4 billion overdue social contributions, 3.7 billion overdue customs and duties and 60 billion overdue mortgage repayments. Tax authorities in 2012 reported that 4,151 individuals (entrepreneurs, footballers, free-lancers, singers) had unpaid tax bills of some 15 billion euros. Evading paying VAT amounted to 6,5 billion euros per year. The bailout agreements forced the Greek cabinets to increase direct and indirect taxation: poll-tax and »solidarity tax« was introduced and VAT went up to 23–24%, including the islands, which enjoyed a lower VAT regime in order to encourage tourism and related professions (tourism's contribution to Greece's GDP stands at 18%). The real disposable income of Greek households has been deteriorating steadily since 2009, whereas the minimum wage was dropped down to the level of 2004 (table 2). This represents a reduction by 22%, although to those under 25 the minimum wage is reduced by 32%. Also, the effects of the crisis and the bailout programmes induced capital flight. In 2012 alone, wealthy individuals expatriated some 280 billion euros, either

20 *To Vima*, 28.3.2016; *Kathimerini*, 7.12.2015 and 2.2.2016.

placing them in foreign banks, mainly German, Austrian, Swiss and British, or investing them in housing and financial assets. Law 4024 of 2011 reduced the personal tax allowance from 12,000 euro a year to 5,000, yet with no effect as tax evasion continued, becoming, effectively, a matter of survival for the impoverished. Economists of the Greek daily *Express* have estimated that pensioners and employees carry the burden of the national tax bill by contributing 53%, whereas free lancers and professionals (lawyers, doctors etc.) contribute by 7%, farmers by 1% and entrepreneurs by 31%.[21] If we look at the effects of the bailout agreements on the employment structure of Greek society, it would become even clearer why tax evasion in Greece is so widespread after 2010.

The picture we have about the government debt and the sources of tax evasion is clear. The private debt presents an interesting trend. As a percentage of GDP, it increased rapidly from 1999 to 2007 and, since the onset of the crisis and the insertion of the country into the bondage of austerity, it skyrocketed (figure 2).

Figure 2: Evolution of general government and private debt as % of GDP (1995–2014)

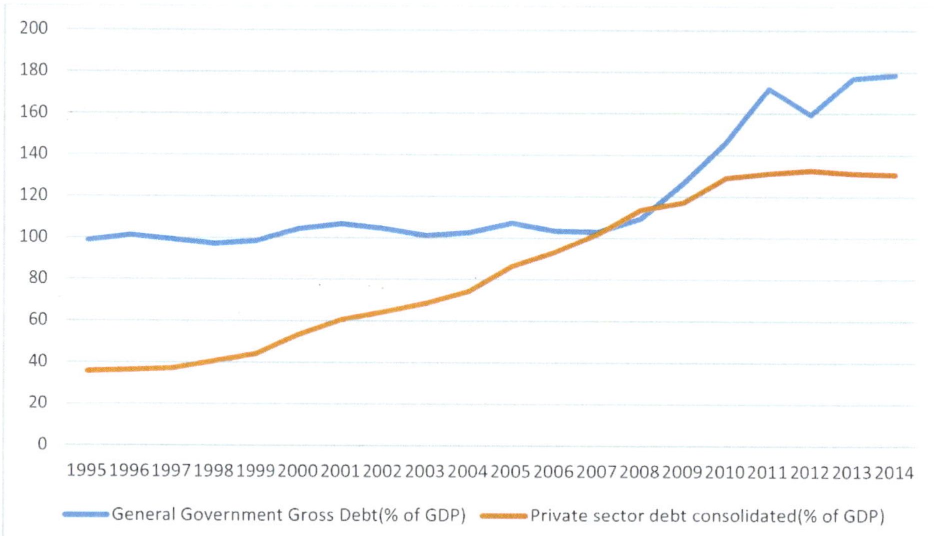

Source: own illustration based on Eurostat

Individuals owe huge amounts of money to Greek state authorities (tax authorities, insurance funds) and banks, whereas, of course, the Greek government owes huge amounts of money to its international lenders that it cannot afford to pay.

21 *Express*, 1.6.2012.

5. Labour market and social security reform

Imperial austerity decimated the middle classes, drawing onto society clear demarcation lines of class polarization with immediate effects on the political and party system. The rise of Syriza to prominence is mainly related to this social transformation, which is typical of a crisis of this magnitude and the social impoverishment and inequality it causes. Moreover, austerity created an even more permanent fissure within Greek class structures, and this goes beyond the extreme polarization between the underpaid and the overtaxed, on the one hand, and the super-rich, on the other. Taking into account the number of unemployed and the increasing number of pensioners, we have come to the conclusion that perhaps the most striking feature of Greek society at present is between those inside and outside of the workforce. More generally, austerity consolidated the structural dynamics of capital centralization and the concentration of wealth in fewer hands while increasing poverty, social inequality and the rate of exploitation for those at work.

Out of a total population of 10,920.000 in 2015, the economically active population, that is, those participating in workforce, are less than 40% (4,038.676 people), whereas the pensioners were more than 2,700.000 (figure 3).

Figure 3: Number of total employment, employees and pensioners in Greece

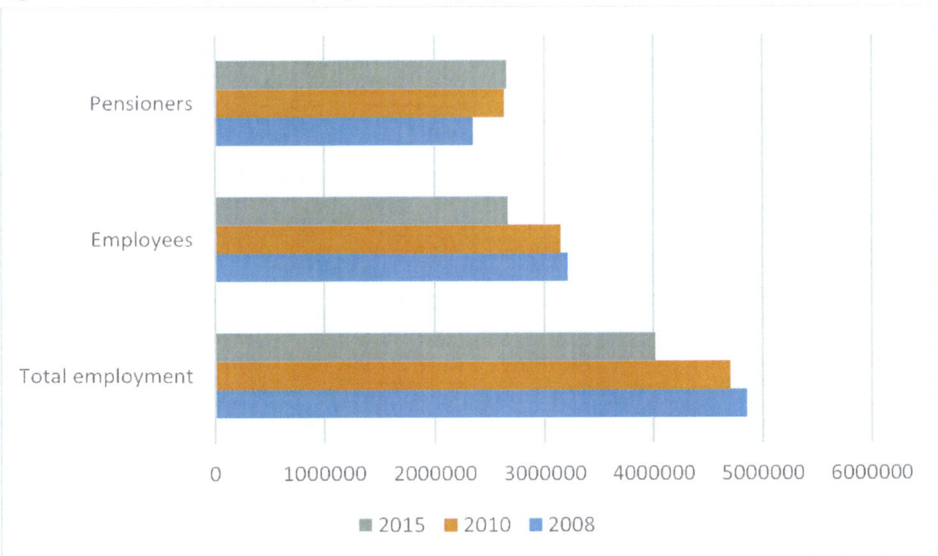

Source: own illustration based on ELSTAT

Having been committed to the austerity of the bailout agreements, all Greek cabinets since 2010 engaged in pension cuts and other measures, such as gradually increasing the pensionable age to 70 years and complicating the eligibility criteria. Yet due to

GDP contraction, Greek pensions, as percentage of GDP, are still the higher in the EU, despite the fact that the minimum national pension has been reduced to 392 euros per month (figure 4).

Figure 4: Expenditure on pensions as % of GDP in EU countries

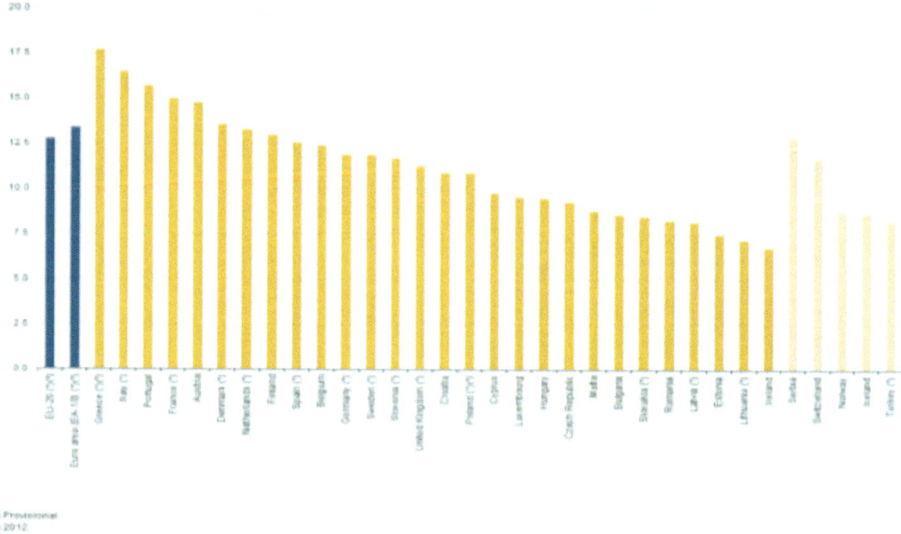

Source: own illustration based on Eurostat

Law 3863 of 2010 introduced a new method in calculating the new pension: whereas before the final pension was defined by the best five years of contributions, the new law stipulated that the final pension results from the average sum of all contributions.

In 2007 the employment rate was 65.8%, but it fell down to 53.3% in 2015 (figure 3). Unemployment rate has always been below 12% since 1998, but it skyrocketed to 27.5% in 2013. Youth (up to 24 years old) unemployment was the highest at 53% during 2012–2015. Long-term unemployment also increased from 34.7% in 2007 to 41.9% in 2012, 70.5% in 2013 and 73.1% in 2014. Part-time, casual and precarious employment also increased, especially after the conversion of contracts from full-time to part-time and rotation work. Following Schäuble's recipe, Greek cabinets, acting under their creditors' diktat, introduced Law 4093 of 2012, in which annual leave became compartmentalized and the costs of hiring and firing workers was minimized. Experts estimate that there is an increase of 44.8% in the conversion of full-time into part-time contracts and an increase of 85.5% in the conversion of full-time contracts into rotation work.[22] In 2013, youth involuntary part-time employment was over 64%.

22 Yianis Kouzis, »Industrial relations, unreliability of enterprises and the threat of joblessness during the recession« in: *Notebooks of the Institute of Labour/General Confederation of Greek Workers* 36 (2012), pp. 7–15.

Figure 5: Evolution of main indicators concerning living standards in Greece, 2004–2015

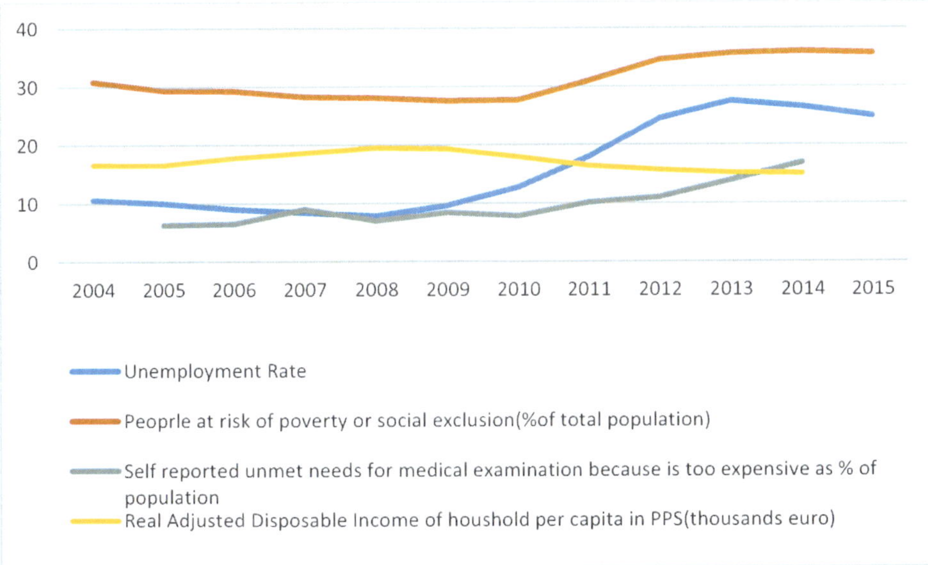

Source: own illustration based on Eurostat

Further, Law 4046 of 2012 dismantled the structure of national collective bargaining by introducing agreements at the level of enterprise. Already in 2010, some 200 sectoral agreements had been signed, covering 80% of employees. By 2015 even sectoral agreements ceased to be the norm: in 2015, there were only 19 sectoral agreements, no national collective agreement, the rest being in-firm agreements, most of which were between ›group of workers‹ and the employer (the trade union was absent).

The institutionalization of the devaluation of labour power via the deregulation of labour market is a substantial part of Greece's »adjustment programme«. In these circumstances, informal employment and unemployment rose to over 30%. Due to high unemployment rate and precarious work, health insurance fees became unaffordable. Free health care for all was provided only by the second Syriza government in August 2015.[23] Greece has now a distinct social group, that of the »new poor«, a social phenomenon quite common in Northern capitalist countries, which first appeared in Europe in Britain in the wake of Thatcher's neoliberal reforms. A substantial number of Greeks, especially pensioners, cannot afford to pay for a full meal a day, and barter be-

23 The creditors pushed for the reform of Greece's fragmented health care system. All health care funds came under a new supervisory agency, the so-called National Organisation for Primary Health Care (EOPYY), whose beneficiaries, according to its president in 2011, were 9 million people (the number was reduced to 6.2 million in 2013). The reform included initial payment of 25% of all medical costs (medicine, diagnostics tests, etc.).

gan to be widespread between 2011 and 2014, although it has now receded. More than 4,000 people committed suicide for reasons related to personal financial difficulties. Researchers note that the rate of extreme deprivation peaked in 2013 at 20% (it was 2.2% in 2009). The standard poverty rate increased from 19.1% in 2009 to 44.3% in 2013, affecting mainly the unemployed, children and the pensioners.[24] Last but not least, the creditors pushed for reduction in public employment. They succeeded on that front too. In 2009, total employment in the broader public sector numbered 1,066.729 civil servants. By February 2013 it decreased to 776,954, and this despite the fact that employment in Greece's public sector as a percentage of economically active population is below the average of OECD countries.[25] Flexibility has also entered the domain of the public sector. Arguably, imperial austerity in Greece has created unsustainable social conditions.

6. Structural reform

The structural reform aspect of all three adjustment programmes was not so disastrous for the dominant classes within Greece. It had had some strong *class* polarization effects within the »historic bloc« ruling Greece since the fall of the Colonels in 1974, supporting some class fractions against others, but it did not destroy capital nor did it damage the process of accumulation. As we argued above, it led to further concentration/centralization of capital and intensified the rate of exploitation through deflation and punitive legislation.

During the expansion period of 1995–2007, housing, transport, metal products, machinery and construction were the sectors that augmented most, whereas capital formation in agriculture remained rather stable (figure 4 and figure 7). As it can be seen from the evolution of gross capital formation, investments began falling after 2007. By 2015, the gross capital formation was reduced by two-thirds, reaching the level of 1995, thus losing all the gains it achieved during the expansion years of 1995–2007. The value of lost capital was nearly 80% in housing, metal products and machinery, whereas agriculture stagnated (see also below). In figure 7, we can see all main macroeconomic indicators over the eight year period of 2006–2014. All of them, with the sole exception of fixed capital consumption which remained rather stable, have deteriorated since 2008.

24 We draw here from the following sources: Dionysis Balourdos / Maria Petraki (eds.), *Poverty in Greece. Trends, Challenges and Policies*, Athens 2012, pp. 16–18; Manos Matsaganis / Chryssa Levendi, *The Anatomy of Poverty in Greece in 2013*, Athens 2013.

25 Ministry of Interior (Greece), *The Truth about the Greek Public Sector. Wages, Employment, Development*, Athens 2016, p. 11. The publication debates the position of the Association of Greek Industrialists (SEV), which argues for massive lay-offs in the public sector in order to reduce salary costs and other expenditure.

Figure 6: Evolution of gross capital formation in Greece, 1996–2015

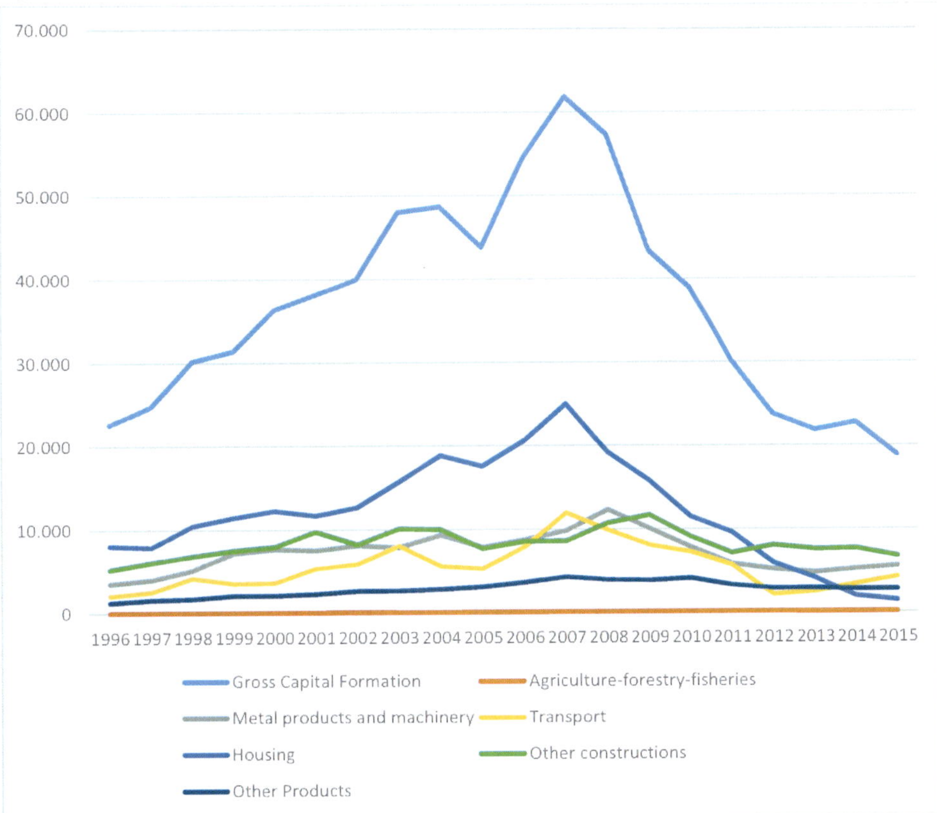

Source: own illustration based on ELSTAT

The real net profits grew throughout the expansion period, reaching their peak in 2007, although, if we trace the data back to 1980, we discern some fluctuations for short periods of time. The economic expansion led to further concentration/centralization of capital, especially in banking, shipping, construction, the media sector and tourism. This trend was further intensified after 2010, that is, when Greece entered the era of imperial austerity. Infrastructural work, such as the Rio-Antirio bridge, the construction of the new Athens airport and works for the 2004 Athens Olympics, had been financed by heavy external and domestic borrowing. When the crisis hit the Greek economy and hot speculation attacked the Greek bond and repo markets, the shaky foundations of the Greek expansion unravelled. As we can see clearly from figure 7, all main macro-economic indicators contracted, the sole exception being that of fixed capital, leaving no space for recovery under this type of deflationary policy.

Figure 7: Main macroeconomic indicators in Greece, 2006–2014

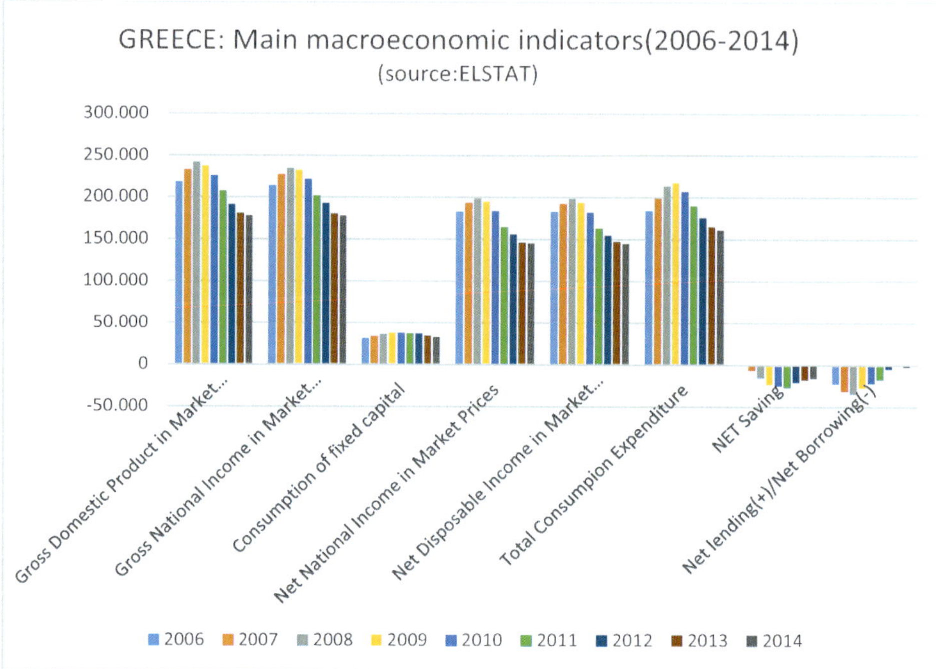

Source: own illustration based on ELSTAT

Interestingly, however, only 18 out of 500 leading enterprises in Greece in 2013 registered losses. The rest continued to register profits throughout the heavy austerity years of 2012–2014, especially the banks.[26] Twenty profitable conglomerates represented 67,6% of all profits in 2013 and controlled 43,8% of the annual payroll of those 500 enterprises. Profits in the banking sector alone totalled 63,5% of all profits recorded, whereas tourism registered 36%. Greece's small manufacturing sector recorded 13% profit, but this covered only 166 firms. In retail, 99 firms covered 8,6% of all profits, although the number of the firms was reduced in 2014 due to bankruptcies and acquisitions.

According to data gathered from Greek national accounts, the sectors affected most from the crisis were the most dynamic ones, simply because they had borrowed heavily. Small family enterprises lost 58.2% of their added value, constructions 52%, social work 45,9%, communication and information services 40.3%, and transport and ware-

26 Tolios, *The Transition to the ›National Currency‹*, op. cit. (note 19), pp. 27–29, passim; Lefteris Tsouflidis / Michel Zoumboulakis, *Greek Sovereign Defaults in Retrospect and Prospect*, MPRA Paper No. 71588, 2016; Marica Frangakis, *Inequality and Financialization: the Case of the EU*, Berlin 2014.

housing 38.5%.[27] Other authors also report that large, long-established firms, such as Nutriat ABEE, declared bankruptcy in 2013. Greece's largest furniture company, NEOSET, employing over 1,000 workers, declared bankruptcy in 2012, as did SATO, another furniture manufacturer.[28] It should be noted that Greece's private sector is dominated by SMEs, of which 98% employ less than 10 workers. Lastly, we can see from figure 8 that FDI inflows in Greece were dominated by German capital (from the late 1940s to early 1980s Greece was dominated by US capital). Before the crisis, the rate of investment was satisfactory. The amount of foreign capital invested in Greece during 2003–2008 was 28,4 billion euros, of which one-third was German (9,1 billion). The average annual investment ranged from 3,4 billion to 7 billion, but in 2012 it was only 2 billion. Unsurprisingly, FDI inflows decreased after 2009. But the most interesting feature has to do with the *type* of FDI Greece experienced since the country entered neoliberal financialization/globalization in the mid-1990s. According to »Enterprise Greece«, a key professional agency recording FDI in Greece, during 2003–2008 71% (19,9 billion) of FDI went to the tertiary sector of the economy, more specifically to finance (33%) and telecommunications (41%). Investment in agriculture, forestry, fisheries and manufacturing was almost zero.[29] From 2009 to 2014, FDI was also directed to services (70% or 11,9 billion), with the breakdown now being 29% to telecommunications, 24% in finance, 18% to the devalued real-estate and 15% to the retail sector. All in all, FDI did not contribute to the development of the real economic sector in Greece during the period of imperial austerity under scrutiny here. Its business concentrated in the acquisition of equities and shares and the floating assets of Greece's privatizing companies (portfolio investment).

27 See www.statistics.gr [22.12.2016].

28 Marica Frangakis, »Public debt crisis, austerity and deflation: the case of Greece« in: *Review of Keynesian Economics* 3, No. 3 (2015), p. 307.

29 Enterprise Greece, *Foreign direct investment*, http://www.enterprisegreece.gov.gr/gr/h-ellada-shmera/giati-ellada/ksenes-ameses-ependyseis [28.12.2016].

Figure 8: Origin of inward FDI, Greece (2003–2014)

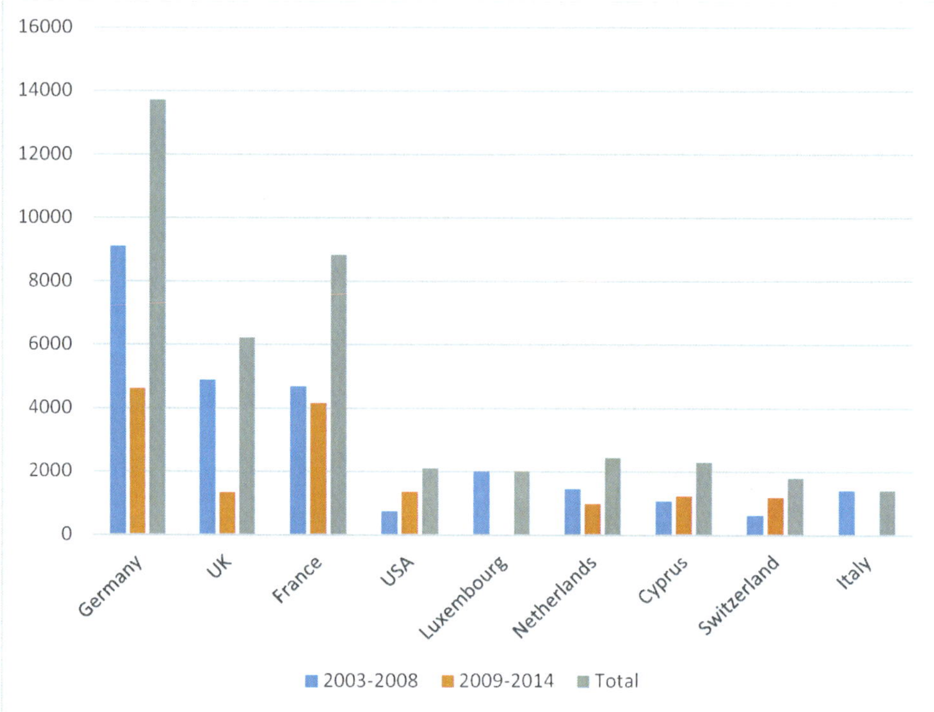

Source: own illustration based on Bank of Greece

As far as the agricultural sector is concerned, it shrank from 8% of GDP in 1995 to 3,1% in 2009, and it began a gentle pick up with the advent of the crisis, when some domestic migration took place as people, due to the crisis, was forced to leave the urban centres, returning to their provinces of origin. Remarkably, though, the EU's CAP (Common Agricultural Policy) did not manage to offset any of the chronic problems of the Greek agricultural sector, namely its labour-intensive character and uncompetitive position (Greece's agricultural sector is dominated by small, family-based farms). If at all, its financing mechanism widened the gap between small and large firms and increased relatively the number of seasonal workers. The overall number of farms, nevertheless, declined from 860,154 in 2007 to 709,449 in 2013.[30]

30 All data from Apostolos G. Papadopoulos, »The impact of CAP on agriculture and rural areas of EU member states« in *Agricultural South: Journal of Political Economy* 4, No. 1 (2016), pp. 22–53 and Spiros Sakellaropoulos, *Crisis and Social Stratification in Greece in the 21st Century* (in Greek), Athens 2014, pp. 123–125, passim.

7. Concluding remarks and prospects for the future

This chapter examined the social and economic consequences of the three »adjustment programmes« imposed on Greece by the EU, the ECB and the IMF. We have called this type of austerity as *imperial*, indeed, *colonial bondage*, especially because specific departments of the Greek state are controlled *directly* by the creditors, thus depriving it of any meaningful (relative) autonomy. Democracy has become meaningless in Greece because state policy (»adjustment programmes«) is the result of the institutionalization of the *merging* of the »national« (the Greek government), the »European« (the EU and the ECB) and the »global« (IMF) into an executive committee, regardless of liberal-democratic processes taking place within Greece.

None of the bailout funds went to the real economic sector, nor did they assist Greece to lower its debt levels despite the harsh austerity measures implemented by successive Greek cabinets from 2010 to 2016. Quite the opposite, the debt/GDP ratio increased, together with class inequality and social polarization. Imperial bondage in Greece has led to the pauperization of the working classes and the disintegration of middle classes, creating a new permanent fissure in society: those in workforce are in minority, the majority being the non-employed (pensioners, unemployed and those looking for work). Within the ensemble of the dominant classes, the class fractions that benefitted most as a result of austerity were rather the most financialized sectors of the economy (e.g., banks).

We have broken down the »adjustment programmes« into three aspects: fiscal consolidation; labour market and social security reform; and structural reform. Our findings suggest that: (a) whatever fiscal consolidation has so far been achieved has failed to induce growth; (b) labour market reform, low wages and flexible forms of employment brought about high profits in certain sectors (finance, tourism) but, time and again, failed to incentivize private capital to invest and thus generate growth; and (c) structural reform offered new opportunities to the finance, shipping and tourist sectors to increase their profiteering, tax-free and speculative activities. Further, FDI, too, is being directed to portfolio investment and services rather than to the real economic sector (manufacturing, agriculture, innovation).

The eurozone seems to act as a straightjacket similar, if not worse, to that of the Gold Standard and whose success or failure depends on the level of participatory democracy within the state in question. If low, as in the 19th century, then the Gold Standard has chances to succeed as a supply-side deflationary recipe and stabilize the exchange rate; if high, as in the inter-war period, when mass political parties, trade unions and universal suffrage won the day, then the Gold Standard is but a recipe for disaster: its deflationary policy breeds authoritarianism, extremism and racism. Following the Troika's programme, the eurozone today resembles a monstrous monetary-deflationary architecture not far from the rigidity of the Gold Standard of the inter-war period. The euro acts as a form of Gold Standard from which no member state is allowed to deviate, let alone to pursue external devaluation in order to address issues of competitiveness. Thus, according to the structural logic of the eurozone, *internal* devaluation, i.e. imperial bondage, is the only option. Is it? In 2010 the Greek cabinet under George A. Papandreou lost a golden opportunity to bargain hard with the creditors to find a reasonable solution to Greece's (and the eurozone's) problems, when large chunks of Greek debt was still held by private lenders all over the world. The bailout agreements, especially the second one, transferred the debt onto public institutions, and the opportunity of driving a hard bargaining was lost. Similarly, a debtor-led default and exit from the eurozone became more difficult, because the debt has now become part of Greece's international obligation adjudicated by the English law.[31] Greece's former Finance Minister, Yanis Varoufakis, has founded and leads a new pan-European party, *DiEM25*, putting pressure on Germany to abandon deflation, low-wages and export-led growth. Varoufakis assesses that there is still life for Greece within the eurozone as long as there is a debt re-structuring and an economic development plan for Greece, taking the country outside the deflationist spiral of austerity. Joseph Stiglitz suggested a »flexible« euro, splitting the currency into Northern and Southern blocs.[32] Other radical Keynesian economists, such as Heiner Flassbeck and Costas Lapavitsas, lead efforts for the abandonment of the eurozone, although their position on the EU remains ambiguous.[33] As we currently write these lines, the Greek government of Syriza has effectively signed a fourth bailout programme. It seems that the so-called »Greek problem« will continue to haunt the eurozone for many years to come. As long as this persists, the future of the eurozone itself remains uncertain.

31 The second bailout agreement stipulated that the law governing the new bonds issued will not be subject to Greek law but to English law. This means, for instance, that the Greek parliament cannot review the legal terms of the deal nor sue in an English court, as this is both complicated and expensive. Further, the framework of the English law renders a quasi-prerogative to the lender, because it is imbued by the colonial tradition protecting the property owner. No legislation could be passed by them, because this deal makes the role of the Greek parliament, that is, the role of formal liberal democracy in one country, redundant.

32 Joseph Stiglitz, »A split Euro is the solution for Europe's single currency« in: *Financial Times*, 17.8.2016. A similar view is put forth by Wolfgang Streeck in his *Buying Time*, referring to a »European Bretton Woods«; see Wolfgang Streeck, *Buying Time. The Delayed Crisis of Democratic Capitalism*, London 2014, pp. 185–187.

33 Heiner Flassbeck / Costas Lapavitsas, *Crisis and Austerity in the Euro-zone*, London 2015, esp. pp. 89–91. The position of Flassbeck and Lapavitsas is not a Marxist position but a left Keynesian one. Orthodox Marxists in Greece and elsewhere do not subscribe to Keynesian analyses of financialization and, having analysed the crisis as a typical crisis of the falling rate of profit, argue for a left exit not just from the eurozone but also from the EU; see, for instance, Stavros D. Mavroudeas, »The Greek crisis: structural or conjunctural?« in: Subasat (ed.), *The Great Financial Meltdown*, op. cit. (note 11), pp. 307–327.

Brian Girvin

The Political Consequences of Austerity in the Republic of Ireland: Domestic Choice, International Constraints and Democratic Deficits

The Great Recession that began in 2008 continues to impact on the lives and income of most Europeans. Austerity and fiscal retrenchment have been the dominant policy choice for governments of the left and the right. Political instability has led to increased support for populist and illiberal movements. Recession and instability also contributed to the UK decision to leave the European Union (EU) in June 2016. Continuing recession has challenged the future of the euro and questioned the goal of European integration itself. This environment has weakened democratic politics and undermined the consensus that characterized Europe since 1945.[1] Notwithstanding the similar circumstances faced by Europeans, individual states have responded in very different ways. Consequently, outcomes vary depending on the political culture, the policy priorities and the state of public opinion in individual states.[2] Small states are particularly vulnerable during periods of crisis. Iceland, Ireland and Greece were seriously exposed during the Great Recession, and each found it difficult to respond to the challenge. What is clear, however, is that the outcome for these three states has been quite different even though their decision making was severely constrained by domestic and international considerations.[3]

The Republic of Ireland (hereafter Ireland) provides an important case study of how a small state responds to austerity and recession. It also demonstrates how constrained policy making can be for a small open economy within the eurozone. Ireland only converged with the European Union at the end of the 1990s after a long period of slow growth and recession.[4] Its economic success during the »Celtic-Tiger« period was actively promoted by the EU as an example for new members from central and Eastern

1 Wolfgang Streeck, »The Crisis in Context: Democratic Capitalism and its Contradictions« in: Armin Schäfer / Wolfgang Streeck (eds.), *Politics in the Age of Austerity*, Cambridge 2013, pp. 262–286.

2 John Hall / John L. Campbell, *The Paradox of Vulnerability: Small Nation-States in the Financial Crisis*, Princeton/New Jersey, forthcoming. I am grateful to the authors for providing me with a draft copy of this book.

3 Hanspeter Kriesi, »The Political Consequences of the Economic crisis in Europe: Electoral Punishment and Popular Protest« in: Nancy Bermeo / Larry M. Bartels (eds.), *Mass Politics in Tough Times: Opinions, Votes, and Protest in the Great Recession*, Oxford 2014, pp. 315–327.

4 Brian Girvin, »Political Culture, Political Independence and Economic Success in Ireland« in: *Irish Political Studies* 12, No. 1 (1997), pp. 48–77; Rona Fitzgerald / Brian Girvin, »Political culture, growth and the conditions for success in the Irish economy« in: Brian Nolan / Philip J. O'Connell / Christopher T. Whelan (eds.), *Bust to Boom? The Irish Experience of Growth and Inequality*, Dublin 2000, pp. 268–287.

Europe.[5] Ireland then confounded international opinion in 2008 when the government unilaterally guaranteed the Irish banking system and, following a fiscal crisis, in 2010 reluctantly accepted a rescue programme sponsored by the EU/European Central Bank and the International Monetary Fund (hereafter the Troika). Ireland exited the bailout in 2013 and experienced sustained growth and recovery by 2016. For the Troika and conservative international opinion, Ireland demonstrated how austerity can work, despite the considerable cost to society. Anti-austerity critics, however, argue that Ireland does not provide a model for successful austerity but that its recovery is due to special circumstances.[6] Nor was the Irish electorate convinced that recovery was underway. In 2016, the two governing parties lost a significant amount of seats at the general election.

The political consequences of austerity in Ireland include the implosion of the Fianna-Fáil-led government in 2010, the end of Fianna Fáil's dominance and dealignment of political system. The political system is increasingly fragmented, but there is little evidence that realignment is occurring.

1. Economic change and political continuity in the Celtic Tiger 1992–2007

The Celtic Tiger made a significant contribution to transforming Ireland between 1992 and 2007. Full employment was achieved for the first time, living standards rose appreciably, and the population reached four million by 2004. Ireland became a more diverse, pluralistic and cosmopolitan society during this time, and attitudes and behaviour were transformed. Ireland was no longer compared to states on the European periphery but with advanced liberal democratic states in northern Europe.[7]

Despite the many social and economic changes that occurred during the Celtic-Tiger period, continuity was the main feature of politics and the political system. Fianna Fáil remained the largest party from 1932 until 2007, attracting over 40 per cent of the vote

5 The EU representation in Ireland emphasizes on its web site that Ireland punches above its weight and specifically notes that »Ireland is recognised as being a great example of how smaller nations can use their status as an EU Member State to help shape a better future for its citizens, and indeed all Europeans.« http://ec.europa.eu/ireland/ireland_in_the_eu/impact_of_ireland_on_eu/index1_en.htm [24.5.2016].

6 Patrick Honohan, »Keynote Speech« in: International Monetary Fund (ed.), *Ireland: Lessons from its Recovery from the Bank-Sovereign Loop*, Washington, DC 2015, pp. 24–32, p. 24; Eoin Burke Kennedy, »Ireland no paradigm of successful austerity – Varoufakis« in: *Irish Times*, 5.11.2015; Philippe Legrain, »Ireland's recovery has nothing to do with austerity« in: *Foreign Policy*, 24.2.2016; William K. Roche / Philip J. O'Connell / Andrea Prothero (eds.), *Austerity and Recovery in Ireland: Europe's Poster Child and the Great Recession*, Oxford 2017 contains the most considered assessment to date.

7 Tony Fahey / Helen Russell / Christopher T. Whelan (eds.), *Best of Times? The Social Impact of the Celtic Tiger*, Dublin 2007; Michael Böss (ed.), *The Nation-State in Transformation: Economic Globalisation, International Mediation and Political Values*, Aarhus 2010, which takes this for granted.

at most general elections.[8] Moreover, during this period the party participated in government on its own or in coalition for 57 out of 75 years. The stability of the system can be seen in figure 1. Persistence has been a key feature of the Irish political system since the 1930s, when Fianna Fáil became the dominant party and Fine Gael the main opposition party in what has been characterized as a two-and-a-half party system (the Labour party being the half).[9]

Figure 1: Party vote 1932–2007

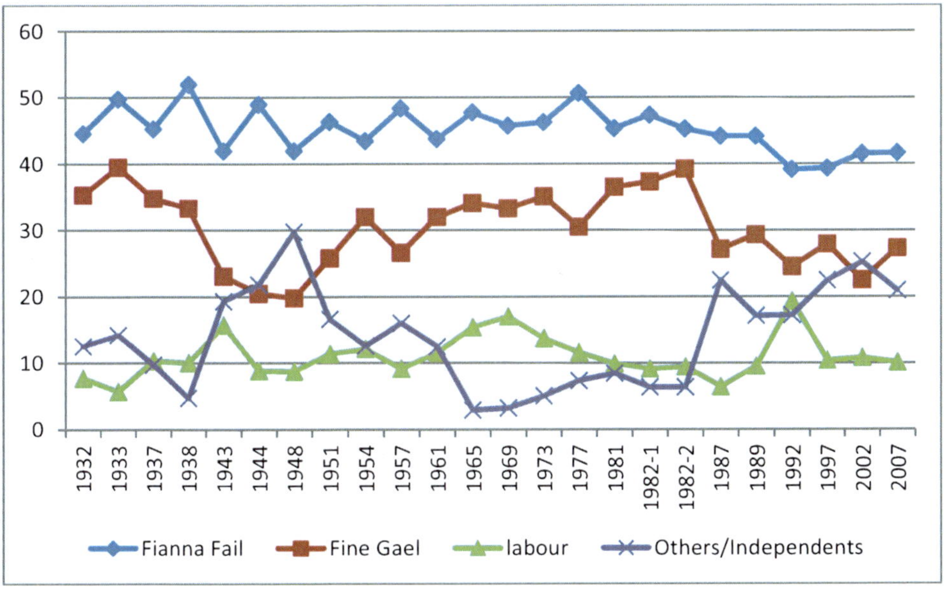

Source: own illustration based on Electionirland.org

Fianna Fáil has been characterized as one of the twentieth-centuries most successful democratic political parties. It has long been accustomed to the prerogatives of office and to thinking of itself as the country's natural governing party.[10] Fianna Fáil drew electoral support from every section of Irish society, from every region and from every age group. At the 2007 general election it was slightly weaker among younger voters and in the Dublin region, but it had a 15 point average lead over its closest rival Fine

8 Until 2011 the party only fell below the 40 per cent mark on two occasions. Gary Murphy, *Electoral Competition in Ireland since 1987: The politics of triumph and despair*, Manchester 2016.

9 Peter Mair, *The Changing Irish Party System*, New York 1987, pp. 12–60, 138–206; Richard Sinnott, *Irish voters decide: Voting behaviour in elections and referendums since 1918*, Manchester 1995, pp. 279–285.

10 R. Kenneth Carty, »Fianna Fáil and Irish party competition« in: Michael Gallagher / Michael Marsh (eds.), *How Ireland Voted 2007: The Full Story of Ireland's General Election*, New York 2008, pp. 218–231, p. 219.

Gael in every category.[11] Fianna Fáil and Fine Gael have dominated the system since the 1930s. Both are national parties competing in every constituency and usually winning at least one seat in each. Furthermore, as nation-wide catch-all parties, both seek to appeal to the widest possible electorate, and this pushes them and the other parties towards the moderate centre. Fianna Fáil secured its position at the centre of the party system and government formation when it entered coalition for the first time in 1989. Once coalition had been accepted, Fianna Fáil was able to seek government partners from its left or right and also from independents. This proved to be an extremely successful formula during the Celtic-Tiger period, and the strategy was closely associated with Bertie Ahern, who successfully led three Fianna-Fáil-dominated governments between 1997 and 2008.[12] Their position at the centre of the political system has been challenged from time to time, but insurgents have been absorbed by both major parties because of their ideological flexibility and a deliberate exclusion of controversial issues from party competition. Such issues have been addressed through referendums and government-appointed commissions, thus reducing the possibility that new parties will successfully mobilize around them.[13]

In these circumstances, it is surprising that, when Bertie Ahern called the general election for May 24, 2007, he told his first press conference that »the consequences of this election will be felt for many years to come.« In retrospect this may seem prescient, yet the election itself has been described as »the earthquake that never happened.«[14] Indeed, the 2007 election could have been any election since 1932. Fianna Fáil won over 40 per cent of the vote, Fine Gael came in second but far behind, and the combined vote for these two parties reached 70 per cent that election year. Ahern was re-elected Taoiseach and negotiated a new coalition government that included for the first time the Green Party. The Green's decision to join the government was an acknowledgement that politics would continue as before and that Fianna Fáil would remain central to government formation. Thus, despite recession during the 1980s, recovery in the 1990s and the subsequent Celtic-Tiger boom, the key features of Irish politics were maintained.

The foundations of continuity and stability were seriously challenged for the first time in 2008, when the Irish economy entered recession and the banking system virtually collapsed. Most policy makers assumed that, though a downturn was inevitable, Ireland would have a soft landing. Taoiseach Brian Cowen insisted as late as 2010 that, »if the unprecedented global collapse had not happened, there would have been a soft landing for the Irish economy.«[15] Cowen and his finance minister Brian Lenihan argued that the fundamentals of Irish policy were sound and that the crisis was a con-

11 Michael Marsh, »Explanations for party choice« in: Gallagher / Marsh (eds.), *How Ireland Voted 2007*, op. cit. (note 10), pp. 105–131, p. 115.

12 Murphy, *Electoral Competition in Ireland since 1987*, op. cit. (note 8), pp. 102–136.

13 This is a brief summary of a very complex discussion. See Seán D. McGraw, *How Parties Win: Shaping the Irish Political Arena*, Ann Arbor 2015, pp. 23–68.

14 Michael Gallagher, »The earthquake that never happened: analysis of the results« in: Gallagher / Marsh (eds.), *How Ireland Voted 2007*, op. cit. (note 10), pp. 78–104.

15 Speech reported in: *Irish Times*, 14.5.2010.

sequence of actions outside the state. However, Lenihan on occasions highlighted an alternative explanation:

»You know we've got to be honest about this as a people. We decided, as a people collectively, to have this housing boom. We decided not to have property taxes, to demand reductions in stamp duties, to demand interest relief for those who bought to-let properties, and there was no questioning in any part of the political system about this.«[16]

Lenihan complained that Fine Gael had promised even more generous incentives for those buying property at the 2007 election, though Fine Gael challenged this. Enda Kenny repeated a very similar claim in 2012 after he became Taoiseach, »what happened in our country was that people went mad borrowing.« After losing office, Cowen argued that unemployment would have been higher and welfare expenditure lower if the government had not pursued the policies it did.[17]

However, evidence suggests that the recession was homemade and would have occurred even if there had not been a global downturn. The Joint Committee of Inquiry into the Banking Crisis concluded that government action and inaction contributed to the crisis. It specifically identified institutional failure, the influence of the electoral business cycle and taxation policy as contributory factors.[18] This was an economic crisis that was created by political decisions made by Irish politicians. Taoiseach Bertie Ahern had dismissed criticism of policy prior to the recession, advising critics to consider killing themselves.[19] In fact, irresponsible budgetary policy from 1999 and arrogance in the face of expert advice and/or criticism undermined the tax base, leaving the state seriously exposed when the property boom ended.

Former Minister for Finance Ray MacSharry recalled the response of the then Minister for Finance Charlie McCreevy to warnings about the unsustainable nature of his budgetary approach:

»The Government felt that they could afford both massive increases in public pay and huge reductions in income tax because of the enormous revenues that property-related taxes were bringing in. The culture of the time seemed to be to spend this revenue without giving a second thought as to whether the level of revenue would

16 »Lenihan: Public to blame for housing collapse« in: *Irish Examiner*, 8.9.2008, http://www.irishexaminer.com/ireland/lenihan-public-to-blame-for-housing-collapse-71791.html [12.7.2017].

17 Interview with Brian Lenihan reported in *Irish Examiner*, 8.9.2008; Kenny's remarks were made at Davos, January 2012; Brian Cowen, *The Euro: From Crisis to Resolution?*, Washington, DC 2012, http://cdn.thejournal.ie/media/2012/03/20120327cowenspeech.pdf [2.7.2017].

18 *Report of the Joint Committee of Inquiry into the Banking Crisis, Volume 1: Report*, Dublin 2016, pp. 7–18; Karl Whelan, »Policy Lessons from Ireland's Latest Depression« in: *The Economic and Social Review* 41, No. 2 (2010), pp. 228–254; Hall / Campbell, *The Paradox of Vulnerability*, op. cit. (note 2) suggest that, when compared to Denmark and Switzerland, Irish institutions were weak. This left the state unprepared for the crisis and ineffective in response to it.

19 Reported in *Irish Times*, 4.6.2007.

be available the following year. When I suggested this was a mistake, McCreevy was far from happy. In one conversation, he said to me ›I have two billion of a surplus. Do you think I should leave that there?‹ I replied, ›yes I do,‹ but he just laughed at me.«[20]

Despite criticism from the central bank and the EU, McCreevy and his successor Brian Cowen maintained an expansionary policy in advance of the 2002 and 2007 general elections. Government and opposition sought to outdo one another in offering benefits to the electorate, with little consideration of cost or implementation.[21] Political parties competed on how much tax to cut rather than assessing whether this was the best policy in the circumstances. Privatization also proved popular, and on one occasion 500,000 people applied for shares in the soon to be privatized Telecom Eireann. When those who had bought shares lost most of their investment, Fine Gael offered to offset losses against tax at the 2002 election.

Throughout this period there is a paradox at the heart of public opinion. The electorate was deeply concerned about health policy and education, agreeing that these areas should take priority.[22] The government and the electorate colluded in the belief that it was possible to improve and expand public service provision without any tax increases. Nor did the main opposition parties challenge these assumptions. Not surprisingly, public opinion strongly supported tax cuts. However, in a 2000 survey nearly two thirds said they would be prepared to sacrifice further tax cuts for an improved health service. Despite this, a later poll reported that the most favoured option for funding health and education involved further privatization (47%). Only 12% in this survey supported tax increases. In October 2003, a majority favoured retaining income tax at existing levels, even if this entailed no additional funding for public services. 48 per cent were in favour of spending cuts to fund such services. Nor had these attitudes changed by 2007. Slightly less than three quarters polled remained opposed to any tax increases to fund public services, while fully 83 per cent agreed that public services should be funded from existing taxes.[23] A downturn in the economy may not have been unexpected, but political considerations in 2007, the resignation of Bertie Ahern in 2008 and a failure to acknowledge or address the fundamental weaknesses in economic policy fatally undermined the prospect of a »soft landing« for the economy.

20 Cited in Murphy, *Electoral Competition in Ireland since 1987*, op. cit. (note 8), p. 110.

21 For a succinct criticism of the political parties for attempting to outbid one another at elections times, Pat Leahy, »The need to Change Our Political Culture is Paramount« in: *Irish Politics Forum*, 28.20.2011, https://politicalreform.ie/2011/10/28/the-need-to-change-our-political-culture-is-paramount/ [16.1.2017].

22 Pat Leahy, *Showtime: The Inside Story of Fianna Fáil in Power*, Dublin 2009.

23 Fiachra Kennedy / Christopher Farrington (eds.), »Data yearbook 2004« in: *Irish Political Studies* 20, No. 1 (2005), pp. 50–51; Christopher Farrington / Liam Weeks (eds.), »Data yearbook 2008« in: *Irish Political Studies* 23, No. 2 (2008), pp. 302–304.

2. The economic and social consequences of austerity

The budgetary strategy pursued by successive governments between 2008 and 2015 was exceptionally severe and has had a disastrous impact on employment, income and living standards. The Irish debt-to-GDP ratio soared from low levels pre-recession to nearly 120 per cent by 2012, but it has fallen back significantly as the austerity programme began to have an impact (table 1). This is in stark contrast to Greece, which despite severe retrenchment continues to suffer from high debt levels. In tables 1, 2 & 3 I have illustrated the contrast between Ireland and a selected number of European states. The EU-28 average provides a base line for comparison. Denmark has been included because Ireland is frequently compared to this Scandinavian state. Greece, Spain and Portugal provide a comparison as they along with Ireland suffered most from austerity. The UK is Ireland's neighbour and remains a major trading partner.

Table 1: Debt-to-GDP ratio 2007–2015

	2007	2008	2009	2010	2011	2012	2013	2014	2015	2016
EU 28	57.6	60.07	72.8	78.4	81.1	83.8	85.7	86.7	84.9	83.5
Denmark	27.3	33.4	40.3	42.9	46.4	45.2	44.7	44.8	40.4	37.8
Ireland	23.9	42.3	61.7	86.3	109.6	119.5	119.5	105.2	78.6	75.4
Greece	103.1	109.4	126.7	146.2	172.1	159.6	177.4	179.7	177.4	179.0
Spain	35.6	39.5	52.8	60.1	69.5	85.7	95.5	100.4	99.8	99.4
Portugal	68.4	71.7	83.6	96.2	111.4	126.2	129.0	130.6	129.0	130.4
UK	42.0	50.2	64.5	76.0	81.6	85.1	86.2	88.1	89.0	89.3

Source: own illustration based on Eurostat

Average real income per adult fell by 7.8 per cent between 2008 and 2011. The poorest 10 per cent suffered a fall of 18.4 per cent. Unemployment soared as a consequence, and the austerity programme had a particularly negative impact on youth unemployment (see tables 2 and 3). An estimated 300,000 jobs were lost, and by 2015 total employment was still only 91 per cent of the 2007 level.

Table 2: Unemployment 2006–2015

	2006	2007	2008	2009	2010	2011	2012	2013	2014	2015
EU-28	8.2	7.2	7.0	9.0	9.6	9.7	10.5	10.9	10.2	9.4
Denmark	3.9	3.8	3.4	6.0	7.5	7.6	7.5	7.0	6.6	6.2
Ireland	4.5	4.7	6.4	12.0	13.9	14.7	14.7	13.1	11.3	9.4
Greece	9.0	8.4	7.8	9.8	12.7	17.9	24.5	27.5	26.5	24.9
Spain	8.5	8.2	11.3	17.9	19.9	21.4	24.8	26.1	24.5	22.1
Portugal	8.9	9.1	8.8	10.7	12.0	12.9	15.8	16.4	14.1	12.6

	2006	2007	2008	2009	2010	2011	2012	2013	2014	2015
UK	5.4	5.3	5.6	7.6	7.8	8.1	7.9	7.6	6.1	5.3

Source: own illustration based on Eurostat

Table 3: Youth unemployment 2013–2015

	2013	2014	2015	2015Q4
EU-28	23.7	22.2	20.3	19.6
Denmark	13.0	12.6	10.8	10.2
Ireland	26.8	23.9	20.9	18.9
Greece	58.3	52.4	49.8	49.0
Spain	55.5	53.2	48.3	46.2
Portugal	38.1	34.7	32.0	32.8
UK	20.7	16.9	14.6	13.1

Source: own illustration based on Eurostat

Emigration increased: over 123,000 more people left the country than entered between 2008 and 2014. In the early years of the recession, EU nationals were the largest group leaving the country, but by 2011 Irish citizens constituted the biggest group. In 2015 the outward trend was maintained but at a lower level. Despite this outflow, the 2016 census reported a further increase in the population, reaching the highest level since the nineteenth century.

Table 4: Migration from Ireland by nationality 2006–2012

	2006	2008	2010	2011	2012	2013	2014	2015
Irish	42.5%	26.7%	41.8%	52.1%	53.4%	57.2%	49.7%	43.6%
EU-27	40.3%	54.9%	44.8%	35.6%	33.9%	31.2%	32.7%	34.5%
Rest of World	17.2%	18.4%	13.4%	12.3%	12.7%	11.6%	17.6%	21.9%
Total	36,000	49,000	69,200	80,600	87,100	89,000	81,900	80,900

Source: own illustration based on Table 5; Geraldine Robbins / Irvine Lapsley, »The Success story of the Eurozone crisis? Ireland's austerity measures« in: *Public Money and Management* 34, No. 2 (2014), pp. 91–98, p. 94; and data for 2015 from Ireland's national statistical office

Between 2008 and 2011, GDP declined by 11.8 per cent and GNP by 14.5 per cent. Between 2007 and 2009, net financial wealth declined by 56 per cent, mostly represented by negative equity in housing. By the end of 2010, 31 per cent of mortgaged properties were in negative equity, constituting 47 per cent of outstanding mortgage loans. By

2011, Irish household debt reached 200 per cent of gross disposable income.[24] The austerity programme contributed to a substantial decline in income, living standards and benefits for all sections of Irish society. Those on welfare suffered most, and the deprivation rate rose from an historic low of 11.8 per cent in 2007 to 24.5 per cent in 2011. The impact of austerity was least severe on retired people and most severe on non-earning lone parents and single unemployed without children (12.6 and 22.4 per cent, respectively). The largest group is single employed without children (34 per cent of families), which experienced an 8 per cent decline in income.[25]

Irish austerity may not have been as severe as that of Greece, but the economic and social consequences were immediate and widely felt. If incumbent governments are rewarded or penalized based on the electorate's assessment of how it performed during its period of office, then Fianna Fáil faced a serious challenge in 2009. Virtually every incumbent government was penalized by the electorate in response to the imposition of austerity politics, and the Irish government was not in a position to avoid this.[26]

3. What happened to Fianna Fáil?

Fianna Fáil had benefitted from its close association with prosperity over two decades. It was also the party considered most likely to maintain continuity and stability in the state. On this occasion, the public quickly lost confidence in the government and Fianna Fáil. Positive attitudes towards the Taoiseach and the government were undermined between June and November 2008, as the seriousness of the crisis became evident. Fianna Fáil was down 15 points in the polls by November, and 76 per cent expressed dissatisfaction with the government. In one poll, Fianna Fáil's share of the vote fell to 26 per cent, behind Fine Gael at 33 per cent. Surprisingly, 50 per cent of the public agreed that former Taoiseach Bertie Ahern, who had resigned earlier in the year, would be the best leader to address the economic downturn. The actual Taoiseach Brian Cowen received 24 per cent while Fine Gael leader Enda Kenny received 28 per cent.[27]

Public opinion became even more volatile in 2009. In the European parliament elections in June, Fine Gael led with 29 per cent of the vote, but Fianna Fáil received a

24 Mary Cussen / Brídín O'Leary / Donald Smith, »The Impact of Financial Turmoil on Households: A Cross country Comparison« in: *Central Bank Quarterly Review* 2 (2012), pp. 78–98; Niamh Hardiman / Spyros Blavoukos / Sebastian Dellepiane-Avellaneda / George Pagoulatos, *Austerity in the European Periphery: the Irish Experience*, Geary Institute Working Paper 2016/04, University College Dublin, 2016.

25 Claire Keane / Tim Callan / Michael Savage / John R. Walsh / Brian Colgan, »Distributional impact of Tax, Welfare and Public Service Pay Policies: Budget 2015 and Budgets 2009–2015« in: *Quarterly Economic Commentary*, 2014, https://www.esri.ie/publications/distributional-impact-of-tax-welfare-and-public-service-pay-policies-budget-2015-and-budgets-2009-2015/ [4.7.2017].

26 Larry M. Bartels, »Ideology and Retrospection in Electoral Responses to the Great Recession« in: Nancy Bermeo / Larry M. Bartels, (eds.), *Mass Politics in Tough times: Opinions, Votes, and Protest in the Great Recession*, Oxford 2014, pp. 185–223.

27 Vanessa Liston / Eimear O'Leary, »Data yearbook 2009« in: *Irish Political Studies* 21, No. 2 (2009), pp. 165–169.

credible 24 per cent. However, more seriously was that Fianna Fáil lost 84 seats in the local elections, and its coalition partner, the Green Party, lost 15 out of its 18 local government representatives. While Fine Gael gained 47 seats and Labour 31, surprisingly Sinn Fein failed to gain any additional seats. While clearly a rejection of the governing coalition, these were still mid-term and second order elections. It was not clear whether the trend against Fianna Fáil would be maintained. If the political foundations of Fianna Fáil dominance were weakening in 2009, opinion remained very hostile to new taxation. 57 per cent expressed opposition to any increase in taxation and 70 per cent believed that public spending cuts should be the priority for government in addressing the economic crisis. Despite this, a majority remained opposed to cuts in welfare benefits; only 1 in 5 supported such a policy. During 2009 Fine Gael became the most popular party, attracting a third of the vote, while Fianna Fáil continued to attract approximately a quarter. Support for Labour also rose significantly: at one point reaching 22 per cent.[28]

It was possible, though difficult, for Fianna Fáil to stabilize its support between 25 and 30 per cent. The electorate might have recognized the necessity for the bailout and the draconian budgets to stabilize the economy. In theory, an election was not due until 2012, and this provided enough time to re-balance the economy and restore confidence in the government. Despite optimistic statements by government ministers, the banking crisis was transformed into a fiscal crisis that threatened the state's sovereignty. As late as October 2010, Brian Lenihan, the Minister for Finance, rejected the claim that Ireland would have to apply for support from the EU and IMF. By this time the government was in denial and deeply divided over policy. In November, the state lost its economic sovereignty when the government was forced into a bailout by the governor of the Irish Central Bank and the international institutions. By December, dissatisfaction with the government reached 90 per cent, and one poll put Fianna Fáil in fourth place after Sinn Fein with 13 per cent support.[29]

The 2011 general election confirmed Fianna Fáil's unpopularity, and its electoral base collapsed. The bailout by the Troika was more serious politically than the 2008 banking guarantee. Fianna Fáil had always emphasized its nationalist and republican character, including the protection of sovereignty and neutrality as expressions of Irish identity. The appearance of the Troika in Dublin undermined these claims and reinforced the crisis of confidence present since 2008. Eamon Gilmore, the Labour leader, gave expression to this sense of betrayal in parliament when he accused the government of economic treason. Gilmore took on the rhetoric of the national interest more often associated with Fianna Fáil and turned it back on the government. A majority of those surveyed believed that Ireland had indeed surrendered its sovereignty by accepting a bailout from the Troika, including 51 per cent of Fianna Fáil supporters.[30] The

28 Murphy, *Electoral Competition in Ireland since 1987*, op. cit. (note 8), pp. 129–154.

29 For a detailed reconstruction of Fianna Fáil's response to the crisis, see John Lee / Daniel McConnell, *Hell at the Gates: The Inside Story of Ireland's Financial Downfall*, Cork 2016.

30 Parliamentary Debates Dáil Eireann, 706, 1, 31.3.2010; Philip Murphy / Neil Matthews (eds.), »Data yearbook 2012« in: *Irish Political Studies* 27, No. 2 (2012), p. 219.

general election destroyed the foundations of Fianna Fáil's traditional dominance, as can be seen in table 5.

Table 5: First preference vote and seats at general elections 2002–2007

	2002	2007	2011
Fianna Fáil	41.5% (81)	41.6% (78)	17.4% (20)
Fine Gael	22.5% (31)	27.3% (51)	36.1% (76)
Labour Party	10.8% (21)	10.1% (20)	19.4% (37)
Sinn Fein	6.5% (5)	6.9% (4)	9.9% (14)
Green Party	3.8% (6)	4.7% (6)	1.8% (--)
Progressive Democrats	4.0% (8)	2.7% (2)	--
Independents and others	10.9% (14)	6.6% (5)	15.2% (19)

Source: own illustration based on Electionirland.org

This was the first election since 1927 that Fianna Fáil did not capture the largest vote. It also lost its status as a national party, and its nationalist credentials were challenged from both the left and the right. Fianna Fáil was now unrepresented in 23 out of 43 electoral constituencies, an unprecedented outcome for such a successful party. It lost nearly two thirds of its support base: 28 per cent of those who deserted the party went to Fine Gael, 15.8 per cent to Labour and 15 per cent to independents. Voter loyalty also weakened appreciably. Historically, approximately 80 per cent of Fianna Fáil voters gave lower preference votes to other Fianna Fáil candidates. In 2011 this fell to 58 per cent. Former PD voters also deserted Fianna Fáil: 44 per cent went to Fine Gael and 25 per cent to independents. Reinforcing Fianna Fáil's failures, Fine Gael and Labour were considered to have the best policies on virtually every issue.[31] The extent of Fianna Fáil's collapse can be seen in tables 6 and 7.

Table 6: Social composition of Fianna Fáil vote 2007 & 2011

	2007	2011
Total	41.6%	17.4%
Men	41.7%	15%
Women	41.6%	15%
AB (middle-class)	37.2%	14.0%
C1 (lower middle-class)	40.8%	14.0%
C2 (skilled working class)	42.7%	15.0%
DE (unskilled working class)	43.9%	16.0%
Farmers	43.9%	23.0%

Source: own illustration based on RTÉ / Millward Brown Lansdowne, *Exit poll*

31 Data from RTÉ / Millward Brown Lansdowne, *General Election Exit Poll*, 25.2.2011.

Table 7: Composition of Fianna Fáil vote by age

	2007	2011
Total	41.6%	17.4%
18–24	35%	12%
25–34	38.8%	12.0%
35–49	40.01%	12.0%
50–64	45.2%	16.0%
65+	48.8%	25.0%

Source: own illustration based on RTÉ / Millward Brown Lansdowne, *Exit poll*

With just 17 per cent of the vote, the future of Fianna Fáil was open to question.

4. The consequences of dealignment, 2011–2016

Fine Gael and the Labour party formed a coalition government with the largest majority in the history of the state. The election was primarily a rejection of the incumbent government, rather than a positive mandate for alternatives or radical policies. Fine Gael was, if anything, more conservative than Fianna Fáil on economic and fiscal questions and was committed to pursuing the recovery programme agreed with the Troika. Despite its anti-austerity rhetoric during the election campaign, Labour was in reality more moderate than this implied. In contrast to Greece, for example, dealignment in Ireland reinforced the influence of the established political parties committed to a conservative consensus on austerity. These tendencies in national politics were reinforced by the influence of the Troika, which insisted that the election would have no effect on the rescue programme. The Troika argued that the November 2010 agreement was binding on the incoming government.[32]

The balance of power between the national government and the Troika was made very clear in March 2011. There was considerable support among the public (and especially in the Labour Party) for »burning the bondholders« and defaulting on outstanding loans. The government agreed to introduce a so called »haircut« for bondholders. Michael Noonan, the Minister for Finance, was threatened by an »irate« Jean-Claude Trichet who warned that a bomb would go off in Dublin's financial sector if the government went ahead with this plan. The government capitulated to the ECB, and Noonan abandoned the plan, rewriting a prepared speech to take account of this.[33] The December 2013 budget confirmed that the government would implement the austerity policies previously agreed by Fianna Fáil.

32 Peter Mair, »Smaghi versus the parties: Representative Government and Institutional Constraints« in: Schafer / Streeck, *Politics in the Age of Austerity*, op. cit. (note 1), pp. 143–168.

33 Murphy / Matthews, »Data yearbook 2012«, op. cit. (note 30), pp. 227–229; Noonan's telephone conversation on 31.3.2011 with Trichet is reported in: *Irish Times*, 9.10.2015.

The consequences of this climb-down were evident to the public, even if they were not aware of the details. Irish sovereignty had been lost and austerity would be maintained on terms dictated by the Troika. If Fine Gael and Labour received a mandate for austerity in 2011, it was a conditional one in the face of a serious economic and financial crisis. Shortly after the new government was formed, nearly two thirds of those polled favoured cuts in public expenditure to reduce the deficit. Only one in five agreed that income tax should be increased. The majority position was close to that expressed by Fine Gael during the election campaign. This suggests a willingness on the part of the public to accept that hard policy choices would be maintained during the lifespan of the new government. There was also some optimism that the new government would have a positive impact on the crisis. 40 per cent believed that the economy would improve. More ominously another 40 per cent thought that government policy would have no impact.[34] Whatever optimism existed after the general election soon evaporated. By the end of 2011, Irish opinion was the most negative in the EU. Satisfaction ratings for the government, which had improved after the election, fell quickly. By 2012 dissatisfaction with the new government had reached 70 per cent, and 59 per cent would not trust the government with the management of the public finances.[35]

The formation of the coalition provided Fine Gael and Labour with the opportunity to consolidate their position as the dominant force in Irish politics. Austerity had created the conditions for dealignment, and the collapse of Fianna Fáil support opened up the political system to a possible realignment. However, this prospect was undermined by the continuation of austerity politics between 2011 and 2013. Budgets remained deflationary, and there was widespread opposition to new taxes including a property tax and water charges. Despite this, a majority recognized the severe budgetary discipline remained »a necessary evil« to restore economic stability. Support for this position was strong among farmers and the middle classes but much weaker among the working class.[36]

Other polling suggests the government faced considerable scepticism about its policies. 71 per cent concluded that the government had gone back on election pledges not to increase taxation, and there was widespread opposition to the imposition of various charges. Irish public opinion during 2012 remained extraordinarily pessimistic in a comparative European context in respect of the country's fortune and its future. Furthermore, the economy contracted further, while unemployment and emigration continued to rise. Only 15 per cent of Irish respondents to a Eurobarometer poll believed that the national economy, the EU or their personal circumstances would improve over the following twelve months. This is also reflected in the collapse of trust in the Irish government and the parliament by the end of the year. Only 18 per cent tended to trust these institutions.

34 »Ipsos-MRBI« in: *Irish Times Poll*, 15–18.7.2011.
35 Philip Murphy, »Republic of Ireland 2012« in: *Irish Political Studies* 28, No. 2 (2013), pp. 207–209 and 215–216.
36 Millward Brown, *Lansdowne Poll*, 28–29.2.2012.

By early 2012, just a year after forming a government, dissatisfaction had increased by 20 points, while satisfaction dropped 20 points. Despite some positive economic signs during 2013, it proved very difficult for the government to restore its credibility. Even the prospect of Ireland exiting the bailout provided only a limited boost to the government's popularity. Dissatisfaction ratings of 70 per cent continued throughout the year. In one poll, Fianna Fáil and Fine Gael received equal levels of support, suggesting that Fianna Fáil were once again in competition politically. Fine Gael was unable to maintain its 2011 support, but Fianna Fáil was also unable to overtake them. Labour performed poorly throughout this period, and a number of TDs left the party due to austerity policies that they could not support. The political system had yet to stabilize, and the main beneficiaries were Sinn Fein and independents, who consistently received between 15 and 20 per cent of first preference intentions.[37]

5. Exit from the bailout and the 2016 general election

While Ireland left the recovery programme at the end to 2013, the exit of the Troika did not mean that austerity was at an end. Ireland's sovereignty might have been restored, but the main policy framework was maintained into 2014. However, there was a considerable amount of self-satisfaction after five years of austerity budgets and politics among government ministers and supporters. Taoiseach Enda Kenny invoked the notion that Ireland was at the end of a prison sentence, from which it was now released: »On Monday, we stand with those shackles around our feet, with the same security as any other country in the Eurozone, same opportunities and we intend to use them.«[38] The Minister for Finance, Michael Noonan, insisted that the impact of the Troika was positive, emphasizing that Ireland was forced to take action in an increasingly difficult economic environment. He acknowledged that the crisis had been home-grown and that correction had been required. Noonan was on less sure ground when he claimed that the key political outcome was maintaining political support for austerity policies. He revealed that the Troika had wanted the incoming government to move faster with the rescue programme agreed in November 2010 (meaning further retrenchment). Noonan argued that some members of the Troika were politically naïve and failed to appreciate the need for electoral accountability. The implications of Noonan's views were that the Irish government had to make difficult decisions which were necessary and in the public interest but that the government also held off demands from the international agencies that might have been even harsher.[39] There was an implication in the government's statements that the end of austerity was in sight. However, the government received very little credit for any achievements in respect of the exit. Only 16 per cent of respondents considered that Fine Gael deserved the most

37 Data drawn from Murphy, »Republic of Ireland 2012«, op. cit. (note 35), pp. 197–216; Philip Murphy / Neil Matthews (eds.), »Data yearbook 2014« in: *Irish Political Studies* 29, No. 3 (2014), pp. 366–380.

38 Kitty Holland, »Ireland ready to cast off shackles says Kenny« in: *Irish Times*, 13.12.2013.

39 Arthur Beesley, »Noonan on tax, the bailout and the Troika« in: *Irish Times*, 13.12.2013.

credit for the exit, and a further 9 per cent identified the current government. For 38 per cent, Irish people/workers were the groups that deserved most credit for achieving an exit.[40]

The government was confident at the end of 2013 that they had achieved a considerable amount in terms of economic recovery and stabilizing the state's finances. However, the electorate was often resentful about the cost of austerity and unwilling to give the government much credit for the success. While there was a slight improvement in those satisfied with the government in December 2013, dissatisfaction still remained above 60 per cent. Fine Gael did receive a temporary increase in support, but the Labour Party remained weak. In polls taken in May and November 2013, the Irish electorate had much less trust in the national government than was the case with the EU average at that time. When asked in February 2013 who had made a positive contribution »to helping Ireland deal with the economic crisis«, only 26 per cent identified the government, while 19 per cent identified the Troika. In stark contrast some 59 per cent thought that the government had had a negative impact on dealing with the crisis, ahead of the Troika at 48 per cent.

The electorate also drew some different conclusions from Noonan on the rescue programme agreed with the Troika. 38 per cent believed that the impact had been negative, while 36 per cent thought it was positive. Surprisingly perhaps, a further 11 per cent concluded that it had had no impact on Ireland's economic situation. The latter position was strongest among Green Party, independent and Sinn Fein supporters (59, 52 & 41 per cent, respectively). There is a pronounced social divide in the responses to this question. Two thirds of Fine Gael supporters believed the programme had had a positive impact, as did the middle classes and farmers. The public also remained sceptical about the status of Ireland's sovereignty. The government stressed the importance of exiting the bailout and restoring the state's sovereignty. However, only 12 per cent believed that sovereignty had been restored in full. 28 per cent believed it had not been restored, and a further 42 per cent thought that it had only been partially restored. Sinn Fein and independent voters were the most likely to believe that sovereignty had not been restored, while Fine Gael voters were most likely to believe that sovereignty had indeed been restored.[41]

In a poll designed to evaluate Irish opinion just as the state was exiting the bailout, Eurobarometer reported that the percentage who believed that the state of the economy was very bad had dropped from 84 per cent in 2010 to 40 per cent in 2013. While this might bring some welcome news to the government, the same report found that 41 per cent also thought the state of the economy to be »rather bad«. This still meant that 81 per cent of Irish respondents thought that the economy situation was either very or rather bad. This cumulative figure compares with a Greek figure of 98 per cent and a Portuguese figure of 96 per cent; even France (not in a bailout) had a figure high-

40 »Ipos-MRBI poll« in: *Irish Times*, 9–10.12.2013.
41 Murphy / Matthews (eds.), »Data yearbook 2014«, op. cit. (note 37).

er than Ireland at 91 per cent. The UK had a figure of 60 per cent, while Denmark's negative appraisal of the economy was at the low end of the EU at 24 per cent.

A further consequence of the bailout was that Irish attitudes to Europe changed from a positive evaluation to a much more critical one. Prior to the crisis in 2008, a majority of Irish respondents tended to trust the EU. This declined after the Banking crisis in 2008 and more dramatically after the rescue package was agreed. Between 2011 and 2013 approximately 60 per cent of Irish respondents tended not to trust the EU, with those trusting it ranging between over 20 to 30 per cent. While 41 per cent of Irish respondents are positive about the EU, 23 per cent have a negative image and some 37 per cent are neutral or don't know. This is much better than Greece which has a negative image at 54 per cent and a positive one of 16 per cent. Interestingly, the positive rating in Ireland at 41 per cent is ten points above the EU average. These figures, however, should be placed against the historic high levels of trust in the EU evident in Ireland. Prior to 2008, positive assessments never fell below 60 per cent and at times reached 75 per cent. What can be seen here is a significant collapse in positive assessments of the EU among Irish public opinion. Despite this, 48 per cent in Ireland continue to believe that Ireland's interests are adequately met by memberships of the EU, significantly higher than that of the UK (29 per cent) or Greece (16 per cent). While there has been a substantial increase in those who have critical attitudes towards the EU, this has not led to the growth of Euroscepticism. Two thirds of respondents disagree with the view that Ireland »could better face the future outside of the EU.« The UK figure is 37 per cent, while even in Greece a majority rejects this proposition.[42]

Consequently, the coalition government faced a number of political challenges in 2014. The first was that exit from the bailout had not provided them with any more than a short term boost in the polls. The public was either ambiguous or sceptical about the government's responsibility for the outcome and was more likely to blame the government for the severe cut-backs that most sections of the population had experienced since 2011. This context was particularly important in 2014 as elections to the European Parliament were due, as were local elections. Trust in politicians was at an all-time low. Only 4 per cent fully trusted politicians, a mere 1 per cent more than the much despised bankers. Dissatisfaction with the Taoiseach was up to 69 per cent by December 2014. Moreover, dissatisfaction with the government and individual members of the government remained extremely high. Dissatisfaction with the government reached 71 per cent in December.[43]

The elections took place in May 2014. European Parliament elections are usually described as second order elections and can provide a midterm assessment of support for both government and opposition. In many respects local elections are of considerable importance in the context of the Irish political system. Most national politicians come

42 European Commission, *Standard Eurobarometer 80: National Report Ireland*, Brussels 2013.

43 Murphy / Matthews (eds.), »Data yearbook 2014«, op. cit. (note 37), p. 372; Yvonne Murphy / Michael Martin, »Data yearbook 2015« in: *Irish Political Studies* 30, No. 3 (2015), pp. 348–350.

to prominence after a period in local politics, and election to a local authority is the normal springboard for an aspiring politician, a minor party or the opposition.[44]

Table 8: Voting at local and European elections, 2009 & 2014

	Local Elections 2009	European Parliament Elections 2009	Local Elections 2014	European Parliament Elections 2014
Fine Gael	32.2%	29.1%	24.0%	22.3%
Labour	14.7%	13.9%	7.2%	5.3%
Fianna Fáil	25.4%	24.1%	25.3%	22.3%
Sinn Fein	7.4%	11.2%	15.3%	19.5%
Other Left	1.8%	2.8%	3.6%	4.7%
Independent and others	16.3%	11.5%	22.5%	20.7%

Source: own illustration based on Kavanagh, »An end to ›Civil War politics‹?«, op. cit. (note 44), p. 75

If the 2014 elections are compared to those of 2009 (probably a more accurate comparison than the 2011 general election), then Labour is the main loser and Sinn Fein is the main beneficiary. Labour loses over half its 2009 vote between the two elections, while Sinn Fein nearly doubles its local election vote and has a substantial increase in the European elections. The other significant feature of this election is the continuing rise of support for independents, which increases by six points for local and eight for the European elections. Surprisingly, Fianna Fáil's vote remains close to its 2009 vote, a relative success for a party that appeared in terminal decline in 2011. Fianna Fáil actually won more votes than Fine Gael in the elections to the European Parliament, but it only won one seat. In the local elections Fine Gael lost 105 seats and Labour 81. Sinn Fein won 125, Fianna Fáil 49 and independents 71. Small left wing parties and the Green Party improved their positions since 2009, though in each case from a very low base.

These elections suggested that the 2011 general elections was a crisis election that undermined some but not all of the traditional foundations of the Irish political system. While Fianna Fáil improved its position in 2014, there was no return to its dominant position in the system. What is now apparent is a party duality between Fianna Fáil and Fine Gael with roughly 20–25 per cent of the vote each; Sinn Fein attracts less than a fifth and independents do likewise. If 2011 was a case of dealignment, there is little evidence for realignment in the political system in 2014. However, what has happened is that Sinn Fein had gradually increased its vote, especially among the Dublin working class. At the 2014 local elections, it was nearly twenty points ahead of Fianna

44 Polling data consistently reports that voters place greater emphasis on choosing a candidate to look after the interests of the constituency than other factors; see McGraw, *How Parties Win*, op. cit. (note 13), pp. 174–180.

Fáil in working class constituencies. Kavanagh has suggested that a »new politics« may be emerging due to the collapse of Fianna Fáil's support and to voter dissatisfaction with other establishment parties.[45]

6. The 2016 general election and the continuation of dealignment

The 2016 general election did not provide a definitive answer to this question. The government clearly lost the election, but it was not entirely clear if anyone actually won it. Fine Gael and Labour lost over 500,000 votes and 57 seats. As table 9 shows, the political system is now heavily fragmented.

Table 9: First preference vote and seats won 2011 & 2016

	Vote 2011	Seats	Vote 2016	Seats
Fine Gael	36.1%	76	25.52%	50
Fianna Fáil	17.4%	20	24.35%	44
Labour Party	19.4%	37	6.0%	7
Sinn Fein	9.9%	14	13.85%	23
Green Party	1.8%	0	2.72%	2
Independents	12.5%	14	17.83%	23
Other Parties	2.7%	5	6.96%	9

Source: own illustration based on Michael Gallagher / Michael Marsh (eds.), *How Ireland Voted 2011*, Houndmills/Basingstoke 2011, pp. 300–303; Gallagher / Marsh (eds.), *How Ireland Voted 2016*, op. cit. (note–45), pp. 293–298

For the Labour Party the election was a disaster. This was the worst performance in the party's history, with 6 per cent of the vote and 7 seats in parliament. The future of the party is now clearly in doubt. It is perhaps ironic that the party received its highest vote ever due to its anti-austerity stance prior to 2011 and its lowest vote as a consequence of widespread anger at its support for austerity once the government was formed.[46] Fine Gael could take some comfort that it was still the largest party. This however was due to the fragmented nature of the party system rather than any positive gain for the party. 2016 was the second most volatile election in Ireland's electoral history after 2011. Ireland has become a multi-party system, and its traditional two-and-a-half party system is no longer a relevant analytical model. The effective number of

45 RTÉ / Behaviour & Attitudes, *European Election Exit Poll May 23, 2014*; Adrian P. Kavanagh, »An end to ›Civil War politics‹? The radically reshaped landscape of post-crash Ireland« in: *Electoral Studies* 38, No. 1 (2015), pp. 71–81.

46 Rory Costello / Paul O'Neill / Robert Thomson, »The Fulfilment of Election Pledges by the Outgoing Government« in: Michael Gallagher / Michael Marsh (eds.), *How Ireland Voted 2016: The Election that Nobody Won*, Houndmills/Basingstoke 2016, pp. 27–45. The authors note that Labour was considered to have not delivered on their promises, though the evidence provided suggests a more nuanced conclusion.

parties (ENP) is now 6.57, while the ENPs represented in parliament is 4.93. This level of fragmentation has not been seen since June 1927, when Fianna Fáil first entered parliament.[47]

Figure 2: First preference vote at general elections 1992–2016 and the combined voter for Fianna Fáil and Fine Gael

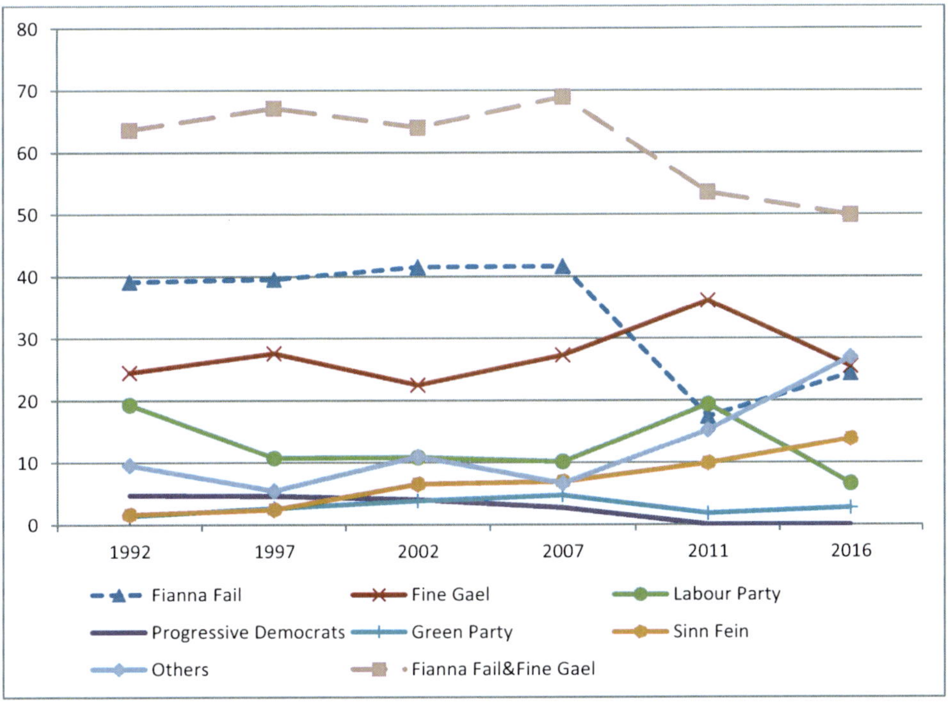

Source: own illustration based on electionirland.org

In 2016 as in 1997, the electorate opted to punish the government rather than reward it. The puzzle in 2016 is why, when the economy appeared to be performing well, Fine Gael and Labour did not attract more support. Between 2013 and 2016 virtually every economic indicator was positive. GDP expanded strongly and private consumer expenditure was up by 3.5 per cent (in 2013 it was –0.3). 127000 new jobs were created and unemployment fell rapidly (see tables 2 & 3). The debt-to-GDP ratio fell below 100 per cent and the fiscal deficit below 3 per cent. The budgets for 2015 and 2016 were mildly expansionary, but not give away.

47 Michael Gallagher, »The Results Analysed: The Aftershock Continues« and David M. Farrell / Jane Suiter, »The Election in Context«, both in: Gallagher / Marsh (eds.), *How Ireland Voted 2016*, op. cit. (note 46), pp. 125–157 and 277–292.

Table 10: GDP per capita 2013–2015

	2013	2014	2015
EU-28	100	100	100
Denmark	128	127	127
Ireland	133	137	177
Greece	72	70	68
Spain	90	90	90
Portugal	77	77	77
UK	107	109	108

Source: own illustration based on Eurostat

Public opinion recognized that circumstances had changed. In December 2013, opinion in Ireland was still overwhelmingly negative about the state of the economy and personal circumstances. By November 2015 this had changed dramatically. 57 per cent now had a positive attitude to the economy, though 43 per cent maintained a negative view. Moreover, Irish respondents were more optimistic on average than other EU respondents. This was a remarkable turnaround as Irish sentiment has been significantly more pessimistic than the EU average from 2008 until 2014.[48]

Despite these favourable findings, Irish opinion continued to distrust the government and the political parties. Other data can be probed to tease out further aspects of this change of mood. Dissatisfaction with the government remained high throughout 2015, averaging two thirds. In July, 16 per cent reported that they were better off than in the previous year. However, 40 per cent considered themselves to be worse off, and 39 per cent were in the same position as previously. When asked to predict what their condition would be a year from the polling, 19 per cent thought they would be better off, 29 per cent worse off and 41 per cent the same. At first glance these data appear to justify the government's confidence that the worst of the recession was over. Nevertheless, the positive mood was restricted to certain social categories, principally farmers and the middle classes. By way of contrast, 50 per cent of the unskilled working class reported that they were worse off than the previous year, as did those aged 55–64. Not surprisingly, those who considered themselves to be worse off were more likely to support either Sinn Fein or independents. Polling during 2015 confirmed that the electorate was more optimistic than it had been previously, but this trend did not enhance the position of the government parties.[49]

Fine Gael adopted the slogan »Let's keep the recovery going« for the election, suggesting that only Fine Gael could do so. It hoped to persuade the electorate that the economy was safe in its hands and that alternatives would endanger the recent successful upturn. Enda Kenny emphasized this in the manifesto, »In an uncertain world, our

48 European Commission, *Standard Eurobarometer 84: National Report Ireland*, Brussels 2015.

49 Millward Brown, »›Political Survey‹« in: *Sunday Independent*, 30.7.2015.

long term economic plan will reinforce Ireland's position as a pro-jobs and pro-family country of stability, growth and opportunity for all«. Fianna Fáil drew a very different conclusion from what had happened over the previous five years. While continuing to support the recovery programme (in effect austerity), Fianna Fáil emphasized the need for a fairer future for our country, but also a more sustainable one. It criticized Fine Gael for making Ireland more unequal and unfair. Fairness was a key word during the election campaign and was persistently used against the government parties. Sinn Fein may have rejected the establishment parties, but it also focused on fairness. Its manifesto »For a Fair Recovery« stressed the uneven nature of the recovery. It echoed other anti-establishment parties, claiming that »it isn't a fair recovery. It is a two-tier recovery that benefits them [Fine Gael and Labour] and their friends at the top, not the majority of hard-working Irish people.«[50] The Labour Party was faced with a different problem. It emphasized what had been achieved in employment creation and welfare but was harassed from all sides for compromising with Fine Gael and the party's contribution to austerity.

If Fine Gael lost the election, Fianna Fáil did not actually win it. Fianna Fáil however can be said to have won the argument about the balance to be struck between careful economic management and expanding public expenditure. Fine Gael retained only 55 per cent of its 2011 vote. Nearly 13 per cent changed to Fianna Fáil, 5.5 per cent to Sinn Fein, 5 per cent to Labour and 7.7 per cent to independent candidates. Labour did badly, only retaining 36.8 per cent of its vote. While Fine Gael attracted 10 per cent of this vote, former Labour voters were more likely to transfer to Sinn Fein (12 per cent), AAA-PBP (8 per cent), independents (7.7 per cent), Social Democrats (7.1 per cent) and the Green Party (3.4 per cent). It is probably safe to conclude that the increase in Labour's vote in 2011 was largely a protest vote against austerity. Given Labour's anti-austerity stance prior to the 2011 election, voters could be forgiven for believing that Labour would maintain that stance while in government. The subsequent collapse in Labour support can be directly attributed to disillusion. Fianna Fáil retained 73 per cent of its 2011 vote while increasing its support and seats overall. Sinn Fein remains the most successful party for voter retention between elections, with a 79 per cent retention rate.[51]

In 2016, as in recent elections, a majority of voters do not consider themselves to be close to a party (73 per cent). As a consequence, party identification and loyalty is weak, and the younger the age group, the less likely it is to remain loyal. In this sense, at least, one traditional feature of Irish politics has continued beyond the collapse of Fianna Fáil and may be accelerated by it. Another feature that continues is the candidate-centred nature of the political system. 53 per cent consider that the candidate was the most important consideration when deciding how to vote, while 44 per cent give priority to a party. A plurality (41 per cent) agreed that the most important considera-

50 Sinn Fein, »A Fair Recovery is Possible«, http://www.sinnfein.brianstanley.ie/a-fair-recovery-is-possible/ [14.7.2017].

51 Unless otherwise indicated, all data is calculated from RTÉ / Behaviour & Attitudes, *2016 General Election Exit Poll Report*, 26.2.2016.

tion involved choosing a candidate who would look after the interests of the constituency. These figures help to explain the continuing significance of independents in the political system. Just a third believe that the policies set out by parties should be the determining feature when choosing, while a further 13 per cent give primary consideration to forming a government. Moreover, 40 per cent would vote for a candidate irrespective of which party she/he stood for. Fully 42 per cent would not vote for a candidate irrespective of the party, while for a further 18 per cent it would depend on the party. These and other data suggest that dealignment has progressed further since 2011, reinforcing long-terms trends of low levels of partisanship and party loyalty. This fragmentation means that political competition remains exceptionally fluid and the environment facilitates the election of independents and smaller parties.

This election also confirmed that the majority of Irish voters place themselves at the moderate-centre of the left-right axis. On a scale where 0 is left and 10 is right, the mean is 4.98. Table 11 sets out the parties on this axis.

Table 11: Left-right placement by party and vote at 2016 general election

	Party vote 2016	Left	Centre	Right	Mean
Total sample		20%	54%	20%	4.98
AAA/PBP	3.9%	50	42	3	3.35
Independents 4Change	1.5%	38	62	--	3.64
Sinn Fein	13.8%	43	41	8	3.71
Green Party	2.7%	26	64	6	4.34
Labour Party	6.6%	25	56	14	4.53
Social Democrats	3.0%	25	61	11	4.62
Independents & Others	11.5%	20	58	13	4.82
Independent Alliance	4.2%	10	68	17	5.26
Renua Ireland	2.2%	13	68	16	5.32
Fianna Fáil	24.3%	10	54	32	5.70
Fine Gael	25.5%	6	56	32	5.84

Source: own illustration based on RTÉ / Behaviour & Attitudes, *2016 General Election Exit Poll*, op. cit. (note 51).

Though maintaining the centrist nature of Irish politics, the electorate in 2016 was more favourable to a moderate expansion of public expenditure. The RTE Exit poll asked respondents to choose between cutting tax and spending much less on public services on the one hand or increasing taxation and spending more on public services on the other. If these questions can be taken as a proxy for specifically left or right policy options, then approximately 11 per cent occupy the right in this dimension, whereas 36 per cent place themselves on the left. The moderate position between the two is supported by 48 per cent. A stronger indicator of left or right wing attitudes can be deduced from the question that asked whether the government should or should not intervene to reduce differences in wealth or income. In response, some 23 per cent opt for non-intervention, 38 per cent are strongly in favour of intervention and 35 per cent favour the moderate position between these two. When asked about the importance of issues that influenced their vote, approximately 20 per cent identified health services and hospitals, two points ahead of those who choose managing the economy.[52]

A poll in February 2016 reported that 35 per cent identified the health services as the most important issue, while managing the economy was identified by 14 per cent. Other important issues included crime and law and order (11 per cent) and job creation (19 per cent). Another poll reported that 39 per cent believed that improving public services should be the main priority for the incoming government. Tax cuts were favoured by 25 per cent, whereas 19 per cent believed that social benefits should be increased. When asked to identify the three most important issues, improving public services received a cumulative 83 per cent, while tax cuts were supported by 68 per cent. The polling data suggests that there was an appetite for some tax increases and increased public expenditure, though it is also the case that there was no support for radical redistribution as advocated by some of the left-wing parties. As a consequence Fine Gael was placed on the defensive during the election campaign and Fianna Fáil occupied the moderate centre ground. Fine Gael's main platform of stability and jeopardy was quickly undermined. Just over a third of those polled agreed that economic stability would be at risk if there was a change of government. However, nearly a half (49 per cent) disagreed with this proposition. More importantly for Fianna Fáil, 57 per cent agreed that a change of government would help create a fairer society, though 23 per cent disagreed.[53] Fine Gael was very successful in attracting votes from those who believed they were personally better off and who considered that the economy was performing better than a year previously. As such the party appealed to sections of the middle classes and to the farming community. However, Fine Gael was unable to attract other social groups who were reluctant to support further austerity. It is likely then that Fine Gael failed in 2016 because it was too closely identified with austerity rather than economic recovery and progress.

Dealignment and the fragmented nature of the political system made it very difficult to form a new government. It took ten weeks of confrontation and negotiation before

52 RTÉ / Behaviour & Attitudes, *2016 General Election Exit Poll*, op. cit. (note 51).

53 Paul Moran, »National Opinion Poll: January/February 2016« in: *Millward Brown*, 2016, http://www.millwardbrown.com/docs/default-source/ireland-downloads/opinion-polls/dublin-bay-south-millward-brown-poll-17th-february-2016.pdf [30.6.2017]; Paul Moran, »Pre-Election Poll Shows Nuanced Opinions« in: *Millward Brown*, 2016, http://www.millwardbrown.com/docs/default-source/ireland-downloads/opinion-polls/pre-election-poll-shows-nuanced-opinions-february-2016.pdf [1.7.2017]; Paul Moran »Some subtle shifts in opinion but not a lot has changed« in: *Millward Brown*, 2016, http://www.millwardbrown.com/docs/default-source/ireland-downloads/opinion-polls/national-millward-brown-poll-21st-february-2016.pdf [1.7.2017].

Fine Gael formed a minority government that included a number of independents who received ministerial posts. However, government formation required Fianna Fáil's agreement, and the two parties secured a »confidence and supply arrangement« to allow this to happen. In an unusual move, Fine Gael accepted that Fianna Fáil »is an independent party in opposition and not a party to a programme for government.« For its part Fianna Fáil agreed to abstain on the election of the Taoiseach and ministers and would vote against or abstain on motions of no confidence in the government. Fianna Fáil also secured the continuation of existing arrangements on public sector pay. Most significantly, Fine Gael agreed to the principle of favouring investment in public services over cutting tax. Enda Kenny was elected Taoiseach and quickly reflected the new reality of minority government. He gave explicit expression to Fianna Fáil's main concerns during the election and subsequent negotiation. He acknowledged that many people had not experienced the benefits of economic recovery, adding:

> *»If economic survival was the urgent priority of the last government then using a strong economy to improve lives, the quality of the lives of our people, must and will be the priority of the new government and that fundamental principle will be the bedrock of our policy programme.«*[54]

These views depart significantly from the tone of Fine Gael's election manifestos and could have been taken from Fianna Fáil's.[55]

7. Conclusion

It will take some time for the political consequences of austerity to work through the political system. The main consequence to date is the end of Fianna Fáil's dominance of the Irish party system and political competition. Without the collapse in the banking system and the loss of sovereignty in 2010, it is likely that Fianna Fáil would have maintained its dominant role. Austerity has also undermined the traditional two-and-a-half party system, which is unlikely to return. It has been replaced by a multi-party and fragmented system that makes government formation and policy implementation much more difficult. This is a clear case of dealignment, but there is little evidence in 2016 for a new realignment. Fine Gael failed to become the dominant party or the lynch pin for a new governing coalition and remains in government with the support of a revived Fianna Fáil. Fianna Fáil regained its position as a national party in the 2016 election, though it remains weak in Dublin. It now has to compete with Sinn Fein for working-class and nationalist voters, but its success in 2016 may have halted the rise of this competitor. Another consequence was increased support for left-wing candidates and parties. The left broadly defined now attracts over 30 per cent of the vote. How-

54 »Enda Kenny re-elected as Ireland's Taoiseach« in: *Independent*, 24.7.2017, http://www.independent.ie/breaking-news/irish-news/enda-kenny-reelected-as-irelands-taoiseach-34690262.html [30.7.2017].

55 Fiach Kelly, »The full document: Fine Gael-Fianna Fáil deal for government« in: *Irish Times*, 3.5.2016; »Enda Kenny announces minority government Cabinet« in: *Irish Times*, 6.5.2016.

ever, this vote should not be treated as a single unit. It needs to be divided between a hard left, Sinn Fein's left nationalism and the more moderate politics of Labour, the Social Democrats and Green Party. There is little agreement among these parties, and the moderate wing is unlikely to cooperate with Sinn Fein or the AAA/PBP. Moreover, the moderate centre remains strong, accounting for nearly 70 per cent of the votes at the election. This vote suggests that change will be moderate and gradual and that political continuity will be strong despite some remarkable changes in the political system.

Christoph Bruckmüller

Striving for More and Falling Behind: How the Swedish Social Democratic Party Became Disadvantaged in the Party System by Institutionalized Austerity

1. Sweden – from crisis-ridden exceptionalism to exemplary mainstream?

Even though Sweden has not been as much concerned with the European debt crisis as members of the eurozone have, it fits the pattern that is used for a common cursory conflict description between fiscally stable northern European countries and Mediterranean ones with notoriously high deficits and public debt. In these categories Sweden can show good numbers (see figures 1, 2 & 3) and seems to be an appropriate role model for an austerity-oriented paradigm.[1] Especially in the aftermath of the recent global financial crisis, the Swedish economy seemed, although not insignificantly affected, to recover relatively quickly. As a reason the argument is used that Sweden, and in particular its banking sector, has been better prepared because of the measures taken during the 1990s subsequent to a deep crisis that struck the financial, the economic, the fiscal and the currency area.[2] It has also been during this phase when Sweden, along with a modernization of the welfare state, introduced permanent austerity as an overarching political goal. This seems not to match very well the typical picture of Sweden as a country with a generous welfare state and a big public sector. Among others, these characteristics, which are historically closely connected to the Social Democratic party, made Sweden a model followed with interest by international observers. »But the days of what has become known as Swedish exceptionalism are over. The country no longer has an exceptionally strong social democracy. Its level of inequality is no longer exceptionally low, and its level of public spending will no longer be exceptionally high. From now on, it will probably be closer to average.«[3] The Swedish political scientist Bo Rothstein is right with this diagnosis[4], although the turning point cannot be identified first with the national election of 2014, in reaction to which he had written his article. The slow and incremental processes are manifold and date back longer in the past, with the mentioned crisis as the initial juncture. There is, however, a general connection between this new paradigm of permanent austerity and Swedish national election results (see table 1), as this chapter will show.

1 Lars Calmfors, »The Swedish Macroeconomic Policy Framework« in: Jon Pierre (ed.), *The Oxford Handbook of Swedish Politics*, Oxford 2016, pp. 592–611, pp. 592–593.

2 Sven Jochem, *Die politischen Systeme Skandinaviens*, Wiesbaden 2012, pp. 162–163.

3 Bo Rothstein, »The End of Swedish Exceptionalism: Why the Elections Mark a New Era for Politics« in: *Foreign Affairs*, 18.9.2014, https://www.foreignaffairs.com/articles/sweden/2014-09-18/end-swedish-exceptionalism [4.2.2017].

4 His proposition has even been taken up by the *Oxford Handbook of Swedish Politics* as the guideline over the different sections. Pierre, *The Oxford Handbook of Swedish Politics*, op. cit. (note 1).

Figure 1: General government gross debt (percentage of GDP)

Source: own illustration based on Anual Macro-Economic Database

Figure 2: General government net lending (percentage of GDP)

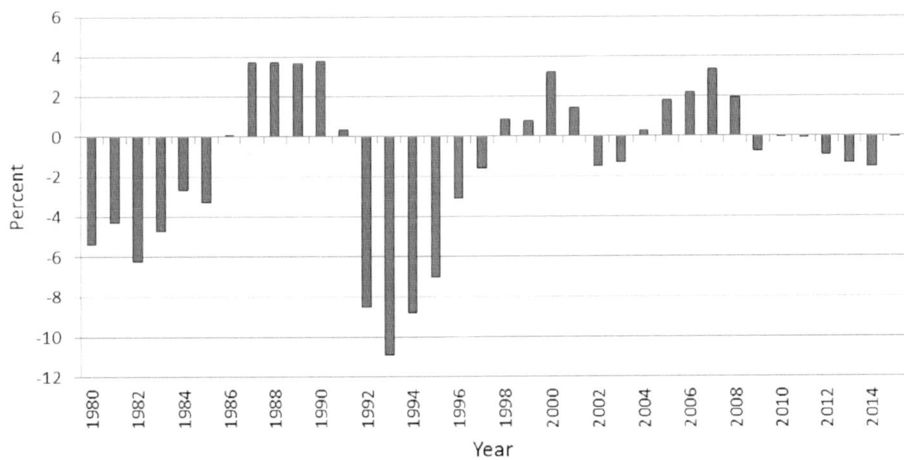

Source: own illustration based on IMF, World Economic Outlook Database

Figure 3: GDP growth rate

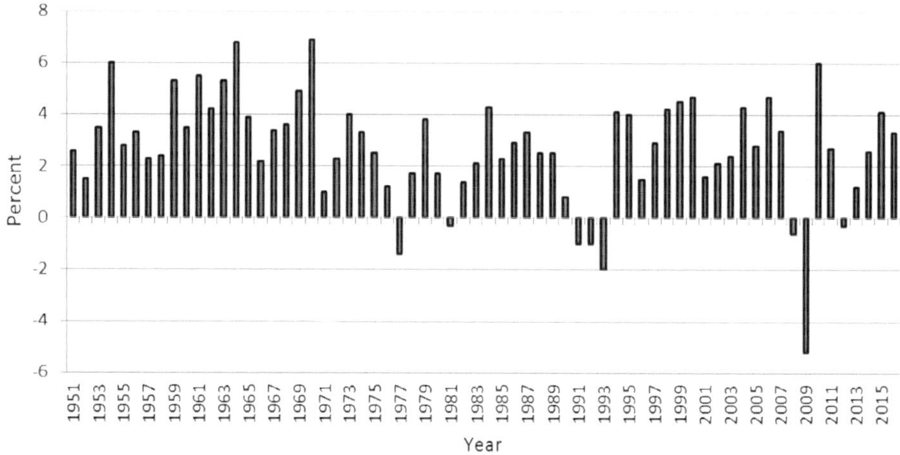

Source: own illustration based on SCB (Statistics Sweden)

To eventually show the impact of austerity on the Swedish party system, a few steps are required. A brief description of the Swedish party system's logic has to be given as well as an explanation of the role the welfare state has been playing in it. Secondly, the main lessons drawn from the crisis in the 1990s have to be attended. By connecting the new fiscal regime to the strategies of the two main parties in the Swedish system, it is shown that there is a structural disadvantage of the Social Democratic party, which is, among others, a major obstacle to return to a predominant[5] position in the party system.

2. *Basic assumptions about austerity and party systems*

To start with a minimal definition, austerity is understood as a policy that is targeting a reduction of budget deficits and gives general precedence to fiscal consolidation. To analyse our case, however, we have to go beyond this because the Swedish version of austerity is the prioritizing of a fiscal policy aiming for improvement of the primary budget balance over the sum of other national policies.[6] Two things are important here: First, this improvement means more than minimizing a budget deficit. So there is no

5 For the term »predominant« in contrast to »dominant«, see Giovanni Sartori, *Parties and Party Systems: A Framework for Analysis Volume I*, Cambridge 1976, pp. 192–195.

6 The minimal definition is very close to Blyth's understanding of »austerity, the policy of cutting the state's budget to promote growth«; Mark Blyth, *Austerity: The History of a Dangerous Idea*, Oxford/New York 2013, p. 2. The term »austerity (policy)« has no exact equivalent in the Swedish language. Closest translations would be »*åtstramning(spolitikv)*« or »*nedskärning (spolitik)*«, both of which can be translated with »reduction (policy)« and imply a more negative connotation than the English »austerity«, which can be used in a more neutral

stop sign for austerity at a balanced budget. Second, how these budget surpluses are reached is left unanswered. So the question how austerity is implemented in various policies is not determined by the definition which implies the assumption that there can be different paths leading to the same result when it comes to austerity.

If we consider that a party system is formed by the different parties and the relations between them, party competition is at the very core of any party system, or to say it in the words of one of the most influential works in the field, a system in general »displays properties that do not belong to a separate consideration of its component elements and [...] results from, and consists of, the patterned interactions of its component parts«[7], which means more specifically that »a party system is precisely the *system of interactions* resulting from inter-party competition.«[8] The parties of a system are – especially amid elections – competing with their programmes, derived from their ideologies, for governmental power. To implement the policies communicated to the voters by programmatic positions, governments need resources, not least financial ones. Thus it is obvious that a set of rules determining the limits of these resources is highly relevant for that competition and thereby for the party system. At the same time this framework was introduced and preserved by partisan actors. This means that there must have been a general agreement to it over time as long as it has not been repealed by governments with different partisan compositions. As will be shown, there are either strategic or ideological reasons for the main parties within the system to keep the framework in place. This mutual logic that the Swedish version of austerity sets preconditions for the party system while the latter is supporting or at least tolerating these regulations is the starting point of this contribution.

It is not possible to quantify this effect; consequently the main aim of this chapter is to demonstrate the logic of this relation rather than trying to measure it. The heuristic argument will be brought forward in several steps: It is important to briefly inform about the main macroeconomic strategies before the collapse as well as the political reactions to it. Furthermore the Swedish party system's general logic and its development has to be explained before the impact of the budgetary surplus regime on it can be examined.

manner. For our purpose the mentioned Swedish version of austerity is more relevant. For its main empirical manifestation, the surplus target, an exact translation exists which is also used in the Swedish public debate within this context (*överskottsmål*).

7 Blyth, *Austerity*, op. cit. (note 6), p. 43.

8 Blyth, *Austerity*, op. cit. (note 6), p. 44, italics in original.

3. The Swedish model and the logic of the Swedish party system

3.1 Traditional Swedish politics

During the major part of the 20th century the Swedish party system had been extraordinary steady and had been »considered the most stable in the west.«[9] It has remained in its frozen state[10] longer than party systems in other liberal democracies. For the first time since the breakthrough of universal suffrage, a party different from the five traditional ones gained enough electoral support to enter the parliament in 1988 (see table 1). This sets a breaking point in the development of the Swedish party system despite the fact that the five established parties have never lost parliamentary representation until today. Not only the lack of new parties in parliament marked the mentioned exceptionalism but also did the strong position of the Social Democratic party which was commonly seen as the natural party of government. Probably its biggest project had been the establishment of a far-reaching welfare state which was generally accepted and supported on the parliamentary and the electoral level.[11] In combination with specific labour market and macroeconomic policies as well as a corporatist policy-making system, this became known as the »Swedish model« and has been the core of the mentioned exceptionalism. During the 1980s and 1990s, however, this model underwent crucial changes.

It is important though to specify the general principles of this model not only to understand it itself and so the (need for) reforms but also because it is persistent in the collective memory of Swedish voters and thus important when we examine the party system. To say it metaphorically, we can, once again, remember Giovanni Sartori: »The question may be raised: What is the present-day relevance of antecedents? Why go back to the origins? The answer is that the past is the original map, the design of the foundations. In the course of time the building grows, and the foundations are covered up. This is why from time to time it is well to look back at the original design.«[12] Here it is reasonable to start to explain this map with the Social Democratic party, because it links the party system to the Swedish model.

9 Martin Bennulf, »Sweden: The Rise and Fall of Miljöpartiet de gröna« in: Dick Richardson / Chris Rootes (eds.), The Green Challenge: *The Development of Green Parties in Europe*, London/New York 1995, pp. 128–145, p. 129.

10 Seymour Martin Lipset / Stein Rokkan, »Cleavage Structures, Party Systems, and Voter Alignments: An Introduction« in: Seymour Martin Lipset / Stein Rokkan (eds.), *Party Systems and Voter Alignments: Cross-National Perspectives*, New York/London 1967, pp. 1–64.

11 Niels Finn Christiansen / Klas Åmark, »Conclusions« in: Niels Finn Christiansen et al. (ed.), *The Nordic Model of Welfare: A Historical Reappraisal*, Copenhagen 2006, pp. 335–354, p. 354. The Conservative party's position as the most critical one towards the welfare state is addressed later.

12 Sartori, *Parties and Party Systems*, op. cit. (note 5), p. 24.

Table 1: National election results (percentage of valid votes; second chamber until 1968)

Year[1)]	Turnout	V	SAP	MP	C	FP	KD	M	SD	Other
1921	54.2	4.6	36.2	/	11.1	19.1	/	25.8	/	3.2
1924	53.0	5.1	41.1	/	10.8	16.9	/	26.1	/	0.0
1928	67.4	6.4	37.0	/	11.2	15.9	/	29.4	/	0.1
1932	67.6	8.3	41.7	/	14.1	11.7	/	23.5	/	0.7
1936	74.5	7.7	45.9	/	14.3	12.9	/	17.6	/	1.6
1940	70.3	4.2	53.8	/	12.0	12.0	/	18.0	/	0.0
1944	71.9	10.3	46.7	/	13.6	12.9	/	15.9	/	0.7
1948	82.7	6.3	46.1	/	12.4	22.8	/	12.3	/	0.1
1952	79.1	4.3	46.1	/	10.7	24.4	/	14.4	/	0.1
1956	79.8	5.0	44.6	/	9.4	23.8	/	17.1	/	0.1
1958	77.4	3.4	46.2	/	12.7	18.2	/	19.5	/	0.0
1960	85.9	4.5	47.8	/	13.6	17.5	/	16.5	/	0.1
1964	83.9	5.2	47.3	/	13.2	17.0	1.8	13.7	/	1.8[2)]
1968	89.3	3.0	50.1	/	15.7	14.3	1.5	12.9	/	2.6[2)]
1970	88.3	4.8	45.3	/	19.9	16.2	1.8	11.5	/	0.4
1973	90.8	5.3	43.6	/	25.1	9.4	1.8	14.3	/	0.6
1976	91.8	4.8	42.7	/	24.1	11.1	1.4	15.6	/	0.4
1979	90.7	5.6	43.2	/	18.1	10.6	1.4	20.3	/	0.8
1982	91.4	5.6	45.6	1.7	15.5	5.9	1.9	23.6	/	0.2
1985	89.9	5.4	44.7	1.5	12.4[3)]	14.2	/[3)]	21.3	/	0.5
1988	86.0	5.8	43.2	5.5	11.3	12.2	2.9	18.3	/	0.7
1991	86.7	4.5	37.7	3.4	8.5	9.1	7.1	21.9	/	7.7[4)]
1994	86.8	6.2	45.3	5.0	7.7	7.2	4.1	22.4	/	2.3
1998	81.4	12.0	36.4	4.5	5.1	4.7	11.7	22.9	0.4	2.2
2002	80.1	8.4	39.9	4.6	6.2	13.4	9.1	15.3	1.4	1.7
2006	82.0	5.8	35.0	5.2	7.9	7.5	6.6	26.2	2.9	2.7
2010	84.6	5.6	30.7	7.3	6.6	7.1	5.6	30.1	5.7	1.4
2014	85.8	5.7	31.0	6.9	6.1	5.4	4.6	23.3	12.9	4.1[5)]

Party abbreviations (for all parties the Swedish party name of 2014 is used): V: Left Party (*Vänsterpartiet*), SAP: Social Democratic Party (*Sveriges socialdemokratiska arbetareparti*), C: Center Party (*Centerpartiet*), FP: Liberal Party (*Folkpartiet liberalerna*), KD: Christian

Democratic Party (*Kristdemokraterna*), M: Conservative Party (*Moderata Samlingspartiet*), SD: Sweden Democrats (*Sverigedemokraterna*).

1) In the years 1970–1994 the election period was three years instead of four.

2) The whole percentage amount of »other« votes was cast for the bourgeois bloc distributed on two cooperative lists (M/C/FP, C/FP).

3) Cooperation between C and KD in 1985: a meaningful differentiation between the votes is not possible since separate and shared lists were existing parallel.

4) Including 6.7 per cent for the party New Democracy (*Ny demokrati*).

5) Including 3.1 per cent for the party Feminist Initiative (*Feministisk initiativ*).

Source: own illustration based on SCB (Statistics Sweden)

Sweden's Social Democratic Workers' Party (*Sveriges socialdemokratiska arbetareparti*, SAP) was founded in 1889 and had rather early developed a moderate ideological position which abandoned the idea of proletarian revolution in favour of reform within a democratic system. Consequentially the party suspended members who were still adhering revolutionary ideas, which gave birth to a communist party in 1917. »Swedish Social Democrats rapidly recognized democratic decision-making as the ultimate standard of legitimacy [...] [and thus] the attainment of political democracy as its first overriding objective. The party never seriously entertained the Leninist idea of an élitist revolutionary cadre.«[13] Hence a major goal at the turn of the century was universal suffrage, which the Social Democratic party had established in government together with the Liberal party between 1918 and 1921. For reducing the number of people not entitled to vote from around twenty to around two per cent of the population that had reached the voting age, the government had to make concessions to the Conservatives who were dominating the first chamber.[14] Most important of these accommodations were the changes to the electoral system of the first chamber: While originally meant to secure the Conservatives foothold, it turned out to be a major institutional reason for the social democratic predominance in the party system later on.[15] This Liberal-Social Democratic cooperation, however, ended after the historical project and when the question of the state's role in the economy became the dominating issue on the political agenda. As elsewhere, the Social Democrats faced the dilemma of representing the core constituency or to gain support in the middle class since the – according to Marxist theory – expected electoral gain of almost the whole society

13 Tim Tilton, *The Political Theory of Swedish Social Democracy: Through the Welfare State to Socialism*, Oxford 1990, p. 257.

14 Bo Särlvik, »Party and Electoral System in Sweden« in: Bernard Grofman / Arend Lijphart (eds.), *The Evolution of Electoral and Party Systems in the nordic countries*, New York 2002, pp. 225–269, p. 241.

15 The electoral system of annual indirect vote of one-eighth of the first chamber members through county and city council representatives intended an element of continuity. It benefited the strongest party in the system, which in the course of the extension of suffrage became the Social Democrats instead of the Conservatives.

was not anticipated to happen soon[16]; especially not in a situation when the economy – after a very short phase of slowdown at the end of the war – was growing again, showing good development also in comparative perspective and when people on the whole were looking forward to the future.[17] In the 1930s the SAP developed two ideological ideas that were leading for the next decades: the universal welfare state, also known as »The People's Home« (*Folkhemmet*)[18], and an active role of the state in the economy based on the ideas of John Maynard Keynes and »The Stockholm School«.[19] The same decade marks the beginning of the exceptionally long time in government for the SAP: After its short-lived minority governments of the 1920s, the party took office after gaining 41.7 per cent of the votes in the election of 1932. Since then this has been the Social Democrats' lowest percentage of votes until 1991, and they remained the ruling party for 44 years with the exception of the short ›summer government‹ of 1936 when the Farmers' party held office on an interim basis.

It was this »Association of Farmers« (*bondeförbundet*) the Social Democratic minority government struck a deal with to secure a majority for their neo-Keynesian policies to fight unemployment in 1933. The successful cooperation led to a formal coalition government between 1936 and 1939, which was replaced by a »national government« consisting of all non-communist parties during the Second World War.[20] The red-green coalition pattern was revisited from 1951 to 1957 and was the last social democratic coalition government until 2014. During the time of the traditional party system, other deviations from the default (SAP minority government) were the phase of non-socialistic governments (1976–1982) and the social democratic one-party majority government in the late 1960s (1968–1970). After the red-green cooperation the parties' division into two blocs in the national parliament was characteristic for the Swedish party system. While there was a distinct senior-junior relation on the socialistic side, proportions in the bourgeois camp[21] were not so clear. The three parties were

16 Adam Przeworski, *Capitalism and Social Democracy*, Cambridge et al. 1987, pp. 7–46, 208–209.

17 Leif Lewin, *Ideology and Strategy: A Century of Swedish Politics*, Cambridge et al. 1988, p. 124.

18 The Peoples' Home became a central narrative for the party and an idea of common knowledge in Sweden after 1928 when the party leader Per Albin Hansson was presenting it in a speech as the society to strive for. Per Albin Hansson, »Folkhemstalet: Tal vid andra kammarens remissdebatt, onsdagen den 18 januari 1928« in: *Fronesis* 34, No. 1 (2010), pp. 57–61.

19 For a discussion if these ideas were developed independently within The Stockholm School, see Bo Gustafsson, »A Perennial of Doctrinal History: Keynes and the ›Stockholm School‹« in: *Economy and History* 16, No. 1 (1973), pp. 114–128.

20 Anders Widfeldt, »The Swedish Centre Party: The Poor Relation of the Family?« in: David Arter (ed.), *From Farmyard to City Square? The Electoral Adaptation of the Nordic Agrarian Parties*, Aldershot et al. 2001, pp. 1–30, p. 4. The crisis agreement has gone down in history as »*kohandeln*«, which is translated to »the cow trade« because of the agrarian context and which has a similar ring as »horse trade« in English at the same time.

21 The term »bourgeois« is used here, as it is in Sweden, in a neutral and not pejorative manner and stands as a synonym for non-socialistic.

alternating in the leading position regarding the proportion of seats in the parliament.[22] While the Liberal Party was the biggest of them from 1948 to 1967 (with the exception of the 1958 election) and the Centre Party (the former Association of Farmers) from 1968 to 1978, the Conservatives have been the strongest one from the implementation of universal suffrage until 1947, in the 1958 election and from 1979 until today. More important than the share of seats was the symptomatic inability to create a united alternative to the SAP governments as a striking characteristic of the traditional party system in Sweden. Consequentially both bourgeois coalition governments that were formed in the second half of the 1970s broke apart before the end of the respective election period. Besides that, the implied support of the SAP by the Communist Party was underpinning the stability of the Social Democratic minority governments, as well as institutional settings like the mentioned first chamber and the principle of negative parliamentarianism have benefited them. The main features of the party system also applied to the neighbour countries Norway and Denmark[23], even though these patterns were eroding earlier there than in Sweden where the system began to thaw in 1988.

While these arguments for the stability of Social Democratic minority governments are plausible, the question remains why the party had so much electoral support in the first place. During the times of the traditional Swedish five-party system, the SAP was easily gaining over 40 per cent of the votes on a regular basis. The quite obvious answer is that the party managed to mobilize electoral support beyond their core constituency of blue collar workers. In the beginning of the 20th century, Sweden was still a rural society with the distinct Nordic historical aspect of independent farmers. The Swedish Social Democrats got access to this group, too, not least because »a clear dividing line between industrial workers and farmers was often difficult to draw, since many workers owned a plot of land and many farmers held part-time jobs, for example as loggers, in the winter.«[24] The SAP reached voters far into the middle class because of their pragmatic ideological position and their cooperativeness towards the bourgeois bloc. The willingness towards compromise – regardless if it is seen as an expression of political culture[25] or as a strategic decision[26] – instead of relying on the left-wing majority assured long-term solutions and broad support behind their policies. These were also targeted at the whole society and not exclusively at the working class: »The feat is one of sustaining a distinctive working-class identity and sense of solidarity while making labor's organized interests and the larger national purpose integral with each

22 Until the reform that changed the system into a unicameral one in 1970, the term »parliament« is referring to the second chamber if no specification is made.

23 It became known also as the Nordic or Scandinavian party system (model), while Sweden always has represented its prototype. David Arter, *Scandinavian Politics Today*, Manchester/New York 2008, pp. 56–61. The classical work concerning the model is Sten Berglund / Ulf Lindström, *The Scandinavian Party System(s): A Comparative Study*, Lund 1978.

24 Arter, *Scandinavian Politics Today*, op. cit. (note 23), p. 75.

25 Leif Lewin, *Votera eller förhandla: Om den svenska parlamentarismen*, Stockholm 1996.

26 Tilton, *The Political Theory of Swedish Social Democracy*, op. cit. (note 13), p. 10.

other.«[27] This national purpose leads us to the relevance of social security policies and the building of the *People's Home*, the Swedish welfare state.

Not only the party system but also the welfare state of the Nordic countries became a model[28] – and again Sweden was considered to be its prototype.[29] »In a comparative perspective, this means that it has generally been seen as more encompassing, more universalistic, and more redistributive than other welfare state systems.«[30] To understand this model, it is less important to wade through the various policy programmes, »which can ultimately be seen in instrumental terms, as devices designed to realize a set of underlying preferences.«[31] These guiding principles matter and are more adequate for our purpose to look at than policies which are, to some extent, more situational. »Especially the following general and structural characteristics make the Swedish welfare state unique in international comparison: a general universalism, equality, the strength in the social civil rights together with effectivity.«[32] Thus social insurances and public services are open to all citizens, tax-financed and indirectly redistributional.[33] Another feature of the idea of the Swedish welfare state is the relation between individual freedom and the role of community. The concept would be misunderstood if one claimed in a more liberal tradition that the goal of equality and a big state would contradict individual freedom. The traditional Social Democratic welfare state in Sweden tries to free individuals from dependence on the market and on other individuals by providing solidarity on the level of society instead of allocating this responsibility to the family.[34] In difference from central or southern European welfare models, care activities traditionally carried out within the household have been socialized in Sweden consequentially. It creates individual independence while it encourages women to participate in the labour market. The consequence, however, is an extensive public sector and high costs for the state. At the same time it creates support for the

27 Hugh Heclo / Henrik Madsen, *Policy and Politics in Sweden: Principled Pragmatism*, Philadelphia 1987, p. 24.

28 Gøsta Esping-Andersen, *The Three Worlds of Welfare Capitalism*, Cambridge 1990.

29 Esping-Andersen, *The Three Worlds of Welfare Capitalism*, op. cit. (note 28), p. 114; Walter Korpi / Joakim Palme, »The Paradox of Redistribution and Strategies of Equality: Welfare State Institutions, Inequality, and Poverty in the Western Countries« in: *American Sociological Review* 63No. 5 (1998), pp. 661–687, p. 682.

30 Bo Rothstein, »Introduction: The Politics of the Welfare State« in: Pierre, *The Oxford Handbook of Swedish Politics*, op. cit. (note 1), pp. 19–21, p. 19.

31 Juhana Vartiainen, »Understanding Swedish Social Democracy: Victims of Success?« in: Andrew Glyn (ed.), *Social Democracy in Neoliberal Times: The Left and Economic Policy since 1980*, Oxford 2001, pp. 21–52, p. 22.

32 Gøsta Esping-Andersen, »Jämlikhet, effektivitet och makt: Socialdemokratisk välfärdspolitik« in: Klaus Misgeld/ Karl Molin / Klas Åmark (eds.), *Socialdemokratins samhälle: SAP och Sverige under 100 år*, Kristianstad 1988, pp. 219–249, p. 219, own translation.

33 For an explanation of the redistributional character of universal welfare states with a flat tax structure, see Bo Rothstein, »The Moral, Economic, and Political Logic of the Swedish Welfare State« in: Pierre, *The Oxford Handbook of Swedish Politics*, op. cit. (note 1), pp. 69–83, pp. 79–80.

34 Henrik Berggren / Lars Trädgård, *Är svensken människa: Gemenskap och oberoende i det moderna Sverige*, Stockholm 2006, pp. 9–11.

welfare state in a twofold way: from its beneficiaries and its employees. Thus the SAP as the constructing engineer of the Swedish welfare state was not only supported by working-class members but also by voters who benefited from this system.

When it comes to unemployment, the strategy was to combine generous benefits for a shortly terminated time with active labour market policies to get people back into work as soon as possible, because this Swedish welfare system was strongly dependent on a high proportion of workforce being employed. Hence a major goal had always been full employment, which binds the welfare state closely to labour market and economic policies. This close connection might be a reason for the lack of a clear discrimination of the term »Nordic« respectively »Swedish model«. While some denominate with it the specific version of the welfare state, others claim that it »has been from the beginning a primarily economic model.«[35] Others again have a broader understanding and include both of the mentioned views and even corporatist elements and political (culture) aspects.[36] Additionally its meaning has been varying over time, and it has also served as »ideological weaponry of the Cold War [...] [when] all five Nordic countries promoted the idea of the Nordic model as a ›middle way‹ between communism and free market capitalism. [...] Although it has some heuristic value as a category of analysis for comparative social scientists, most of its power was derived from its role as a discourse: a means of imagining and describing this part of the world.«[37] In this way the Swedish model must also be understood as a »discursive battlefield«[38], and therefore it remains fairly unclear what is meant if someone is talking about it today when »the concept has become a common denominator for both left- and right-wing politics.«[39] Political actors are fighting for it[40] and trying to take advantage of the fact that it activates positive associations in the electorate. So even though its meaning as a *floating signifier*[41] is unclear if not specified, it is obviously very present in the political debate until today, when Stefan Löfven put it on top of the agenda of the SAP again in

35 Detlef Jahn, »Das schwedische Modell: Zukunfts- oder Auslaufmodell?« in: Gunilla Rising Hintz (ed.), *Das Schwedische Modell: Zukunfts- oder Auslaufmodell?*, Marburg 1994, pp. 21–38, p. 22, own translation.

36 Rothstein, »Introduction«, op. cit. (note 30), p. 19.

37 Mary Hilson, *The Nordic Model: Scandinavia since 1945*, London 2008, p. 114.

38 Jenny Andersson, »A Model of Welfare Capitalism? Perspectives on the Swedish Model, Then and Now« in: Pierre, *The Oxford Handbook of Swedish Politics*, op. cit. (note 1), pp. 563–577, p. 564.

39 Andersson, »A Model of Welfare Capitalism?«, op. cit. (note 38), p. 564.

40 The SAP even tried to obtain approval of the term »Nordic Model« as a registered trademark. Urban Lundberg, »Das nordische Modell: Sozialdemokratisches Markenzeichen oder gemeinsames kulturelles Erbe?« in: Bernd Henningsen / Sven Jochem / Siegfried Frech (eds.), *Das politische Skandinavien: Gesellschaft, Wirtschaft, Politik & Kultur*, Schwalbach 2015, pp. 37–62, pp. 38–39.

41 A floating signifier is a term which has no clear and commonly accepted definition and whose ambivalent meaning is dependent on the context. In practice this means that it is used by adherents of different ideologies, who also »load« the term with a different meaning. Lundberg, »Das nordische Modell«, op. cit. (note 40), pp. 56–57.

2016, announcing in a speech: »Therefore here and now I blow to battle for the Swedish model.«[42]

The electoral strength of the SAP cannot be explained without mentioning the far-reaching tie between the party and the labour unions, especially the powerful umbrella organization for blue collar workers LO (*Landsorganisationen i Sverige*). They have always considered themselves as the two branches of the Swedish labour movement, and until today there are many financial and personal linkages, which have led to the description of a »symbiotic relation.«[43] Clearly the benefits were for the party a channel to mobilize voters and to make blue-collar workers politically aware, while the LO could have more political influence. Furthermore the close collaboration was contributing to the SAP's predominant position in the party system through the collective membership. With this system of party membership by default, which required union members to actively resign from the SAP, the Social Democrats not only acquired financial support through membership fees but also had a better opportunity to deliver their political message directly to their core constituency. Both organizations put massive efforts into political education, and the Swedish labour movement reached far into the cultural and personal lives of its supporters, thus providing a cradle-to-grave structure that helped to generate a feeling of common identity and to channel inevitable conflicts within the broad-based party.[44] LO could also be seen as a Social Democratic think tank, and it had great influence especially on the labour market policies, which are a definitive feature of the Swedish model.

The social democratic labour market policy was based on the Rehn-Meidner model, which was developed within LO, and on the main principle of equal wages. The foundations for this narrow understanding of the Swedish model were laid with the Saltsjöbaden Agreement in 1938, when LO and the employers' association SAF decided to reconcile conflicts without state intervention. This compromise between capital and labour served as a blueprint for other labour market agreements and was a precondition for the powerful position social partners should get later in the Swedish system. The goals the model was supposed to fulfil were full employment and equality, which at the same time should not undermine the ability of the small export-oriented country to compete internationally. »Both inflation and lack of efficiency are serious threats to the competitiveness of the Swedish economy. To make full employment compatible with price stability, and equality with efficiency have been the crucial challenges of the Swedish Model.«[45] In the logic of the Rehn-Meidner model, the government's role is

42 Stefan Löfven, »Striden om den svenska modellen« in: *Website of the Swedish Social Democrats*, http://www.socialdemokraterna.se/Stefan-Lofven/Tal-och-artiklar/2016/Striden-om-den-svenska-modellen/ [4.2.2017].

43 Christian Steffen, »Die Parteiensysteme Dänemarks, Norwegens und Schwedens« in: Oskar Niedermayer / Richard Stöss / Melanie Haas (eds.), *Die Parteiensysteme Westeuropas*, Wiesbaden 2006, pp. 67–108, p. 70, own translation.

44 Heclo / Madsen, *Policy and Politics in Sweden*, op. cit. (note 27), pp. 323–324; Tilton, *The Political Theory of Swedish Social Democracy*, op. cit. (note 13), pp. 2–3.

45 Rudolf Meidner, »The Rise and Fall of the Swedish Model« in: *Studies in Political Economy* 39 (1992), pp. 159–171, p. 161.

to actively keep total demand somewhat lower than the balance level and engage in active labour market measures to equalize in and between the affected geographical and economical areas. At the core there are central wage negotiations by the two head organizations according to the principles of same pay for same work and modest increases which were also meant to prevent a price-wage spiral caused by inter-union rivalry. This has a structure-transformative consequence with the most productive companies making more profit and the least competitive ones being either forced to reform or squeezed out of the market. The resulting unemployment in the least productive sectors and firms is taken care of in the form of re-education and mobility with state support, the main cause for the denomination as *active* labour market policy. There was an incentive within the Social Democratic party to make sure that the overall goal of equality would not be undermined by the profits of the over-average employers. Except the idea of reinvesting, the possibility of wage-drift[46] and the use for pension funds, the Rehn-Meidner model implied the concept of wage-earner funds. This gradual shift of ownership was »originally conceived as a logical repercussion of the labour-market model«[47] while at the same time it was not only strongly refused by employers but also controversial within the SAP. After years of debate a diluted version was implemented, but later it was abolished by the bourgeois government in the beginning of the 1990s.[48]

3.2. The erosion of traditional patterns and the crisis of the early 1990s

The Swedish labour-market model seemed to be very successful in the beginning, given that the objectives of equality and full employment were largely fulfilled. Also the predicted effect of accelerated productivity growth and flows of workers applied. The problems, however, started in the 1970s with increasing inflation (see figure 4 & 5). The specific Swedish system of multi-level wage bargaining already had an inbuilt logic of causing wage drifts. Additionally, as Juhana Vartiainen points out, the unions changed their strategy of wage solidarity in the more radicalized atmosphere of the late 1960s, »starting to embark on an ambitious extension of this policy. First, the solidaristic wage policy, originally conceived as ›same pay for similar work‹ was increasingly transformed into ›same pay for all work‹. Secondly, the LO launched its controversial initiative for wage-earner funds.«[49] The former meant a change from balancing between sectors and enterprises »to a dramatic equalization of wages within firms and between tasks and competence levels. [... The] striving for a radical evening out of all wage differentials was the most important factor that contributed to the Swedish em-

46 Of course the wage drifts were not supposed to get out of hand, since they would undermine the objective of equality. Still they were needed as »a necessary safety valve within a centralized bargaining system.« Vartiainen, »Understanding Swedish Social Democracy«, op. cit. (note 31), p. 31.

47 Vartiainen, »Understanding Swedish Social Democracy«, op. cit. (note 31), p. 34.

48 Meidner, »The Rise and Fall of the Swedish Model«, op. cit. (note 45).

49 Vartiainen, »Understanding Swedish Social Democracy«, op. cit. (note 31), pp. 32–33.

ployers' rejection of coordinated bargaining.«[50] While the prior goal was promoting productivity growth, this was slowed down by the new approach. Also the collective character of bargaining only by the two head organizations got lost early, and the system got more internally differentiated.[51] »The LO member unions remained mostly loyal to the principles of coordination, but the white-collar and public-sector unions gradually became tired of adjusting their wages according to the wage claims of others. «[52] With developing away from centralized bargaining, the main mechanism against increasing wage drifts and inflation was invalidated. Eventually the separate agreement in the metal industry in 1983 can be seen ex post as the point of no return; consequentially the SAF abrogated its central bargaining organization in 1992.

Figure 4: Inflation (CPI growth rate in per cent)

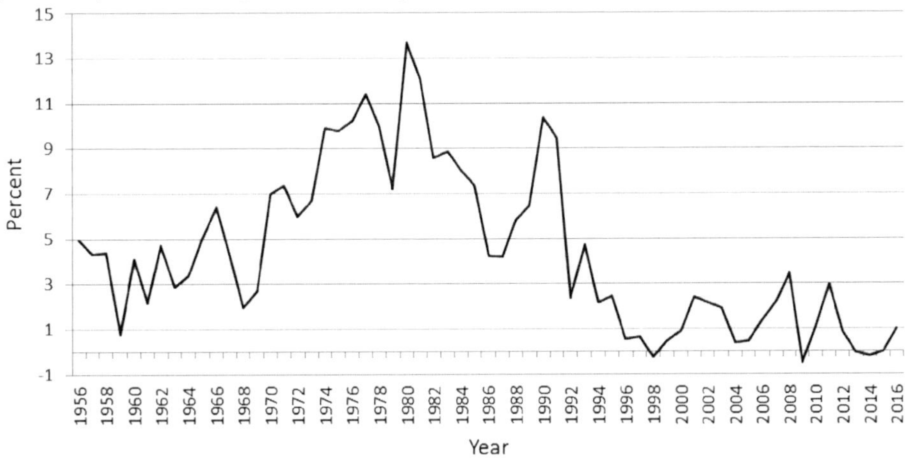

Source: own illustration based on OECD

50 Vartiainen, »Understanding Swedish Social Democracy«, op. cit. (note 31), p. 33.

51 Nils Elvander, *Den svenska modellen: Löneförhandlingar och inkomstpolitik 1982-1986*, Stockholm 1988, p. 253.

52 Vartiainen, »Understanding Swedish Social Democracy«, op. cit. (note 31), p. 35.

Figure 5: Unemployment rate (percentage of the labour force)

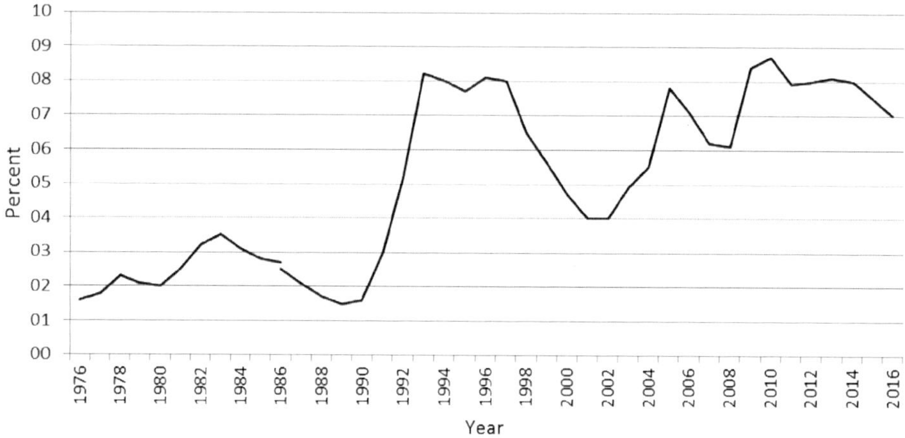

Source: own illustration based on SCB (Statistics Sweden)

Additionally the SAP returned into government in 1982 with its new political programme of the »third way«, which was meant to position the party between old-fashioned Keynesianism respectively the fiscal expansionary stance which was tried in France under Mitterrand and austerity respectively monetarism as it was represented by Thatcher or Reagan. In the Bretton Woods era monetary policy did not play a major role compared with fiscal and labour market policy; in the subsequent phase, though, Swedish governments used the tool of currency devaluation comparatively frequently since the Keynesian countercyclical requirements have not been met in times of economic boom.[53] Thus it was not an unknown measure when the new SAP government devaluated the krona with 16 per cent in 1982.[54] »The idea was to make a final, big devaluation that would be followed by austere fiscal policies that were expected to transfer resources from sheltered economic sectors – including the public sector – to the export-oriented sector.«[55] While the first step enhanced international competitiveness, the continuity in welfare policies – meaning the reluctance to implement the second step – required increasing resources for the state. But since the public debt had already risen to a critical point (see figure 1) and the tax burden was at a level which did not allow further heightening, deregulation of the financial market seemed

53 This is one of the decisive reasons why the Rehn-Meidner model collapsed in the end according to Rudolf Meidner, one of its architects. Meidner, »The Rise and Fall of the Swedish Model«, op. cit. (note 45), p. 164.

54 Even though there was a goal of a fixed exchange rate to bind the inflation to the one of other countries, it was never prioritized over the goal of full employment, which weakened its credibility, especially since the central bank was highly dependent on the government. Calmfors, »The Swedish Macroeconomic Policy Framework«, op. cit. (note 1), p. 596.

55 Leif Lewin / Johannes Lindvall, »One Hundred Years of Swedish Economic Policy« in: Pierre, *The Oxford Handbook of Swedish Politics*, op. cit. (note 1), pp. 578–591, p. 587.

to be a solution of this problem. The opening of the highly protected and regulated domestic capital market[56] from 1985 onwards coincided with another increase of inflation, which was not counteracted by the government but further intensified through tax reductions. The consequences of increasing prices and wages, growing demand and supply of credits, the formation of a real estate bubble and a more and more overheated economy led to the unusual Social Democratic policy-package proposal in the beginning of 1990, which included a wage freeze and a strike ban combined with austerity measures. After not getting a parliamentary majority for this proposition because the Left party denied support, the government resigned, even though it took office again shortly thereafter because of the lack of an alternative government and the constitutionally fixed election period. The main difference, though, was the resignation of finance minister Kjell-Olof Feldt, who was highly respected but could not get through his ideas of a more restricted fiscal policy within the SAP ever since the third way was proclaimed. »The austerity plan itself proved that the government had lost control of the economy. It came too late, and the effects of its proposals were very doubtful. Feldt himself later revealed that he did not believe in its regulatory nature.«[57] This means, in short, that right before the outbreak of the crisis not only the economy faced huge problems but also the main pillars the Swedish model had rested on were broken. The on all levels deeply divided SAP could not rely on the support of the Left party anymore, centralized wage bargaining was dead and the cohesion of the labour movement was unprecedentedly disrupted.[58]

»Around 1991, the boom turned into bust and deep recession, the most severe in the post-war era. Unemployment increased. The budget deficit accelerated. In real terms, national income declined three years in a row – a unique pattern without parallel in Sweden during the twentieth century.«[59] Already in October 1990 the government finally announced that the fight against inflation will be the overriding goal from now on, which can be seen as the moment when Sweden lost its exceptionalism in macroeconomic policy. Nevertheless, the higher priority of the exchange rate could not help – no matter if pegged to a trade-weighted currency basket or to the European Currency Unit, as from 1991 onwards – to avoid the international expectation of another devalu-

56 Peter Englund, »The Swedish Banking Crisis: Roots and Consequences« in: *Oxford Review of Economic Policy* 15, No. 3 (1999), pp. 80–97, p. 83.

57 Anders Widfeldt, »The Swedish Parliamentary Election of 1991« in: *Electoral Studies* 11, No. 1 (1992), pp. 72–77, p. 73.

58 David Arter, »›The War of Roses‹: Conflict and Cohesion in the Swedish Social Democratic Party« in: David S. Bell / Eric Shaw (eds.), *Conflict and Cohesion in Western European Social Democratic Parties*, London 1994, pp. 70–95. Sven Jochem, »Reformpolitik im schwedischen Sozialstaat: Formen, Gründe und Konsequenzen der Austeritätspolitik« in: *Wirtschaftspolitische Blätter*, No. 3, 2015, pp. 601–614.

59 Lars Jonung, »Reforming the Fiscal Framework: The Case of Sweden 1973–2013« in: Torben M. Andersen / U. Michael Bergman / Svend E. Hougaard Jensen (eds.), *Reform Capacity and Macroeconomic Performance in the Nordic Countries*, Oxford 2015, pp. 190–215, pp. 199–200. Even if it is mostly referred to as a banking crisis, it had exceptionally hard consequences for the economy (GDP) also in comparative perspective. Lewin / Lindvall, »One Hundred Years of Swedish Economic Policy«, op. cit. (note 55), p. 588.

ation. After the Central Bank had desperately tried to protect the *krona* with an interest rate of 500 per cent, Sweden had to let it float on November 19, 1992. While exchange rates were unsure in general at that time in Europe, this kind of anchor was not an option to take again. Another mechanism to ensure credibility for the announced inflation control was needed; thus the Central Bank adopted an inflation target of 2 (+/- 1) per cent per annum in January 1993. The argument for implementing Central Bank independence, which the SAP was refusing at first, was twofold and can be explained with Sweden joining the European Union in 1995. First of all the Maastricht treaty was requiring more independence, but it was also necessary because Sweden did not want to participate in the monetary union, »which made it clear that credibility for low-inflation policy had to be built at home.«[60] Since then Sweden actually managed to keep inflation within acceptable borders; in fact the problem was rather low inflation than a high one in recent years.

The currency directly dropped by 9 per cent on November 20, 1992 (by 20 per cent at the end of the year), which caused an end to the acute phase of the crisis, because it was stabilizing the (export-oriented) economy. Another problem was persisting though, and it was more complex to solve. The Swedish welfare state had been supported by the former macroeconomic policy because of its dependency on low unemployment, which was rising during the crisis up to over 12 per cent total unemployment (including people in labour market programmes) in 1993 and 1994, which was, back then, an unacceptable rate in a country used to full employment (see figure 5 for the open unemployment rate). Bearing in mind the national debt, the tax burden and the size of the public sector, options were limited for the Swedish government; public expenditure needed to be reduced. What had only been the plan in the 1980s was realized in the 1990s: fiscal consolidation through austerity measures in combination with economic growth which was made possible with the last (unintended) depreciation.

4. A new consensus in Swedish politics

4.1 The fiscal policy framework

The Swedish government was reacting with expansive fiscal policy as a direct response to the crisis and gradually initiated austerity reforms, which were more tightened once the economy started to recover in 1994–95, and in a third step introduced a rule-based fiscal policy regime, thus »seeking to lock in the gains from the fiscal consolidation process in the second half of the 1990s.«[61] The changes within the welfare state are widely seen as an improvement in sustainable financing rather than a radical change and were implemented during both bourgeois as well as SAP governments. As mentioned, one of the main problems was that the arrangement of social security and welfare was based on the assumption of very low unemployment, which is also why it

60 Calmfors, »The Swedish Macroeconomic Policy Framework«, op. cit. (note 1), p. 598.
61 Calmfors, »The Swedish Macroeconomic Policy Framework«, op. cit. (note 1), p. 606.

cannot be called unconditionally universal. »The Swedish welfare state has never been universal in a strict sense. [...] Programs like unemployment benefits, sickness cash benefits and the supplementary pension (ATP) all required previous participation in the labour market.«[62] Universality was only indirectly ensured by safeguarding full employment, but with the change of goals and the subsequently higher rate of people out of work this indirect logic became visible. The reforms taken were serving the purposes of defending the universal character of the welfare state and of fighting the deficit problem. A stronger element of workfare could build on the country's history of active labour market policy, which made it manifest to concentrate on a »strengthened emphasis on skill formation and activating social policies, [... since] the main aim was to stimulate and upgrade labor supply, thereby increasing revenues and reducing expenditures.«[63] Again the various policy changes (i.e. replacement rate cuts, reintroduction of waiting days in health and unemployment insurance, pension reform) will not be examined here. This has two reasons: First, it is widely accepted that, although the Swedish welfare state was tightened, the reforms did not fundamentally change it in its defining characteristics.[64] Second, most of the measures taken in reaction to the crisis had been decided upon in cross-bloc agreements.

The continuity of measures to fight the crisis in the 1990s – including the new fiscal regime – taken by the different governments led by both of the leading parties in the respective bloc, from SAP (until 1991) to centre-right (1991–1994) and to SAP again (from 1994 on), is not surprising, given that they all were minority governments and the historical fact that the bourgeois parties in the 1970s – even after the very long period of Social Democratic rule and in a majority position – had not changed the macroeconomic and fiscal policy, i.e. »to accept temporary inflation and current account deficits in order to maintain full employment«, and they »went *even further* than the Social Democrats in the pursuit of full employment.«[65] So already in this situation of government change from left to right it can be stated: »If anything changed after the takeover, it was the fact that the amount of expansive social reforms increased and that public spending actually grew.«[66] In the 1990s Sweden was facing the most severe economic crisis since the 1930s, and it was clear that small adjustments would not solve the problem. This made it a project of national interest, for which broad agreements are common in Sweden. Very few and smaller reforms have been repealed after the change of government in 1994, but in general there was a consensus between the major

62 Christina Bergqvist / Anders Lindbom, »The Swedish Welfare State: Neo-liberal Challenge and Welfare State Resilience« in: *Österreichische Zeitschrift für Politikwissenschaft* 32, No. 4 (2003), pp. 389–401, p. 394.

63 Jonung, »Reforming the Fiscal Framework«, op. cit. (note 59), p. 257.

64 Bergqvist / Lindbom, »The Swedish Welfare State«, op. cit. (note 62); Christoph Arndt, *The Electoral Consequences of Third Way Welfare State Reforms: Social Democracy's Transformation and Its Political Costs*, Amsterdam 2013, pp. 159–167.

65 Lewin / Lindvall, »One Hundred Years of Swedish Economic Policy«, op. cit. (note 55), p. 586, 590, italics in original.

66 Andreas Bergh / Gissur Ó. Erlingsson, »Liberalization without Retrenchment: Understanding the Consensus on Swedish Welfare State Reforms« in: *Scandinavian Political Studies* 32, No. 1 (2009), pp. 71–93, p. 86.

parties in parliament.[67] Even though the party system is divided into two blocs, there is a long tradition for agreements reaching across this borderline, which is why there is the possibility for viable minority governments in Sweden.[68] To a certain degree this is a mutually conditioning, respectively strengthening, mechanism. So, once again, also in this case the traditional characteristics of Swedish policy making were facilitating continuity in political actions across periods of different parties in central government. »Compared to most other countries, policy making in Sweden is known to be particularly rational, pragmatic and consensual. Furthermore, government commissions and interest groups play an important role, and in general, decisions are not made hastily. [...] Taken together, the influence of social science on policy making and the commission system have helped to produce a culture of political consensus.«[69] When it comes to the main long-term stabilizing instrument, that is the new fiscal framework, both of these elements are pronounced as well: it is based on a broad agreement and on scientific expertise.[70]

The current fiscal framework was put in place gradually and consists of several elements. At first the parliamentary decision about the annual budget was reorganized into a specific top-down mode, which has been applied since 1996. Secondly, the parliament now decides over an expenditure ceiling proposed by government for central governmental expenditure three years ahead to secure stability orientation on the expenditure side. Third, regions and municipalities are required to have their annual budgets in balance; possible deficits must be equalized within three years. Together with the sub-national rule a surplus target for the central government was fully implemented in 2000. The Budget Act does not specify the exact percentage which is set by parliament, but it had been introduced with an excess claim of revenues over expenditures by one per cent of GDP over the business cycle and stayed at this number until recently. Later, in 2007, an independent Fiscal Policy Council was established to audit the sustainability of public finances from the outside. Its annual report is discussed in a public hearing in the parliament's finance committee, and the government, i.e. the finance minister, is referring to the report in the budget proposal.[71]

67 For a more sceptical assessment of the consensus spirit, especially for the second half of the period 1991–1994, see Anders Widfeldt, »The Swedish Parliamentary Election of 1994« in: *Electoral Studies* 14, No. 2 (1995), pp. 206–212, p. 207.

68 There are as a matter of fact other reasons why Swedes primarily run their country out of a minority position, but these had been discussed elsewhere before. Torbjörn Bergman, »Sweden: When Minority Governments are the Rule and Majority Coalitions the Exception« in: Wolfgang C. Müller / Kaare Strøm (eds.), *Coalition Governments in Western Europe*, Oxford/New York 2000, pp. 192–230.

69 Bergh / Erlingsson, »Liberalization without Retrenchment«, op. cit. (note 66), p. 81.

70 Calmfors, »The Swedish Macroeconomic Policy Framework«, op. cit. (note 1), pp. 604–606.

71 For an explanation of the framework, see Jonung, »Reforming the Fiscal Framework«, op. cit. (note 59); Calmfors, »The Swedish Macroeconomic Policy Framework«, op. cit. (note 1). For a presentation of the Fiscal Council, specifically see Lars Calmfors, »Sweden: Watchdog with a Broad Remit« in: George Kopits (ed.), *Restoring Public Debt Sustainability: The Role of Independent Fiscal Institutions*, Oxford 2013, pp. 189–211.

According to the new parliamentary mode of budgeting, an amount of total expenditure and its distribution among 27 expenditure areas as well as changes in fees and tax rates are set by parliament after the finance committee's proposal in a first step.[72] Then the allocations within the expenditure areas are made while they are not allowed to exceed their respective expenditure limit. While at the second step every committee leaves a proposal to the chamber, they report in the first one to the finance committee only, which is handing in one proposal for all the 27 expenditure areas, considering the suggestions from government and those statements. This procedure puts the finance committee in a primus inter pares position and gives it a filter function.

4.2 Austerity and the Swedish party system

When the relation between this rule-based fiscal regime and the party system is to be examined, it has to be clear that it is not an externally imposed straitjacket on the parties in government; it is based on inter-party consensus. The Conservative Party had always constituted the right margin of the parliamentary parties in the dominant left-right conflict, while in international comparison it has been more moderate than other members of its party family, which it also communicated by changing its name into »Moderate Unity Party« (*Moderata sammlingspartiet*) in 1969. While the party in the beginning of welfare-state expansion had an opposed stance, which was more directed at the basic principles, favouring a more residual type of welfare state than the encompassing one, it later accepted it in general since it had broad public support.[73] Instead the Moderates have been focusing on lowering taxes and incremental change like introducing or increasing private alternatives to public welfare services.[74]

The argument which is brought forward in the rest of this chapter is that by and large the Conservatives were part of a consensus on the Swedish model (even in a broader understanding). Still this was ideologically closer to the SAP than to them. After the collapse of this model a new consensus was reached, although this time it has been closer to the Moderates than to the Social Democrats.

With the big Social Democratic project of the People's Home, the SAP managed to gain broad support also from conservative voters and so from the Conservative Party.

72 Of course there are several steps before that, most important the parliament's decision about the guidelines of fiscal policy in the spring proposition and the so-called »scope for reform« (*reformutrymmet*), which exposes »the total sum of permanent tax reductions and government expenditure increases that can be actively decided by Parliament and that are compatible with the surplus target.« Calmfors, »The Swedish Macroeconomic Policy Framework«, op. cit. (note 1), p. 601. The identification of what is possible without being explicitly financed is usually a non-politicized technical matter.

73 The path-dependent character of welfare regimes contributes also to this acceptance, of course, since it involves high costs to change such a system more generally. But it is reasonable that a party would still consider it if there was more electoral support for such a change.

74 Anders Lindbom, »The Swedish Conservative Party and the Welfare State: Institutional Change and Adapting Preferences« in: *Government and Opposition* 43, No. 4 (2008), pp. 539–560.

This was also an intrinsic goal of the idea, since the welfare state was meant to be a universal one for the whole society. »Solidarity and equality of consideration characterize the good home; there consensus is the objective and democratic persuasion the method of governance.«[75] When the Swedish model started to crumble, some parts of it had to be reassessed and changed. While this was done, the welfare state was the main part which was not questioned in general but needed to become more efficient and adjusted to social changes. It was put in a nutshell by others in a regional perspective: »In essence the reform efforts under social democratic rule from the mid-1990s were aimed to preserve as much as possible ›as it was‹ in the Nordic welfare states.«[76] The need for a cost reduction had become obvious during the crisis; so it was not that difficult for the parties to agree to a reform process into this direction. But while the SAP had to be careful not to sell out their most supported project and their identity, it did not mean an ideological struggle for the Moderates; thus they could handle the situation pragmatically, even though while in government in a difficult parliamentary constellation.[77] In general they were doing so and engaging in problem-solving. Only the abolishment of the Ghent system – which was re-established when the SAP returned to power – had no fiscal motive and was supposed to weaken the Social Democratic power resources.[78] The main cut-backs the bourgeois government had introduced had not been repealed by the SAP afterwards; some of them were even tightened.[79] But this line did not have ideological reasons; indeed, »the extensive austerity programme enacted by the Göran Persson [Social Democratic prime minister 1996–2006] government – budget savings amounting to about 8 per cent of GDP – was motivated by fiscal reasons instead of being inspired by a fundamental political reorientation.«[80] It also has to be emphasized that the election result of 1994 gave the SAP a very strong mandate in this turbulent times, because the Social Democrats still had the electoral monopoly on the capability of crisis management.[81] So the Social Democratic welfare policies in the 1990s can be seen as a reaction to external pressure and a strate-

75 Tilton, *The Political Theory of Swedish Social Democracy*, op. cit. (note 13), p. 259.

76 Jon Erik Dølvik / Jørgen Goul Andersen / Juhana Vartiainen, »The Nordic Social Models in Turbulent Times: Consolidation and Flexible Adaptation« in: Jon Erik Dølvik / Andrew Martin (eds.), *European Social Models from Crisis to Crisis: Employment and Inequality in the Era of Monetary Integration*, Oxford 2015, pp. 246–280, p. 256.

77 The Moderate Unity Party and its coalition partners formed a minority government that could either work together with the undisciplined and hardly reliable parliamentary group of the populist New Democracy or make agreements with a party out of the socialistic bloc, which in practice meant the SAP. Even though the government did not fall apart this time, the bourgeois bloc was far from resembling a united team.

78 Arndt, *The Electoral Consequences of Third Way Welfare State Reforms*, op. cit. (note 64), p. 160.

79 To the author it is more convincing that the economic development widened the scope for further cut-backs than applying the blame avoidance hypothesis to the actions of the SAP government. To explain the election result of the SAP in 1994, however, this logic seems appealing. Lindbom, »The Swedish Conservative Party and the Welfare State«, op. cit. (note 74), p. 541.

80 Vartiainen, »Understanding Swedish Social Democracy«, op. cit. (note 31), p. 25.

81 This has changed, however, as recently as with the world financial crisis after 2007.

gic decision to fulfil the voters' expectations of problem-solving, which also applies for the long-term stability oriented construction of a new fiscal framework. With this Social Democratic orientation a consensus was not difficult to find, since the measures were coherent with the ideologies of the bourgeois parties, which returned to power in 2006, this time in a majority coalition.

It must be stressed that at the time when the centre-right parties won the parliamentary election in 2006 and returned into office, the goal of stabilization can be deemed successfully accomplished. Even though there might be strong arguments for a balanced budget in this situation, the question can be raised if there had been a justification for maintaining a surplus goal, particularly since »there is no mainstream school of economic thought – from either the ›left‹ or the ›right‹ – that is advocating for constant surpluses.«[82] The answer to the question why the pursuit of budget surpluses has been continued is to find in the logic of the party system. Both major parties have an interest in keeping up the Swedish version of austerity paradigm, as will be shown.

Two main lessons the Moderate Unity Party learned from the heavy defeat in the parliamentary election of 2002, when they suffered their worst election result in almost 30 years: First of all, the campaign, which mainly focused on significant tax cuts, did not go down well with the voters who preferred to keep the SAP in government, which took a clear position against any tax cuts and for social reform. Secondly, the disunited situation in the non-socialistic bloc – until the election day it was not clear who would be the next prime minister in case of a change of government – was unfavourable. So after this fiasco the Moderate Unity Party changed not only its leadership but also developed a new strategy with the central element of »an ideological charge for the centre ground, with several sacred cows cheerfully slaughtered on the way. Lower taxes, which had become central to the Moderates' platform, were retained as an objective [… and] the Alliance clearly pledged to adjust the Swedish model, not to overturn it.«[83] The non-socialistic bloc put also great effort in providing a clear alternative government to the voters, which was realized with a joint election platform, »Alliance for Sweden«. This was not only a historical novelty but also turned out as a big success since this time the government question had been settled before the election and a joint programme could be presented. The Moderates took the leading role and gained a plus of 11 percentage points compared to 2002. In hindsight it is clear that a big part of their changed position was merely of rhetorical nature. The Alliance, as it was commonly referred to and to which the name was changed later also formally, introduced the Fiscal Council relying on their parliamentary majority and against the Left, the Green and the Social Democratic Party. As it turned out later, this independent fiscal monitoring institution was less biased in favour of the Conservatives than the opposition parties suspected and the Alliance might have hoped. So the other par-

82 Scott Brenton / Jon Pierre, »Budget Surplus Goal Experiments in Australia and Sweden« in: *New Political Economy*, 29.12.2016, http://www.tandfonline.com/doi/full/10.1080/13563467.2017.1270924 [3.1.2017], p. 7.

83 Nicholas Aylott / Niklas Bolin, »Towards a Two-Party System? The Swedish Parliamentary Election of September 2006« in: *West European Politics* 30, No. 3 (2007), pp. 621–633, p. 625.

ties gave up their resistance against the Fiscal Council and even agreed to strengthen its position in 2011.[84]

To get a better understanding for the persistence of the Swedish version of austerity, we have to look at the partisan motives behind it. While Anders Lindbom might be right when he states »that the distinction between a real change of preferences and strategic change largely disappears in a highly path-dependent context«[85], it is exactly this discrimination that elucidates the relation between the party system and the reforms. In this chapter two major consensuses were presented, about (1) the general character of the Swedish welfare state and (2) the austerity measures and their »lock in«. For number one the SAP had ideological reasons and for number two, strategical ones, while for the Moderates the strategical (1) and the ideological motivations (2) were the other way around. Since »there are absolutely no signs of any weakening support for the welfare state in any respect«[86], a strategy of promoting a fundamental change of the welfare state would be doomed. Thus for the Alliance it makes sense »to adapt to welfare state popularity. This adaptation is, though, only strategic; their real preferences remain the same.«[87] In such an environment the only possible way (without losing significant voter support) is incremental change. As Philip Mehrtens has shown, this gradual change works in a combination of decentralization, market creating liberalization and privatization. With the surplus goal in place, it is hard to reverse and puts public welfare services under pressure as well as it is targeted to weaken the public support for it in the long run.[88] After another change of government in 2014, the SAP finds itself in a minority coalition government with the Green party and faces a difficult situation being trapped in the *trilemma of the service economy*. This means in short that governments in a service-economy context cannot satisfy the three goals of income equality, high employment and fiscal discipline at the same time.[89] To fulfil the surplus target, the SAP has to lower the priority of the other objectives, which are both at the core of their ideology. This is why the Social Democrats were never eager to have the surplus target as a permanent solution, which was not only indicated by their concern about the Fiscal Council but also by the attempt to abolish the surplus target and to replace it by a balanced budget requirement.[90] It had always been a tough task for the SAP to criticize the Alliance's rigid fiscal policy since the former Social Democratic government promoted to lower public debt, too. At the same time the surplus goal has broad support within the electorate, and budget deficits are linked to

84 Calmfors, »The Swedish Macroeconomic Policy Framework«, op. cit. (note 1), pp. 603–604.

85 Lindbom, »The Swedish Conservative Party and the Welfare State«, op. cit. (note 74), p. 544.

86 Stefan Svallfors, »A Bedrock of Support? Trends in Welfare State Attitudes in Sweden, 1981–2010« in: *Social Policy and Administration* 45, No. 7 (2011), pp. 806–825, p. 816.

87 Lindbom, »The Swedish Conservative Party and the Welfare State«, op. cit. (note 74), pp. 542–543.

88 Philip Mehrtens, *Staatsschulden und Staatstätigkeit: Zur Transformation der politischen Ökonomie Schwedens*, Frankfurt/New York 2014, pp. 189–272.

89 Torben Iversen / Anne Wren, »Equality, Employment, and Budgetary Restraint: The Trilemma of the Service Economy« in: *World Politics* 50, No. 7 (1998), pp. 507–546.

90 Stefan Löfven / Magdalena Andersson / Per Bolund, »Bättre framtidsutsikter utan åtstramande överskottsmål« in: *Dagens Nyheter*, 3.3.2015, p. 6.

governmental mismanagement, even though the Fiscal Council had repeatedly criticized the Alliance government for not reinvesting; even the question of a reasonable minimum debt level was raised.[91] »The size of the surplus has become a proxy measure of the government's economic management skills.«[92]

The Social Democrats were traditionally identified with economic competence and always owned the issue on the electoral level since it has been measured by the *Swedish National Election Studies*, except in 1991 when they also lost government.[93] But in 2006 they had lost the issue again to the Moderates and never won it back. In combination this explains why the SAP is very careful with changing the surplus target and is maintaining its strategy even though ideologically it would make sense to give it up according to the mentioned trilemma, especially if it is considered that both income equality and unemployment are not satisfying for the party at present. In June 2016 a broad compromise across the blocs was found to lower the surplus target from 1 to 0.33 per cent starting in 2019. At the same time the parties agreed upon a debt level of 35 per cent of GDP, which means that the government has to explain deviations of more than 5 per cent (in both directions!) to parliament.[94] This means that the Swedish version of austerity is continued, although in a milder version. Also there is a chance that, once the targeted debt level is reached, there will be more scope for reinvesting.

5. Conclusion

Until this happens – if this happens at all – the Swedish version of austerity is putting the Social Democrats in a disadvantaged position in the party system, because their policies to fight unemployment are more expensive for the state than the bourgeois ones, which, during their latest time in office, were mainly to strengthen incentives to work by lowering taxes for the employed part of the population and thereby widening the gap between them and recipients of unemployment benefits, which were cut first and then frozen while wages were increasing.[95] ›Equality‹ could be the title of Swedish Social Democratic ideology because it has always been the major goal of the party's policies. While inequality is still comparatively low in Sweden, it is increasing rapidly (see figure 6) also in international comparison. If the SAP wants to stop this development and wants to fulfil their self-imposed objective of having the lowest unemployment rate inside the European Union by 2020, it might need to give up the surplus goal according to the model of the trilemma of the service economy. With the current constellation in parliament they cannot expect to get a majority for that, though. Being de-

91 Mehrtens, *Staatsschulden und Staatstätigkeit*, op. cit. (note 88), pp. 192–201.

92 Brenton / Pierre, »Budget Surplus Goal Experiments in Australia and Sweden«, op. cit. (note 82), p. 13.

93 Henrik Oscarsson / Sören Holmberg, *Svenska väljare*, Stockholm 2016, p. 192.

94 Fredrik Öjemar, »Bred enighet om sänkt överskottsmål« in: *Dagens Industri*, 30.6.2016, http://www.di.se/artiklar/2016/6/30/bred-enighet-om-sankt-overskottsmal/ [3.1.2017].

95 Anders Lindbom, »Political Partisanship and Policy Feedback: The Swedish Welfare State after Eight Years of Center-Right Government« in: Pierre, *The Oxford Handbook of Swedish Politics*, op. cit. (note 1), pp. 37–54, pp. 43–47.

pendent on cooperation across the blocs means also that a deliberate and obvious breach of the surplus target would be a risky strategy with consequences on the electoral level and for the willingness to cooperate in the bourgeois bloc. There might be an attempt though to convince the electorate of a stronger element of discretionary fiscal policy in the election campaign in 2018.

Figure 6: Distribution of disposable income (Gini coefficient)

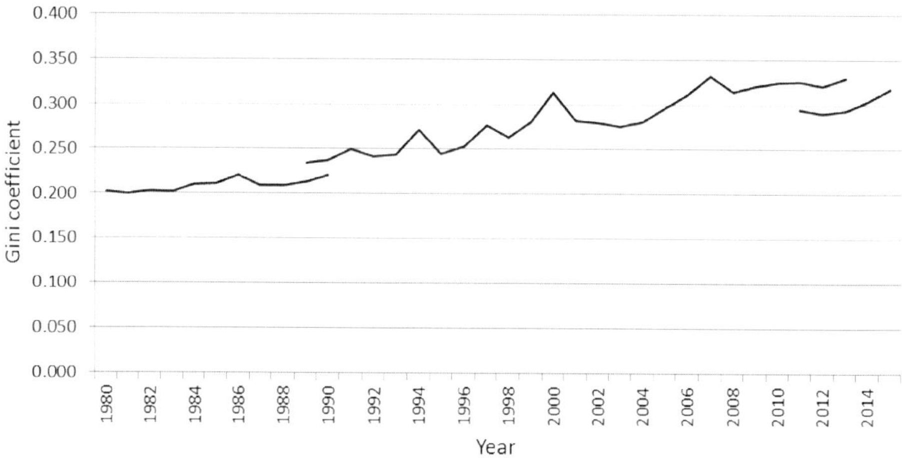

Note: The first disruption is caused by a tax reform, the second one by a change of method.

Source: own illustration based on SCB (Statistics Sweden)

Philipp Adorf

Austerity and the Rise of Populism in European Debtor and Creditor States

2016 proved to be the year of populism. Whether it was the British vote to leave the European Union, the election of Donald Trump, the ability of right-wing populist Norbert Hofer to unite almost 50 per cent of the Austrian electorate behind him, or the fact that a right-wing populist party managed to secure double digit shares of the vote in five different state elections across Germany, populism dominated political discussions in Western democracies for good reason. These actors seemed to lend a voice to significant parts of the electorate that expressed disillusionment and sometimes outright contempt for a political elite deemed as not guided by the concerns of the »common man« but rather primarily interested in securing spoils for themselves and a select few at the very economic top. 2016 thereby saw a surge of indignation that catapulted populist parties and movements to heights previously assumed impossible or at least highly unlikely.

One of the central questions regarding the study of populism is its relationship with crisis, a particularly pertinent topic to assess in light of the recent eurozone and migrant crises and the aforementioned populist groundswell. Work in the comparative field has demonstrated that certain societal crisis constellations – what American historian Lawrence Goodwyn refers to as »populist moments« – are usually a prerequisite for the spawning of populist parties and movements that thrive on a widespread sense of elite failure. At the same time, however, it is of course virtually impossible to quantify »crisis« and use it to predict populist success. The fact that the recent rise of populist actors across a wide variety of EU member states coincided with the union's worst economic crisis and austerity policies nonetheless appears to indicate that the two are to a certain extent interconnected – even in countries that managed to weather the economic storm relatively unscathed. This essay uses a twofold approach concerning a number of political parties that have either emerged in recent years or have seen their electoral fortunes increase rather remarkably during or after the *Great Recession*. It will on the one hand assess to what extent a variety of upstart parties can be classified as populist (of both the left- and right-wing variety) and then at the same time chart how these populist players of various stripes have incorporated the financial and economic crisis and the resulting upheaval into their political programmes. It will analyse how and why populists on the far left succeeded in an environment of almost complete economic depredation, while their counterparts on the far right used the crisis to lambast the political construct of the European Union, an entity presented as distant and uninterested in – if not outright opposed to – the will of the people.

1. Populism, the role of crisis and the distinction between creditor and debtor nations

»Populism« can come in various guises: as an ideology (usually »thin-centred,« which requires the attachment to a more comprehensive one)[1], a mere discourse involving certain »stylistic« elements[2], a manner of organizing political movements[3], or a political style in a political environment that has been »[reduced] to neat us-against-them antagonisms.«[4] At the most basic level, the definition of populism states that those subscribing to its basic tenets see society as being divided into two camps that are engaged in a struggle for power: on the one side the valiant people, on the other the self-serving political elite that is only governing in the interests of a select few (itself, the financial elite, ethnic and sexual minorities). While populists on the left and right may differ about what exactly constitutes »the people« (a class or nationality), »›the people as sovereign‹ […] is the always-present key feature of populism in democracies.«[5]

Failure at the hands of an existing government and political elite to, for example, bring an end to a prolonged economic downturn can provide an opening for populists to exploit, particularly those outside the political class that can present themselves as having wholly clean hands. To what extent a »crisis« truly aids the electoral fortunes of populists is nonetheless not always easy to discern. There is the most basic question of what exactly constitutes a crisis, a concept that is moreover, as mentioned, difficult to quantify. A causal link between an economic crisis, strategies to overcome a crisis such as austerity, and the success of populist parties, particularly those on the right, is less than clear. In their analysis on the success of right-wing parties, Kai Arzheimer and Elisabeth Carter, for example, found a negative correlation between unemployment and votes for the extreme right.[6] This can be explained by the historical negligence concerning economic topics by right-wing populist actors. Traditionally, when socio-economic topics have dominated the national political agenda, right-wing populists have had little to say on the matter outside of perhaps blaming out-groups for the economic downturn. As will subsequently be shown, these parties have nonetheless been able to incorporate the eurozone crisis into their agenda, leading to success in those countries that made it through the *Great Recession* relatively unscathed.

1 Ben Stanley, »The thin ideology of populism« in: *Journal of Political Ideologies* 13, No. 1 (2008), pp. 95–110.

2 See for example Jan Jagers / Stefaan Walgrave, »Populism as political communication style: An empirical study of political parties' discourse in Belgium« in: *European Journal of Political Research* 46, No. 3 (2007), pp. 319–345.

3 Kurt Weyland, »Clarifying a Contested Concept: Populism in the Study of Latin American Politics« in: *Comparative Politics* 34, No. 1 (2001), pp. 1–22.

4 Benjamin Moffitt / Simon Tormey, »Rethinking Populism: Politics, Mediatisation and Political Style« in: *Political Studies* 62, No. 2 (2014), pp. 381–397, p. 387.

5 Daniele Albertazzi / Duncan McDonnell, *Populists in Power*, London/New York 2015, p. 5.

6 Kai Arzheimer / Elisabeth Carter, »Political opportunity structures and right-wing extremist party success« in: *European Journal of Political Research* 45, No. 3 (2006), pp. 419–443, p. 434. Also: Alexandre Afonso, »The far right vote in the European elections: It's not the economy, stupid«, https://alexandreafonso.me/2014/05/26/the-far-right-vote-in-the-european-elections-its-not-the-economy-stupid/ [10.1.2017].

A variety of scholars do contend though that »crisis«, austerity, and populism go hand in hand, with Hanspeter Kriesi even going as far as to refer to right-wing populist movements as »movements of crisis«[7] that mobilize segments of society fearing a personal economic decline, as these parties on their part promise to maintain and defend the status and privileges of their electorate. Ernesto Laclau argues that populism presents itself »both as *subversive* of the existing state of things and as the starting point for a more or less radical *reconstruction* of a new order wherever the previous one has been shaken.«[8] According to him, »some degree of crisis in the old structure is a necessary precondition of populism.«[9] Pablo Iglesias, current secretary-general of Podemos and a scholar himself who has studied the topic of populism extensively, argues in a similar manner that, rather than populism being »an ideology or a collection of policies, it is a way of building politics from an ›outside‹ that expands at moments of crisis.«[10]

Assessments of the topic of »crisis« should by no means be limited to external factors though. Benjamin Moffitt, for example, contends »that rather than just thinking about crisis as a trigger of populism, we should also think about how populism attempts to act as a trigger for crisis,«[11] as »populist actors actively participate in the ›spectacularization of failure‹.«[12] Populists thus have an incentive to play up crises and use them to their own advantage, »provoking [crises] in order to benefit from the ensuing sense of elite incompetence and loss of control.«[13] Therefore, rather than merely focusing on the external existence of a crisis and the role this may play in facilitating populist fortunes, »the performance of crisis should be seen as an essential core feature of populism itself«[14], as these populist actors use a variety of perceived government failures to foster a sense of crisis while pitting those responsible for said crisis against »the people« who bear no responsibility whatsoever.[15]

The financial and eurozone crisis and their consequences were incorporated into the programmes and narratives of populists on both the left and right, albeit in a somewhat different manner. Right-wing populists from creditor countries have taken issue with decreases in welfare spending at home while debtor countries are supposedly treated in

7 Hanspeter Kriesi, »Bewegungen auf der Linken, Bewegungen auf der Rechten: Die Mobilisierung von zwei neuen Typen von sozialen Bewegungen in ihrem politischen Kontext« in: *Swiss Political Science Review* 1, No. 1 (1995), pp. 1–46, p. 16.

8 Ernesto Laclau, *On Populist Reason*, London 2005, p. 177.

9 Laclau, *On Populist Reason*, op. cit. (note 8), p. 177.

10 Quoted in: Elsa García de Blas / Francesco Manetto, »Spain's Podemos party rejects parallels with Trump« in: *El País*, 11.11.2016.

11 Benjamin Moffitt, »How to Perform Crisis: A Model for Understanding the Key Role of Crisis in Contemporary Populism« in: *Government and Opposition* 50, No. 2 (2015), pp. 189–217, p. 190.

12 Moffitt, »How to Perform Crisis«, op. cit. (note 11), p. 190.

13 Ben Stanley, »The Post-Populist Non-Crisis in Poland« in: Hanspeter Kriesi / Takis S. Pappas (eds.), *European Populism in the Shadow of the Great Recession*, Colchester 2015, pp. 251–269, p. 252.

14 Benjamin Moffitt, *The Global Rise of Populism: Performance, Political Style, and Representation*, Stanford 2016, p. 131.

15 Benjamin Moffitt, »How to Perform Crisis«, op. cit. (note 11), pp. 198–202.

a too lenient manner by European and international institutions. In the eyes of these right-wing populists, real and true austerity has never been imposed on the peripheral eurozone countries. The nationalist narrative furthermore presents the crisis as a tale of virtuous and industrious nations that have not lived beyond their means now being required to foot the bill for the spendthrift ways of the periphery that still lacks the desire to enact the necessary reforms (reforms which the very same right-wing populist parties would object to if they were proposed at home [e.g. increasing the retirement age and cutting a wide variety of welfare programmes]). They moreover see European solutions such as Eurobonds as nothing less than a new power grab by – in their eyes illegitimate and unelected – European elites. »Austerity« in its broader context is seen as a tool in the hands of the European political elite to protect their landmark project of the common currency and expand their own reach at the expense of national economic sovereignty.

Left-wing populists on their part object to austerity from a primarily economic perspective as they reject what are seen as neoliberal policies intended to bailout banks and the financial elites at the cost of the average citizen. Objections to further European cooperation are less frequently voiced; as a matter of fact, the opposite quite frequently is the case, as Eurobonds and some sort of European institution for economic governance are regarded as integral to overcoming the financial crisis. At least with regards to Syriza, Giorgos Katsambekis furthermore contends that another distinguishing feature of left-wing populism is that »the elite« is not presented in strictly moralist terms as corrupt or outright evil; instead it is to be opposed primarily on the basis of ideological and political concerns. In this portrayal, members of the elite are not inherently evil but merely support faulty economic policies that have wide-ranging negative repercussions for the broader public.[16] The central focus lies on those policies and their cessation rather than on an abstract »elite« that needs to be removed. This approach can be altered though when a party obtains power and is confronted with the simple fact that the policies in question appear to be set in stone – as has been the case with Syriza, whose populist rhetoric has become significantly more moralist in the wake of the 2015 bailout referendum, which did not yield the desired outcome of less austerity.[17]

Generally speaking, right-wing populism in Europe has received the strongest boost in areas least affected by austerity measures (e.g., Austria, Sweden, Germany), whereas countries such as Spain, Portugal, and the Republic of Ireland have up until now not have had to contend with significant players on the populist right. Voting for the populist radical right therefore is in some sense a luxury one has to be able to afford. Material concerns about job security likely drive voters into the hands of parties that are perhaps not liked but trusted to provide a safe pair of hands during economic downturns, while populist parties on the right have, as already mentioned, traditionally ne-

16 Giorgos Katsambekis, »Radical Left Populism in Contemporary Greece: Syriza's Trajectory from Minoritarian Opposition to Power« in: *Constellations*, 2016, online version of record published before inclusion in an issue, p. 5–8.

17 Katsambekis, »Radical Left Populism in Contemporary Greece«, op. cit. (note 16), p. 13.

glected the economic conflict dimension altogether.[18] One relevant side-effect of the recent economic crisis is the fact that it has forced virtually all of these parties to address this issue area in a more comprehensive manner, not infrequently incorporating these economic questions into their more encompassing cultural narrative.[19] In that sense, then, right-wing populist actors may have indirectly profited from the crisis because it compelled them to address shortcomings in their programmatic foundations whose rectification now puts them in a position to present a more comprehensive programmatic profile to the electorate (see for example the Front National's increased emphasis on socio-economic topics).

A comparison between the recent economic development of different EU member states whose partisan shifts (bar Germany's) are assessed over the following pages serves to illustrate how these countries have been affected by the *Great Recession* and its aftermath. The following table shows the evolution in GDP per capita in Purchasing Power Standard (PPS) of a number of EU member states in relation to the GDP per capita in PPS for the entire European Union[20] during the 2007 through 2015 period with a 2007 base value of 100 for each country. As we can see, Germany has fared the best in this particular group, slightly improving its GDP per capita in PPS vis-à-vis the EU-28 by roughly 7 per cent over the nine-year period. France's economy has remained largely stagnant, while Greece and Spain have seen the strongest downturns. Italy's slow but steady decline is also reflected in the table with its 2015 GDP per capita in PPS standing at 90 per cent of its 2007 value (once again in relation to the entire EU). The past decade has also proven to be a mediocre economic period for the Netherlands. As will be illustrated over the coming pages, this diverging economic development has also had different effects on the respective party systems.

18 Elisabeth Ivarsflaten, »The vulnerable populist right parties: No economic realignment fuelling their electoral success« in: *European Journal of Political Research* 44, No. 3 (2005), pp. 465–492. The author contends that »populist right parties in Western Europe are limited by or vulnerable to the salience of the economic dimension.«

19 Alexandre Afonso / Line Rennwald, »The Changing Welfare State Agenda of Populist Radical Right Parties in Europe« in: Philip Manow / Bruno Palier (eds.), *Electoral Realignments in Welfare State Transformations in Europe*, New York 2016.

20 The value of the EU-27 or subsequently 28 is a constant 100.

Table 1: GDP per capita in PPS, 2007–2015. 2007 base value equalling 100[21]

	2007	*2008*	*2009*	*2010*	*2011*	*2012*	*2013*	*2014*	*2015*
France	100	99	100	101	101	100	101	100	99
Germany	100	101	99	103	106	106	106	108	107
Greece	100	102	102	95	84	80	80	79	77
Italy	100	100	99	98	97	96	93	91	90
Netherlands	100	101	100	98	98	96	96	96	94
Spain	100	98	98	94	91	89	88	88	89

Source: own illustration based on Eurostat

2. Syriza

Populism has played a central role in Greece's political discourse for decades now, having been employed by mainstream parties both on the left and right (with Takis S. Pappas going so far as to call it a »populist democracy« for example), which, along with a general distrust towards the state as an entity, laid the groundwork for a left-wing populist party like Syriza to unify forces on the radical left and eventually take PASOK's place within the party system (by employing a rhetoric and ideology not dissimilar to the brand of populism used by Andreas Papandreou's PASOK during the 1980s).[22] The two main centrist parties suffered an unheard of implosion at the ballot box over the course of a single decade (although New Democracy has recovered as of late) as Syriza rose to become the strongest party in the country in the two 2015 elections:

21 Eurostat, *GDP per capita in PPS*, http://ec.europa.eu/eurostat/tgm/table.do?tab=table&plugin=1&language=en&pcode=tec00114 [20.8.2016].

22 Takis S. Pappas, »Populist Democracies: Post-Authoritarian Greece and Post-Communist Hungary« in: *Government and Opposition* 29, No. 1 (2014), pp. 1–23; Yannis Stavrakakis / Giorgos Katsambekis, »Left-wing populism in the European periphery: the case of SYRIZA« in: *Journal of Political Ideologies* 19, No. 2 (2014), pp. 119–142, p. 124.

Figure 1: Percentage share of the vote in Greek parliamentary elections, 2004–2015

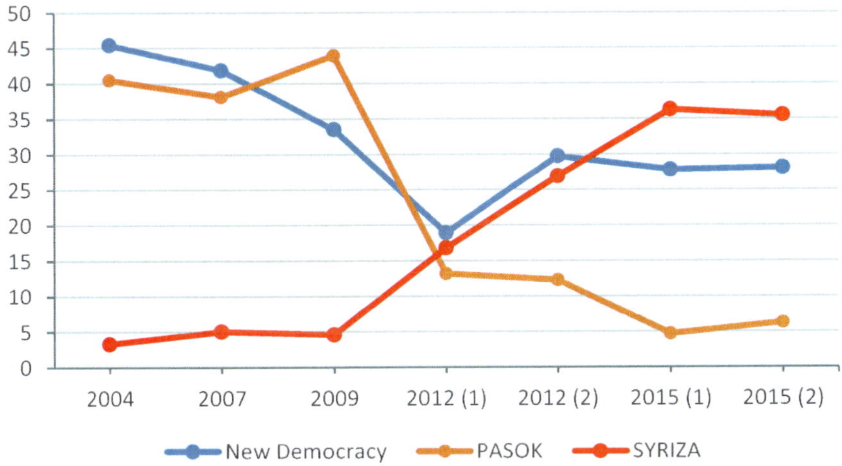

Source: own illustration based on ypes.gr

Contrary to Podemos, which has been more open to using the populist label for itself from the very beginning, Syriza's journey to populism took considerably longer. After the party's founding as an alliance in 2004, Syriza and the largest member within this alliance of the left (Synaspismos) still espoused something that Giorgios Katsambekis has dubbed »minoritarian populism.«[23] The party primarily targeted its appeals by employing the epithets of »the youth«, »movements«, or »society« when referring to protests against government policies.[24] Presenting itself as »a party of the young people«, Syriza did indeed make use of an *us-vs.-them* narrative with the intention of driving up polarization in society as populists regularly do, doing so however by primarily presenting the youth as an inter-class group whose future had been robbed of them by the establishment rather than presenting the entirety of the Greek people as the victims of the political and financial elite.[25] At this point, Syriza still »[failed] to establish an effective dialectic of representation between particularity [›the youth‹] and universality [›the people‹].«[26] Paris Aslanidis and Nikos Marantzidis also note that it took the emergence of Greece's counterparts to the Spanish »indignados« as a result of the eurozone crisis to bring about a change in Syriza's political appeals, as the party »consciously revamped its political rhetoric to align itself closely with the populist zeitgeist of the indignados.«[27] These *aganaktismenoi* saw the crisis in deeply populist terms as

23 Katsambekis, »Radical Left Populism in Contemporary Greece«, op. cit. (note 16).
24 Stavrakakis / Katsambekis, »Left-wing populism in the European periphery«, op. cit. (note 22), p. 127.
25 Katsambekis, »Radical Left Populism in Contemporary Greece«, op. cit. (note 16), p. 5.
26 Katsambekis, »Radical Left Populism in Contemporary Greece«, op. cit. (note 16), p. 5.
27 Paris Aslanidis / Nikos Marantzidis, »The Impact of the Greek Indignados on Greek Politics« in: *Southeastern Europe* 40, No. 2 (2016), pp. 125–257, p. 149.

they did any sort of resolution to it. Greece's disastrous downturn had in their eyes been caused by a political elite that had betrayed the people; the antidote was to be a »real democracy« in the form of more direct democratic participation of the people.[28]

Having failed to fully embrace a populist conception of society for the first few years of its existence, the Grand Coalition between PASOK and New Democracy formed by Lucas Papademos in late 2011 to implement more welfare cuts (a coalition which also included the right-wing populist *Popular Orthodox Rally* [LAOS]) moreover provided Syriza with an opportunity to cast off its »proto-populism« and instead adopt a more traditional populist narrative.[29] Syriza had finally been given the opportunity to become the sole non-extremist voice of Greeks opposed to the »memorandum« imposed by the troika. Subsequently, Tsipras and media institutions affiliated with the party began to increasingly invoke »the people« in stories and on the campaign trail in 2012, whereas all those who had backed austerity measures received the label of »the others.«[30] Now the party was no longer merely appealing to the young or other specific groups but instead sought to unite all segments of society that had been harmed by austerity measures under a single banner of *the people*, whose banner would and could only be carried by Syriza and Tsipras. As one member of Syriza's political secretariat put it, the party now addressed »[a]ll those who are affected by the economic crisis. The lower middle class is also hit by the crisis. Even industrialists are hit by the crisis.«[31] Because the crisis had thoroughly affected virtually every part of Greek society, »›the people‹ takes a very broad meaning. It goes much beyond the people of the left.«[32]

The party's 2012 election manifesto made extensive use of the antagonistic narrative between the people and the elite, the latter embodied by PASOK and New Democracy along with the troika. »They decided without us, we move on without them« was one rallying cry in the document, calling on the people to support a programme that would »overthrow the rotten two-party political system and create alternative governance structures, where the people will be a protagonist.«[33] Another central enemy could be found in both Berlin and Brussels, as Tsipras lambasted Angela Merkel as a sinister figure who, »in alliance with a neoliberal bureaucratic elite in Brussels, treat social solidarity and human dignity as economic distortions and national sovereignty as a nuisance.«[34] Key terms like the reference to a »bureaucratic elite« in the EU capital

28 Katsambekis, »Radical Left Populism in Contemporary Greece«, op. cit. (note 16), p. 2.
29 Katsambekis, »Radical Left Populism in Contemporary Greece«, op. cit. (note 16), p. 5.
30 Stavrakakis / Katsambekis, »Left-wing populism in the European periphery«, op. cit. (note 22), pp. 127–133.
31 Quoted in: Myrto Tsakatika, »SYRIZA's Electoral Rise in Greece: Protest, Trust and the Art of Political Manipulation« in: *South European Society and Politics*, published online October 25, 2016, pp. 1–22, p. 10.
32 Quoted in: Tsakatika, »SYRIZA's Electoral Rise in Greece«, op. cit. (note 31), p. 10.
33 Quoted in: Katsambekis, »Radical Left Populism in Contemporary Greece«, op. cit. (note 16), p. 8.
34 Alexis Tsipras, *The Europe we want*, 13.1.2014, http://www.syriza.gr/article/THE-EUROPE-WE-WANT---article-by-Alexis-Tsipras-in-the-New-Europe-magazine1.html#.V6dKKa3D7l8 [10.1.2017].

along with the defence of national sovereignty indicate a certain ideological overlap with populist counterparts on the right as well. This new embrace of populism paid off handsomely, as Syriza was able to jump from 4.6 per cent in the 2009 elections to 26.9 per cent in the second Greek parliamentary election of 2012 (see figure 1). By the time of the July 2015 bailout referendum, Tsipras and his party had completely embraced the populist narrative of representing *the people* against *the* elites, calling the referendum a »people's verdict«[35] that was opposed by European finance ministers who on their part »attempted to blackmail the will of the Greek people and to hinder democratic processes«[36], employing the populist narrative that direct democracy trumps all other forms. Two months after the referendum, Tsipras once again justified his position and ultimate acceptance of a new bailout at a Syriza party conference. Rather than specifically being about the proposed terms of a new memorandum, the Greek vote was now portrayed as something more extensive, more populist. Interpreting the »no« vote, Tsipras argued, »[i]t was a ›no‹ to a regime that is not wanted by the people anymore; and the elites will not be able to restore it.«[37] Moreover it was also »a no to dependency, guardianship, limitations to national sovereignty, devaluation of popular sovereignty.«[38] In a similar vein, an editorial in the leftist newspaper *I Avgi* interpreted Syriza's victory in the January 2015 elections as a clear choice by »our people« against »the memorandum policies«, as »[t]he people said ›no‹ to the austerity [...] imposed by Samaras.«[39]

What does the future hold for anti-austerity parties in Greece? Spyros Plakoudas makes the case that the failure of the Syriza-ANEL government to live up to its anti-austerity promises means that the country's anti-memorandum movement has passed its heyday, the sole remaining opponents being extremist parties like Golden Dawn.[40] All other parties have begrudgingly accepted the simple fact that the EU is calling the shots on the topic and that Greece can either remain a member of the eurozone or discard austerity policies – both are not possible. Polls as of the spring of 2017 reflect this development, as Greek voters appear to have migrated back into the New Democracy camp (polling at around 35 per cent of the vote, up from 28 per cent in the last elec-

35 Alexis Tsipras, *Prime Minister Alexis Tsipras' message*, 1.7.2015, http://www.primeminister.gov.gr/english/2015/07/01/prime-minister-alexis-tsipras-message/ [10.1.2017].

36 Alexis Tsipras, *Prime Minister Alexis Tsipras' statement on the latest developments*, 28.6.2015, http://primeminister.gr/english/2015/06/28/prime-minister-alexis-tsipras-statement-concerning-on-the-latest-developments/ [10.1.2017].

37 Alexis Tsipras, *Alexis Tsipras speech at the nationwide SYRIZA conference*, 29.8.2015, http://www.syriza.gr/article/Alexis-Tsipras-speech-at-the-nationwide-SYRIZA-conference-.html#.V6dU5q3D7l8_[10.1.2017].

38 Tsipras, *Alexis Tsipras speech at the nationwide SYRIZA conference*, op. cit. (note 37).

39 Analyze Greece, *The editorial of the newspaper »I Avgi«: A historic victory in Greece, a message to Europe*, 26.2.2015, http://www.analyzegreece.gr/topics/elections-250102015/item/83-the-editorial-of-the-newspaper-i-avgi-a-historic-victory-in-greece-a-message-to-europe. [10.1.2017].

40 Spyros Plakoudas, »The debt crisis and Greece's changing political discourse«, in: *Byzantine and Modern Greek Studies* 40, No. 2 (2016), pp. 207–314, p. 314.

tion) with Syriza's support significantly lower than the 35.5 per cent it won in the September 2015 elections (around 20 to 23 per cent).[41]

3. Podemos

Just as has been the case in Greece, the turmoil of the economic crisis seems to have brought about, or at least expedited, major changes in Spain's political party system, namely the notable shrinkage of the main centre-left and centre-right parties, whose share of the popular vote in parliamentary elections had dropped from a record-high of around 84 per cent in 2008 to a little over 50 per cent in 2015 before recovering to around 56 per cent in the most recent election in June of 2016.

Figure 2: Combined share of the popular vote in Spanish parliamentary elections by the main centre-right parties (Union of the Democratic Centre 1977/1979, People's Alliance 1982/1986, Popular Party 1989 onwards) and Spanish Socialist Workers' Party (PSOE) since the restoration of democracy in Spain, 1977–2016

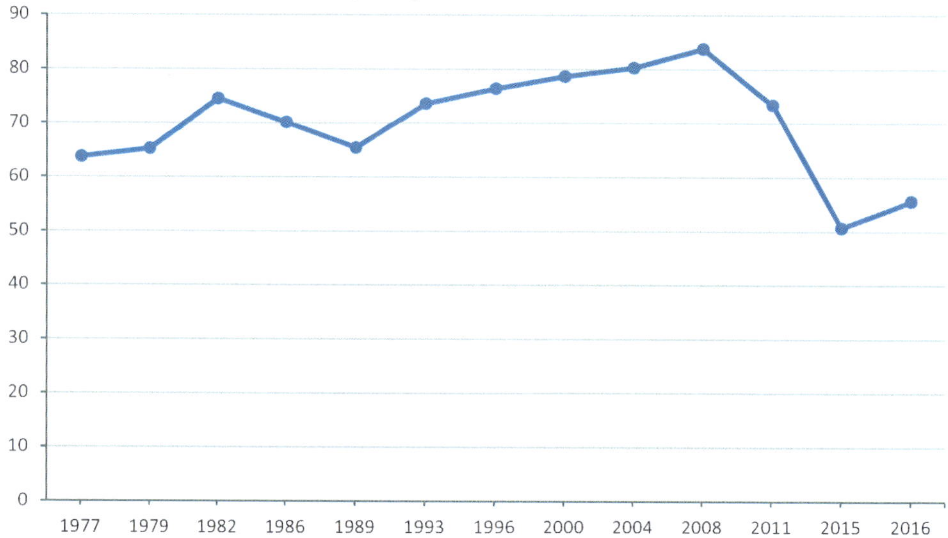

Source: own illustration based on infoelectoral.mir.es

In the wake of substantial spending cuts by the Socialist government, youth-led protests arose across Spain in 2011 (the 15-M Movement, also known more widely as the *indignados*), providing the foundation for the formation of Podemos (We can). Rather than focusing on extra-parliamentary efforts to bring about political change, the party's leadership cadre looked at the »inclusionary populism« of Latin America as

41 Electograph, *Polls, Greece*, 15.5.2017, http://www.electograph.com/search/label/Greece [15.5.2017].

an example to be emulated. These were examples that Podemos' leaders had had first-hand experiences with: Pablo Iglesias (the party's current secretary-general) had worked as an advisor to Hugo Chavez, while Íñigo Errejón (the party's current political secretary and in some sense its chief ideological theorist) had written his dissertation on the path to power of Evo Morales' Movement for Socialism.[42] Speaking in Bolivia in 2014, Pablo Iglesias paid homage to his party's Latin American roots, telling his audience that »the genealogy – the DNA – of Podemos [is] directly connected to Bolivia in a way that's closer than many can imagine.«[43]

As the existing far left offered few indications of wanting to change its rigid, rather ideologically orthodox ways[44], and as Podemos' leading figures saw themselves as the spearheads of an all-encompassing political movement that intended to represent the *people* and not just a narrow segment of the electorate[45], the only alternative left was to establish a new party in January of 2014. According to Errejón, the demise of the »left« in Spain led to certain parts of it »fight[ing] for the truth of the word ›left‹« as in »we're the true left.«[46] Errejón always rejected that path for Podemos: »[F]rom the beginning we said ›you can keep it, we hand it over to you. We're interested in constructing a people, not in constructing the left‹.«[47]

While nonetheless undoubtedly an ideologically leftist party (something neither Iglesias nor Errejón have ever sought to hide), the party has actually undergone a process of moderation since its early days. The close ties between Podemos and Syriza (in conjunction with the latter's disastrous handling of the debt negotiations) were seen as an obstacle to appealing to more moderate leftist voters in Spain. While Podemos leader Pablo Iglesias still joined Alexis Tsipras on the campaign trail ahead of the January 2015 Greek elections, telling supporters »Syriza, Podemos – venceremos [we will win] «, the relationship between the two leaders cooled significantly afterwards. By the time of the 2015 Spanish general election in December, the party's platform looked substantially different from previous incarnations and had little in common with the more radical proposals espoused by Syriza. Proposals for a universal minimum wage for all citizens, unilateral action against Spain's public debt, and the demand for converting

42 John B. Judis, *The Populist Explosion: How the Great Recession Transformed American and European Politics*, New York 2016, p. 122.

43 Quoted in: Bécquer Seguín, »Podemos's Latin American Roots« in: *Jacobin Magazine*, 27.3.2015, https://www.jacobinmag.com/2015/03/podemos-spain-iglesias-morales-chavez/ [3.5.2016].

44 Pablo Iglesias, »Understanding Podemos« in: *New Left Review* 93 (2015), pp. 8–22, p. 15. Iglesias laments the »stubborn conservatism of the IU [United Left] leaders, incapable of taking on other styles or perspectives.«

45 Concerning Iglesias' aspirations, see his comments in a debate with IU politician Alberto Garzón: »I don't want to be the 20 or 15 per cent. I don't want my biggest political aspiration to be taking three regional ministries from the Socialist Party. I don't want to be a ›hinge‹, I want to win.« Quoted in: Luke Stobart, »Understanding Podemos (2/3): Radical populism« in: *Left Flank*, 14.11.2014, http://left-flank.org/2014/11/14/understanding-podemos-23-radical-populism/#sthash.57mur4Rm.dpuf [10.1.2017].

46 Íñigo Errejón / Chantal Mouffe, *Podemos: In the Name of the People*, London 2016, p. 120.

47 Errejón / Mouffe, *Podemos*, op. cit. (note 46), p. 120.

the ECB into a »democratic institution« were all dropped in favour of more moderate positions. Rather than a universal income, Podemos now merely called for a »subsidy« for »all those people without an income.«[48] Concerning the ECB, the party now proposed adjusting the central bank's statutes to also include »the maintenance of an adequate level of economic activity and also job creation.«[49] And rather than striking all »illegitimate debt« from the record, »coordinated« action with European partners as part of a European conference was now the desired path to restructure debt within the eurozone.[50]

In terms of its ideological worldview, Podemos has been influenced by the writings of both the late Ernesto Laclau and his wife Chantal Mouffe, whose interpretations of populism present it as a central component of the way politics is structured and a central tool to establish a »radical democracy« rather than a threat to it.[51] In his seminal work *On Populist Reason*, Laclau, for example, lamented that populism had »not only been demoted; it has also been denigrated.«[52] Building upon Laclau and Mouffe's analysis of populism, Podemos has therefore sought to essentially cleanse the term of »populism« within Spain's domestic context from its less savoury connotations, instead presenting the party's interpretations and usage of populist means as a vital component in their attempts to democratize society and return political power to the hands of the people, representing a European example of an »inclusionary populism« that has its roots in Latin America.[53] Differing approaches to populism are also one of the reasons why Podemos' leadership was reluctant to seek change through established leftist parties. Germán Cano, member of Podemos' citizens' council and in charge of the party's relationship with Argentina, Uruguay, and Chile, argues his party sees »populism as a space that has been undervalued and underestimated as much by the liberal tradition as by the Marxist tradition, which hasn't understood that the social composition doesn't respond to fixed and already constituted identities.«[54] Íñigo Errejón in particular has made the case that, in order to be successful, Podemos had to broaden its appeal through using the *pueblo-* or *gente-* (the people) against the *casta-* (the caste of elites) divide rather than the traditional left/right cleavage. In his words, Podemos' decision to »[offer] the dichotomies ›democracy/oligarchy‹, ›citizenship/caste‹ or even ›new/old‹ instead [...] established new borders to isolate elites and propose a new identifica-

48 Quoted in: Francesco Manetto, »Podemos abandons most radical proposals in economic program« in: *El Pais*, 28.11.2014, http://elpais.com/elpais/2014/11/28/inenglish/1417170085_999647.html [10.1.2017].

49 Podemos, *Queremos, Sabemos, Podemos – A programme to change our country*, 2015, pp. 54–55.

50 Podemos, *Queremos, Sabemos, Podemos*, op. cit. (note 49), pp. 55–56.

51 Judis, *The Populist Explosion*, op. cit. (note 42), p. 123.

52 Laclau, *On Populist Reason*, op. cit. (note 8), p. 19.

53 »Podemos: the ambiguous promises of left-wing populism in contemporary Spain« in: *Journal of Political Ideologies* 21, No. 2 (2016), pp. 99–120.

54 Quoted in Seguín, »Podemos's Latin American Roots«, op. cit. (note 43).

tion to better position ourselves in relation to them.«[55] In the eyes of Errejón this new dichotomy is central to Podemos' success because it creates a political environment that the »old regime« is largely inexperienced in. As he notes, »[w]ith the left-right frontier, the cards are comfortably dealt by the traditional actors, who place themselves at the centre of the distribution of positions.«[56] The new »citizenry-casta« (or people v. anti-people, us vs. them) division of society has the consequence that the »casta« is »suddenly forced to play on a very difficult terrain«[57]; the elite, which had previously been able to place »themselves at the centre-right/centre-left« as challengers were confined to »the margins«, is in this new frontier »confused« and »out of their comfort zone.«[58] In a similar vein, party leader Pablo Iglesias contends that »he who sets the rules of the game is highly tipped to win«[59], underscoring the centrality of using your own definitions of political cleavages and terms in the fight for political power – a fight whose future outcome may very well make Podemos a model to follow for other populist actors on the left.

4. Five Star Movement

Italy's economic demise has been more gradual but also more enduring than, for example, that of Spain. With the demise of Silvio Berlusconi and his *Forza Italia*, the primary challenger to the centre-left Democratic Party has turned out to be a populist party that defies easy classification: the *Movimento 5 Stelle* (M5S). The party's roots predate the economic crisis, but it is now »progressively filling the ›void‹ left by the traditional parties«[60] – a void that began to widen significantly after the ascent of technocrat Mario Monti to the office of prime minister in late 2011 and with the subsequent grand coalition of the Letta government that received the support of both the major centre-right (»People of Freedom«) and left parties (Democratic Party). In the 2013 Italian parliamentary election, the M5S received 25.5 per cent of the vote, the largest share of any single party. In municipal elections in 2016, the party scored electoral wins in a number of mayoral contests, obtaining the office in Rome and the industrial hub of Turin, capturing both cities from the Democratic Party in the process. Current polls indicate a neck-and-neck race for first place between the centre-left Democratic Party and the M5S.[61]

55 Íñigo Errejón, »¿Qué es ›Podemos‹?« in: *Le Monde Diplomatique*, 07.2014, http://www.monde-diplomatique.es/?url=articulo/0000856412872168186811102294251000/?articulo=8c640f81-5ccc-4723-911e-71e45da1deca Translation found at: http://links.org.au/node/3969 [4.7.2017].

56 Errejón / Mouffe, *Podemos*, op. cit. (note 46), p. 122.

57 Errejón / Mouffe, *Podemos*, op. cit. (note 46), p. 122.

58 Errejón / Mouffe, *Podemos*, op. cit. (note 46), p. 121.

59 Pablo Iglesias, *Politics in a Time of Crisis: Podemos and the Future of Democracy*, London 2015, p. 103.

60 Fabio Bordignon / Luigi Ceccarini, »Five Stars and a Cricket. Beppe Grillo Shakes Italian Politics« in: *South European Society and Politics* 18, No. 4 (2013), pp. 427–449, p. 428.

61 Electograph, *Polls, Italy*, http://www.electograph.com/search/label/Italy [12.12.2016].

The M5S is difficult to categorize in the context of a left-right divide, as it is a party that sees itself as one without »ideologies, but ideas«[62] instead. The party's co-founder Beppe Grillo shares a sentiment popular among many other populists about the old left-right political divide having become obsolete: »Right and Left do not exist. What exists is a business group. Italy is its business.«[63] One unifying factor has nonetheless proven to be a sense of dissatisfaction with domestic and European political elites and the argument that they are acting in contravention of the interests of the people, indicating a populist understanding of society standing at the heart of the party. Candidates' political inexperience is praised, as they are presented as »people like you. They are your mirror, democracy back to front.«[64] The current state of the political system and democracy along with the political actors seen as responsible for its pitiful state are scolded in no uncertain terms: »Italy is not a democracy, the citizen is not represented in parliament. […] Parliament is elected by the mafia, by the freemason system, by the leadership of the parties, not by the citizens.«[65] Opposition to the eurozone crisis management is moreover central to the party's self-identity. An entry ahead of the 2014 European elections on Beppe Grillo's blog, for example, lamented that »Europe is not a bank, yet we are in effect governed by the ECB« while calling for a Europe in which »a country in need – such as Greece – is not left to die to save the balance sheets of German and French banks.«[66] Speaking in the Italian senate, M5S-senator Vito Crimi criticized the »hegemony of the banks and finance« within the eurozone, adding that it had been turned »into a banking union rather than a union of peoples.«[67] The senator finished his speech with a populist rallying cry of »power to the people and not the banks!«[68]

M5S-voters tend to reflect the party's diverse set of ideas rather than ideologies. While around half (48 per cent) of the party's voters self-identified as left/centre-left shortly after the party's establishment in 2010, whereas a mere 11 per cent considered themselves to be part of the right/centre-right, those respective shares stood at 32 and 28 per cent respectively in May of 2012.[69] On specific issues, a variety of both left and right positions can be found among M5S-voters, as they are simultaneously more like-

62 Political communique on beppegrillo.it, quoted in Bordignon / Ceccarini, »Five Stars and a Cricket«, op. cit. (note 60), p. 436.

63 Beppe Grillo, *Political Press Release number 10*, 28.4.2008, http://www.beppegrillo.it/en/2008/04/political_press_release_number_9.html [12.1.2017].

64 Grillo quoted in: Bordignon / Ceccarini, »Five Stars and a Cricket«, op. cit. (note 60), p. 435.

65 Beppe Grillo, *We are alive! We are alive! We are alive!*, 27.9.2010, http://www.beppegrillo.it/en/2010/09/we_are_alive_we_are_alive_we_a.html [12.1.2017].

66 Il Blog di Beppe Grillo, *Il M5S alle elezioni europee*, 16.10.2013, http://www.beppegrillo.it/2013/10/il_m5s_alle_elezioni_europee.html [15.12.2016].

67 Il Blog di Beppe Grillo, *Referendum sull'euro in Italia: la proposta M5S in Senato*, 8.7.2015, http://www.beppegrillo.it/2015/07/referendum_sulleuro_in_italia_la_proposta_m5s_in_senato.html [15.12.2016].

68 Il Blog di Beppe Grillo, *Referendum sull'euro in Italia*, op. cit. (note 67).

69 Luigi Ceccarini / Fabio Bordignon, »The five stars continue to shine: the consolidation of Grillo's ›movement party‹ in Italy« in: *Contemporary Italian Politics* 8, No. 2 (2016), pp. 131–159, p. 143.

ly than Italians in general to support Italy's exit from the eurozone as well as gay marriage, a universal basic income, and the right for the children of immigrants to hold Italian citizenship.[70] The ability of the party to attract voters from radically different ideological backgrounds and to unite them within a single political movement has led some scholars to therefore attach the label of a »catch-all (anti-party) party«[71] to it. The voting behaviour of the party in the European Parliament (and the fact that it joined the same parliamentary group as UKIP and the Sweden Democrats) is a testament to the eclectic mix of issue positions found within the party's ranks – as was the surprising announcement in January of 2017 that the party intended to change parliamentary groups, hoping to move from one of the most eurosceptic to one of the most pro-European factions. While this manoeuvre was ultimately stopped by members of the liberal ALDE faction, voting records from the Five Star Movement's MEPs indicate strong disagreements with its other partners within the eurosceptic *Europe of Freedom and Direct Democracy* (EFDD) parliamentary group. Rather than share a common platform, Grillo's group has seen the strongest overlap with the *United Left-Nordic Green Left* (GUE/NGL) and *Greens/European Free Alliance* groups.[72] Recent data that assessed the voting patterns on over 4,700 policy items between 2014 and 2016, for example, illustrated that M5S MEPs voted with GUE/NGL and the Greens 74 and 73 per cent of the time respectively, compared to just 27 per cent with UKIP.[73] Only on the topic of the euro have EFDD and M5S MEPs shared a somewhat similar stance.[74]

Ultimately data like these indicate the central role the euro and not European integration in general play in the M5S's objections to the broader European project. This behaviour in Brussels and Strasbourg reflects the disillusionment the Italian public has shown on the topic of the common currency. The Eurobarometer's 2015 autumn data showed a gap of twelve points between the share of Italians who felt the euro was a »good thing« for their country and the eurozone average (49 and 61 per cent, respectively).[75] Data from two years earlier (autumn 2013) still showed a substantially narrower gap of just five points (52 per cent in Italy, 57 per cent across the eurozone)[76], while data from 2012 illustrated that Italians essentially had a no more negative attitude towards the common currency than eurozone citizens in general (»good thing«:

70 Ceccarini / Bordignon, »The five stars continue to shine«, op. cit. (note 69), p. 150.

71 Ceccarini / Bordignon, »The five stars continue to shine«, op. cit. (note 69), p. 154.

72 Paolo Franzosi / Francesco Marone / Eugenio Salvati, »Populism and Euroscepticism in the Italian Five Star Movement« in: The International Spectator 50, No. 2 (2015), pp. 109–124, pp. 119–120.

73 Votewatch Europe, *Anti-euro Italian opposition party to join ALDE?*, 8.1.2017, http://www.votewatch.eu/blog/anti-euro-italian-opposition-party-to-join-alde/ [9.1.2017].

74 Franzosi / Marone / Salvati, »Populism and Euroscepticism in the Italian Five Star Movement«, op. cit. (note 72), p. 120.

75 European Commission – Economic and Financial Affairs, *Eurobarometer: Rising overall support for the single currency in the euro area*, 11.11.2015, http://ec.europa.eu/economy_finance/articles/euro/2015-11-06-eurobarometer_en.htm [15.12.2016].

76 European Commission, Directorate-General for Economic and Financial Affairs, *Flash Eurobarometer 386*, 2013, p. 9.

54 per cent in Italy, 55 per cent eurozone).[77] Eurobarometer data from the spring of 2016 also showed that in only one other eurozone member state was support for the common currency and monetary union lower than in Italy. While 54 per cent of Italians favoured a European economic and monetary union with a single currency, so did 53 per cent of Cypriots (with an EU-28 average of 55 per cent). Even in the worst crisis-hit countries of Greece (62 per cent), Spain (68 per cent), and Portugal (69 per cent) support for the euro was substantially higher.[78]

5. Front National

The Front National can be seen as the poster child of the changes many parties of the populist radical right have undergone on economic topics. During the 1980s, former leader Jean-Marie Le Pen still espoused the values of the anti-tax Poujadist movement of the 1950s, styling himself as a leader in the ideological mould of Thatcher or Reagan.[79] Then President Mitterrand's policies were decried by Le Pen as a »Marxist revolution« while objecting to a »dictatorial imposition of tax by an insolent administration« that he likened to a »system of fiscal inquisition comparable to the Gestapo.«[80] Eventually his steadfast anti-leftist position on these topics somewhat mellowed though, allowing Le Pen to make significant inroads into the working class in the 1990s. In the first round of the 1995 French presidential election, for example, Le Pen came in first among skilled and unskilled manual labourers, obtaining 21 per cent of their vote.[81] His daughter Marine has even more so recognized the potential electoral windfall that an alteration of the party's programmatic foundations on economic matters and an increased emphasis on them can entail (while simultaneously presenting a more electable, outwardly moderate face to the public), as she has cast herself as a working class heroine all the while incessantly railing against the main centre-right and centre-left parties, »who represent the interests of financial markets and the banks.«[82] Her self-described focus, on the other hand, is to act in the interests of the »farmers, unemployed, workers, pensioners […] the forgotten, invisible majority, crushed by a

77 European Commission, Directorate-General for Economic and Financial Affairs, *Flash Eurobarometer 362*, 2012, p. 8.

78 European Commission, Directorate-General for Communication, *Standard Eurobarometer 85*, Spring 2016, p. 33.

79 Hans-Georg Betz / Susi Meret, »Right-wing populist parties and the working-class vote: what have you done for me lately?« in: Jens Rydgren (ed.), *Class Politics and the Radical Right*, Milton Park/New York 2013, pp. 107–121, p. 117.

80 Quoted in: J. G. Shields, *The Extreme Right in France: From Pétain to Le Pen*, Abingdon 2007, p. 206.

81 Nonna Mayer, »From Jean-Marie Le Pen to Marine Le Pen: Electoral Change on the Far Right« in: *Parliamentary Affairs* 66, No. 1 (2013), pp. 160–178, p. 171.

82 Marine Le Pen quoted in: Joseph Bamat, »Far-right candidate attacks ›deadly‹ globalisation, immigration« in: *France* 24, 3.6.2012, http://www.france24.com/en/20120219-france-far-right-candidate-french-presidential-election-marine-le-pen-lille-convention-sarkozy [10.1.2017].

financial system gone mad.«[83] As part of this, the Front National has completely embraced protectionist measures and the supposedly benevolent role the state can play in protecting the »forgotten«, a development not dissimilar to what has transpired on the other side of the Atlantic.

Overall, Marine Le Pen regards the French state as the sole entity capable of protecting the French people in the face of a globalist onslaught, as other countries are able to manufacture goods at a far more competitive price. As Le Pen put it in 2011, »[a]t a time when the crisis and globalization rage, when everything collapses, there is still the state.«[84] A rebirth of the French industrial sector therefore requires a »strong state« that is »capable of imposing its authority on the forces of money.«[85] Only a strong state, which has in recent decades been weakened »from above and from below«, can act as the »spearhead« for the country's »reindustrialization and national recovery.«[86] The European Union's role in all of this is perceived as wholly negative (seen as the actor that has weakened the French state from above), being described in the 2012 programme as a »Trojan horse for ultraliberal globalization«, with the union's treaties imposing a »dogma of free and undistorted competition«[87] that prevents state aid to national companies solely for ideological reasons. Recent crises, both of the financial and migrant variety, have provided Le Pen and her party with plenty of ammunition to be used against the EU, as she has attacked the union as »a prison of peoples«, in which »[m]ember nations no longer determine their own budgets« and »are called upon to open their borders against their will.«[88]

Applying the tried and tested narrative of the old left-right divide having become obsolete, Marine Le Pen has pursued a strategy of turning the party into a home for an electorate not just located at the fringes of the political spectrum, attempting to normalize the FN's image while still nonetheless retaining some of its ideological distinguishing features that differentiate it from the rest of the French party system in order to attract voters dissatisfied with the status quo.[89] A central part of this scheme have been attempts to cleanse the party of her father's more racist legacy, embarking on a course of mainstreaming with the intention of placing the FN in a position to actually

83 Quoted in: Michel Wieviorka, »The Front National's new clothes« in: *Open Democracy*, 15.4.2013, https://www.opendemocracy.net/michel-wieviorka/front-national%e2%80%99s-new-clothes [10.1.2017].

84 Quoted in »Front National: Marine Le Pen défend un Etat fort«, in: *Le Parisien*, 16.1.2011, http://www.leparisien.fr/election-presidentielle-2012/front-national-marine-le-pen-defend-un-etat-fort-16-01-2011-1229689.php [10.2.2017].

85 Front National, *Notre Projet. Programme Politique du Front National*, 2012, p. 5.

86 Front National, *Notre Projet*, op. cit. (note 85), p. 5.

87 Front National, *Notre Projet*, op. cit. (note 85), p. 5.

88 Marine Le Pen, »After Brexit, the People's Spring Is Inevitable« in: *New York Times*, 28.6.2016, http://www.nytimes.com/2016/06/28/opinion/marine-le-pen-after-brexit-the-peoples-spring-is-inevitable.html?_r=0 [10.1.2017].

89 Gilles Ivaldi, »A new course for the French radical right? The Front National and ›de-demonisation‹« in: Tjitkse Akkerman / Sarah L. de Lange / Matthijs Rooduijn (eds.), *Radical right-wing populist parties in western Europe: Into the mainstream?*, Abingdon 2016, pp. 225–246.

hold power rather than merely expressing dissent. The most prominent casualty of this strategy has been Marine Le Pen's father and predecessor Jean-Marie himself, who was expelled from the party in August of 2015 for remarks which referred to the Holocaust as »a detail of history.« On the policy level this detoxification of the party has included a move away from solely focusing on the issue of immigration towards the formation of a more comprehensive and encompassing programme that also addresses economic concerns, albeit through an anti-immigration and anti-globalist lens.[90] Analyses of party manifestos reflect this greater emphasis on economic and welfare topics. While around 15 per cent were devoted to socio-economic questions during the mid-1990s, 37 per cent of the FN's 2012 presidential manifesto addressed this issue area.[91]

Despite attempts to capture more left-leaning segments of the electorate, the FN's rhetoric on France's debt has even in recent years in certain parts sounded far from left wing and more reminiscent of the free-market capitalist positions espoused by Marine Le Pen's father. The 2012 presidential manifesto considered controlling France's public debt as »an urgent national imperative« that required »restoring control of the country's finances through a responsible spending policy.«[92] Marine Le Pen's comments concerning her proposals for public debt reduction also read more like something to be found in a Tory manifesto, as her goal was to »clear the debt smoothly [...] and to restore a virtuous cycle and fiscal orthodoxy.«[93] The Front National's stance on the euro, on the other hand, combines a nationalist rejection of European integration and a more leftist tone, as both financial and political elites are attacked for their detrimental actions against the interests of the people. Austerity at home and the usage of French funds to help save other countries are presented as the common currency's negative side effects as the euro is portrayed as a »symbol of [...] brinkmanship by absurd financial elites ready to sacrifice the people on the altar of their interests.«[94] Going forward, the 2012 presidential manifesto therefore called for a course to »reject to commit to a policy of austerity in the name of preserving a currency that stifles Europe.«[95] Simply put, »unnecessary and ruinous bailouts« had to end while »[t]he money of the French has to remain in France.«[96]

The FN's programmatic shift under Marine Le Pen appears to offer something for everyone, indicative of the trend seen among other populist parties that defy conventional classification along the traditional left-right divide. The FN's political manifesto

90 Hans-Georg Betz, »The Revenge of the *Ploucs*: The Revival of Radical Populism under Marine Le Pen in France« in: Kriesi / Pappas (eds.), *European Populism in the Shadow of the Great Recession*, op. cit. (note 13), pp. 75–90, p. 79.

91 Ivaldi, »A new course for the French radical right?«, op. cit. (note 89), p. 230.

92 Front National, *Notre Projet*, op. cit. (note 85), pp. 58-59.

93 Front National, *Notre Projet*, op. cit. (note 85), p. 94.

94 Front National, *Notre Projet*, op. cit. (note 85), p. 68.

95 Front National, *Notre Projet*, op. cit. (note 85), p. 68.

96 Front National, *Notre Projet*, op. cit. (note 85), p. 68.

speaks to a growing share of French voters that object to European integration[97] while attempting to bridge the gap between voters who see a burgeoning government deficit and debt as the most serious problem facing the country and those citizens on the other hand whose primary concerns are about job security. Judging by the party's recent electoral performances, Marine Le Pen's course correction appears to have paid off. She won 6.4 million votes in the first round of the 2012 French presidential election, an increase of over 2.5 million votes over her father's first round performance five years earlier and at the time the best result ever obtained by a Front National presidential candidate. In the first round of the 2015 French regional elections, the party managed to increase its share of the vote from 11.4 per cent in 2010 to 27.7 per cent, winning a plurality in six of the 13 regions of metropolitan France in that round. Its arguably biggest (or at least most widely reported) success came in the 2014 European elections, in which the Front National managed to win a plurality of French seats and almost quadruple its share of the popular vote from 6.3 per cent (2009) to 24.9 per cent. The recent French presidential elections also saw Marine Le Pen win around twice as many votes in the second round as her father had obtained 15 years earlier.

6. Partij voor de Vrijheid (PVV)

Founded in 2006, the party's path to success had to a certain extent been paved by Pim Fortuyn and his party *Lijst Pim Fortuyn*, which managed to become the second strongest party in the 2002 Dutch general election after the assassination of its leader. Fortuyn's brand of right-wing populism was distinctive in the sense that it did not mirror the general objection to immigration rooted in a worldview focused on ethnicity or race, which is traditionally ubiquitous among the far right, but instead focused on Islam and its supposed incompatibility with Western liberal values.[98] These liberal values were presented as quintessentially Dutch and under threat from Islam, something that represented quite a personal matter for an openly homosexual man like Fortuyn. In this sense of course the approach of Fortuyn and his party was not dissimilar to that of other right-wing populists who also profess to defend their homeland's national identity; it was just that in this instance the Dutch national identity of social liberalism and its defence of gay rights, for example, was rather different and distinctive from the conservative idealized world that many others on the far right tend to long

97 According to the September 2015 Eurobarometer, 52 per cent of the French considered EU membership to be a good thing, marginally above the British share of 47 per cent and significantly below Germany (71 per cent), the Netherlands (70 per cent), or Belgium (68 per cent). European Commission, Directorate-General for Communication, *European Parliament Eurobarometer (EB/EP 84.1) Parlemeter 2015 – Part II*, November 2015, p. 20; European Parliament, *European Parliament Eurobarometer: Parlemeter 2015, Part II*, 30.11.2015, http://www.europarl.europa.eu/pdf/eurobarometre/2015/2015parlemeter/eb84_1_synthese_analytique_partie_II_en.pdf [4.7.2017].

98 Merijn Oudenampsen, »Explaining the Swing to the Right: The Dutch Debate on the Rise of Right-Wing populism« in: Ruth Wodak / Majid KhosraviNik / Brigitte Mral (eds.), *Right-wing populism in Europe: Politics and Discourse*, London 2013, pp. 191–207, p. 203.

for. Wilders has, in a somewhat less progressive form, picked up Fortuyn's torch on socio-cultural issues. His defence of gay rights, however, appears to be rooted less in a genuine conviction of sexual equality than in his rejection of Islam, which is portrayed as the foremost threat to sexual minorities.[99]

On economic topics, Dutch right-wing populism has also defied easy classification. Both Pim Fortuyn and Wilders (initially) espoused economically liberal positions, calling for welfare cuts and a further deregulation of the labour market. In recent years, Wilders has taken a turn to the left though as Dutch governments have had to slash public expenditure as well with the Rutte government even going as far as to announce an end to the Dutch welfare state.[100] Developments like these resulted in a 2010 party manifesto that contained an »eclectic mix« concerning welfare and economic policies while also placing a far bigger emphasis on socio-economic topics than the previous one from 2006.[101] One former PVV MP, Joram van Klaveren, summed up the PVV's policies as »tough on safety and migration, soft on care.«[102] In 2012, Wilders withdrew his support for the minority Rutte government over objections to budget cuts, justifying his decision with a mixture of anti-austerity and anti-EU rhetoric: »We don't want our pensioners to bleed just to meet the dictates coming from Brussels. Today, I can look my electorate directly in the eye and say we didn't cave in to the bureaucrats in Brussels.«[103]

The 2012 manifesto clearly focused on the EU and the eurozone. Its introduction is a jeremiad against the EU and its leaders, which laments a perceived loss of popular sovereignty and the preferential treatment supposedly bestowed on other Europeans, placing little emphasis on spending cuts at home. While Romanians are »laugh[ing] themselves silly« as Greeks »drink another ouzo on behalf of Henk and Ingrid« (a fictional couple the PVV uses to describe the average Dutch citizen) and Bulgarians send »their gypsies [...] to our streets«, the Dutch are left with nothing but the »burdens« of EU membership.[104] This election was therefore supposed to be a stark choice between democracy, wealth and freedom (all presented as incompatible with EU mem-

99 Stijn Van Kessel, »Right-wing populism in contemporary Dutch politics« in: Frank Decker / Bernd Henningsen / Kjetil Jakobsen (eds.), Rechtspopulismus und Rechtsextremismus in Europa: Die Herausforderung der Zivilgesellschaft durch alte Ideologien und neue Medien, Baden-Baden 2015, pp. 205–216, p. 209.

100 »Not so Calvinist any more« in: *The Economist*, 3.10.2013, http://www.economist.com/news/europe/21586887-party-freedom-benefits-dutch-austerity-fatigue-not-so-calvinist-any-more [10.1.2017].

101 Van Kessel, »Right-wing populism in contemporary Dutch politics«, op. cit. (note 99), pp. 208–209. In 2006, socio-economic topics played at best a marginal role in the PVV's manifesto. Four years later its salience was almost at the level of socio-cultural topics on the other hand. Tjitkse Akkerman, »The Party for Freedom: Balancing between mission, votes and office« in: Akkerman / de Lange / Rooduijn (eds.), *Radical right-wing populist parties in western Europe*, op. cit. (note 89), pp. 144–168, pp. 149–150.

102 Quoted in: Akkerman, »The Party for Freedom«, op. cit. (note 101), p. 154.

103 Quoted in: »Dutch government on brink of collapse« in: *RNW Media*, https://www.rnw.org/archive/dutch-government-brink-collapse [9.12.2017].

104 Partij voor de Vrijheid, *Hún Brussel, óns Nederland*, 2012, p. 13.

bership) and, on the other side, »Brussels slavery.«[105] For Wilders, the answer to the question »are we still a country that wants to govern itself«[106] could therefore only be answered affirmatively if the country left the EU. On economic matters and austerity-related questions, the 2012 party manifesto nonetheless continued to straddle the line between more traditional liberal proposals and an opposition to broader cuts while nonetheless still constituting the most left leaning manifesto on socio-economic topics in the party's history.[107]

The PVV therefore illustrates one of the key dilemmas right-wing populist parties can face regarding economic topics. On the one hand their electorate does tend to favour some form of state intervention, primarily to protect natives though. At the same time, the »state« (at least in its current form) is run by an elite presented as disconnected from the concerns of the average citizen. The PVV's more liberal »get the government off your back« positions are thereby in line with traditional populist notions about freeing the ordinary man from the shackles imposed on him by an elite that uses tax money to further their own influence and prosperity.[108] Squaring the circle of combining leftist and anti-elitist sentiments is accomplished by putting forth the argument that safeguarding the welfare state (limited to its own citizens) is possible by simply withdrawing funds from elitist institutions (»government« in general and the EU). Taxes for »Henk and Ingrid« could be cut as long as Brussels is put »on a diet of water and bread«[109] – a necessary step since the EU is seen as standing for »More Socialism. More rules. More bureaucratic nightmares.«[110] More left-leaning positions, on the other hand, become evident on the issue of unemployment benefits, with the party vowing to not slash them since »[w]orkers are not disposable napkins.«[111] Leaving the government over austerity cuts in 2012 was thus part of a broader effort to brand the PVV as the staunchest defender of the welfare state. The manifesto bluntly stated that »our compatriots did not want the eurozone crisis, yet they now have to foot the bill.«[112] Defending the welfare state would allow the Dutch worker to »catch their breath and find another job. That is why the Freedom Party is outspoken in its defence of <u>our</u> [emphasis in original] welfare state.«[113] In the eyes of the PVV, welfare cuts would moreover not be necessary if it wasn't for the costs incurred by immigration, a tried and tested approach of the populist radical right that links welfare to this policy area. A defence of the welfare state therefore »automatically leads to a rejection of mass immigration which costs us €7.2 billion annually.«[114]

105 Partij voor de Vrijheid, *Hún Brussel, óns Nederland*, op. cit. (note 104), p 13.
106 Partij voor de Vrijheid, *Hún Brussel, óns Nederland*, op. cit. (note 104), p. 7.
107 Akkerman, »The Party for Freedom«, op. cit. (note 101), p.148.
108 Jeffrey Bell, *Populism and Elitism: Politics in the Age of Equality*, Washington, D.C. 1992, p. 14.
109 Partij voor de Vrijheid, *Hún Brussel, óns Nederland*, op. cit. (note 104), p. 19.
110 Partij voor de Vrijheid, *Hún Brussel, óns Nederland*, op. cit. (note 104), p. 23.
111 Partij voor de Vrijheid, *Hún Brussel, óns Nederland*, op. cit. (note 104), p. 23.
112 Partij voor de Vrijheid, *Hún Brussel, óns Nederland*, op. cit. (note 104), p. 22.
113 Partij voor de Vrijheid, *Hún Brussel, óns Nederland*, op. cit. (note 104), p. 22.
114 Partij voor de Vrijheid, *Hún Brussel, óns Nederland*, op. cit. (note 104), p. 22.

The PVV's electoral results do indicate that the country's poor economic performance (see table 1) has not coincided with an increasing popularity of the populist right-wing outfit. Its best showing came before the country had to implement austerity measures of its own, as it won 17 per cent of the vote in the 2009 European elections. One year later it won 15.5 per cent in national elections (increasing its number of seats from 9 to 24 in the Dutch lower house), only to lose more than a third of its support two years later as Wilders' decision to bring down the Rutte government over objections to its austerity measures was not too popular with the Dutch electorate (the PVV won 10.1 per cent in the 2012 general election). The party's modest improvement in the 2017 general election once again coincided with a socio-cultural topic (the migrant crisis and its ramifications) rather than the economy dominating the headlines, as the party increased its number of seats in the Dutch house of representatives from 15 to 20.

7. Conclusion

Austerity policies have played into the hands of populists both on the left and right while moreover making an already bad economic situation even worse, a deterioration in living standards and employment that only served to damage people's trust in democratic institutions and democracy itself. Left-wing populists were able to harness the indignation of parts of the electorate whose own interpretation of the *Great Recession* overlapped with the populist narrative of an elite attempting to make the people pay for the mistakes of the former. Right-wing populists in creditor countries on their part focused on the role played by the political elite that implemented unpopular bailouts while providing unelected European institutions (such as the ECB) with a bigger say in financial and fiscal matters. The result has turned out to be an increase in the electoral fortunes of populist parties across a variety of European countries, particularly pronounced in the southern part of the continent though.[115] Greece and Spain's left-wing populist parties have in the process wholly embraced the people-vs.-elite dichotomy as they have become (or were on the verge of becoming) the biggest forces on the left in their respective countries. Podemos in particular provides an interesting case study because its leadership consciously drew conclusions from the lessons taught by other leftist populist movements about how to achieve widespread electoral success. It will remain to be seen whether other far-left actors will also be willing to disavow parts of their socialist or communist orthodoxy in order to appeal to wider swathes of the electorate – an approach indeed adopted to at least initially great success by Syriza. Podemos' approach of fighting populism with populism may therefore offer a window into the future of political conflict in Europe.

115 Takis S. Pappas / Hanspeter Kriesi, »Populism and Crisis: A Fuzzy Relationship« in: Kriesi / Pappas (eds.), *European Populism in the Shadow of the Great Recession*, op. cit. (note 13), pp. 303-324, p. 323.

The role of austerity in the increasing electoral fortunes of populist actors by itself should not necessarily be overstated though. The support of centre-left parties for austerity measures and the inherent dismantling of the welfare state represent a continuation of a long-term trend that has in previous decades also aided the rise of populist parties on both fringes of the political spectrum. The financial crisis of 2008 and beyond therefore did not constitute a major source of upheaval or an about-face by Europe's social democrats but just another opportunity for populist parties to point out the increasingly neoliberal policy outlook of centre-left parties on economic issues. Combining the unpopularity of these policies among working class voters with a broader anti-elitist narrative provided populist parties both on the right and left with an opportunity structure they were well placed to exploit for political gain. Particularly in creditor countries, right-wing populist parties frequently did not take issue with the austerity measures imposed on other countries themselves (that were often deemed to be too lenient to begin with) but a further Europeanization of politics and the perceived undemocratic nature of these processes as said parties have championed the argument that these integrationist measures require the direct consent of the people through plebiscitary means. An indirect effect of the Great Recession has been that it has forced right-wing populist parties to address their past neglect of economic issues, arguably providing them with a more solid programmatic base for future electoral campaigns while not necessarily increasing their chances of actually obtaining political office due to a lack of ideological overlap with other potential coalition partners on the right on economic matters. When it comes to the declining electoral fortunes of centre-left parties, of course one also has to remember that their demise is not limited to countries affected by the Great Recession. Case in point Sweden, where in 2010 the local social democrats obtained their worst election result since the introduction of universal suffrage (30.7 per cent, only to marginally improve to 31 per cent four years later, thus constituting its second worst showing). In general, social democratic parties across Western Europe are today in the worst shape in decades.[116]

We can expect some of the topics that have helped fuel the rise of populist parties to remain at the top of the political agenda, thereby ensuring continued populist strength in the short- to mid-term. This is especially true for right-wing populist parties whose focus has not necessarily been on austerity measures – that might eventually be phased out anyway – but the more extended European integration process (epitomized by the euro) and the refugee crisis. The eurozone crisis may very well flare up again with its resolution requiring a further Europeanization of fiscal policy, thereby narrowing the room for manoeuvre afforded to domestic political actors even further – a process that has always stood at the heart of the right-wing populist argument against Europe. A further Europeanization will also allow right-wing populists to continue to use the people-vs.-elite dichotomy even if they have become part of the governing elite, as

116 Chris Hanretty, »Electorally, West European social democrats are at their lowest point for forty years« in: *Medium*, 5.10.2015, https://medium.com/@chrishanretty/electorally-west-european-social-democrats-are-at-their-lowest-point-for-forty-years-ac7ae3d8d-db7#.edt8nycbk [13.1.2017].

Brussels is presented as the »real« elite with national governments relegated to the status of merely carrying out orders from the European capital. At least in the short- to mid-term future, European politicians therefore face the conundrum that moves to bring about resolutions to the myriad of the crises the continent is facing can be exploited by populists on the left and right. As Pappas and Kriesi conclude, »populism's upward tendency in Europe is non-negligible and probably enduring.«[117]

117 Pappas / Kriesi, »Populism and Crisis«, op. cit. (note 115), p. 323.

Claudia Wiesner

Representative Democracy in Times of Austerity: New Challenges in the EU Multi-level System

European integration has brought about a crucial change with regard to representative democracy and balance of powers in the EU multi-level system: they are no longer shaped either on the level of the member states or the EU level alone. Nowadays, also the vertical interplay between the different levels influences representative democracy and balance of powers in the whole of the multi-level system. The EU's austerity regime has had some decisive effects on this complex setting both on the EU level and in the member states. The governance mechanisms that have been designed in the sovereign debt crisis have intensified already existing tensions. Balances of powers have been changed on the EU level as well as on the national level and between the member states; moreover, core institutions and mechanisms of representative democracy have been challenged. The chapter analyses the changes and the new imbalances and discusses their consequences for representative democracy and balances of powers in the whole of the multi-level system. It ends with a discussion of possible solutions to the new dilemmas. The chapter aims at filling a gap in the current debate: while the financial crisis as such has been discussed in a number of contributions, the democratic dilemmas it brought about have been much less in the focus.

1. Representative democracies and balances of powers in the EU multi-level system

Representative democracies are usually marked by a balance of powers between legislative, judicative and executive branches. In nation states, these are situated on the same level, i.e. the national polities. The EU's multi-level system brings together member states with their representative democratic systems and their respective balances of powers on the one hand and the EU polity with its specific political system on the other. In consequence, the setting of representative democracy and balance of powers in the EU multi-level system is getting more complex and the different levels are intertwined.

When discussing balance of powers and democracy in the multi-level system, it is important to mention that balance of powers regards at least three different levels, or types of relationships[1]: (a) there is a horizontal separation of legislative, executive and judiciary on both for the EU level and in the member states. This horizontal balance of powers can be differentiated into (aa) a horizontal separation of powers and (ab) a hor-

1 Miriam Hartlapp / Claudia Wiesner, »Gewaltenteilung und Demokratie im EU-Mehrebenensystem – neu, anders, oder weniger legitim?« in: Miriam Hartlapp / Claudia Wiesner (eds.), *Gewaltenteilung und Demokratie im EU-Mehrebenensystem*, Wiesbaden 2016, pp. 3–16; Arthur Benz, »Föderale Demokratie und das Problem der Gewaltenbalance« in: ibid., pp. 37–52; Ingeborg Tömmel, »Gewaltenteilung in der EU – Problem oder Baustein demokratischer Ordnung?«, in: ibid., pp. 53–70.

izontal internal linkage of powers; (b) there is a vertical balance of powers between the different levels in the EU multi-level system; and (c) there is a horizontal balance of powers between the EU's member states. Furthermore, in analysing the respective balance of powers we find differences between their formal and their de facto realization. This means that formally fixed powers can differ from the ones that are practised. These differences are particularly relevant for the EU, as will be discussed below.

Democracy in the EU in the last decades has mainly been discussed with regard to the question whether there is a »democratic deficit«. While the positions are clear, the underlying problems are important also for the question that is to be discussed here.

For a start, academics do not agree on the nature of the EU. While one standpoint claims the EU to be an intergovernmental entity[2] that should not be further democratized as the member states legitimize it sufficiently, another, more recent standpoint claims it to be a political system that can be compared to others[3] and that also should be further democratized. Whereas this discussion at first sight might seem to be of purely academic character, it is, however, important for understanding different ways of judging the EU. If one adheres rather to the position that it is an intergovernmental entity, one will be rather sceptical to mention or think about »democracy« in, let alone »democratizing«, the EU, while the fact that one regards the EU as a political system nearly implies that it can be a representative democratic system, too.

The following argument is based on the position that a) the EU is to be seen as a political system that b) has continuously been and still can be further democratized. From that standpoint, there are a number of critical points to be mentioned regarding democracy on the EU level itself.[4] It is moreover important to underline that a judgement of the EU's democratic quality should take into account not only the EU but also the whole multi-level system, i.e. the EU and its interrelations with the current 28 member states. From this standpoint, there are a number of flaws and challenges to democracy to be mentioned on the institutional side. There are also a number of questions regarding the political-cultural dimension of *demos* formation that shall not be discussed here.[5]

2 Giandomenico Majone, »Europe's ›Democratic Deficit‹: The Question of Standards« in: *European Law Journal* 4, No. 1 (1998), pp. 5–28; Andrew Moravcsik, »In Defence of the ›Democratic Deficit‹: Reassessing Legitimacy in the European Union« in: *Journal of Common Market Studies* 40, No. 4 (2002), pp. 603–624.

3 Ingeborg Tömmel, *The European Union: what it is and how it works*, Houndsmills, 2014; Simon Hix / Bjørn Høyland, »Empowerment of the European Parliament« in: *Annual Review of Political Science* 16, No. 1 (2013), pp. 171–189.

4 For overviews see Andreas Føllesdal / Simon Hix, »Why there is a Democratic Deficit in the EU: A Response to Majone and Moravcsik« in: Journal of Common Market Studies 44, No. 3 (2006), pp. 533–562; Simon Hix, *What's wrong with the European Union and how to fix it*, Cambridge, M.A. 2008.

5 Claudia Wiesner, *Demokratisierung der EU durch nationale Europadiskurse? Strukturen und Prozesse europäischer Identitätsbildung im deutsch-französischen Vergleich*. Baden-Baden 2014.

First, EU policies no longer are merely regulative, but they have redistributive effects.[6] The EU hence does interfere severely with the everyday life of its citizens. This fact raises the necessity for a solid democratic legitimation of the EU and its policies, also in terms of input-legitimacy.

Second, legitimation chains in the EU are still long and rather non-transparent, and accountability is not easily claimed. Council members, for instance, are legitimized via national elections and national parliaments, i.e. in a long chain. Commission members are appointed by the member states' governments, even if the EP, following some successful political struggles, has by and by obtained the right to vote upon the Commission's approval and also to influence the Commissioner setting to a certain degree.[7]

Third, input-legitimacy is still weaker on the EU level than in member states' democracies.[8] National representative democracies therefore comply better with the needs of democratic input-legitimacy, but they continually lost competencies to the EU level by different ways and means. In sum, European integration thus has led to a net loss of input legitimacy in the multi-level system.[9]

Fourth, EU institutions increased their competencies over the last decades without adding a representative-democratic legislative component that equals the ones in the nation states. As at the same time the representative democracies and their legislatives in the member states lost competencies, executive powers increased on the whole in the EU multi-level system, and legislative powers decreased.[10] Moreover, powers also shifted to the judiciary realm.

Fifth, in sum, decision-making powers in the EU multi-level system are constantly withdrawn from the realm of representative democracy and political participation.[11] The balance switches in favour of an executive and judiciary dimension of politics.[12]

6 Føllesdal / Hix, »Why there is a Democratic Deficit the EU«, op. cit. (note 4), pp. 551; David Beetham / Christopher Lord, »Legitimacy and the European Union« in: Albert Weale / Michael Nentwich (eds.), *Political Theory and the European Union*, London1998, pp. 15–33, pp. 17–19.

7 Teija Tiilikainen / Claudia Wiesner, »Towards a Political Theory of EU Parliamentarism? « in: Pasi Ihailainen / Cornelia Ilie / Kari Palonen (eds.), *Parliament and Parliamentarism. A comparative history of disputes on a European concept*, New York 2016, pp. 292–310.

8 Beetham / Lord, »Legitimacy and the European Union«, op. cit. (note 6), pp. 17–19; Richard Bellamy / Dario Castiglione, »Legitimizing the Euro-›Polity‹ and its ›Regime‹. The Normative Turn in EU Studies« in: *European Journal of Political Theory* 1, No. 2 (2003), pp. 7–34.

9 Jürgen Habermas, »Braucht Europa eine Verfassung? Eine Bemerkung zu Dieter Grimm«, in: Jürgen Habermas, *Die Einbeziehung des Anderen*, Frankfurt/Main 1999, pp. 185–191, pp. 186–187; Beetham / Lord, »Legitimacy and the European Union«, op. cit. (note 6), p. 17–19.

10 Føllesdal / Hix, »Why there is a Democratic Deficit the EU: A Response to Majone and Moravscik«, op. cit. (note 4), pp. 534–536; Yves Mény, »De la démocratie en Europe: Old Concepts and New Challenges« in: *Journal of Common Market Studies* 41, No. 1 (2003), pp. 1–13.

11 Jürgen Habermas, »Euroskepsis, Markteuropa, oder Europa der (Welt-)Bürger« in: Jürgen Habermas, *Zeit der Übergänge*, Frankfurt/Main 2001, pp. 85–103.

12 Mény, »De la démocratie en Europe«, op. cit. (note 10); Jeffrey T. Checkel / Peter Katzenstein, »The politicization of European Union identities« in: Jeffrey T. Checkel (ed.), *Euro-*

The Lisbon Treaty has brought some remedies to some of these points, especially by according more powers to the directly elected European Parliament (EP), which today in a number of policy areas is the first chamber of legislation and co-decides with the Council. But the short account of the democratic deficit has also indicated that the problem is complex. To put the finger on the »where« of the EU's institutional democratic deficit is far from simple and involves a careful account of the dynamics of legitimacy, democracy and balance of powers in the whole of the multi-level system.

2. Governance of financial aid: horizontal balance of powers and representative democracy on the EU level

The problems and difficulties relating to democracy and the balance of powers in the EU multi-level system that have been sketched above have been severely increasing by the governance of financial aid in the sovereign debt crisis, as I will argue in the following. All dimensions sketched are concerned in the whole of the multi-level system: the EU level, the member states, vertical and horizontal balance of powers, and also the formalized situation as well as the de facto practice. In the following, five interrelated problems will be discussed.

In this section 2, the consequences the governance of financial aid brought for the EU level, i.e. for democracy and the horizontal balance of powers there, will be analysed. On this level, first, new intergovernmental treaties between the euro-countries created new institutions such as the European Stability Mechanism (ESM) and the Fiscal Compact, as well as new agents such as the Troika. In consequence, an intergovernmental parallel structure to the EU's institutions has been developing. Second, the European Parliament is the only one of the EU's institutions that is formally excluded from this structure (2.1.). Third, competencies and accountability of the Troika are opaque (2.2.).

Regarding the member state level, there are further problems to be mentioned: fourth, parliamentary decision-making and parliamentary powers have been cut down in both debtor and donor states (3.1. & 3.2.), and fifth, the horizontal balance of powers between the member states is damaged by this constellation.

2.1. Creating an intergovernmental parallel structure

New intergovernmental Treaties in the financial aid governance de facto created a parallel structure to the EU's institutional system. The actors that figure in the ESM Treaty are largely identical to those in the EU Treaties – including the Commission, Council members, the European Central Bank and even the Court of Justice of the European Union. There are, however, two crucial differences: non-Euro countries are formally excluded, and so is the European Parliament.

pean identity, Cambridge 2009, pp. 1–25; Juan Diez Medrano, »The public sphere and the European Union's political identity« in: ibid., pp. 81–107.

When financial aid for Greece was started in May 2010, the basis was an intergovernmental declaration of the eurozone's heads of state and government. Shortly afterwards, the European Financial Stabilization Mechanism (EFSM) and the European Financial Stabilization Facilty (EFSF) were created. EFSF is the predecessor of today's ESM, guaranteeing the larger part of the financial aid programmes (440 billion euro) by member state and IMF bonds. The EFSM, in exchange, was based on the EU Treaties but guaranteed only up to 60 billion euro.[13] While the financial aid for Greece was paid out of the EFSF, aid for Portugal and Italy was paid at least partly by the EFSM.[14] This setting, then, already mixed the EU's institutions and Treaties with a newly created structure, adding the International Monetary Fund (IMF) as a new player outside the EU. Monetary policy is regulated by the EU Treaties, but not the policies of financial aid.

The basis for these moves can be found in the Treaties, however. Formally, only the 19 euro countries are responsible for financial aid. As article 137 of the Treaty on Functioning of the European Union (TFEU) rules, they constitute the »Eurogroup«.[15] Formally as well as de facto, the Eurogroup is closely related to the Council: The Eurogroup's members, i.e. the ministers for finance of the euro states, belong to the Council, and the eurozone's heads of state and government belong to the European Council. But the Eurogroup is much less transparent and much more informally structured than the Council. Protocol No. 14 of the Lisbon Treaty especially states that Eurogroup meetings are *informal*.[16] The Council's official website does present the Eurogroup as an informal institution as well.[17] While Council meetings are public when the Council is acting in its legislative function, this is not the case for the Eurogroup.

The European Stability Mechanism ESM was officially started on October 8, 2012. It took over the tasks and programmes formerly carried out by EFSF and EFSM. The ESM is related to the Eurogroup and based on an intergovernmental Treaty. Formally, as the German Ministry of Finance explains, the ESM is an intergovernmental Financial Institution (IFI) and therefore subject to international law[18] – and hence clearly outside the EU's institutional system.

13 Peter Christian Müller-Graff, »Euro-Budgethilfenpolitik im rechtlichen Neuland« in: *Integration* 4 (2011), pp. 289–307.

14 Bundesfinanzministerium, *Europäische Finanzhilfen: EFSF und EFSM*, http://www.bundesfinanzministerium.de/Content/DE/Standardartikel/Themen/Europa/Stabilisierung_des_Euro/Zahlen_und_Fakten/europaeische-finanzhilfen-efsf-efsm.html [24.3.2015]; European Commission, *European Stabilisation Actions – the EU's response to the crisis*, http://ec.europa.eu/economy_finance/eu_borrower/european_stabilisation_actions/index_en.htm [2.10.2012].

15 Europäische Union, *Konsolidierte Fassung des Vertrags über die Europäische Union und des Vertrags über die Arbeitsweise der Europäischen Union*, 2016, p. 107.

16 Europäische Union, *Konsolidierte Fassung des Vertrags über die Europäische Union und des Vertrags über die Arbeitsweise der Europäischen Union*, op. cit. (note 15), pp. 283.

17 Europäischer Rat, *Die Euro-Gruppe*, http://www.consilium.europa.eu/de/council-eu/eurogroup/ [27.7.2015].

18 Bundesfinanzministerium, *Fragen und Antworten zum Europäischen Stabilitätsmechanismus (ESM)*, http://www.bundesfinanzministerium.de/Content/DE/FAQ/2012-08-16-esm-faq.html [24.3.2015].

The ESM currently disposes of a capital of 701 billion Euros. The single member states hold shares that are equal to their shares in the European Central Bank. Their maximum risk hence is limited to the capital they invested. Moreover, a reserve fond consisting of benefits gained by the ESM and sanctions paid by the members subject to the Stability and Growth pact allows for some additional capital which reduced the ESM members' risks.[19]

Despite this intergovernmental setup, again, the ESM de facto is closely linked to the EU's institutions. First, it was founded on the occasion of a European Council meeting in December 2010.[20] The EC decided to add a new third paragraph in article 136 TFEU that enabled the eurozone states to create such a mechanism.[21] The ESM Treaty, moreover, explicitly relates to the EU.[22] Representatives of two of the EU's institutions can be invited to meetings to the ESM governor board: the Commissioner for economic and monetary affairs of the European Commission and the ECB President.[23] The Court of Justice can be called upon in case of conflict.[24]

In sum, the governance structures of budgetary aid around the European Stability Mechanism ESM represent an intergovernmental parallel structure to the institutional system of the EU Treaties. The current European Stability Mechanism (ESM) is an intergovernmental construction, based on a treaty concluded by the eurozone member states only.[25] However, the actors involved in the ESM are to a large extent identical to EU actors under the Lisbon Treaty: heads and/or ministers of member states, the EU commission and the European Central Bank (ECB). But the ESM, even if it relates to the EU Treaties, is not part of the EU's institutional framework and its checks and balances.

The new structures also represent a decisive regression behind the Lisbon Treaty's new standards. The Lisbon treaty brought the EU some considerable advances regarding the democratic quality and the balance of powers on the EU level. The European Parliament became the first chamber of legislation in the areas of co-decision between Council and Parliament, which has now been termed the ordinary legislative proce-

19 Bundesfinanzministerium, *Fragen und Antworten zum Europäischen Stabilitätsmechanismus (ESM)*, op. cit. (note 18); Bundesfinanzministerium, *Europäische Finanzhilfen: ESM*, http://www.bundesfinanzministerium.de/Content/DE/Standardartikel/Themen/Europa/Stabilisierung_des_Euro/Zahlen_und_Fakten/europaeische-finanzhilfen-esm.html [24.3.2015].

20 ESM, *European Stability Mechanism*, http://www.esm.europa.eu/ [24.3.2015].

21 Europäischer Rat, *Tagung des Europäischen Rats. 16./17. Dezember 2010. Schlussfolgerungen*, https://www.consilium.europa.eu/uedocs/cms_data/docs/pressdata/de/ec/118604.pdf [6.10.2016].

22 Article 2, ESM Treaty; *Vertrag zur Einrichtung des europäischen Stabilitätsmechanismus (ESM)* 2015.

23 Article 5, 3, ESM Treaty.

24 Article 37, ESM Treaty.

25 European Council, *Treaty establishing the European Stability Mechanism*, http://www.efsf.europa.eu/attachments/esm_treaty_en.pdf [11.9.2012].

dure.[26] The European Parliament is the part of the EU's legislative that possesses a direct input-legitimacy accorded by the EU's citizens. The new structures represent a decisive regression in that respect. Intergovernmental institutions dominate and the European Parliament is formally excluded. As Colin Crouch emphasizes, this bypassing of the EP relates to a British veto, the UK opposing the idea that the euro crisis was managed through the EU's institutional system proper.[27]

Regarding the dimensions of a balance of powers that were named in the beginning, two critical effects can be noted. First, the EP and hence the directly legitimized part of the legislative is excluded on the horizontal EU level. Second, and regarding the vertical balance of power, it is to be noted that the member states' governments are considerably strengthened and hence the executive and with it the intergovernmental component in the EU. In sum, the representative-democratic dimension is weakened on the whole.

It has to be noted, however, that these moves have been prepared by Treaty changes and protocols, concluded in the European Council and ratified in the member states if and where necessary. They can therefore be termed to be formally legitimized and for sure legal. Nevertheless their legitimation must be termed weak. Transparency and publicity of the decisions are considerably reduced compared to legislative processes in the standard legislative procedure. The Eurogroup does not hold public meetings, parliaments are only formally involved on the member state level, and the processes are dominated by governments, experts and non-majoritarian institutions. The electorates hence only indirectly relate to most of these actors. Since the new institutions take on decisions with far-reaching redistributive consequences, this legitimation basis seems to be insufficient.[28]

2.2. The Troika: a player with an opaque role

The governance of financial aid is mostly operated by the often cited »Troika«, consisting of representatives of the EU commission, the ECB and the International Monetary Fund (IMF). Formally, the Troika is their agent and is charged with a) negotiating the

26 Tiilikainen / Wiesner, »Towards a Political Theory of EU Parliamentarism?«, op. cit. (note 7). Regarding the overall picture in the balance of powers among Council, Parliament and Commission, it might be questioned whether the EP not lost some competencies in the budgetary procedure and, moreover, the Council received considerable new competencies. Tömmel, »Gewaltenteilung in der EU«, op. cit. (note 1).

27 Colin Crouch, »Comment on Wolfgang Merkel, ›Is capitalism compatible with democracy?‹« in: Zeitschrift für Vergleichende Politikwissenschaft 9, No. 1–2 (2015), pp. 61–71, p. 69.

28 Henrik Enderlein, »Das erste Opfer der Krise ist die Demokratie: Wirtschaftspolitik und ihre Legitimation in der Finanzmarktkrise 2008–2013« in: *PVS Politische Vierteljahresschrift* 54, No. 4 (2013), pp. 714–739.

conditions of financial aid and b) controlling that these conditions are kept. This role had already been fixed in the EFSF Treaty.[29]

The ESM treaty continues to fix these responsibilities. The ministers of finance and economics of the euro states decide on financial aid and the conditions for it (Art. 5, 5f) – *after* the Troika has negotiated these conditions and fixed them in a »Memorandum of Understanding« (MoU). This MoU will be signed by representatives of the Commission in the name of the ESM.[30] This means that the Troika not only is the agent that controls all conditions linked to any financial assistance; it is also in charge of *negotiating* these terms and putting them down in Memoranda of Understanding.

This structure is non-transparent, and accountability remains unclear. The Troika has a decisive but highly non-transparent role in the crisis management. The ESM Treaty defines the members and the general tasks of the Troika, but it neither sets limits for its competencies nor establishes standards for its accountability. In particular, it remains unclear which competencies the Troika has over the member states, their governments and their parliaments, how those competences refer to the Troika's principals, ECB, Commission and IMF, and how they relate to the Eurogroup's governments.

It might be argued that such undefined competencies are an outcome of »incomplete contracting« as part of a principal-agent relation.[31] Nevertheless the structure is so opaque that it is difficult to see how the principals control the agent in the end. The European Parliament – trying to exert at least some informal oversight and trying also to create publicity – held a number of hearings on the financial aid governance. At one of these occasions, Troika members argued that in each case not their institution was responsible for a critical outcome but the other institutions – i.e. the Commission's representative would argue that ECB and IMF were responsible, and so on.[32]

3. Governing austerity: effects on democracy and on balance of powers in and between member states

Governance of financial aid has had several backfire effects into the national democracies of the member states. These backfire effects regard all three dimensions of the balance of powers that have been named: horizontal balances of powers in the member states and the EU, the vertical balance of powers between the EU and the member states, and the horizontal balance of powers between the member states.

29 EFSF, *EFSF Framework Agreement (as amended with effect from the Effective Date of the Amendments)*, http://www.efsf.europa.eu/attachments/20111019_efsf_framework_agreement_en.pdf [11.9.2012], p. 5.

30 Article 13, 3, European Council, *Treaty establishing the European Stability Mechanism*, http://www.efsf.europa.eu/attachments/esm_treaty_en.pdf [11.9.2012].

31 Eugenia Da Conceiao-Held, »Verantwortungszurechnung im EU-Mehrebenensystem während der Krise: wer kontrolliert die Troika?« in: Hartlapp / Wiesner (eds.), *Gewaltenteilung und Demokratie im EU-Mehrebenensystem*, op. cit. (note 1), pp. 115–130.

32 Udo Bullmann, *Die neue institutionelle Struktur der EU*, Contribution to Discussion Forum Rhein-Main-Runde, Frankfurt, 24.5.2012.

First of all, in general national parliaments have a much weaker role in financial aid governance than in the Lisbon Treaty and the EU Policies. Article 12 of the Lisbon treaty defines a number of formal possibilities for national parliaments to be involved into EU policies.[33] But financial crisis governance, as has been said, for a large part is placed outside the EU's Treaties. This means that the question of involvement of national parliaments into governance of financial aid is crucially decided by the competencies they have in the national systems and by the ways the respective balances of powers are shaped. The next decisive question then is whether the respective national balances of power work well or not. Another decisive criterion is whether the parliaments are situated in debtor or in donor states of financial aid.

3.1. Donor states: the German example

In donor states the crucial question is whether parliaments have the right to co-decide on financial aid. Taking the German example, Article 59, 2 of the Basic Law (*Grundgesetz* or GG) defines that intergovernmental Treaties must be ratified in parliament. Nevertheless the German government first tried to keep the *Bundestag* involvement into financial aid governance limited. As a result, a number of MPs carried out constitutional complaints, and a number of resulting judgements of the German Constitutional Court (*Bundesverfassungsgericht*) underlined that the first chamber of parliament, the *Bundestag*, had to be regularly, clearly and strongly involved[34]: The Court neither regarded a small board of nine MPs as sufficient to decide on urgent matters in financial aid, nor did it agree that the German government had sufficiently informed the German MPs before voting on the EFSF. Furthermore, the Court judged that the ESM Treaty was to be regarded as a kind of EU Treaty subject to Article 23 Basic Law that secures a considerable degree of influence in EU matters for the *Bundestag* and the second parliamentary chamber, where the federal states are represented, the *Bundesrat*.[35]

Moreover, the *Bundestag* obtained considerable co-decision rights in the areas of ESM and financial aid. In September 2011 the Constitutional Court judged that financial assistance must be voted first in the budgetary committee of parliament.[36] After that, in a kind of anticipatory obedience, the ratification laws for fiscal compact and ESM foresaw a strong parliamentary role, explicitly stating that and where both the

33 European Union, Lisbon Treaty (2010).

34 Bundesverfassungsgericht, *Pressemitteilung Nr. 14/2012 vom 28.2.2012*, http://www.bverfg.de/pressemitteilungen/bvg12-014.html [11.9.2012]; Bundesverfassungsgericht, *Pressemitteilung Nr. 67/2012 vom 12.09 2012*, http://www.bverfg.de/pressemitteilungen/bvg12-067.html [12.9.2012].

35 Bundesverfassungsgericht, *Pressemitteilung Nr. 42/2012 vom 19.6.2012*, http://www.bverfg.de/pressemitteilungen/bvg12-042.html [11.9.2012].

36 Bundesverfassungsgericht, *Pressemitteilung Nr. 55/2011 vom 7.9.2011. Verfassungsbeschwerden gegen Maßnahmen zur Griechenland-Hilfe und zum Euro-Rettungsschirm erfolglos – Keine Verletzung der Haushaltsautonomie des Bundestages*, http://www.bundesverfassungsgericht.de/SharedDocs/Pressemitteilungen/DE/2011/bvg11-055.html [24.3.2015].

budgetary committee and the plenary of the *Bundestag* had to give their approval.[37] In sum, the *Bundestag* received considerable new competencies in the financial aid policies – but it earned those competencies via constitutional complaints and via Constitutional Court judgements. This means that the German balance of powers worked quite well and the judiciary defended and even strengthened the legislative.

3.2. Debtor states: the Greek example

It has been said above that the Troika's role and accountability remains opaque. In particular, it remains unclear which competencies the Troika has over the member states, their governments and their parliaments, and whether it only negotiates the Memoranda or also imposes conditions on where, how and what to cut in the budget. The key questions are: do member states and their parliaments lose all power over their budgets under the austerity regime, since they can only accept the Troikas conditions or face bankruptcy, or can they define political priorities? Is the budgetary right of national parliaments only *limited*, or is it *suspended*? And to whom (actors or institutions) is the Troika accountable?

These questions are not answered in the ESM Treaty. The problem of lacking transparency of financial aid governance discussed above is hence increased, as parliamentary and executive competencies in a decisive area, the budget, are left unclear. This also means that accountability is opaque, i.e., it is unclear who accounts for austerity policies as they are carried out in the debtor states.

The interplay between the EU, the member state level and the Troika is decisive here. The Greek case is instructive in this respect. The results of the Greek bailout negotiations, the Memoranda of Understanding and the related economic recovery programmes, hint at the budgetary rights of the Greek parliament being at least severely impeded. These documents define very detailed measures and spending cuts, naming percentages and also areas or programmes where the cuts need to be carried out in the public sector, regarding pensions, and in labour market policies.[38] The first economic recovery programme for Greece states the following[39]:

37 Sascha Kneip, »Mehr (nationale) Demokratie wagen? Die Europarechtsprechung des Bundesverfassungsgerichts im Lichte des Demokratie- und Gewaltenkontrolldefizits im EU-Mehrebensystem«, in: Hartlapp / Wiesner (eds.), *Gewaltenteilung und Demokratie im EU-Mehrebenensystem*, op. cit. (note 1), pp. 131–148; Andreas Wimmel, »Verhandeln im Schatten von Vetomacht: Der Einfluss der Opposition im Bundestag auf die Euro-Rettungspolitik«, in: ibid., pp. 195–214.

38 European Commission, *Memorandum of Understanding between the European Commission and the Hellenic Republic and the Bank of Greece*, http://ec.europa.eu/economy_finance/assistance_eu_ms/greek_loan_facility/pdf/01_mou_20150811_en.pdf [18.10.2016]; European Commission, *Memorandum of Understanding*, http://ec.europa.eu/economy_finance/eu_borrower/mou/2012-03-01-greece-mou_en.pdf [30.10.2012].

39 European Commission, *Financial assistance to Greece*, https://ec.europa.eu/info/business-economy-euro/economic-and-fiscal-policy-coordination/eu-financial-assistance/which-eu-countries-have-received-assistance/financial-assistance-greece_en [20.3.2017].

»Large cuts in public wages and pensions are inevitable. [...] Cuts in wages consist of the abolition of the Easter, summer and Christmas bonuses and their replacement by a flat bonus (EUR 1000) for those earning less than EUR 3000 per month (gross). Moreover, the allowances (wage top-ups) paid to the highwage earners are also reduced. [...] Cuts in pensions also consist of the abolition of the Easter, summer and Christmas bonuses and their replacement by a flat bonus (EUR 800), for monthly pensions of less than EUR 2500 (gross). The higher pensions, exceeding EUR 1400 per month in gross terms, are reduced by an average of 8 percent, starting in 2010. This affects about 10 percent of pensioners.«

This means that the budgetary competencies of the Greek parliament have been at least severely impeded. This is the case notwithstanding the fact that the Greek parliament in most cases approved of the austerity programmes – albeit not always. In the first decisions on financial aid in 2010 the Greek government tried to bypass parliament: when the minister for finance signed the first Memorandum of Understanding, he did not previously consult the parliament, which represented a breach of the Greek constitution. The next Memorandum in 2012 was discussed only as an emergency law, i.e. in a very limited parliamentary procedure.[40]

Besides these internal questions of the Greek balance of powers, another decisive question is whether the parliament disposed of a margin of decision-making that enabled to define details of the budget, or whether the decision merely was one between acceptance or decline of an austerity package designed by the Eurogroup and Troika in detail. In the Greek case there are strong indicators that the latter has been happening.

The conflict between Syriza government and the Eurogroup in 2015 made these tensions public. It became apparent that the Eurogroup exercised a considerable pressure on the Greek government and the Greek parliament. Despite a referendum result that spoke against accepting austerity, the Greek government in July 2015 was forced to either accept new austerity rulings or to stop negotiations. The third Memorandum of Understanding again fixed detailed spending cuts and austerity measures.[41]

This means that the Eurogroup and the Troika did not take the decision of the majority of the Greek electorate into account that in the referendum had voted against austerity. Parliament and government in Greece experienced time pressure, and the new austerity measures were approved of a parliamentary majority consisting of part of the Syriza faction and the opposition. Formally, then, the Memorandum was approved of parliament. In practice and de facto, again, the margin of decision left for parliament was minimized and the vote was one between yes or no.

But budgetary right is for good reasons understood as one of the crown jewels of a parliament: a budget symbolically and materially expresses the will of the parliamentary majority by defining the policies to be carried out in a country. Even when the

40 Anthoula Malkopoulou, »Eurozone Crisis and parliamentary democracy: The Greek case«, in: Claudia Wiesner / Meike Schmidt-Gleim (eds.), The Meanings of Europe, London 2014, pp. 160–178.

41 European Commission, *Memorandum of Understanding between the European Commission and the Hellenic Republic and the Bank of Greece*, op. cit. (note 38).

Greek parliament voted for the Memoranda, this does not mean that it actually had something substantial to decide upon. The conditions were so detailed that little room for any substantial parliamentary decision on the budget could have been left. But a parliament that in the end cannot decide on details and between true alternatives regarding the budget has lost the core of its role as a parliament. Decisions then not only are de-politicized but also void of the substance of parliamentarism. In such cases, parliament takes on a referendum role (voting just Yes or No) rather than the parliamentary function of deliberation and vote.

What is more, the interventions into the Greek parliament's budgetary rights took place outside of the structure of the EU Treaties. The agents intervening were the Eurogroup, the European Commission and the Troika, bringing about once more all problems of non-transparency and lack of accountability and legitimacy that have been named. In sum, the vertical balance of powers between the Eurogroup and Greece has been severely impeded.

3.3. Austerity and the national political systems

Austerity, moreover, had consequences on the political systems in the debtor states. Most states that received financial aid experienced changes in government and the founding of new political parties.

As has been said above, the Greek parliament has been bypassed by the governments in the beginning of austerity politics. But what would have happened if the Greek parliament had been fully involved? In other states that installed austerity programmes, such as Italy (which did not receive financial aid from ESM but was governed by a »technocrat government« under Mario Monti after the Berlusconi government had resigned) or Portugal and Spain (that received financial help via the Eurogroup), severe consequences occurred. In both Italy and Portugal heads of governments resigned because their austerity packages did not obtain parliamentary majorities. Italian Prime Minister Monti in consequence said that heads of government needed more independence from their parliaments.[42] Regarding the fact that government also tried to bypass parliament in the donor state Germany, one general question to be raised is whether it is inherently related to crisis politics and crisis management to at least try and concentrate powers on the executives.

Besides such effects of power concentration and changes in government, there have been effects on the party systems. Again, the Greek case is particularly pertinent. After the Papandreou-government had resigned early on in the Greek crisis, a »technocrat government« was installed. After that, Greece experienced a series of politicians leaving their factions and parties, the founding of new parties and also several elections following one another. A severe decline in trust in the Greek political class followed, as

42 »Italiens Premier Monti warnt im SPIEGEL vor Auseinanderbrechen Europas« in: *Spiegel Online*, 5.8.2012, http://www.spiegel.de/politik/ausland/italiens-premier-monti-warnt-im-spiegel-vor-auseinanderbrechen-europas-a-848280.html [12.9.2012].

well as protests, demonstrations and open disobedience.[43] Other debtor states experienced similar developments – Spain is another pertinent example here, where the old opposition of the people's party and the socialist party has been complemented by new, or relatively new, movements like Podemos and Ciudadanos.

These developments are mirrored by a decline of citizen's support for the EU throughout the crisis, which indicates that EU citizens are not willing to simply accept the crisis management and its effects. During the financial crisis identification, trust and support into democratic institutions both on the EU and national level have been shrinking decisively.[44] For instance, between 2011 and 2013, more than 60% of those polled by Eurobarometer did *not* feel that their voice counts in the EU, and only around 30% of those polled felt that it counted at that time. Trust in EU institutions declined by approximately 20 percentage points between 2007 (around 50%) and 2015 (just above 30%). What is more, trust in national parliaments and national governments, which is usually lower than trust in EU institutions, also declined in parallel from 35% (parliaments) and 34% (governments) to 28% (parliaments) and 27% (governments). While trust in the EU thus declined more decisively, national institutions also were severely affected by the effects the financial crisis had on citizen's trust.

This indicates, first, that in the multi-level system legitimacy beliefs no longer are solely fixed on either the EU or the nation state; now the two are linked. Second, it indicates that the sovereign debt crisis has not been passing unnoticed by the citizens. Input-legitimacy of the EU and the member states has been shrinking in this respect, and it shows that the EU's legitimacy problems have been increasing on the input side during the financial crisis.

3.4. The horizontal balance of powers is hampered

Last not least, the horizontal balance of powers between the member states is impeded by the new developments, as donor state parliaments co-decide on the conditions for budgetary aid. Once more, the cases of Germany and Greece underline the problematic best.

When the German *Bundestag* decided on supporting the German share for financial aid for Greece, it did so based on the conditions of the austerity programmes and the Memoranda of Understanding. This means that the German *Bundestag*, at least by means of deciding upon the conditions of austerity for Greece, obtained a co-decision right on details of the Greek budget. Surely this side-effect never was intended by the EU Treaties, and probably neither by the ESM Treaty.

Now it seems inevitable that a donor, especially one as big and powerful as the Federal Republic of Germany, in a Weberian sense disposes of power over a debtor. But

43 Malkopoulou, »Eurozone Crisis and parliamentary democracy: The Greek case«, op. cit. (note 40).

44 Eurobarometer results of the last years; Eurobarometer, *Public Opinion – European Commission*, http://ec.europa.eu/COMMFrontOffice/publicopinion/index.cfm/Survey/index#p=1&instruments=STANDARD&surveyKy=2130 [8.11.2016].

these imbalances in power shares went along with a *Bundestag* co-decision right on the Greek budget that was as big, or even more important, than the one of the Greek parliament: the *Bundestag* decided upon the conditions of financial aid and hence details of the Greek budget – and, moreover, it could debate, influence and possibly change them in the course of its parliamentary deliberations, different from the Greek parliament. As has been said, the margin of decision of the Geek parliament compared to this seems to be quite small, as it could only decide upon accepting or not the conditions that thus had been set by others.

This means that the decisive question is not whether the *Bundestag* as a parliament disposes of more influence in the German political system than the Greek parliament in the Greek political system (which is quite probable). The *Bundestag*'s co-decision rights on financial aid, as has been discussed above, have to be regarded as a sign of checks and balances that work well in the German political system. The decisive point is that the setting that has just been sketched indicates a limitation of the horizontal balance of powers between the EU member states.

The German *Bundestag* – and not only the *Bundestag* but also all other parliaments of donor states where they have been involved – was able to directly intervene into the Greek budget decisions and hence into matters of the Greek parliament and the Greek government. De facto this created a link between *Bundestag* decisions and budgetary policies in Greece. This link is an outcome of the power imbalances between donor and debtor states, as well as the governance structures in financial aid that have been sketched above, and it is mediated by the vertical relations of member states and Eurogroup. As a result, not only the budgetary rights of debtor state parliaments are impeded, but also the competencies of national parliaments are mixed up.

4. Concluding discussion

The discussion has raised a number of problems that austerity governance created for representative democracies and balances of powers in the EU's multi-level system. Crisis governance institutions, first, bypass the progresses to supranational representative democracy obtained in the EU over the last decades and take a shortcut back into intergovernmentalism. It is a decisive legitimization problem, second to have set decisions of such impact as in the crisis management both outside the EU's and most of the national representative institutions.

This fallback indicates that the middle ground between intergovernmentalism and democracy in the EU is marked by a crucial imbalance due to the policy orientation on market-driven economic integration: Economic and monetary integration are far advanced – far beyond a mere intergovernmental integration. But they have not been equipped with democratic governance mechanisms on the whole: We have a functioning inner market, yet member states since many years do not set or implement their own rules for it. A common currency has been introduced, but the economic and budgetary policies have not been integrated, neither have they been subject to representative democracy on EU level; they were decided upon in the member states. But now their representative democratic decisions are circumnavigated by the fiscal crisis governance, which may be supranational, but is not democratic.[45]

Third, crisis governance severely impedes national representative democracies and their balances of powers in the EU's multi-level system. It needs to be discussed, though, which alternatives would have existed especially in the Greek case. If the Greek parliament had voted no on one or several of the Memoranda, a Greek state bankruptcy might have followed. In that case, as according to an argument that is frequently made, Greece would have been subject to IMF emergency measures that would have been even less democratically legitimate. This argument certainly is true, but it is no excuse for safeguarding the pitfalls and legitimacy problems in financial aid governance more or less permanently, neither does it justify the austerity measures being fixed in such detail by the Eurogroup, Commission, IMF and Troika. On the contrary the argument that opposes state bankruptcy and acceptance of the Troika's austerity programmes underlines the problematic that has been sketched above, i.e. the fact that parliamentary decision making powers have been limited to a mere yes or no vote.

Fourth, the financial crisis has given rise to two general challenges for democratic nation states.[46] The first one is the conflict of creditworthiness versus national sovereignty. In case a state does not have the confidence of the financial market actors any more, its sovereignty is severely impeded, as again the Greek case demonstrates. The second challenge relates to the role of austerity regulations in this setting. The conditions of financial help, in a much more explicit way than the EU's convergence criteria, have the effect of hidden national objectives – hidden because not even the EU treaties define financial austerity as a goal. Nevertheless most EU states today are subject to austerity rules. In the debtor states this is flagrant, and the Portuguese president made it explicit when he claimed after an election that he would only name a new government that accepted the Troika conditions. But also donor states and all other member states that are subject to the fiscal compact or the European Semester regulations have to accept austerity conditions.[47]

Fifth, the problematic effects of austerity governance on representative democracies and balances of powers in the EU multi-level system are complemented by apparent deficits and problems of effective governance. The opaqueness of the structures that has been sketched favours conflicts between the Troika's members and within the Eurogroup. This is why the »presidents' report«, issued in 2015 by the presidents of European Commission, European Council, Eurogroup, European Parliament and European Central Bank, emphasizes that financial aid needs to be organized in a more

45 Claudia Wiesner, »From Safeguarding Peace in Europe to Financial Crisis: Old questions and new challenges of EU integration«, in: Wiesner / Schmidt-Gleim (eds.), *The Meanings of Europe*, op. cit. (note 40), pp. 91–106.

46 Claudia Wiesner, »Capitalism, democracy, and the European Union« in: *Zeitschrift für Vergleichende Politikwissenschaft* 10, No. 3–4 (2016), pp. 219–239.

47 Claudia Wiesner, »Gewaltenteilung und Demokratie in der EU-Finanzhilfenpolitik«, in: Hartlapp / Wiesner (eds.), *Gewaltenteilung und Demokratie im EU-Mehrebenensystem*, op. cit. (note 1), pp. 231–249.

transparent and more efficient way.[48] This »presidents' report«, however, does not focus on safeguarding representative democracy on the EU level and in the member states. It only suggests that national parliaments should be heard and that they should use the existing means of intergovernmental cooperation.

But the discussion above clearly underlined that the existing structures of governance of financial aid harm representative democracy on several levels of the multi-level system. Is there a chance to deal with these problems? Can sustainable representative-democratic structures and institutions be kept or even strengthened under conditions of financial crisis and austerity rules instead of simply keeping up an intergovernmental crisis governance mechanism? And is it possible to limit or avoid side-effects such as the German parliament intervening into budgetary competencies of the Greek parliament?

These questions touch upon a question of principle, i.e., they touch upon the question how policy areas are to be treated that are not ruled by the EU and the EU treaties but still intervene a) into the EU's policies and b) into the member states and their representative systems. In the following it is argued that there are two possible ways to approach this dilemma. The following[49] sketches the principles and does not, at first, regard whether they are realistic:

1) There is a defensive or a narrow solution. In this solution, the EU continues to rule only part of the policies that are carried out in the multi-level system and the member states, and hence only part of those policies that are ruled as according to the EU Treaties and the checks and balances they establish. The defensive component then would consist in a safeguarding and protection mechanism for national representative systems.
2) There is an offensive or broad solution that would consist in broadening the policy areas the EU rules to include all, or almost all, of the policies that are currently ruled by democratic nation states. This system of full integration would stop differentiated integration and submit all policy areas to one mode of legitimation.

When discussing which of these solutions is realistic, however, it soon becomes apparent that the first one, the defensive or narrow solution, will be much easier to obtain than the second, for the broad solution would require to overcome the differentiated integration that we currently experience. There are different degrees of integration in different policy areas, and there are different degrees of integration among different groups of member states. The EU is hence dispersed into a great variety of different regulation regimes and schemes, ranging from co-decision in the inner market, over the intergovernmentally structured Common Foreign and Security Policy, the Eurogroup that just unites the euro countries, to the Schengen System that is another

48 Jean-Claude Juncker / Donald Tusk / Jeroen Disselbloem / Mario Draghi / Martin Schulz, *Die Wirtschafts- und Währungsunion Europas vollenden*, https://www.ecb.europa.eu/pub/pdf/other/5presidentsreport.de.pdf?4b942c5f6fc385ea3624ec18a85f3fe4 [30.6.2017].

49 Wiesner, »Capitalism, democracy, and the European Union«, op. cit. (note 46); Claudia Wiesner, »Möglichkeiten und Grenzen repräsentativer Demokratie in der EU-Finanzhilfenpolitik« in: Integration, 1 (2017/1), pp. 33-47.

structure half apart. This dispersion of a polity as big as the EU also creates differing patterns of legitimization and control. But it is not likely that this might change soon. So far, there is not even agreement on the basic goals of the EU: Should it just continue to create an inner market, as it did? Should we rebuild and cut down the EU? Or should it become a truly supranational federation? The last declaration by Commission president Juncker accordingly sketches five possible paths for the EU's future development[50] that also range from a minimum to a maximum solution.

Therefore the chances to reduce differentiated integration seem doubtful, and the same is true for another question: In order to remedy part of the problems sketched, a policy change away from financial austerity across the EU would be required. But the political majorities in the European Parliament and in the member states, or those in the eurozone, would need to support this approach. This means that a political battle in the 28 (or soon 27) member states, or the eurozone member states, would have to be led – and won – on this matter first. As this does not seem realistic either, the possible solutions are limited to the question of how the consequences of austerity governance on representative democracies and balances of powers can be limited. The following scenarios seem possible.

1) *Changes for financial aid governance in the narrow solution:* The smallest solution is to defend what there is to be defended, i.e. to hedge the backfire effects on national representative democracies. EU-led policies, as has been discussed, threaten democratic standards and rights in the member states. To remedy this problem, transparency, accountability and vertical balance of powers need to be better protected.

First, key decisions have to be taken away from indirectly legitimized agents such as the Troika. Even if financial aid governance is not decisively changed, the Troika's competencies and accountability could be made more transparent. Second, the substance of parliamentary decision-making competence needs to be safeguarded also under austerity conditions. This means basically that austerity conditions can fix the sums to be cut in the budget, but they shouldn't intervene in detail into the budget itself and hence determine the policies of a country in detail. Third, the results of national elections and referenda need to be respected, as well as the core powers of national parliaments and governments. As long as austerity and monetary stability are not fixed as national objectives, a margin of decision making needs to be safeguarded for them. Explicit or implicit mutual interventions of national parliaments into each other's areas of competencies should be regulated. It does not seem to be possible to exclude them in the current system of financial aid, at least as long as donor state parliaments vote on the conditions for support, but it seems possible to define more explicit rules and limits for them – such as, again, the condition that austerity goals may only fix sums but not budget details and, accordingly, that donor state parliaments may co-decide on sums to be saved but not on details of budgets and policies in debtor states.

50 European Commission, *White Paper on the future of Europe: Avenues for unity for the EU at 27*, http://europa.eu/rapid/press-release_IP-17-385_en.htm [30.3.2017].

2) *In the offensive version*, and hence in the path that seems much less realistic in the moment, the governance of financial aid and also the Eurogroup would need to be submitted to the EU treaties' framework. In that case, the EP as the EU's legislative could be included. It is however to be taken into account that non-euro countries should not decide upon policies carried out in euro countries. This means that a Eurochamber could be created in the European Parliament to become the democratic co-legislator for the Eurogroup. In addition, a full-fledged and democratically legitimized transfer union in the EU could be created – even if it must rightfully be discussed whether such a transfer union would be sustainable given the persisting economic differences in the EU.[51] Finally, the most far-reaching solution would be to stop differentiated integration and re-integrate the EU. Differences between fully and partly integrated policy fields and different modes of regulation, law- and policy-making could be reduced and finally abolished. At the same time, co-decision should become the legislative procedure in all of the EU's policy fields.

51 Wolfgang Streeck, *Buying time. The delayed crisis of democratic capitalism*, Brooklyn 2014.

List of contributors

Philipp Adorf is Research Assistant at the Department for Political Sciences and Sociology at the University of Bonn.

Christoph Bruckmüller is Research Assistant at the Institute of Political Science at Friedrich-Alexander-University Erlangen-Nuremberg.

Constantine Dimoulas is Assistant Professor in Social Administration and Evaluation of Social Programmes at the Department of Social Policy at Panteion University, Athens.

Vassilis K. Fouskas is Professor if International Politics and Economics at the School of Business and Law and Director of STAMP at the University of East London.

Brian Birvin is Honorary Professor at the School of Social and Political Sciences at the University of Glasgow.

Tim Griebel is Assistant Professor at the Institute of Political Science at Friedrich-Alexander-University Erlangen-Nuremberg.

Klaus Gretschmann is President of CATE and former Director-General of EU Council of Ministers.

Reiner Grundmann is Professor of Science and Technology Studies at the University of Nottingham.

Bob Jessop is Distinguished Professor of Sociology, Lancaster University.

Kim-Sue Kreischer is Research Student and Teaching Affiliate at the University of Nottingham.

Sabina Monza is a PhD Candidate in Politics, Policies and International Relations at the Autonomous University of Barcelona.

Wolfram Ridder is Lecturer at the Institute of Political Science at Friedrich-Alexander-University Erlangen-Nuremberg.

Mike Scott is developer of WordSmith and Visiting Research Fellow at Aston University.

Roland Sturm is Professor of Political Science at Friedrich-Alexander-University Erlangen-Nuremberg.

Erik Vollmann is Doctoral Candidate at the Institute of Political Science at Friedrich-Alexander-University Erlangen-Nuremberg.

Claudia Wiesner is Visiting Fellow at the Robert Schumann Centre for Advanced Study at the European University Institute, Florence.

Thorsten Winkelmann is Assistant Professor at the Institute of Political Science at Friedrich-Alexander-University Erlangen-Nuremberg.